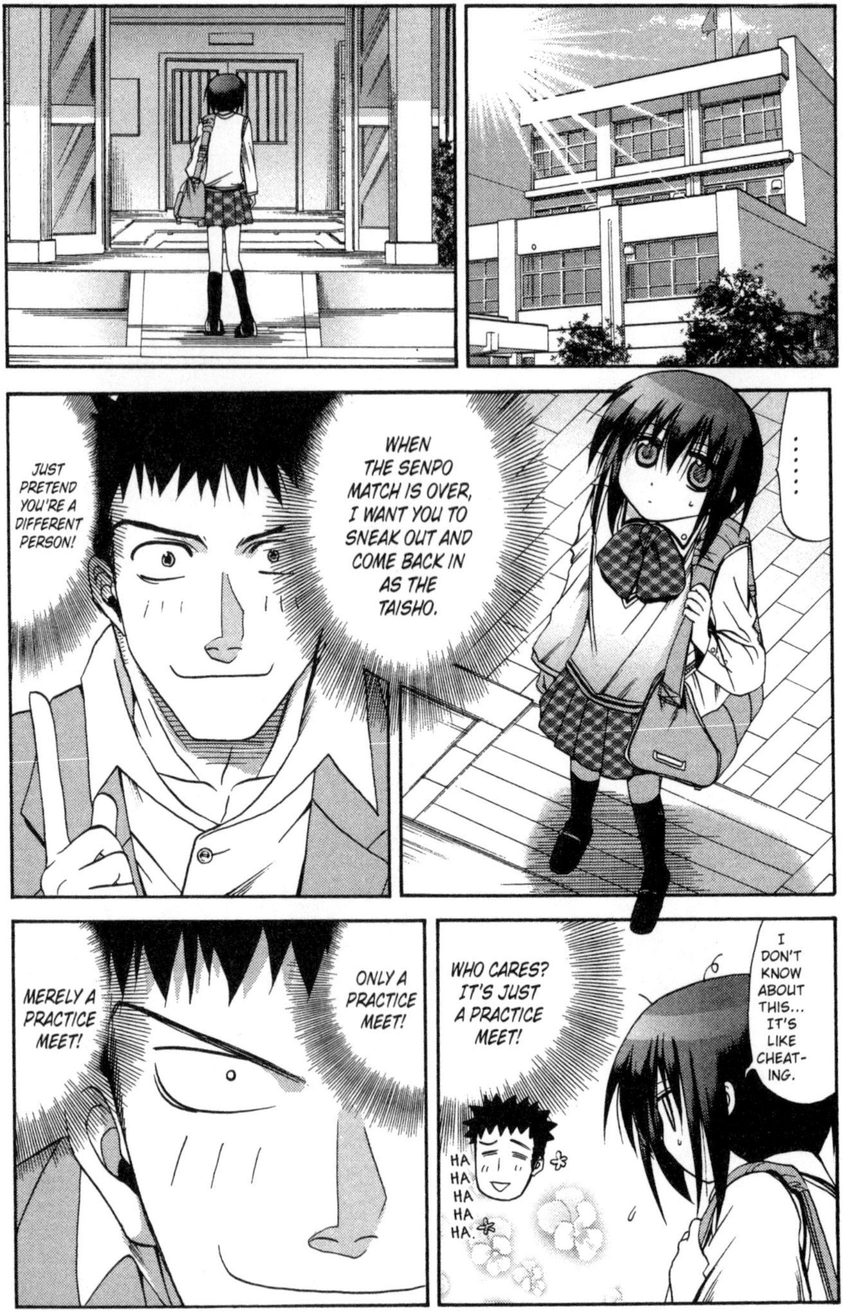
......
WHEN THE SENPO MATCH IS OVER, I WANT YOU TO SNEAK OUT AND COME BACK IN AS THE TAISHO.
JUST PRETEND YOU'RE A DIFFERENT PERSON!
I DON'T KNOW ABOUT THIS... IT'S LIKE CHEATING.
WHO CARES? IT'S JUST A PRACTICE MEET!
HA HA HA HA HA.
ONLY A PRACTICE MEET!
MERELY A PRACTICE MEET!

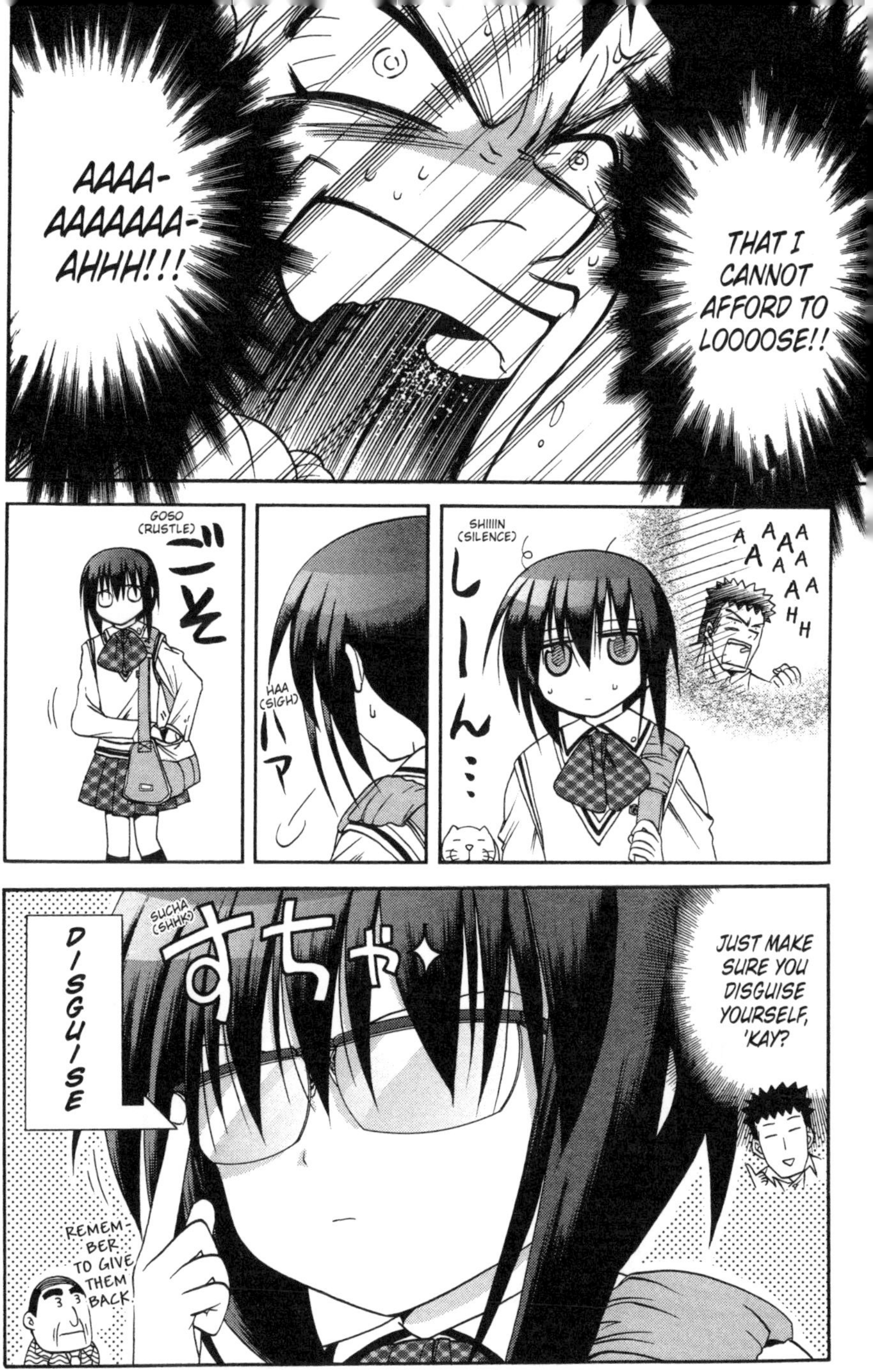
THAT I CANNOT AFFORD TO LOOOOSE!!
AAAA-AAAAAAA-AHHH!!!
SHIIIN (SILENCE)
しーん…
AAAAAAAAAAAHH
HAA (SIGH)
ハァ
GOSO (RUSTLE)
ごそ
JUST MAKE SURE YOU DISGUISE YOURSELF, 'KAY?
DISGUISE
SUCHA (SHHK)
すちゃ
REMEMBER TO GIVE THEM BACK

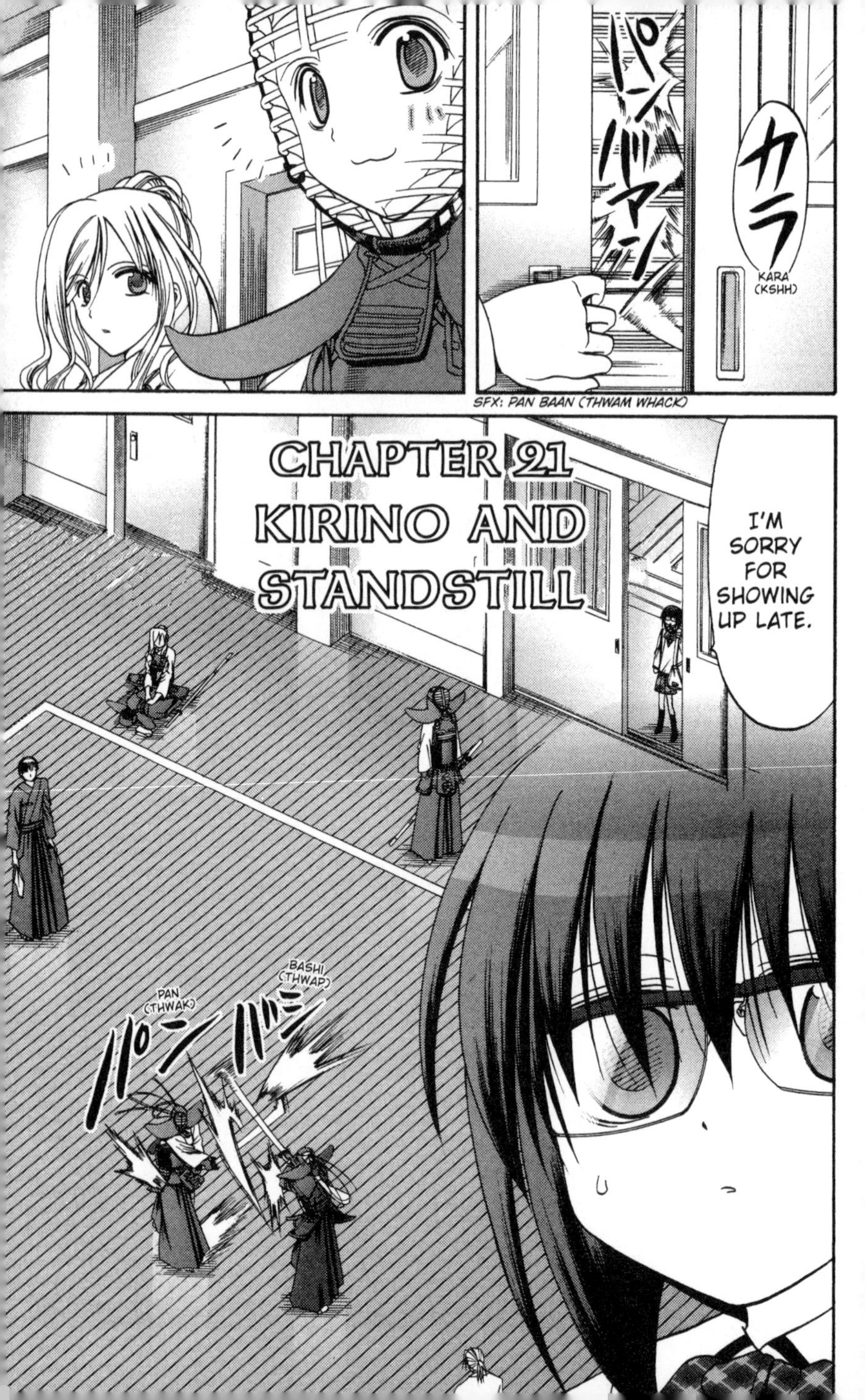

カラ
KARA (KSHH)
SFX: PAN BAAN (THWAM WHACK)
I'M SORRY FOR SHOWING UP LATE.
CHAPTER 21
KIRINO AND STANDSTILL
BASHI (THWAP)
PAN (THWAK)

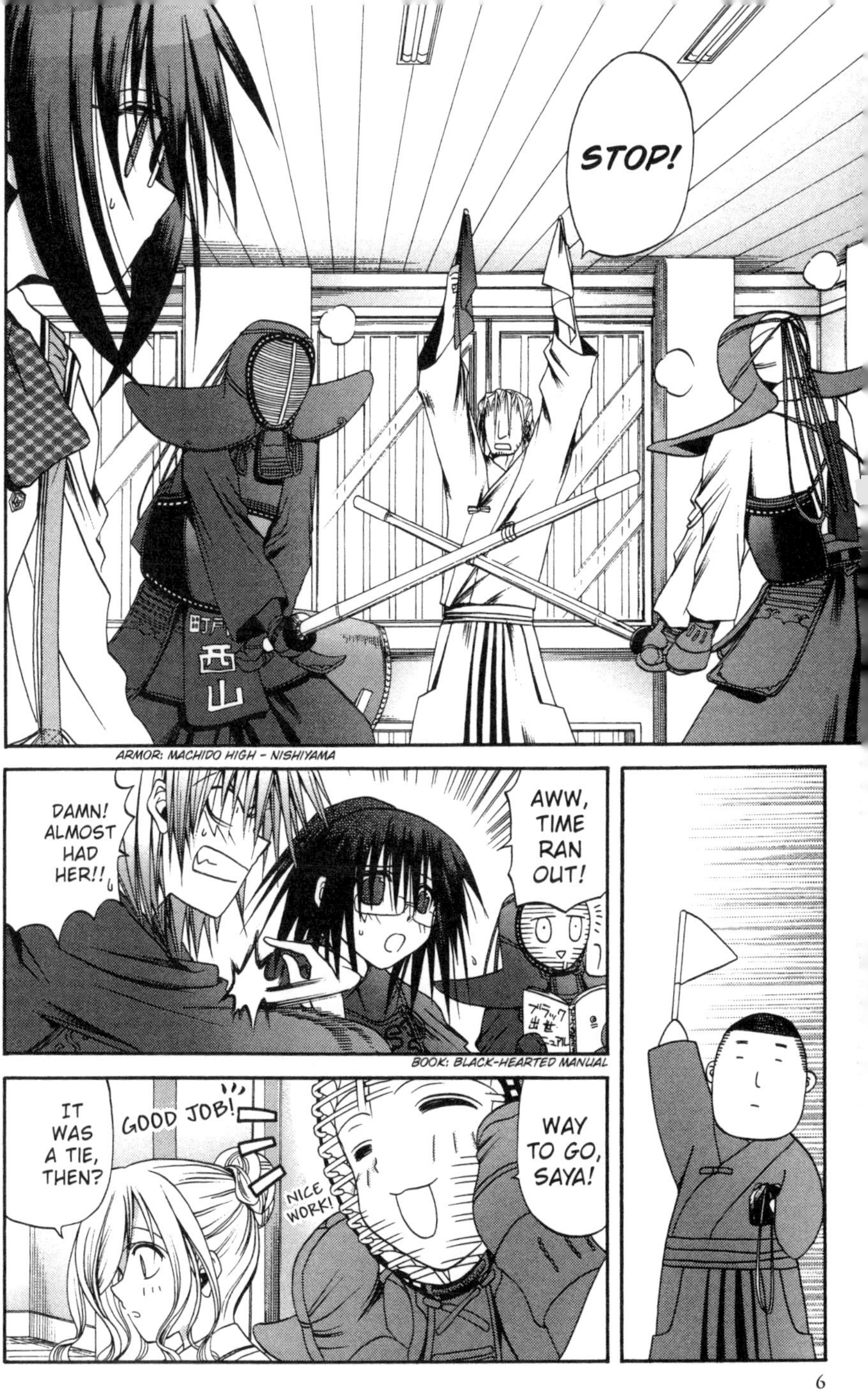
STOP!
ARMOR: MACHIDO HIGH - NISHIYAMA
AWW, TIME RAN OUT!
DAMN! ALMOST HAD HER!!
BOOK: BLACK-HEARTED MANUAL
WAY TO GO, SAYA!
NICE WORK!
GOOD JOB!
IT WAS A TIE, THEN?

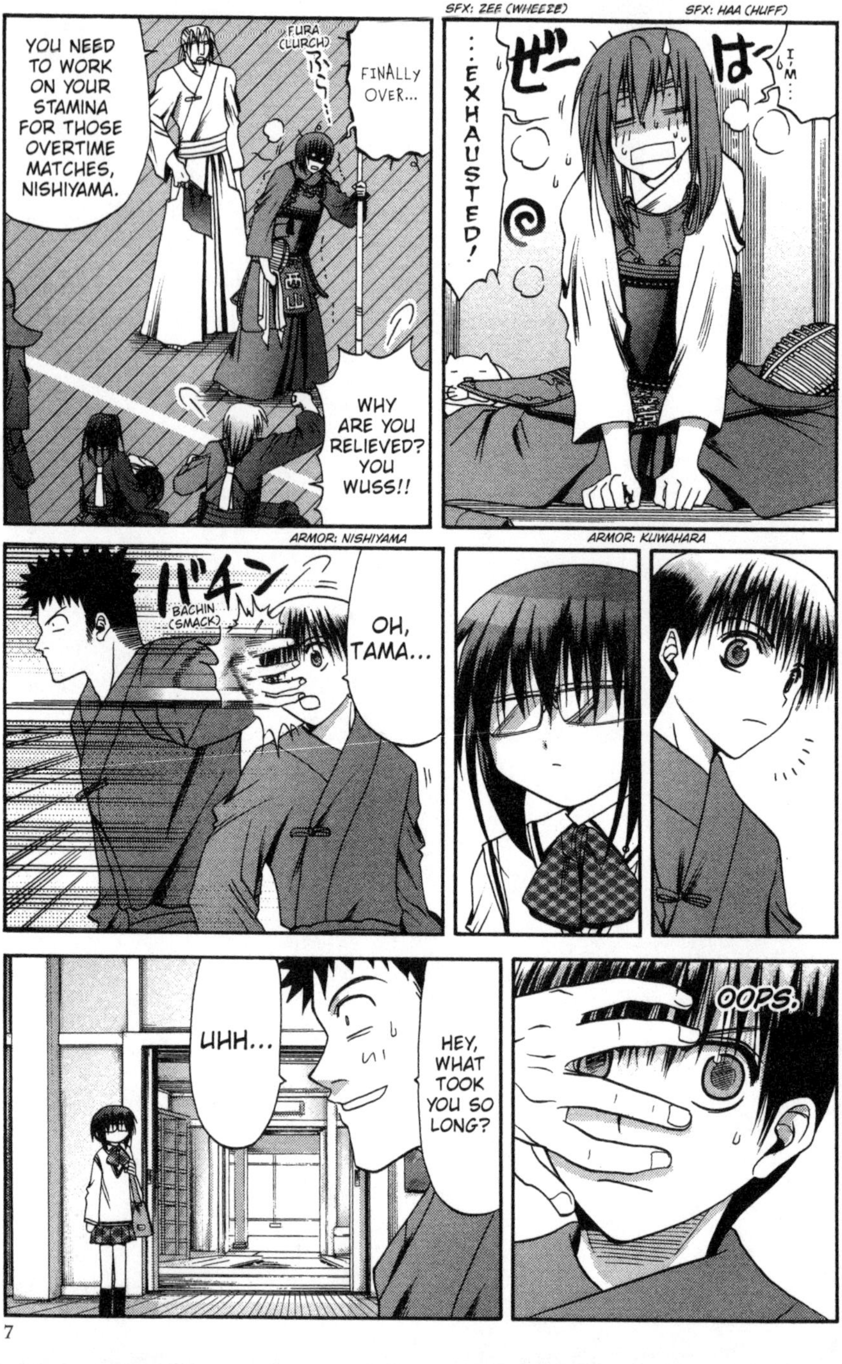
SFX: ZEE (WHEEZE)
SFX: HAA (HUFF)
ぜー
は-
I, I'M...
...EXHAUSTED!
ARMOR: KUWAHARA
FINALLY OVER...
FURA (LURCH)
ふら
YOU NEED TO WORK ON YOUR STAMINA FOR THOSE OVERTIME MATCHES, NISHIYAMA.
WHY ARE YOU RELIEVED? YOU WUSS!!
ARMOR: NISHIYAMA
OH, TAMA...
バチン
BACHIN (SMACK)
OOPS.
HEY, WHAT TOOK YOU SO LONG?
UHH...

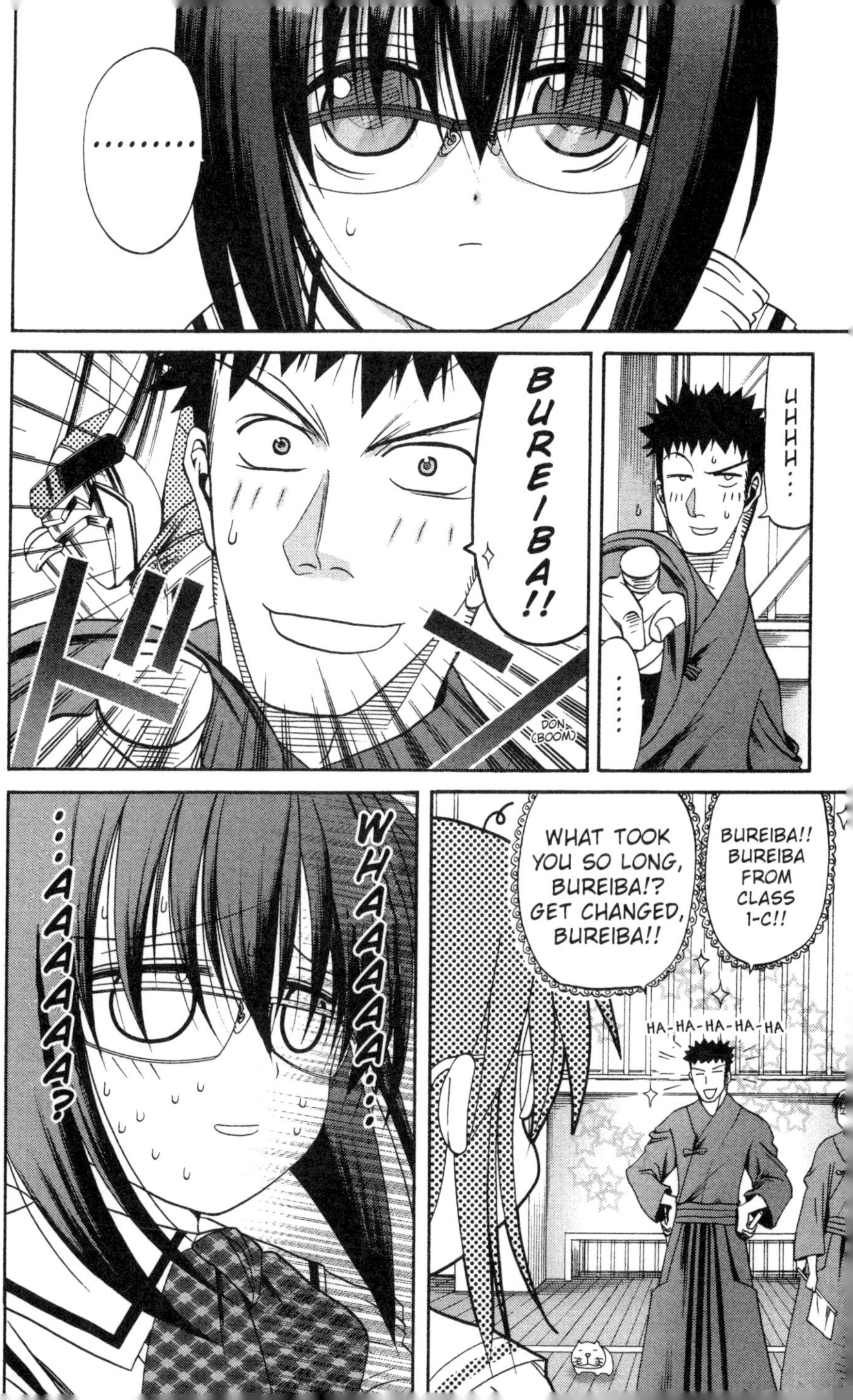
....
UHHH...
......
BUREIBA!!
DON (BOOM)
BUREIBA!! BUREIBA FROM CLASS 1-C!!
WHAT TOOK YOU SO LONG, BUREIBA!? GET CHANGED, BUREIBA!!
HA-HA-HA-HA-HA
WHAAAAAA...
...AAAAAAA?

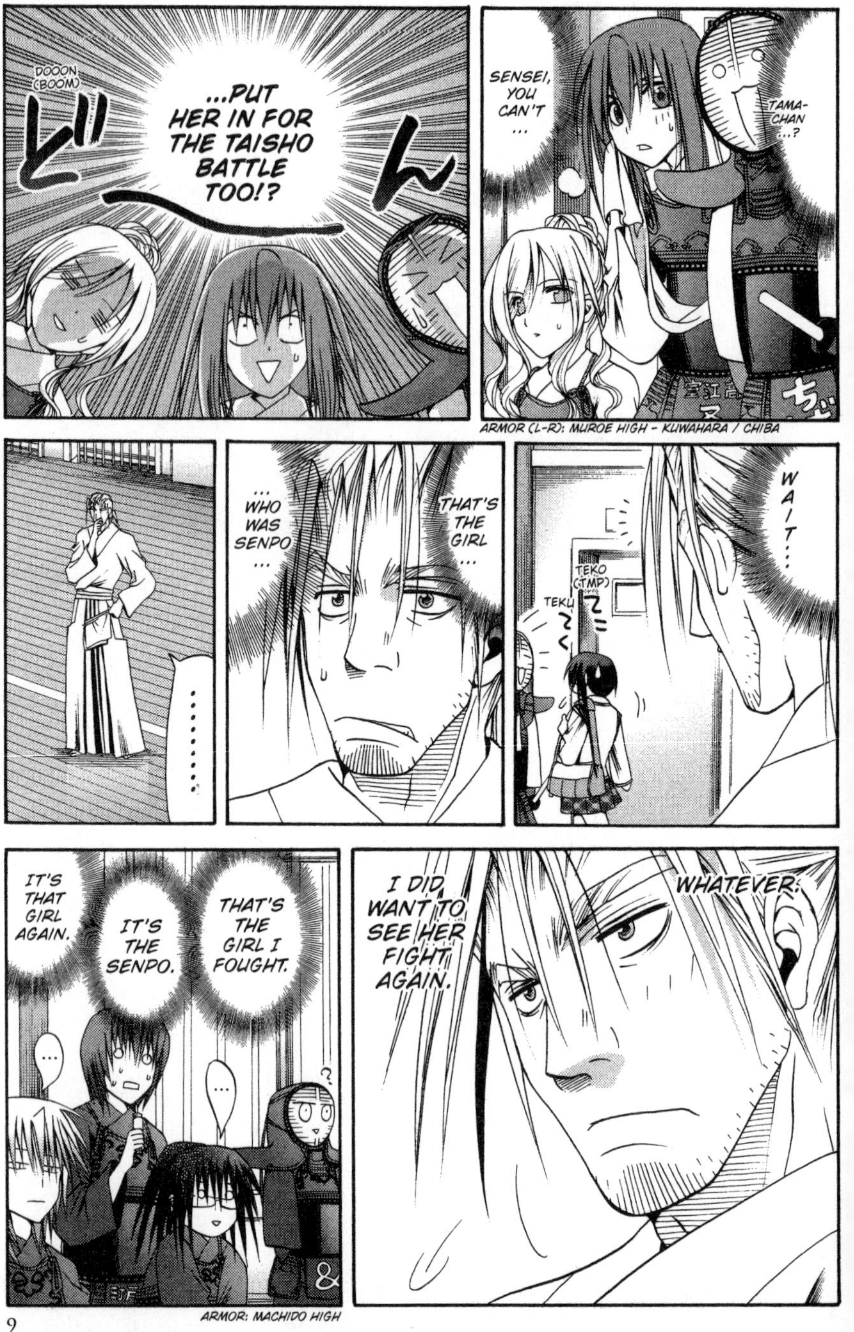
SENSEI, YOU CAN'T ...
TAMA-CHAN ...?
DOOON (BOOM)
...PUT HER IN FOR THE TAISHO BATTLE TOO!?
WAIT...
TEKO (TMP)
TEKU
THAT'S THE GIRL ...
... WHO WAS SENPO ...
....
WHATEVER.
I DID WANT TO SEE HER FIGHT AGAIN.
THAT'S THE GIRL I FOUGHT.
IT'S THE SENPO.
IT'S THAT GIRL AGAIN.
...
...
?
ARMOR (L-R): MUROE HIGH - KUWAHARA / CHIBA

ARMOR: MACHIDO HIGH

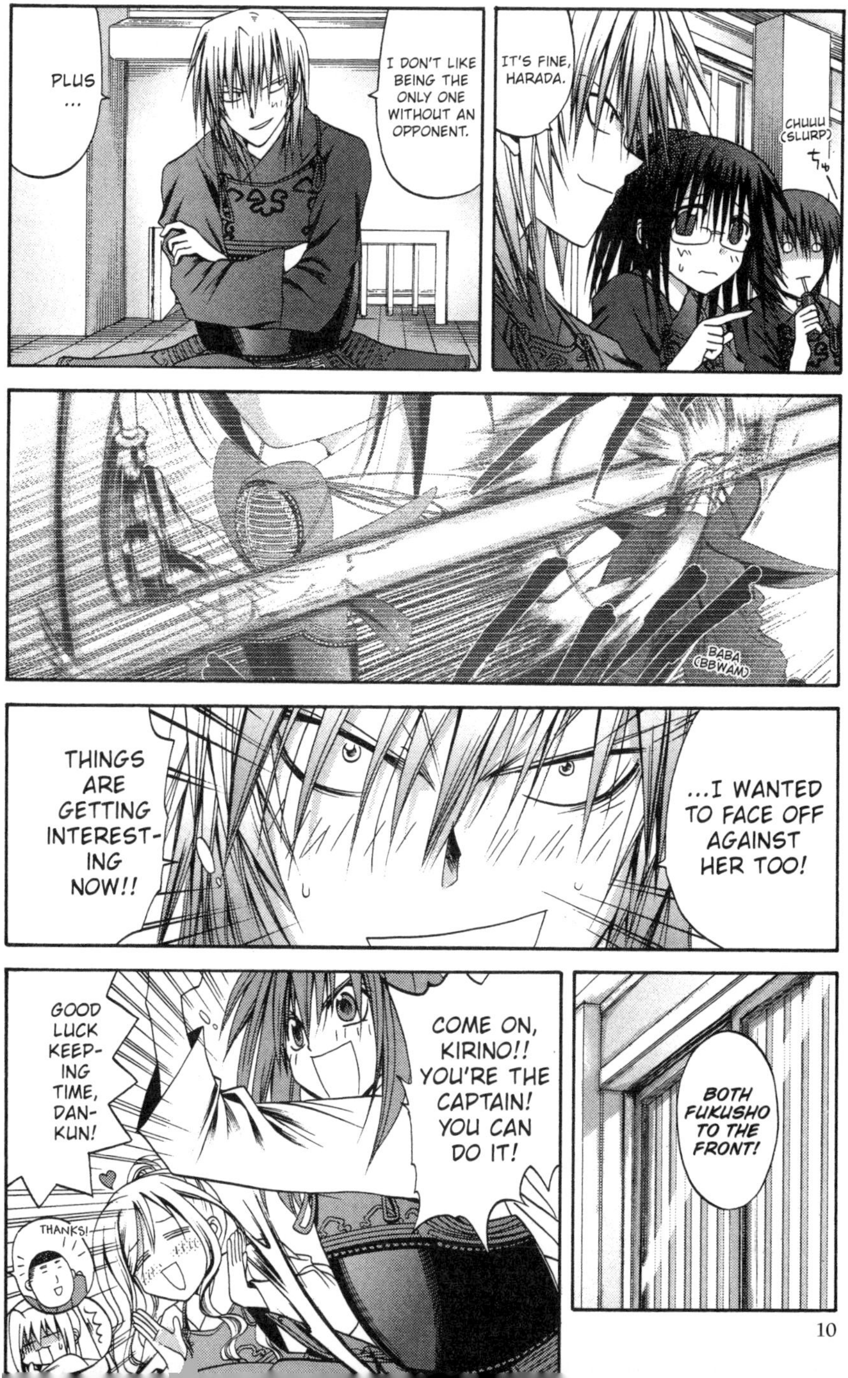
IT'S FINE, HARADA.
CHUUU (SLURP)
I DON'T LIKE BEING THE ONLY ONE WITHOUT AN OPPONENT.
PLUS ...
BABA (BBWAM)
...I WANTED TO FACE OFF AGAINST HER TOO!
THINGS ARE GETTING INTEREST-ING NOW!!
BOTH FUKUSHO TO THE FRONT!
COME ON, KIRINO!! YOU'RE THE CAPTAIN! YOU CAN DO IT!
GOOD LUCK KEEP-ING TIME, DAN-KUN!
THANKS!

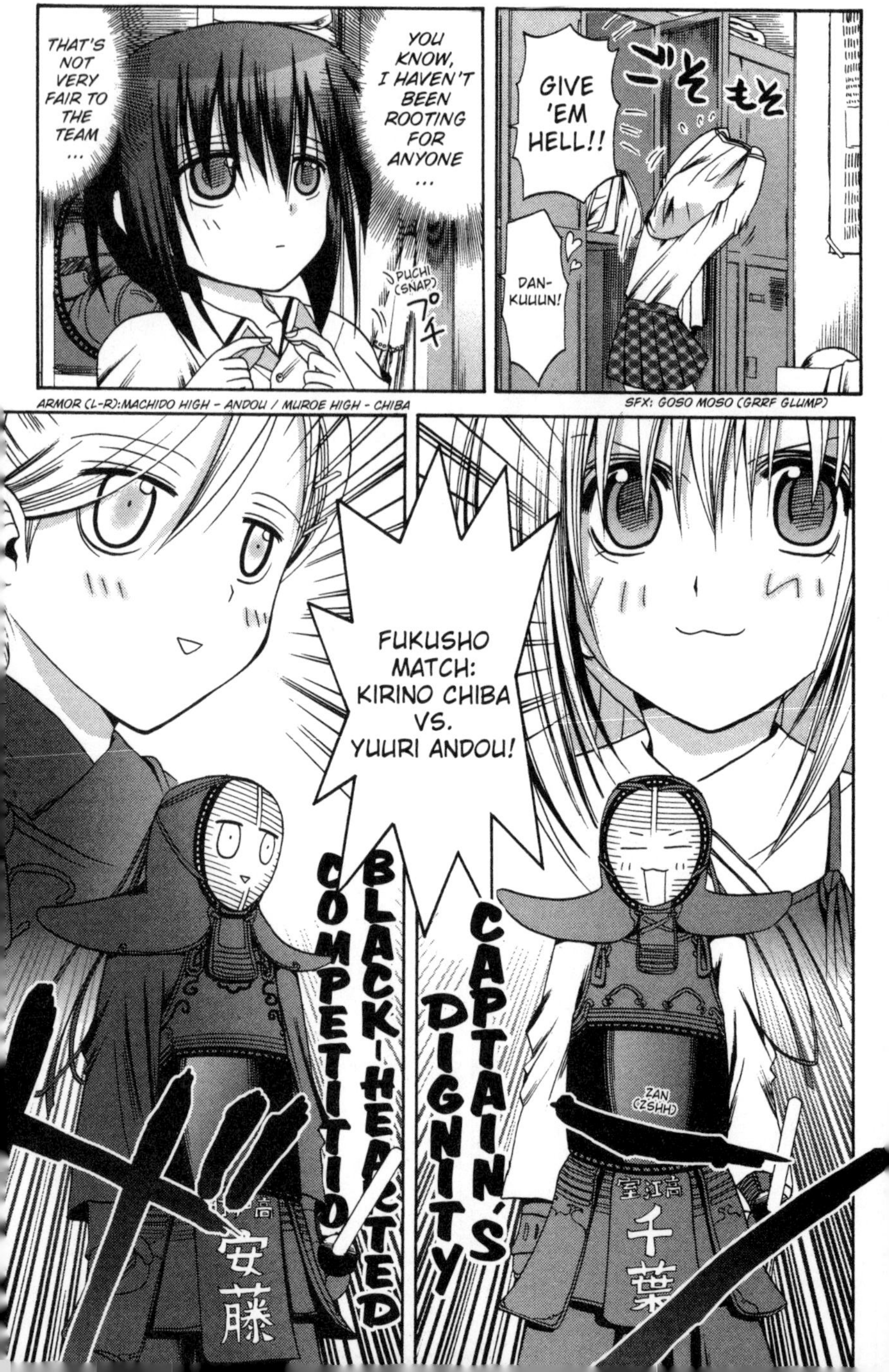
GIVE 'EM HELL!!
DAN-KUUUN!
SFX: GOSO MOSO (GRRF GLUMP)
YOU KNOW, I HAVEN'T BEEN ROOTING FOR ANYONE ...
THAT'S NOT VERY FAIR TO THE TEAM ...
PUCHI (SNAP)
ARMOR (L-R):MACHIDO HIGH - ANDOU / MUROE HIGH - CHIBA
FUKUSHO MATCH: KIRINO CHIBA VS. YUURI ANDOU!
CAPTAIN'S
DIGNITY
BLACK-HEARTED
COMPETITION
ZAN (ZSHH)
室江高
千葉
安藤

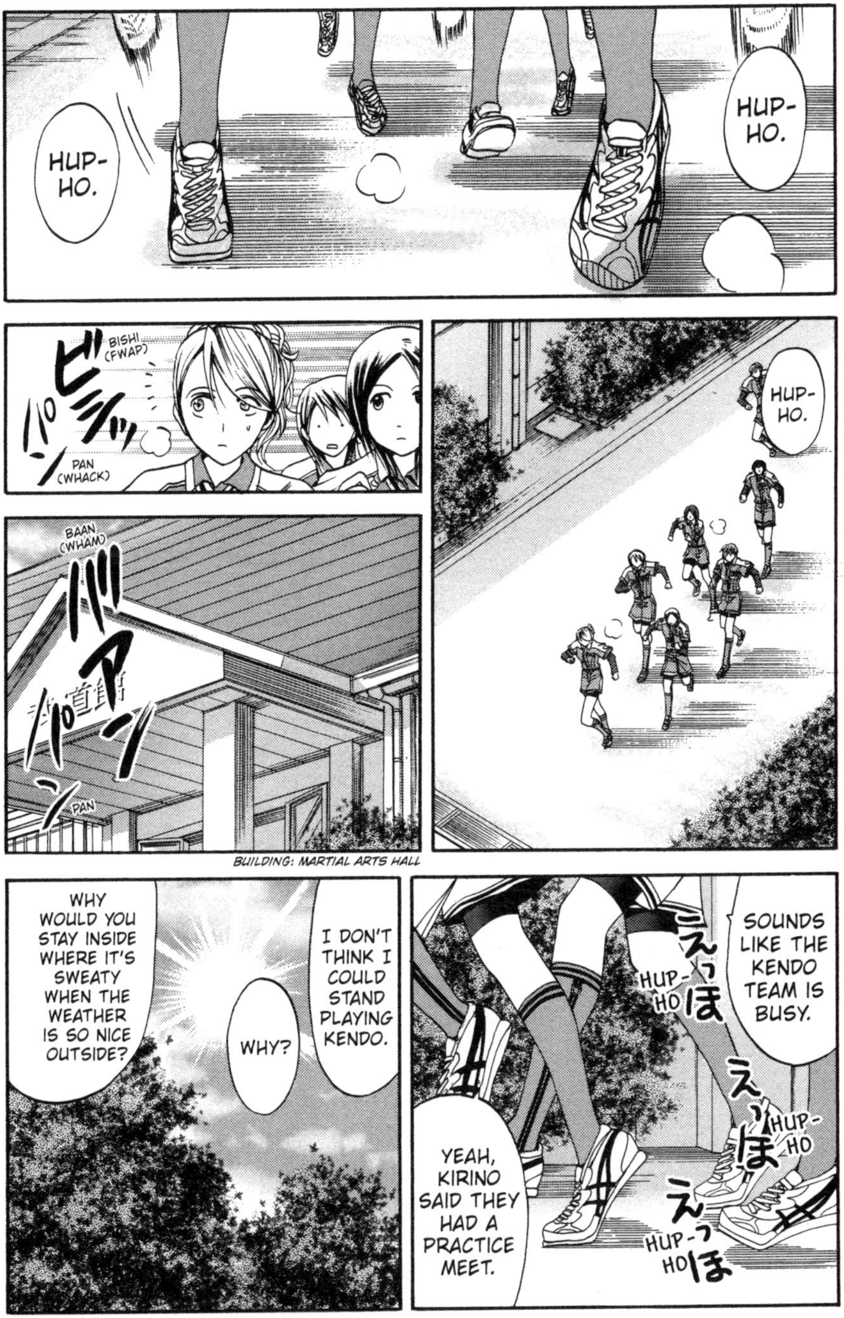
HUP-HO.
HUP-HO.
HUP-HO.
BISHI (FWAP)
PAN (WHACK)
BAAN (WHAM)
PAN
BUILDING: MARTIAL ARTS HALL
SOUNDS LIKE THE KENDO TEAM IS BUSY.
HUP-HO
HUP-HO
HUP-HO
YEAH, KIRINO SAID THEY HAD A PRACTICE MEET.
I DON'T THINK I COULD STAND PLAYING KENDO.
WHY?
WHY WOULD YOU STAY INSIDE WHERE IT'S SWEATY WHEN THE WEATHER IS SO NICE OUTSIDE?

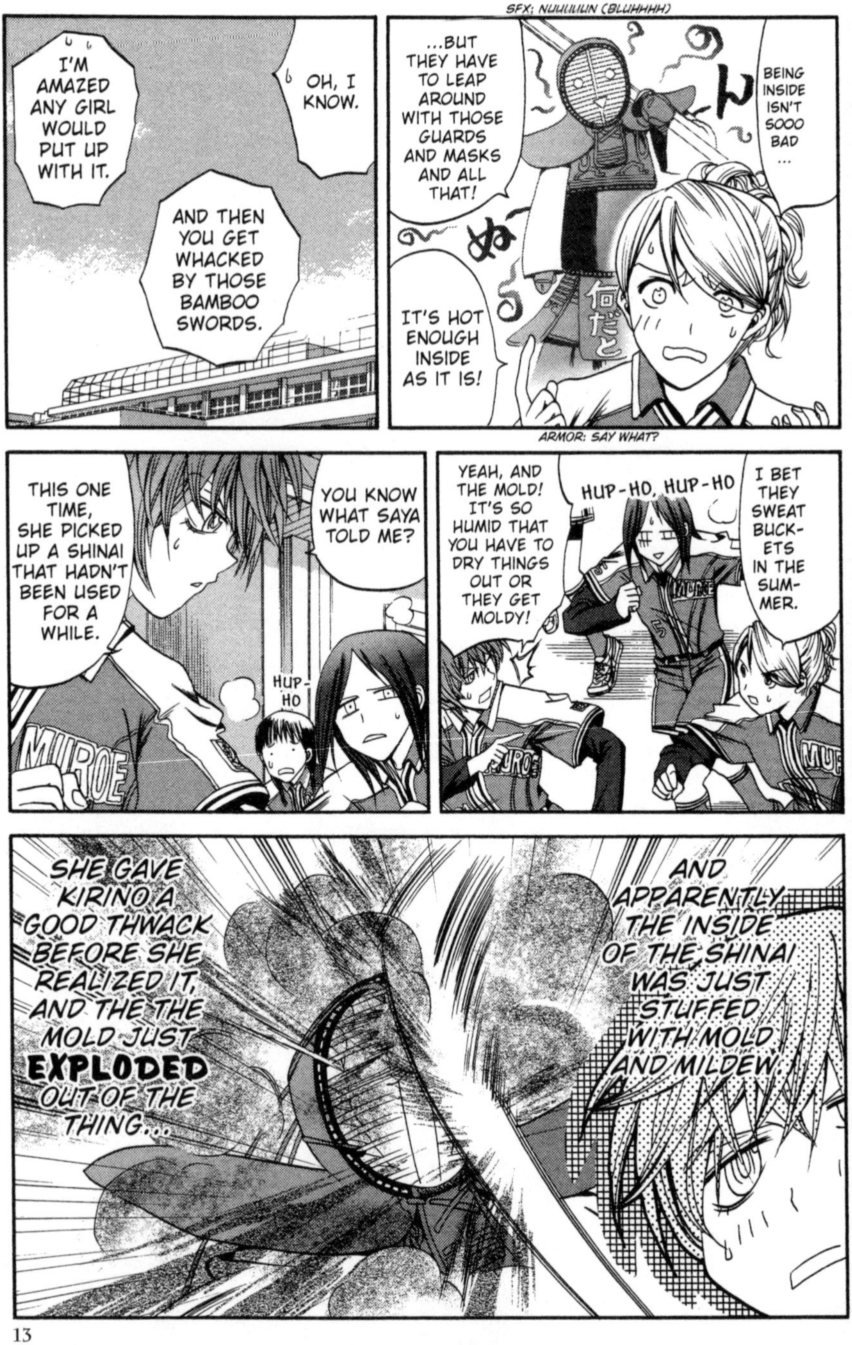
SFX: NUUUUUN (BLUHHHH)
...BUT THEY HAVE TO LEAP AROUND WITH THOSE GUARDS AND MASKS AND ALL THAT!
IT'S HOT ENOUGH INSIDE AS IT IS!
BEING INSIDE ISN'T SOOO BAD ...
ARMOR: SAY WHAT?
I'M AMAZED ANY GIRL WOULD PUT UP WITH IT.
OH, I KNOW.
AND THEN YOU GET WHACKED BY THOSE BAMBOO SWORDS.
I BET THEY SWEAT BUCKETS IN THE SUMMER.
HUP-HO, HUP-HO
YEAH, AND THE MOLD! IT'S SO HUMID THAT YOU HAVE TO DRY THINGS OUT OR THEY GET MOLDY!
YOU KNOW WHAT SAYA TOLD ME?
THIS ONE TIME, SHE PICKED UP A SHINAI THAT HADN'T BEEN USED FOR A WHILE.
HUP-HO
SHE GAVE KIRINO A GOOD THWACK BEFORE SHE REALIZED IT, AND THE THE MOLD JUST **EXPLODED** OUT OF THE THING...
AND APPARENTLY THE INSIDE OF THE SHINAI WAS JUST STUFFED WITH MOLD AND MILDEW.

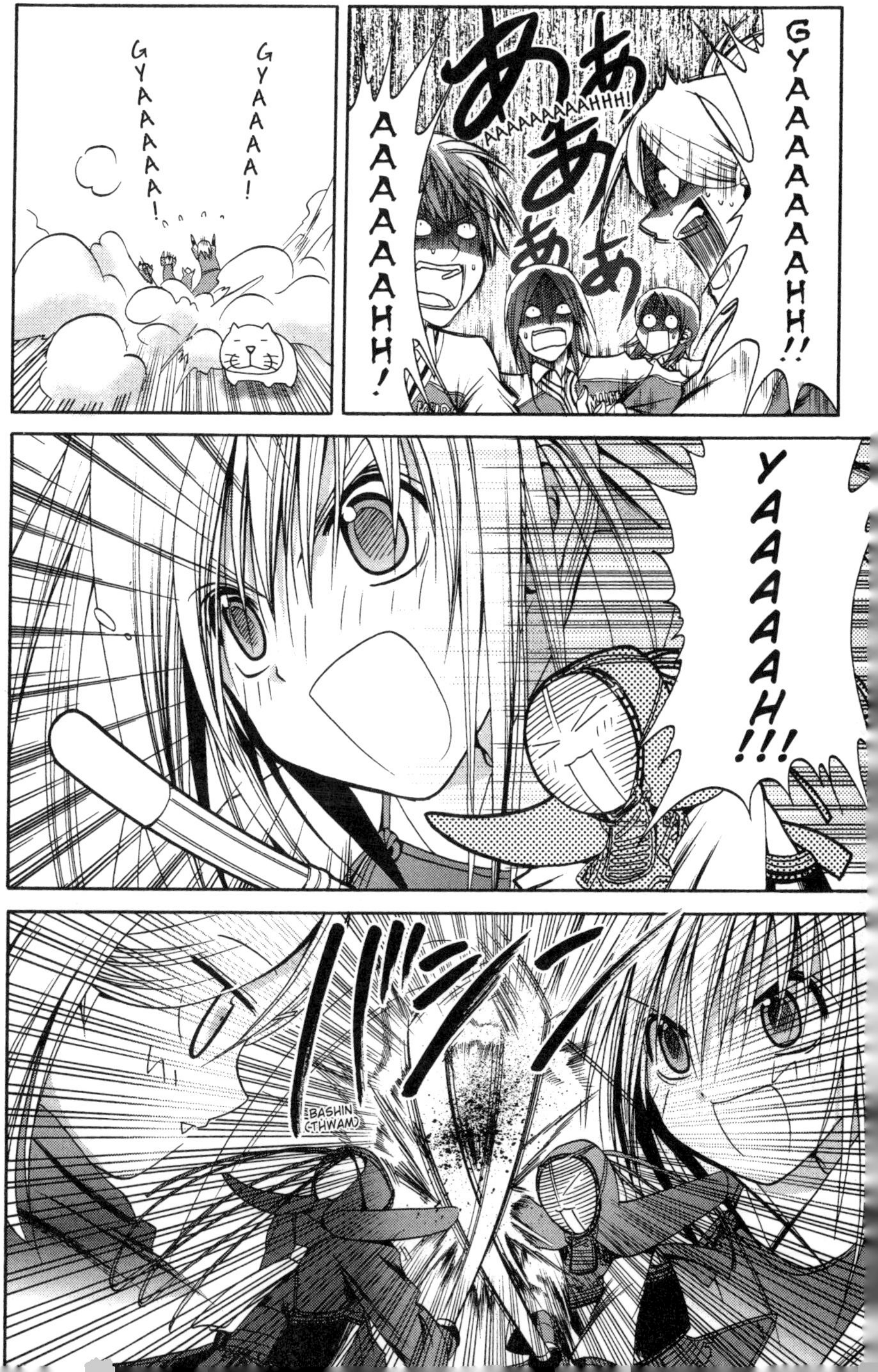
GYAAAAAAAAAH!!
ああああ
AAAAAAAAAHHH!
AAAAAAAAHH!
GYAAAA!
GYAAAAAA!
YAAAAAAAH!!!
BASHIN (THWAM)

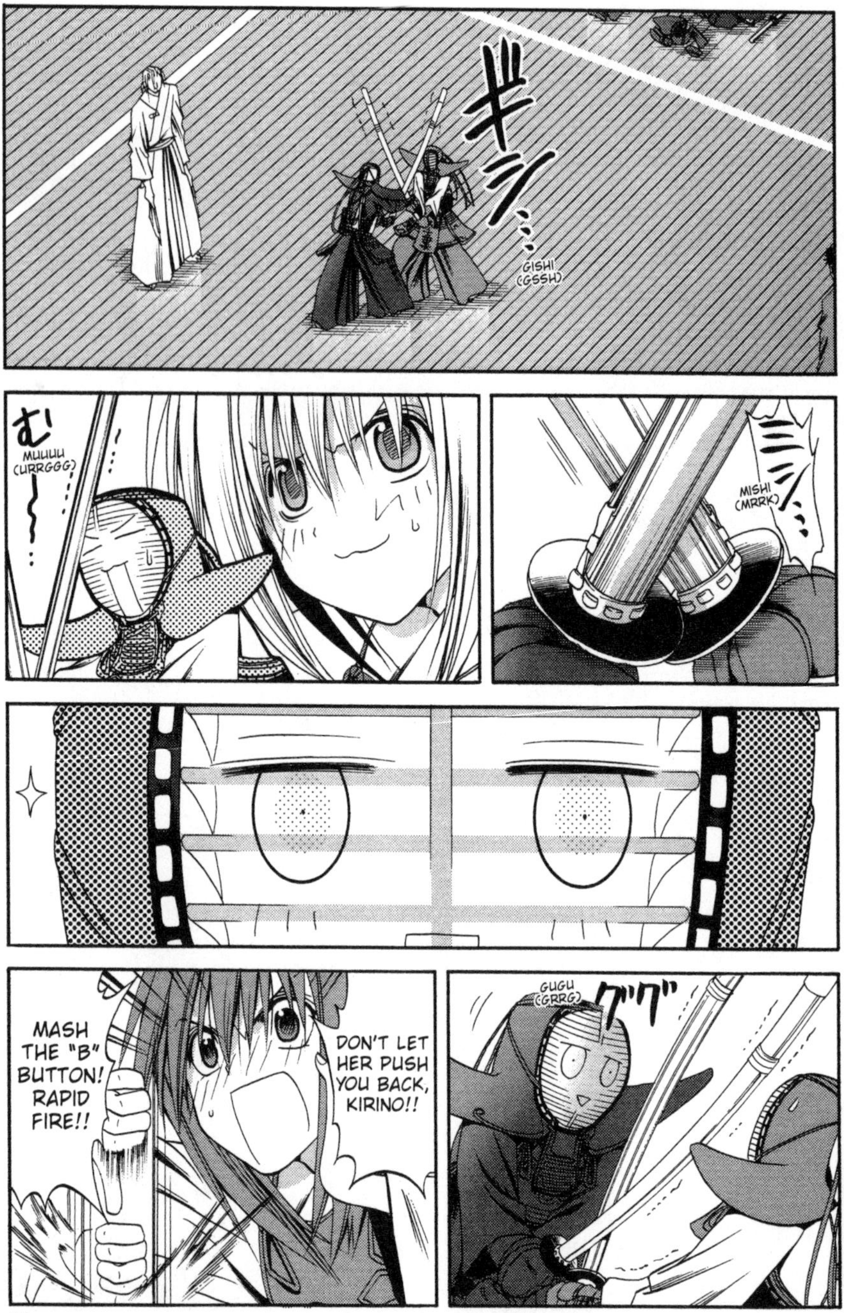
ギシ…
GISHI (GSSH)
ミシ…
MISHI (MRRK)
む
MUUUU (URRGGG)
DON'T LET HER PUSH YOU BACK, KIRINO!!
MASH THE "B" BUTTON! RAPID FIRE!!
グググ
GUGU (GRRG)

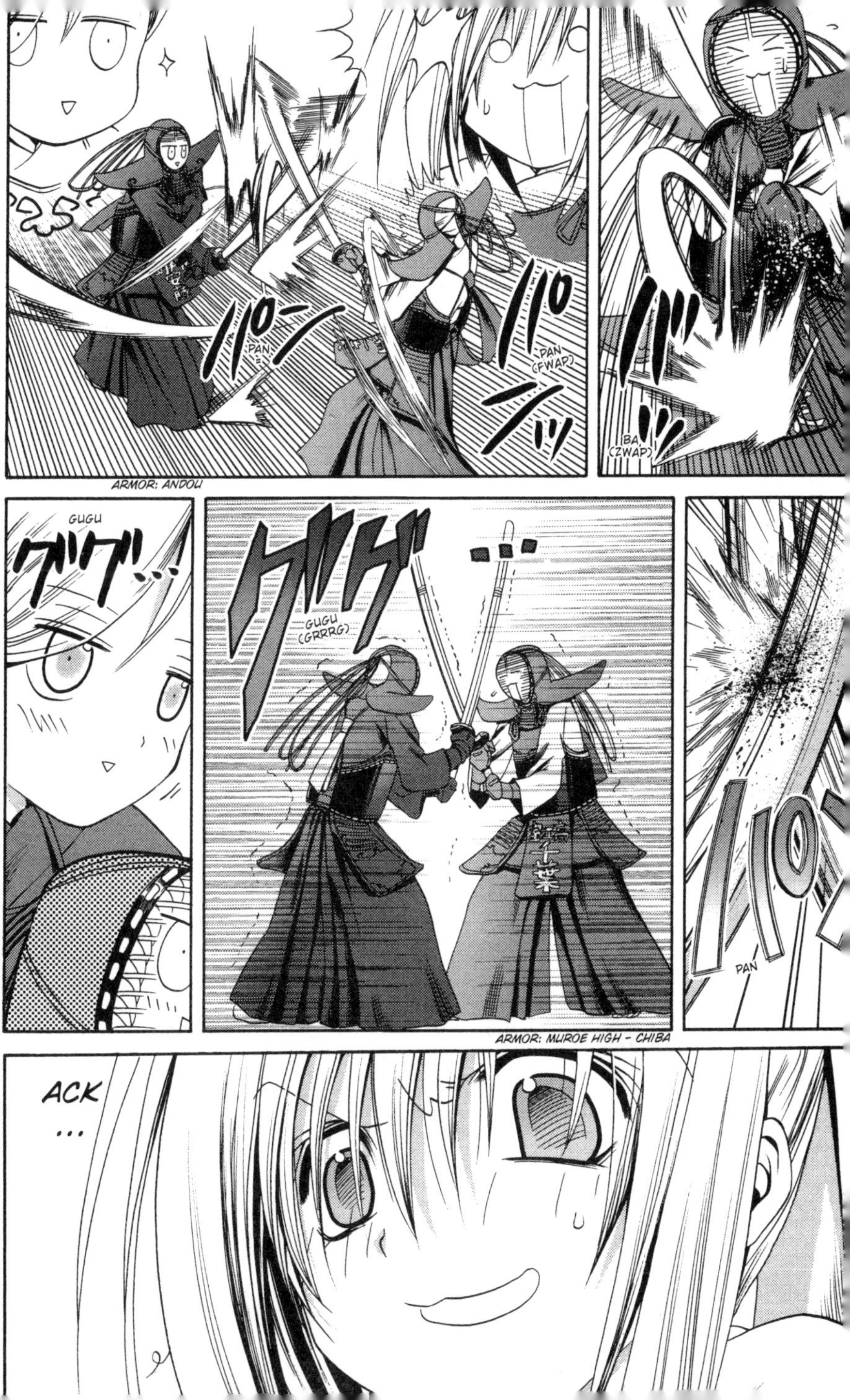
BA (ZWAP)
PAN (FWAP)
PAN
ARMOR: ANDOU
PAN
GUGU (GRRRG)
...
ARMOR: MUROE HIGH - CHIBA
GUGU
ACK
...

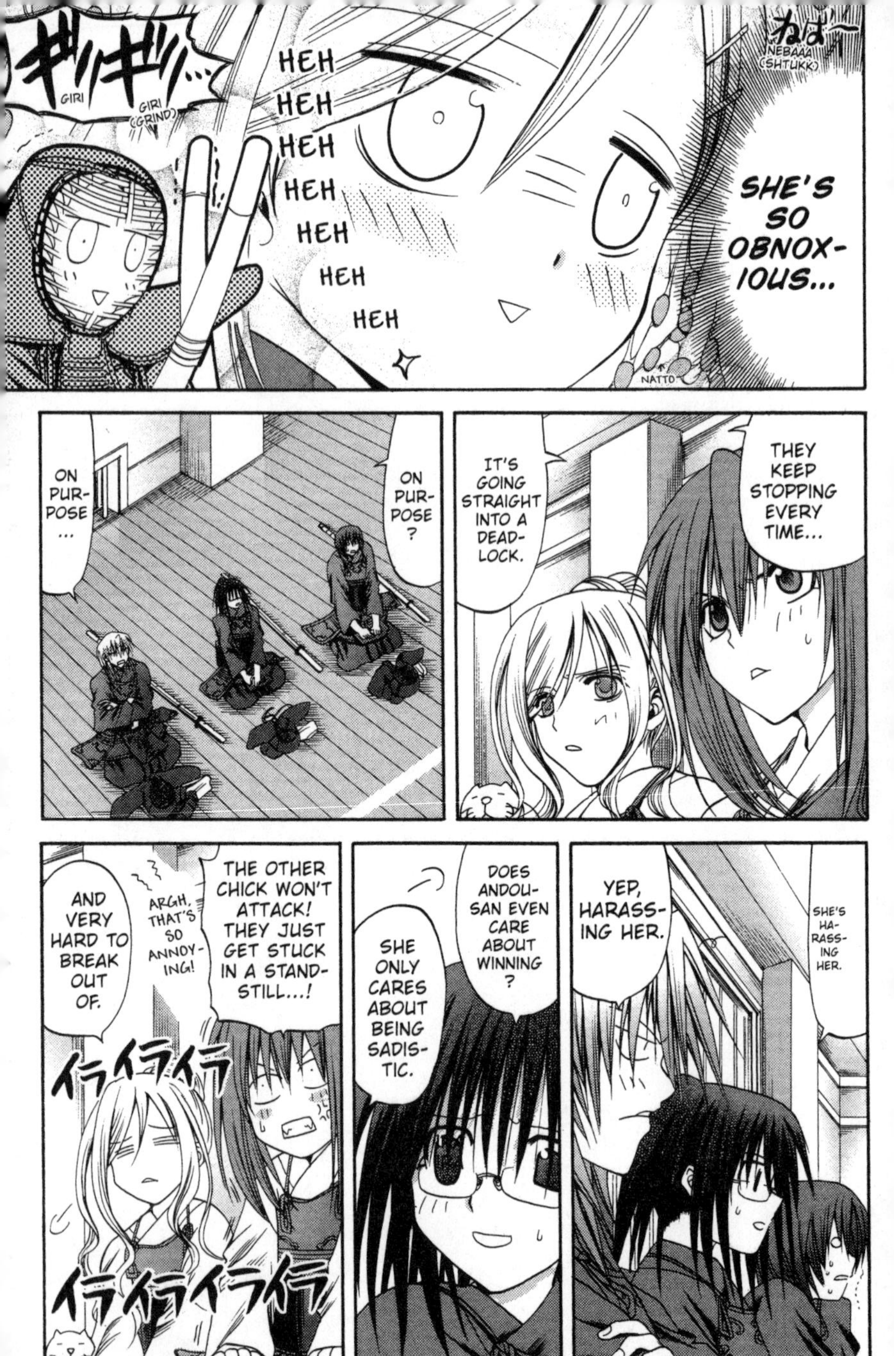
ねばー
NEBAAA (SHTUKK)
SHE'S SO OBNOX-IOUS...
NATTO
HEH HEH HEH HEH HEH HEH HEH
ギリギリ...
GIRI
GIRI (GRIND)
THEY KEEP STOPPING EVERY TIME...
IT'S GOING STRAIGHT INTO A DEAD-LOCK.
ON PUR-POSE?
ON PUR-POSE...
SHE'S HA-RASS-ING HER.
YEP, HARASS-ING HER.
DOES ANDOU-SAN EVEN CARE ABOUT WINNING?
SHE ONLY CARES ABOUT BEING SADIS-TIC.
THE OTHER CHICK WON'T ATTACK! THEY JUST GET STUCK IN A STAND-STILL...!
ARGH, THAT'S SO ANNOY-ING!
AND VERY HARD TO BREAK OUT OF.
イライライラ
イライライライラ
SFX: IRA (RRRGH) IRA IRA IRA IRA IRA IRA

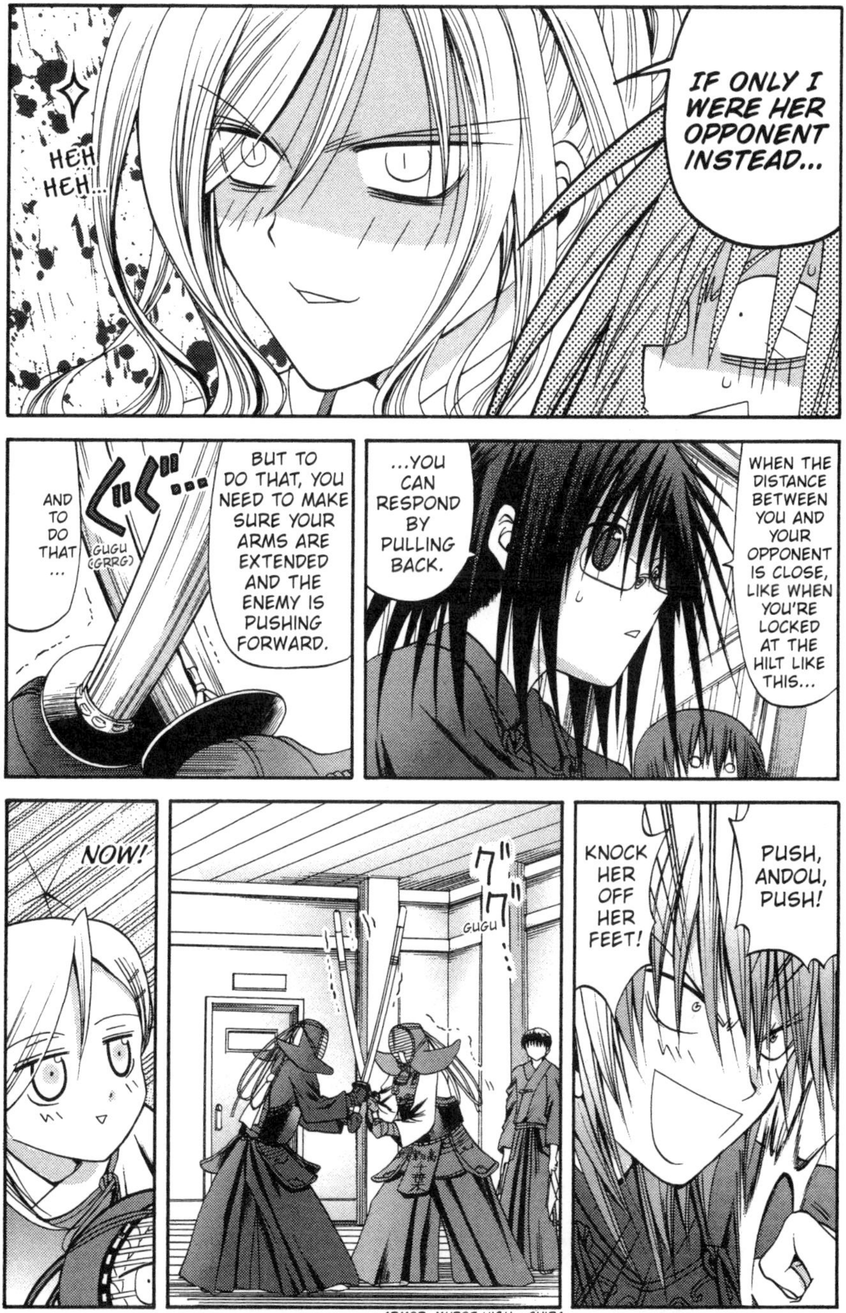
IF ONLY I WERE HER OPPONENT INSTEAD...
HEH HEH...
WHEN THE DISTANCE BETWEEN YOU AND YOUR OPPONENT IS CLOSE, LIKE WHEN YOU'RE LOCKED AT THE HILT LIKE THIS...
...YOU CAN RESPOND BY PULLING BACK.
BUT TO DO THAT, YOU NEED TO MAKE SURE YOUR ARMS ARE EXTENDED AND THE ENEMY IS PUSHING FORWARD.
GUGU (GRRG)
AND TO DO THAT...
PUSH, ANDOU, PUSH!
KNOCK HER OFF HER FEET!
GUGU
NOW!

ARMOR: MUROE HIGH - CHIBA

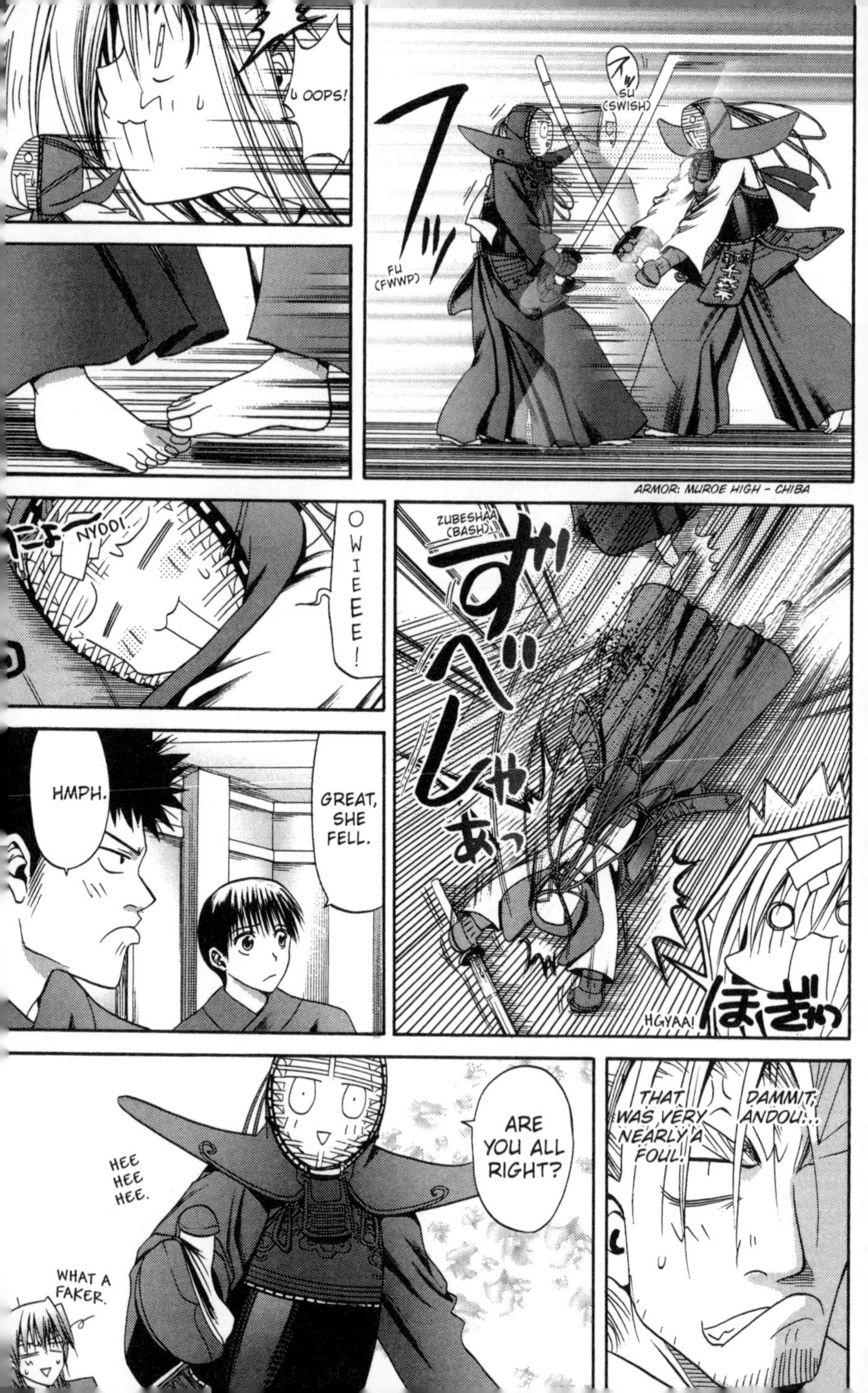
SU (SWISH)
FU (FWWP)
OOPS!
ARMOR: MUROE HIGH - CHIBA
ZUBESHAA (BASH)
HGYAA!
NYOO!
OWIEEE!
GREAT, SHE FELL.
HMPH.
DAMMIT, ANDOU...
THAT WAS VERY NEARLY A FOUL!
ARE YOU ALL RIGHT?
HEE HEE HEE.
WHAT A FAKER.

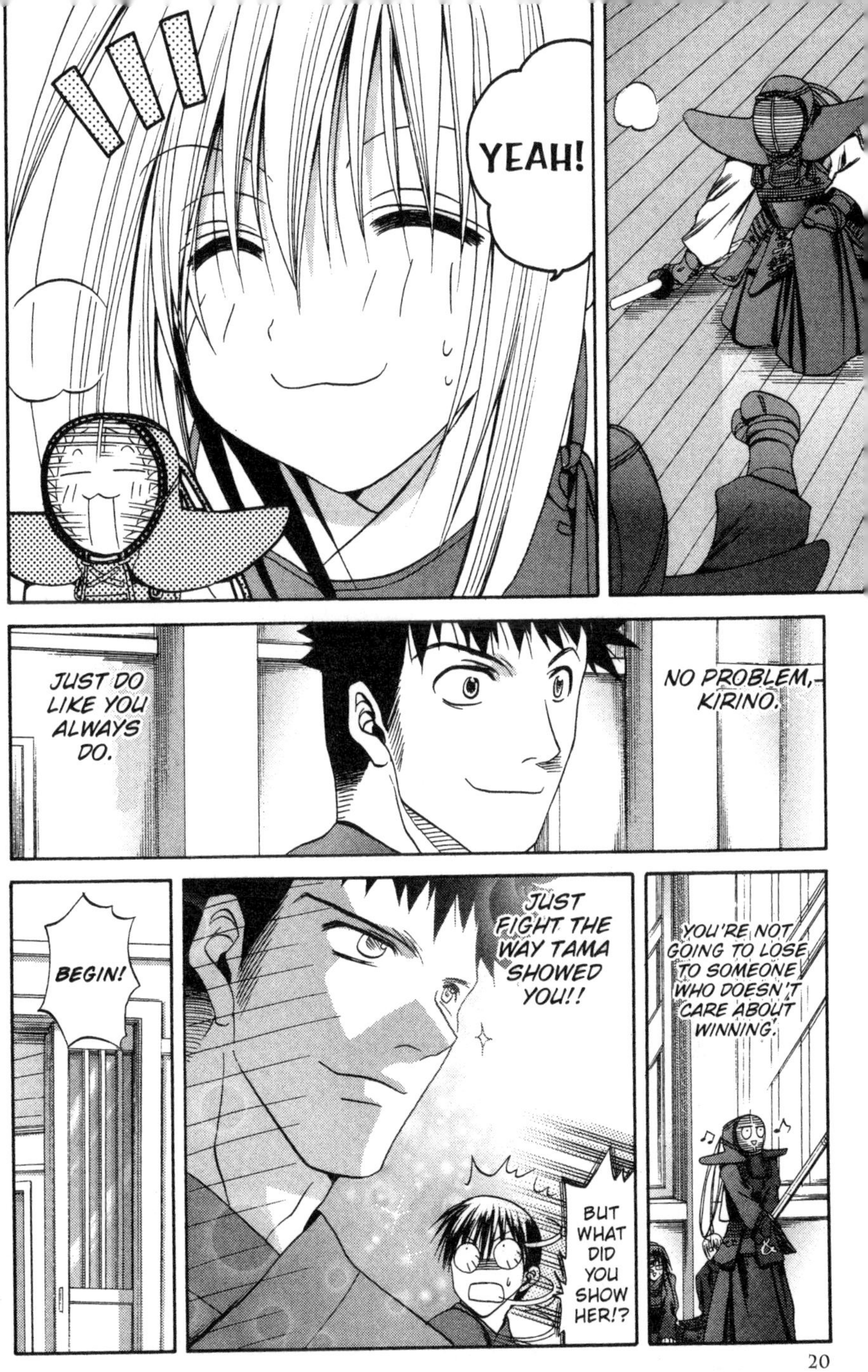
YEAH!
NO PROBLEM, KIRINO.
JUST DO LIKE YOU ALWAYS DO.
YOU'RE NOT GOING TO LOSE TO SOMEONE WHO DOESN'T CARE ABOUT WINNING.
JUST FIGHT THE WAY TAMA SHOWED YOU!!
BUT WHAT DID YOU SHOW HER!?
BEGIN!

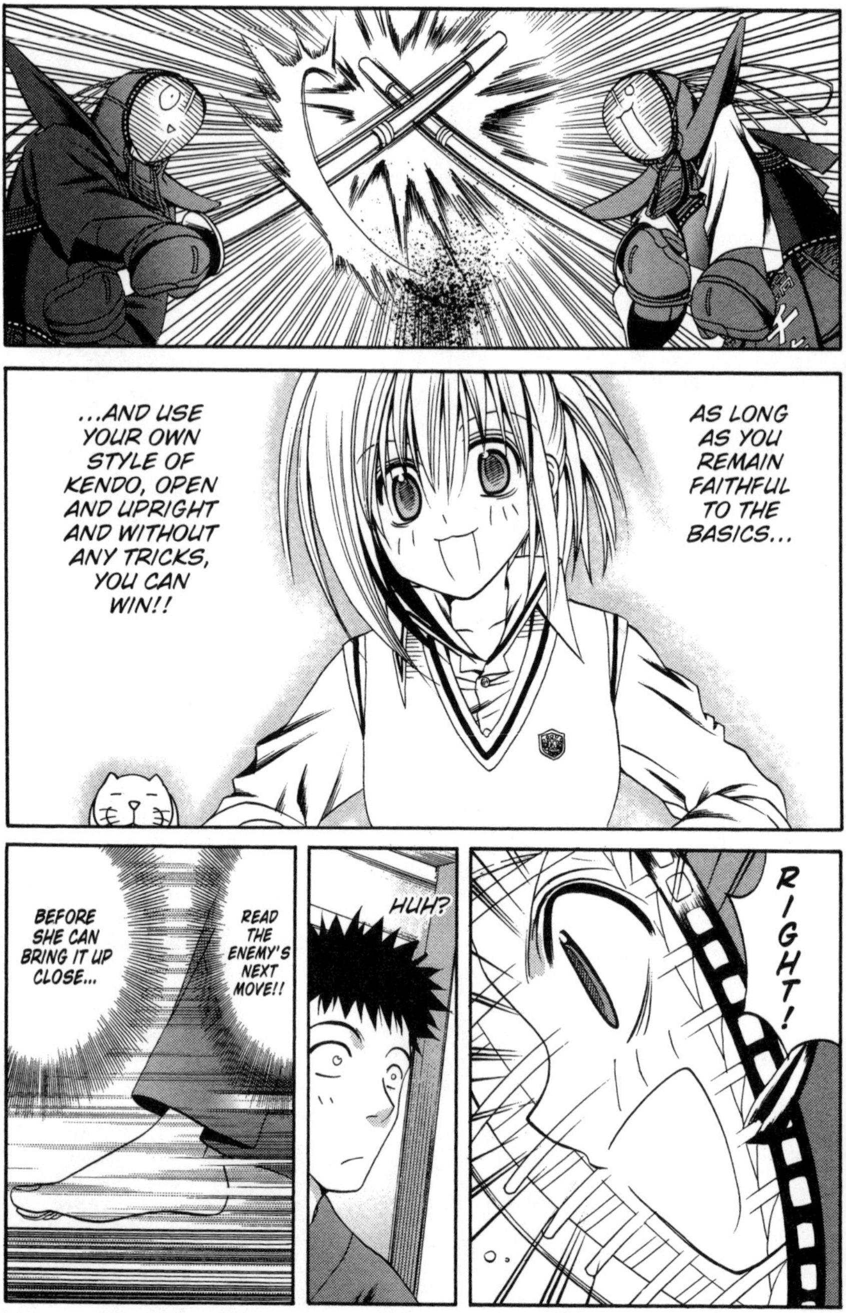
AS LONG AS YOU REMAIN FAITHFUL TO THE BASICS...
...AND USE YOUR OWN STYLE OF KENDO, OPEN AND UPRIGHT AND WITHOUT ANY TRICKS, YOU CAN WIN!!
RIGHT!
HUH?
READ THE ENEMY'S NEXT MOVE!!
BEFORE SHE CAN BRING IT UP CLOSE...

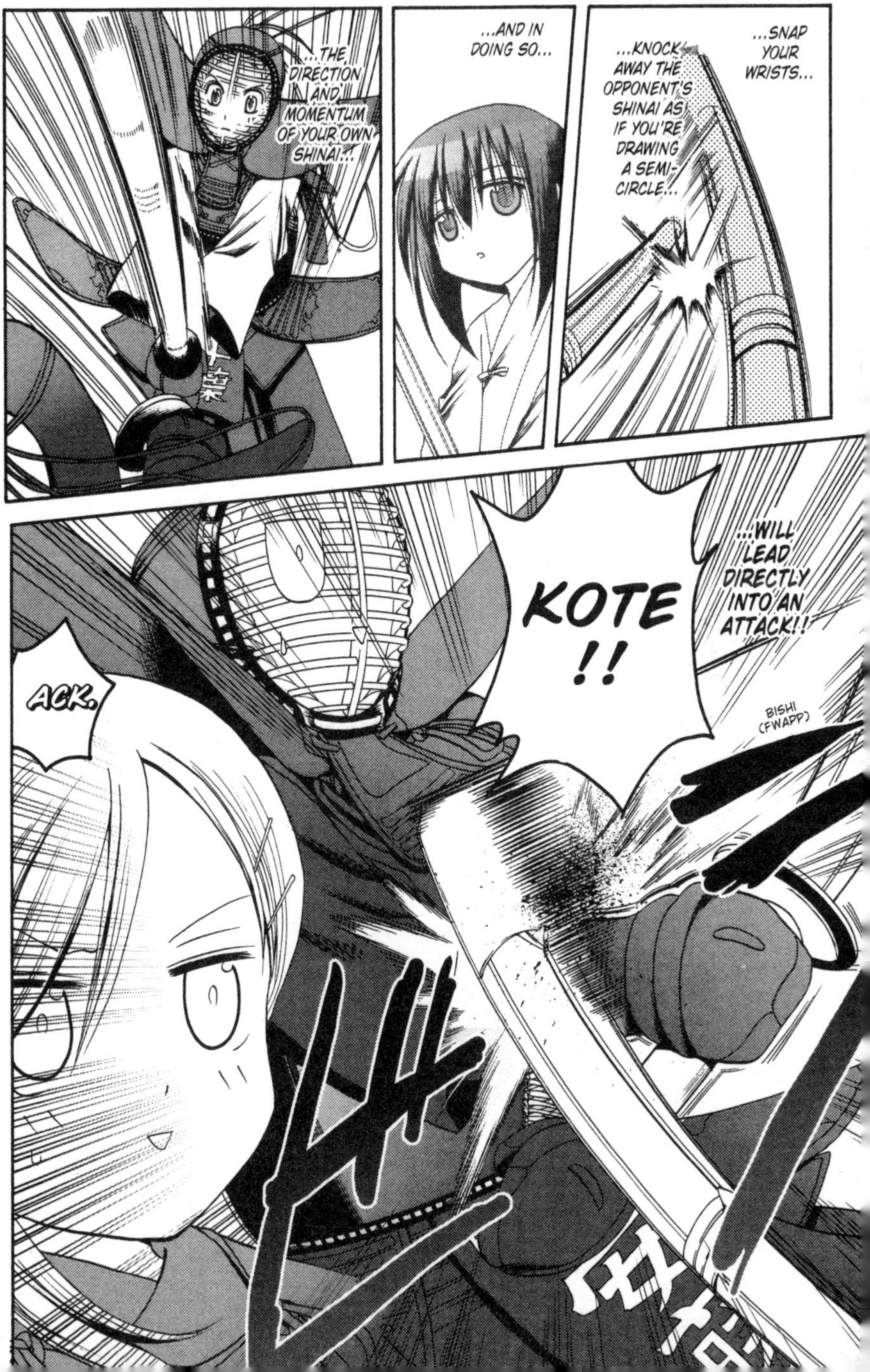
...SNAP YOUR WRISTS...
...KNOCK AWAY THE OPPONENT'S SHINAI AS IF YOU'RE DRAWING A SEMI-CIRCLE...
...AND IN DOING SO...
...THE DIRECTION AND MOMENTUM OF YOUR OWN SHINAI...
...WILL LEAD DIRECTLY INTO AN ATTACK!!
KOTE !!
BISHI (FWAPP)
ACK.

BAMBOO BLADE

KAWAZOE-SAN AND GLASSES

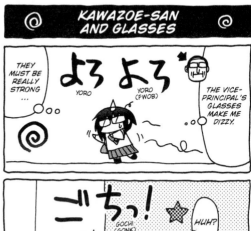

THE VICE-PRINCIPAL'S GLASSES MAKE ME DIZZY.
よろよろ
YORO YORO (FWOB)
THEY MUST BE REALLY STRONG ...
HUH?
ごちっ!
GOCHI (GONK)
ごちっ!
GOCHI
WHAT THE-?
ぷく
PUKUUU (PWOOP)
WELL, WELL.
I'VE GOTTEN TALLER.

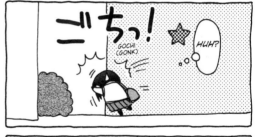

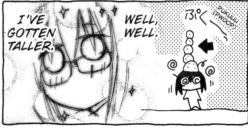

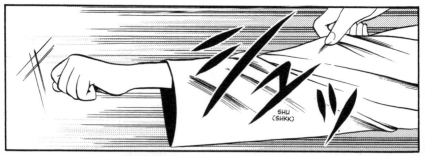

SHU
(SHKK)

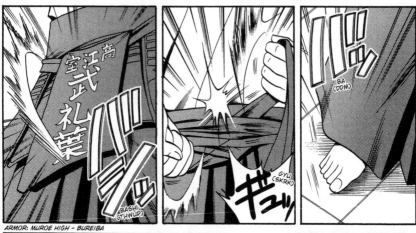

BASHI
(THWUP)

GYU
(SKRK)

BA
(DDM)

ARMOR: MUROE HIGH - BUREIBA

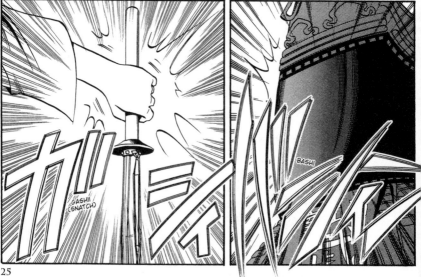

GASHII
(SNATCH)

BASHI

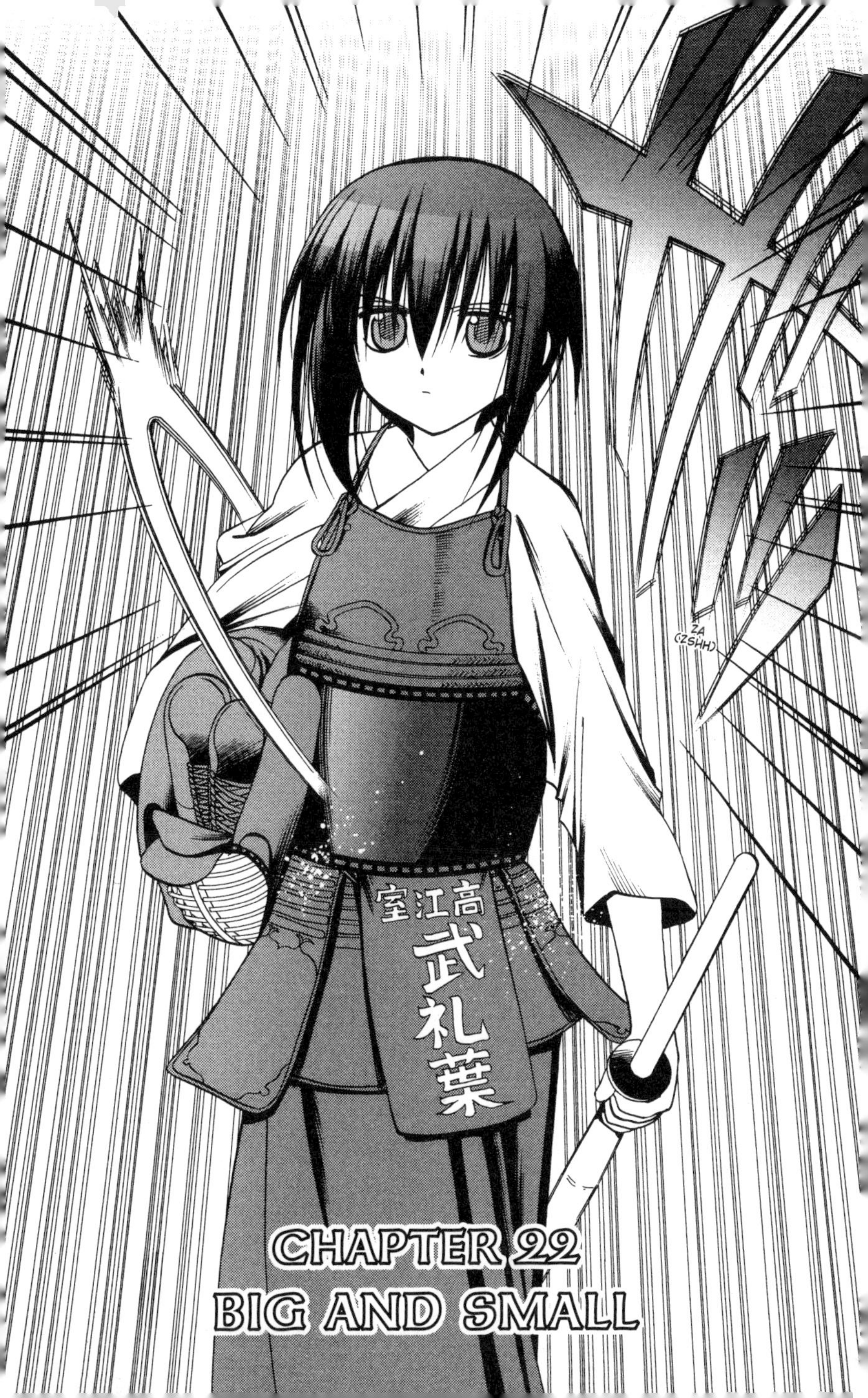
ZA
(ZSHH)
室江高
武礼葉
CHAPTER 22
BIG AND SMALL

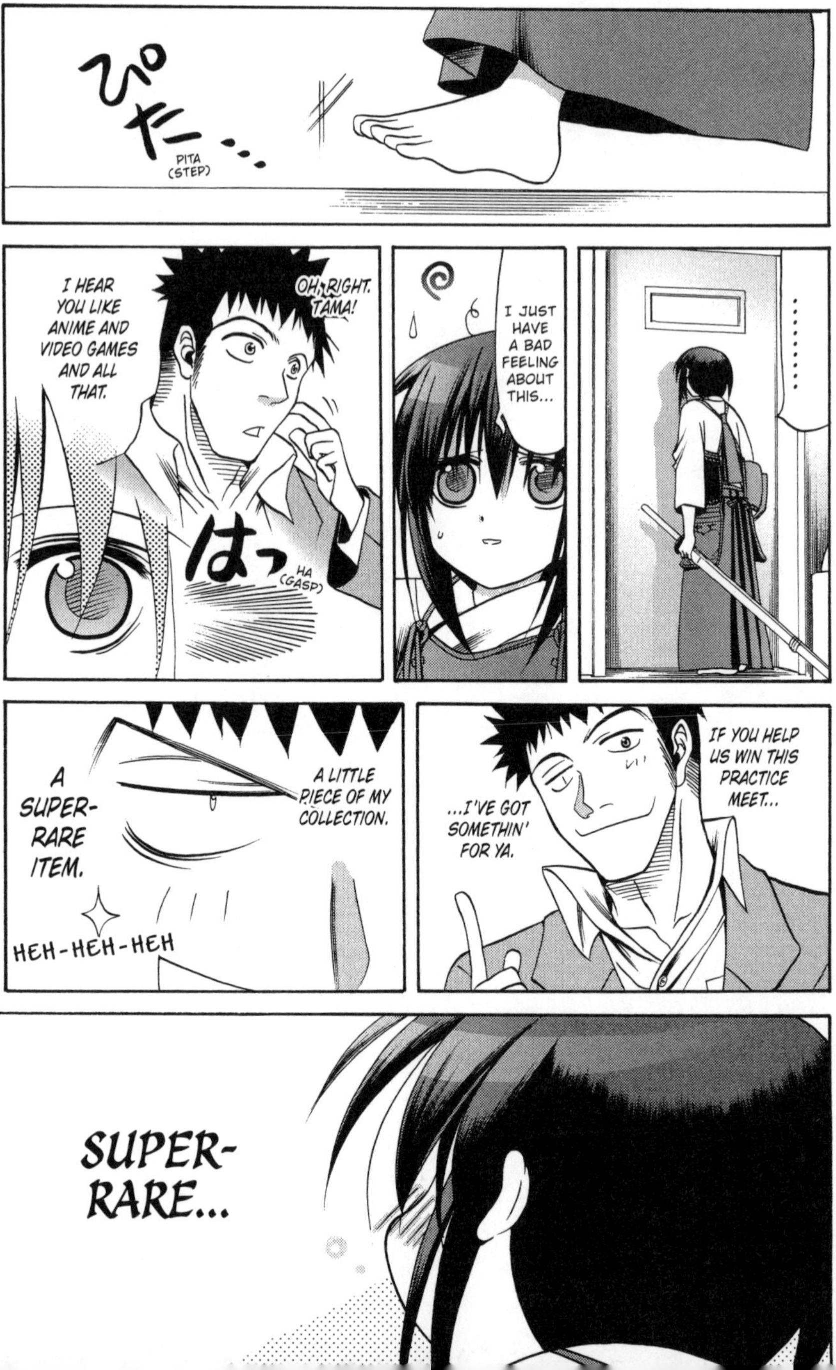
ぴた…
PITA (STEP)
……
I JUST HAVE A BAD FEELING ABOUT THIS…
OH, RIGHT. TAMA!
I HEAR YOU LIKE ANIME AND VIDEO GAMES AND ALL THAT.
はっ
HA (GASP)
IF YOU HELP US WIN THIS PRACTICE MEET…
…I'VE GOT SOMETHIN' FOR YA.
A LITTLE PIECE OF MY COLLECTION.
A SUPER-RARE ITEM.
HEH-HEH-HEH
SUPER-RARE…

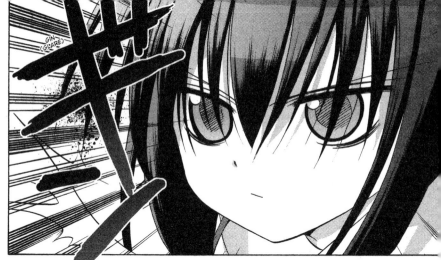
GIN
(GLARE)

FLY AT HER!!

GO, KIRINO, GO!!

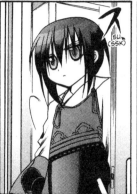
ス
SU
(SSK)

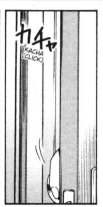
カチャ
KACHA
(CLICK)

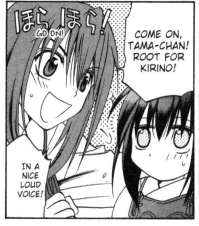
ほら ほら!
GO ON!

COME ON, TAMA-CHAN! ROOT FOR KIRINO!

IN A NICE LOUD VOICE!

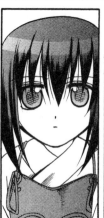

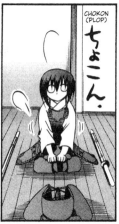
CHOKON
(PLOP)
ちょこん。

28

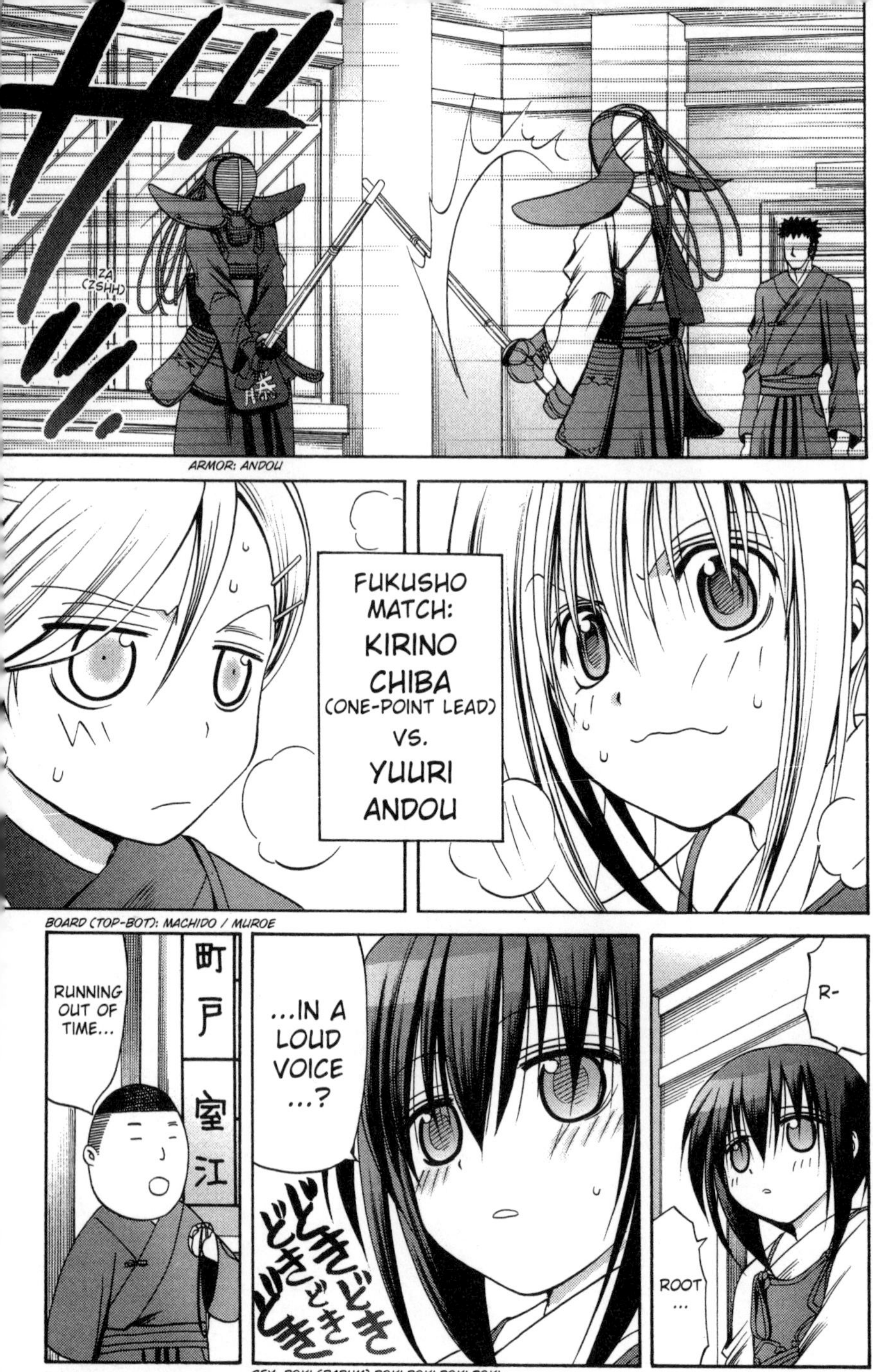
ZA (ZSHH)
FUKUSHO MATCH: KIRINO CHIBA (ONE-POINT LEAD) VS. YUURI ANDOU
R-
ROOT ...
...IN A LOUD VOICE ...?
どきどきどきどきどき
RUNNING OUT OF TIME...
町戸
室江

ARMOR: ANDOU

BOARD (TOP-BOT): MACHIDO / MUROE

SFX: DOKI (BADUM) DOKI DOKI DOKI DOKI

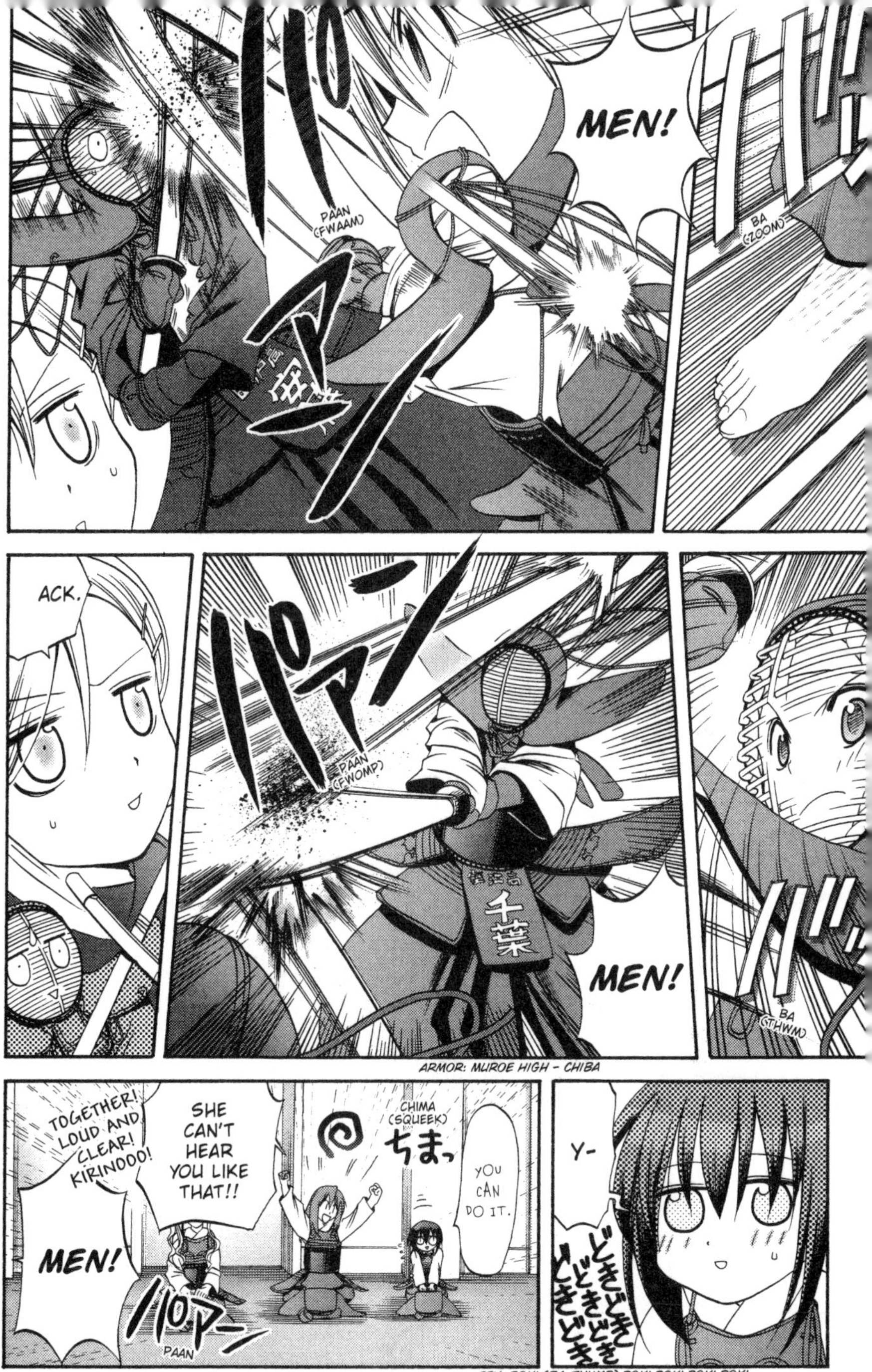
MEN!
BA (ZOOM)
PAAN (FWAAM)
MEN!
BA (THWM)
PAAN (FWOMP)
ACK.
Y-
CHIMA (SQUEEK)
ちまっ
YOU CAN DO IT.
SHE CAN'T HEAR YOU LIKE THAT!!
TOGETHER! LOUD AND CLEAR! KIRINODOO!
MEN!
PAAN

ARMOR: MUROE HIGH - CHIBA

SFX: DOKI (BA-THUMP) DOKI DOKI DOKI DOKI

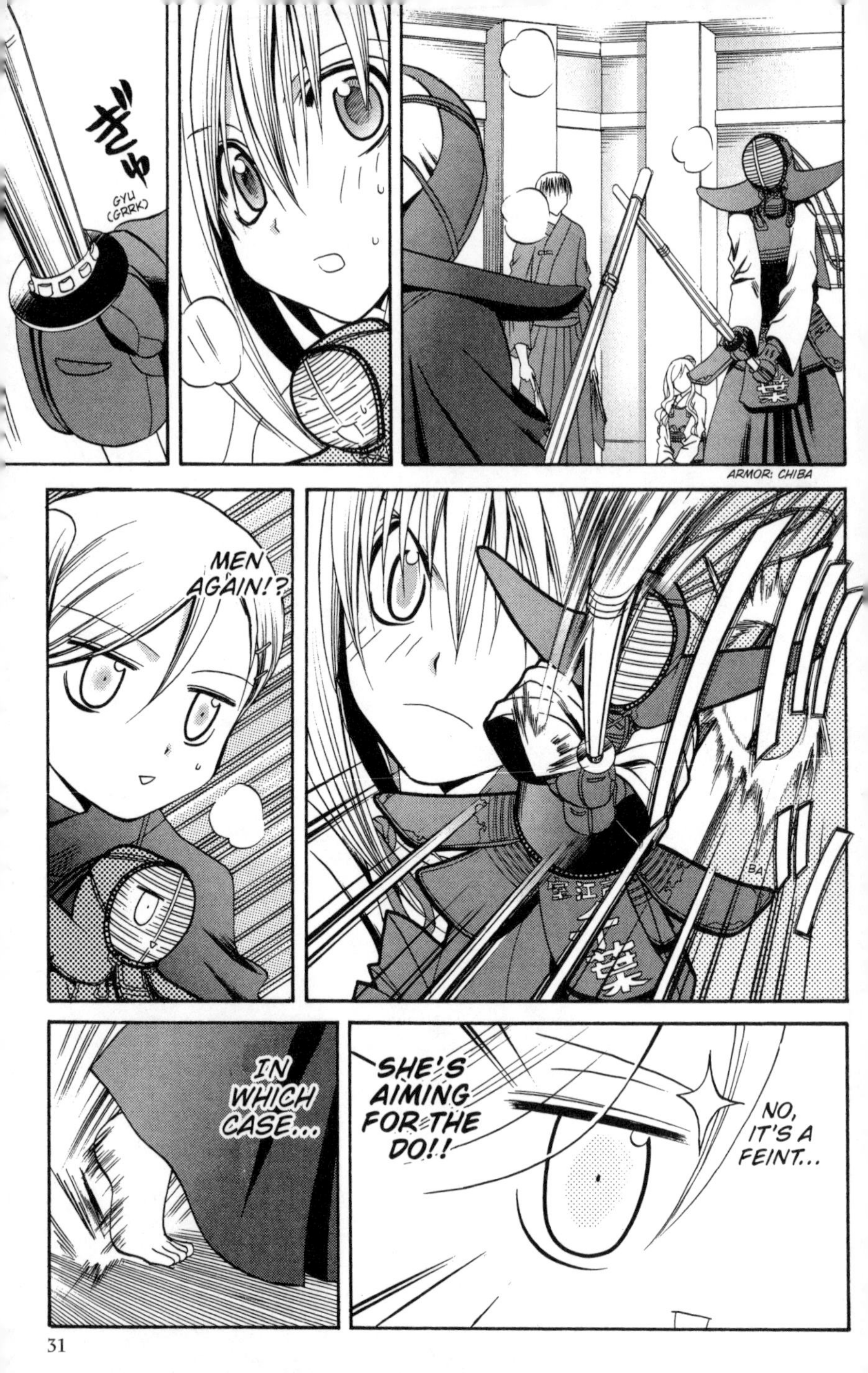
ARMOR: CHIBA
ぎゅ
GYU (GRRK)
BA
MEN AGAIN!?
SHE'S AIMING FOR THE DO!!
NO, IT'S A FEINT...
IN WHICH CASE...

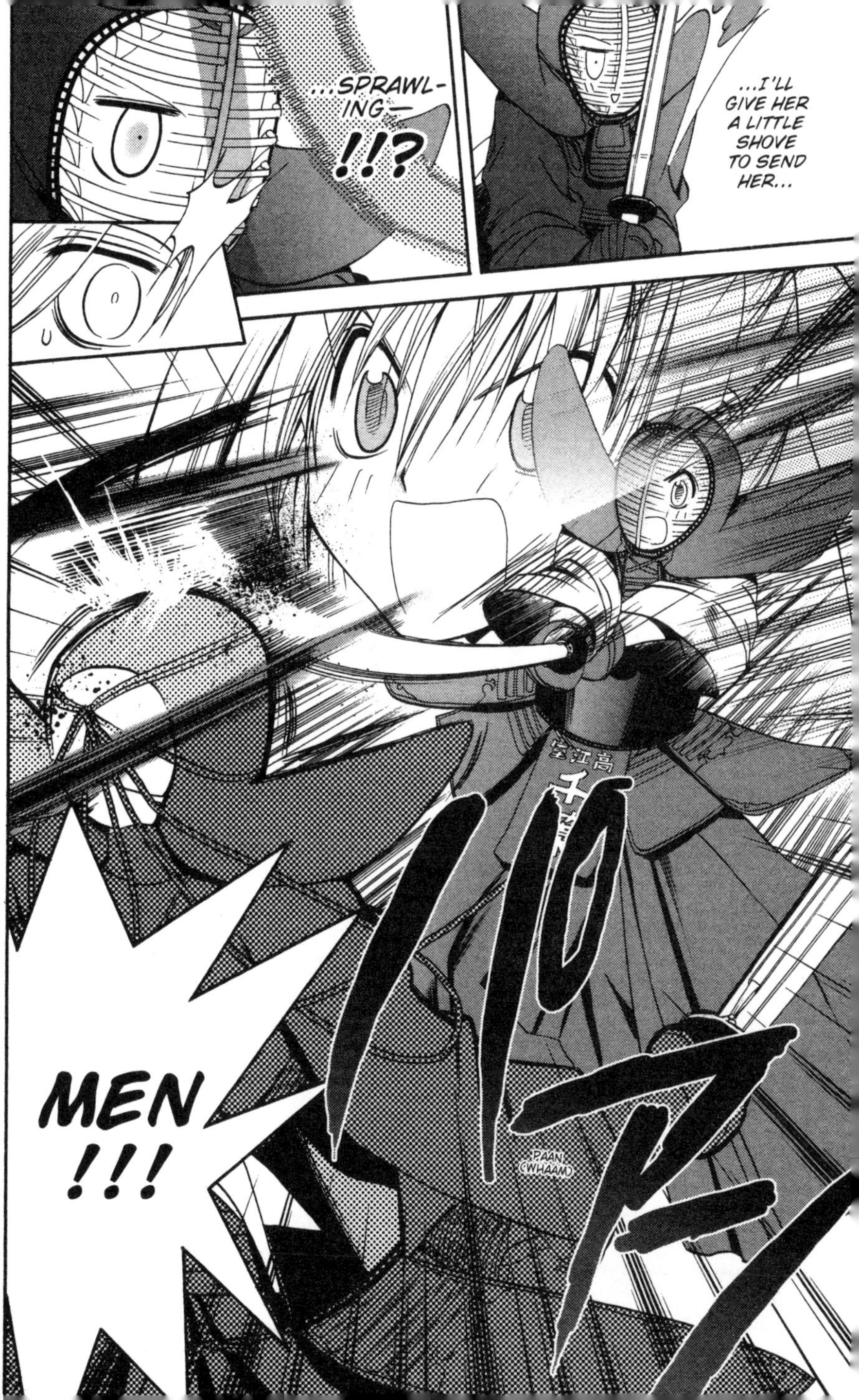
...I'LL GIVE HER A LITTLE SHOVE TO SEND HER...
...SPRAWL-ING—
!!?
MEN!!!
PAAN (WHAAM)

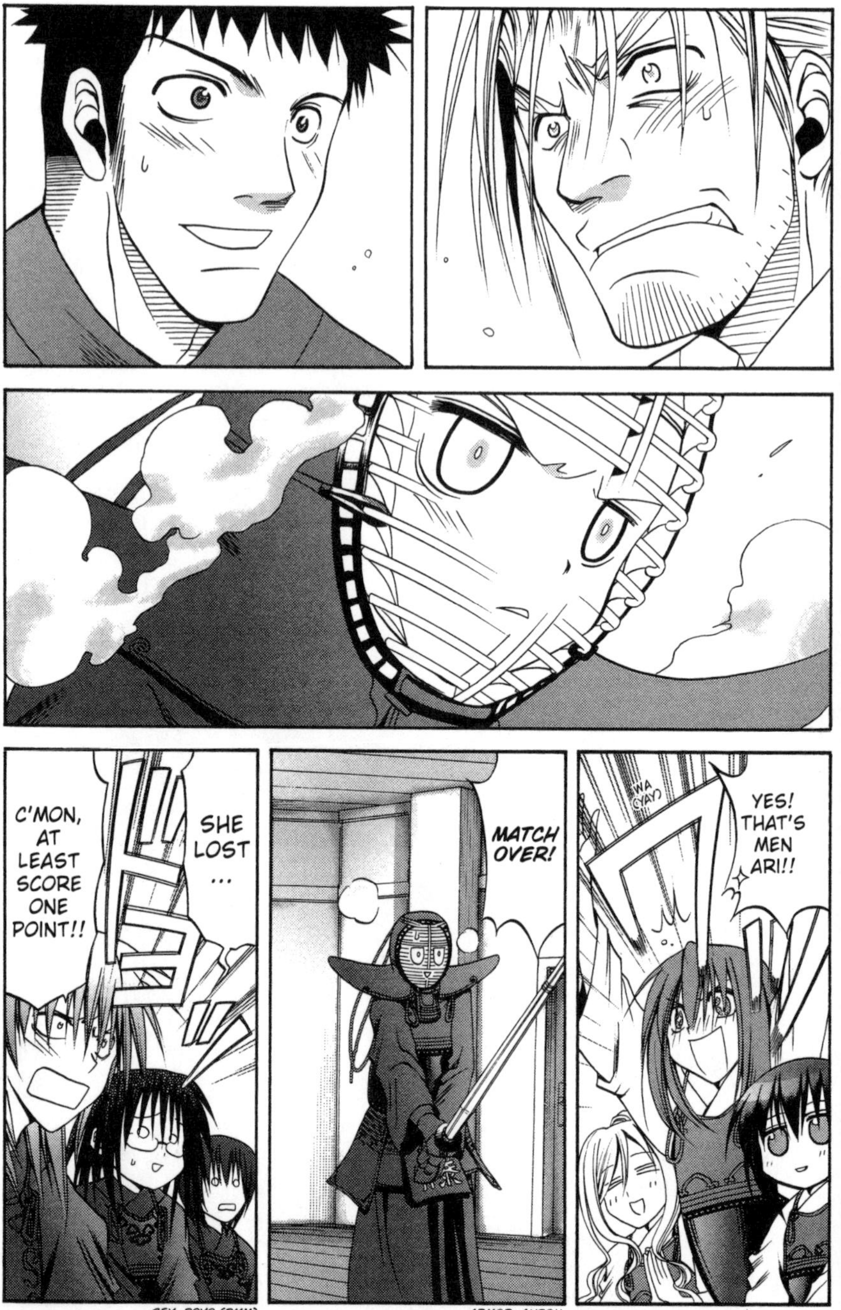
WA (YAY)
YES! THAT'S MEN ARI!!
MATCH OVER!
SHE LOST ...
C'MON, AT LEAST SCORE ONE POINT!!

SFX: DOYO (DMM)

ARMOR: ANDOU

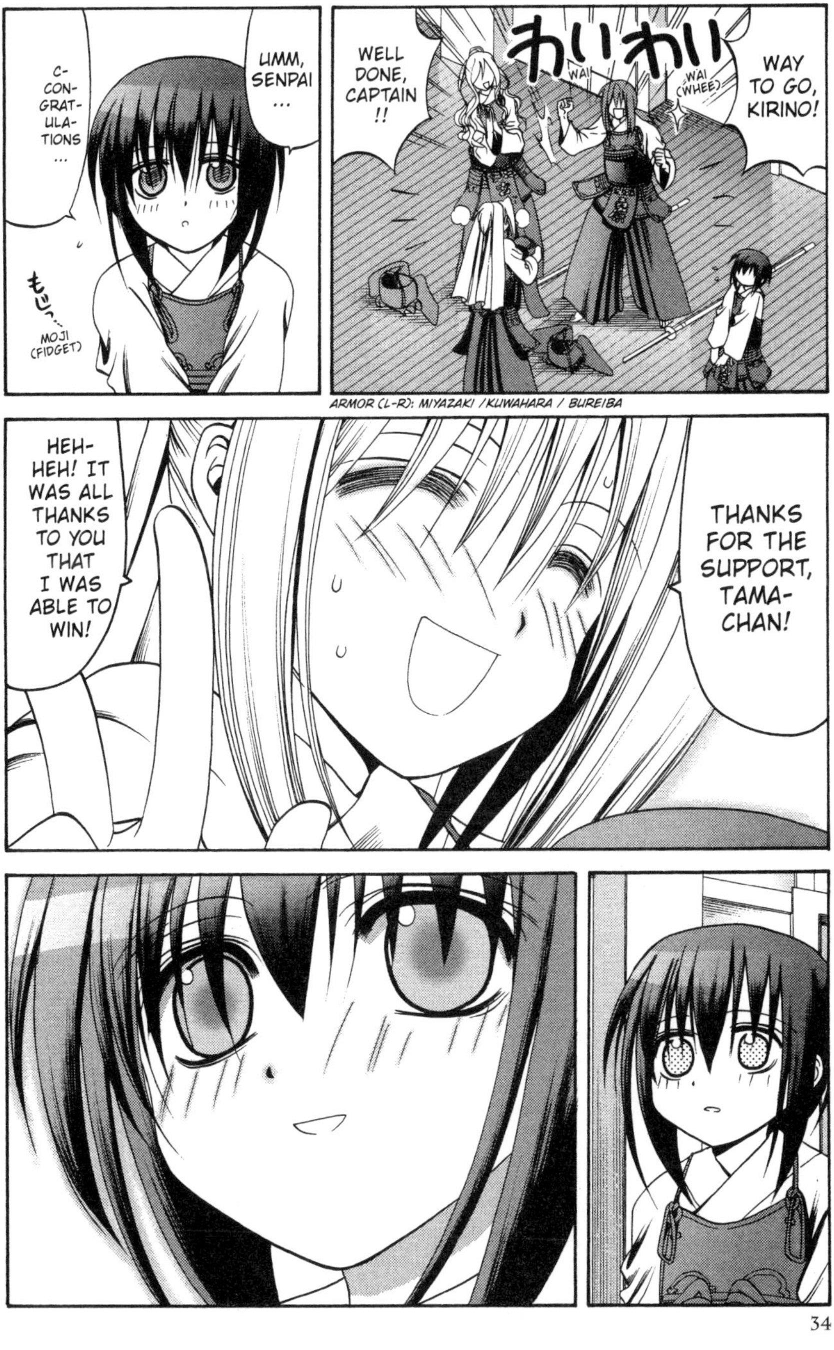
WAY TO GO, KIRINO!
わいわい
WAI WAI (WHEE)
WELL DONE, CAPTAIN!!
UMM, SENPAI...
C-CONGRATULATIONS...
もじっ...
MOJI (FIDGET)
ARMOR (L-R): MIYAZAKI / KUWAHARA / BUREIBA
THANKS FOR THE SUPPORT, TAMA-CHAN!
HEH-HEH! IT WAS ALL THANKS TO YOU THAT I WAS ABLE TO WIN!

SFX: POKA (THWOK) POKA

SFX: POKA POKA

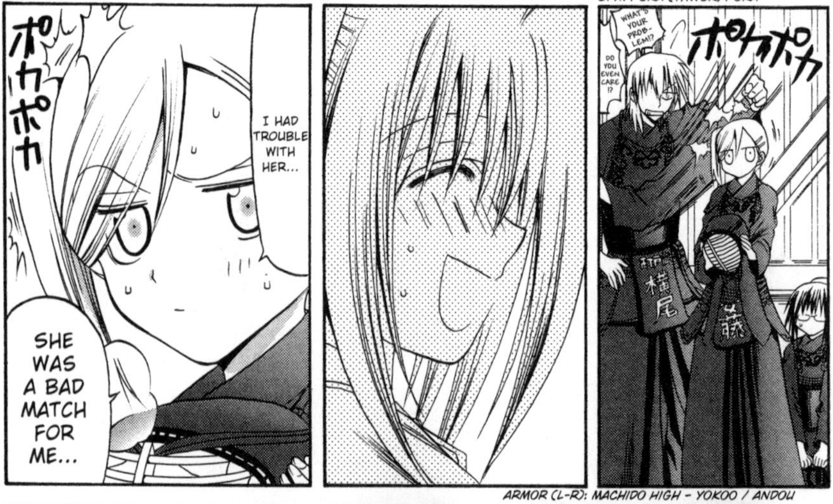
WHAT'S YOUR PROB-LEM!?
DO YOU EVEN CARE!?
ポカポカ
I HAD TROUBLE WITH HER...
SHE WAS A BAD MATCH FOR ME...
ポカポカ

ARMOR (L-R): MACHIDO HIGH - YOKOO / ANDOU

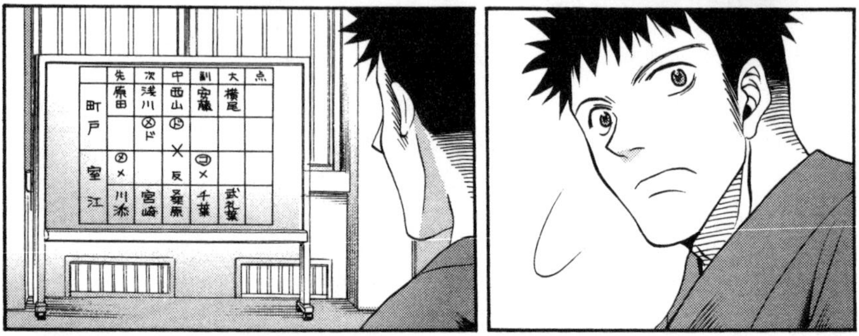

MACHIDO	HARADA	ASAKAWA	NISHIYAMA	ANDOU	YOKOO	
		(M) D	(D)			
			X			
	(M) M		F	(K) M		
MUROE	KAWAZOE	MIYAZAKI	KUWAHARA	CHIBA	BUREIBA	

NOTE: "○" INDICATES FIRST STRIKE. THE LETTERS CORRELATE WITH FIRST LETTER OF THE PART HIT. "D" FOR DO (CHEST), "M" FOR MEN (MASK), AND "K" FOR KOTE (GAUNTLET). "F" STANDS FOR FOUL, AND AN "X" ON THE MIDDLE LINE INDICATES A DRAW.

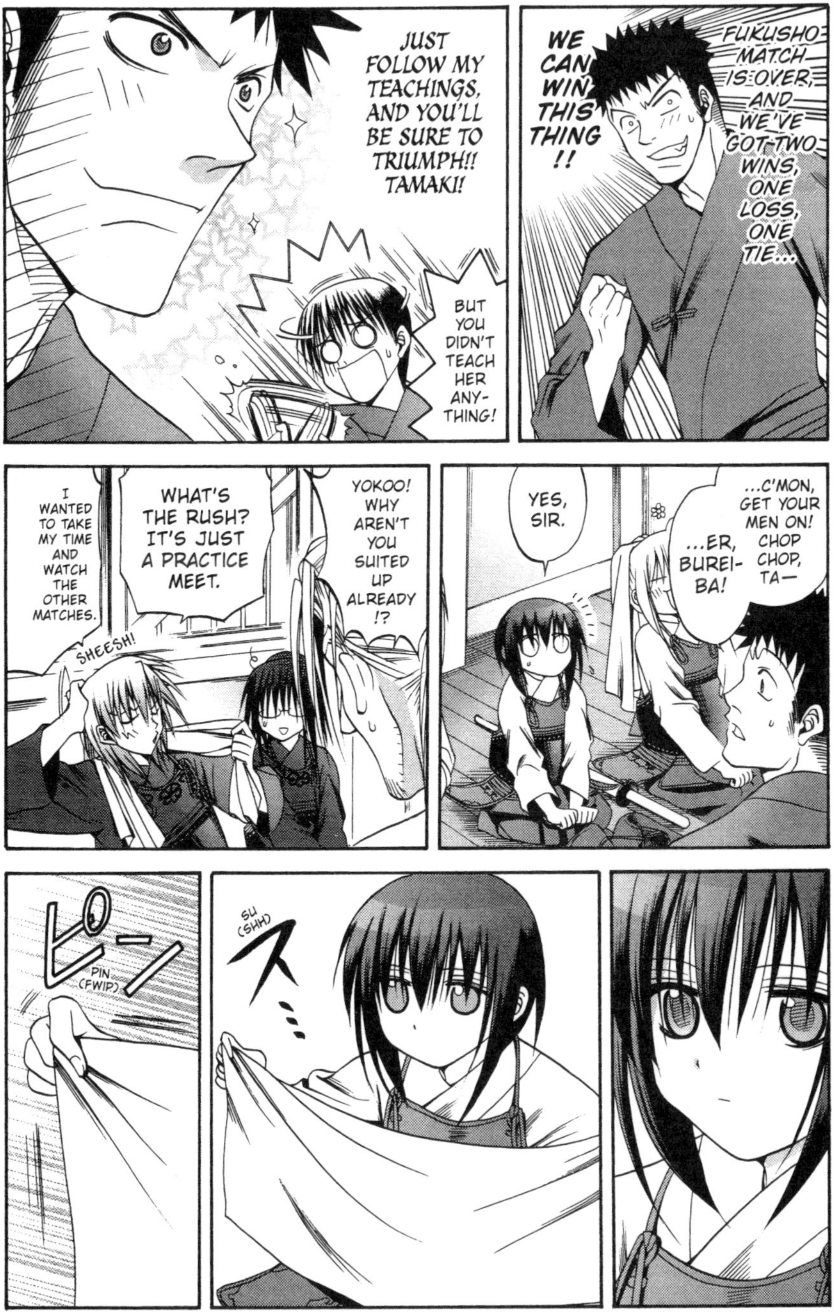
FUKUSHO MATCH IS OVER, AND WE'VE GOT TWO WINS, ONE LOSS, ONE TIE...
WE CAN WIN THIS THING!!
JUST FOLLOW MY TEACHINGS, AND YOU'LL BE SURE TO TRIUMPH!! TAMAKI!
BUT YOU DIDN'T TEACH HER ANYTHING!
...C'MON, GET YOUR MEN ON! CHOP CHOP, TA—
...ER, BUREI-BA!
YES, SIR.
YOKOO! WHY AREN'T YOU SUITED UP ALREADY!?
WHAT'S THE RUSH? IT'S JUST A PRACTICE MEET.
I WANTED TO TAKE MY TIME AND WATCH THE OTHER MATCHES.
SHEESH!
SU (SHH)
ス
ピーン
PIN (FWIP)

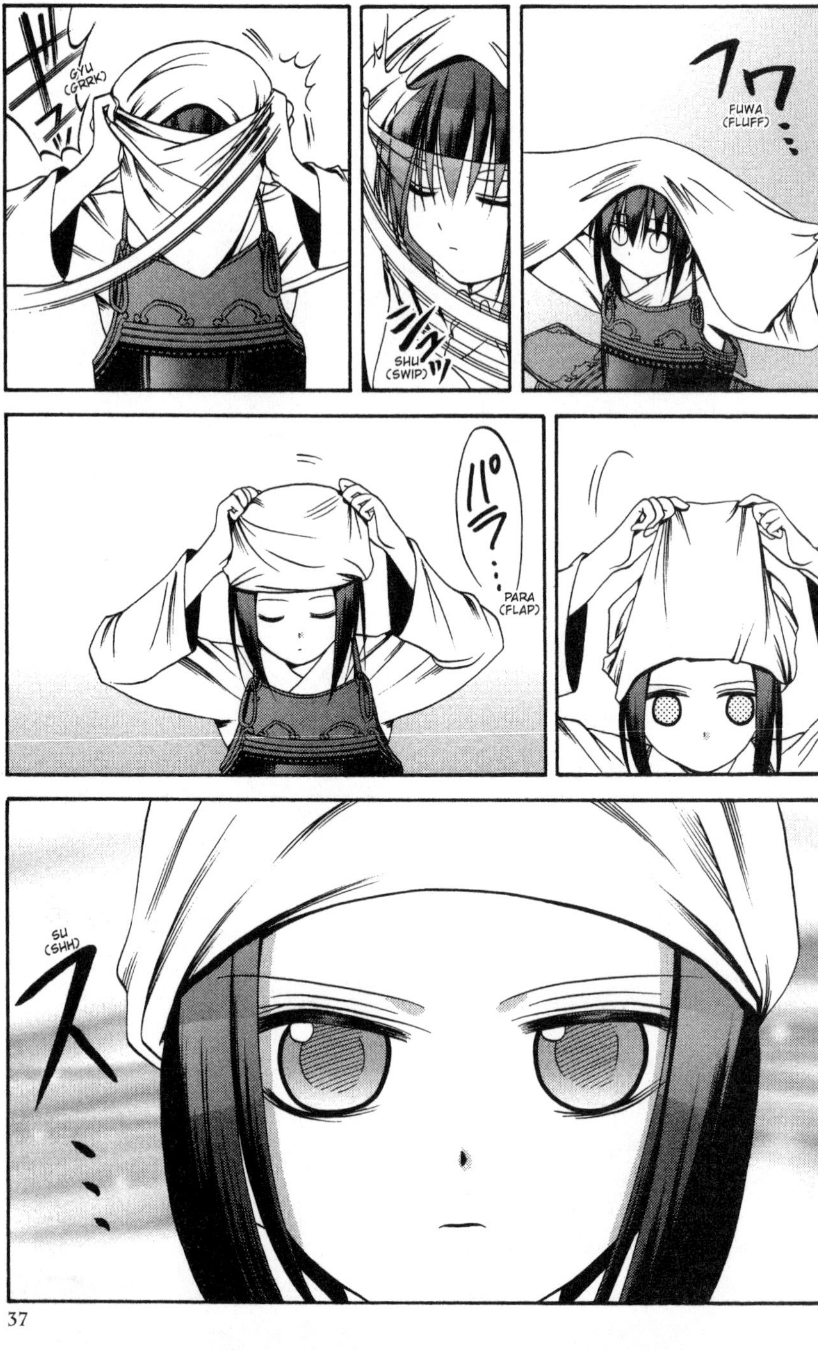
FUWA
(FLUFF)
SHU
(SWIP)
GYU
(GRRK)
PARA
(FLAP)
SU
(SHH)

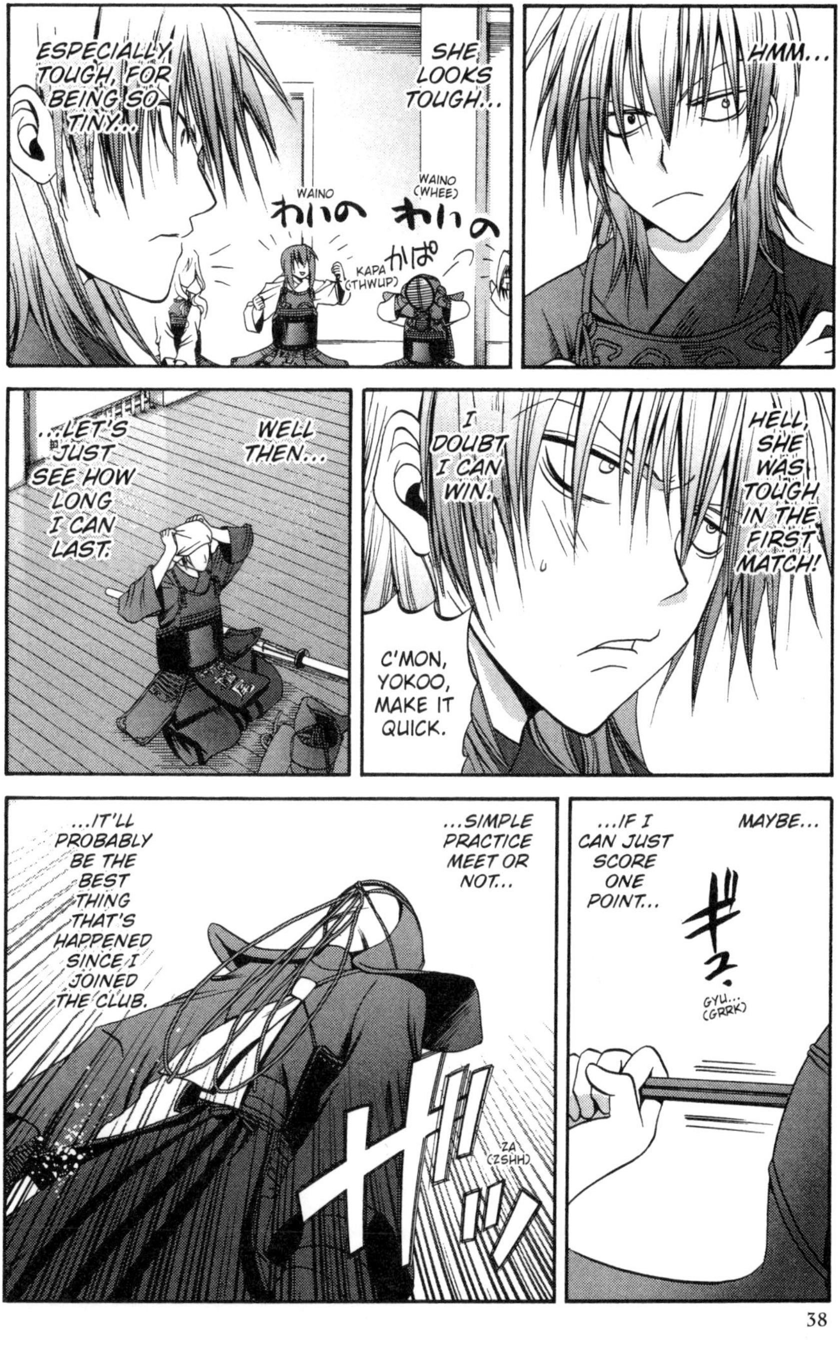
HMM...
SHE LOOKS TOUGH...
ESPECIALLY TOUGH, FOR BEING SO TINY..
WAINO
わいの
WAINO (WHEE)
わいの
KAPA (THWUP)
かぱ
HELL, SHE WAS TOUGH IN THE FIRST MATCH!
I DOUBT I CAN WIN.
C'MON, YOKOO, MAKE IT QUICK.
WELL THEN...
...LET'S JUST SEE HOW LONG I CAN LAST.
MAYBE...
...IF I CAN JUST SCORE ONE POINT...
GYU... (GRRK)
...SIMPLE PRACTICE MEET OR NOT...
...IT'LL PROBABLY BE THE BEST THING THAT'S HAPPENED SINCE I JOINED THE CLUB.
ZA (ZSHH)

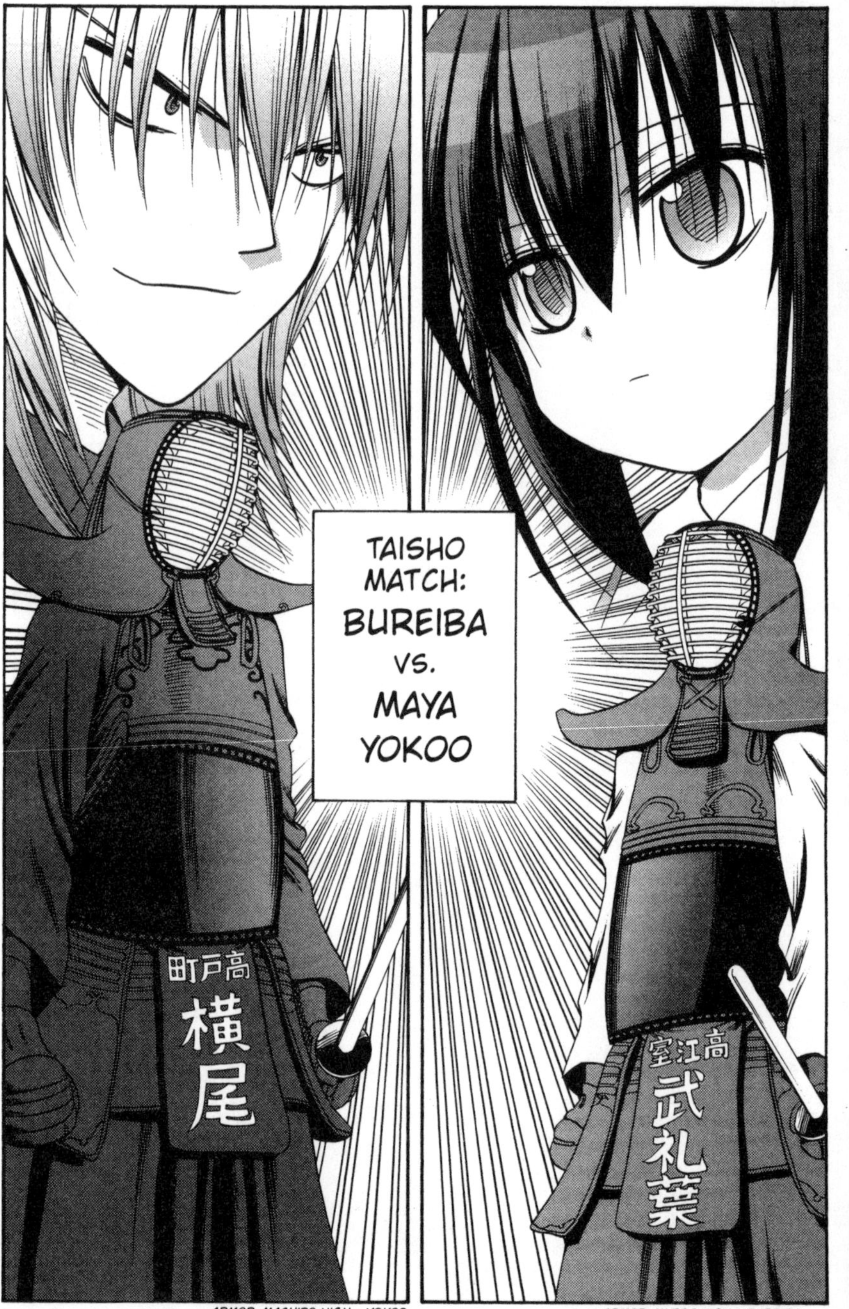
室江高
武礼葉
TAISHO MATCH: BUREIBA VS. MAYA YOKOO
町戸高
横尾

ARMOR: MUROE HIGH - BUREIBA

ARMOR: MACHIDO HIGH - YOKOO

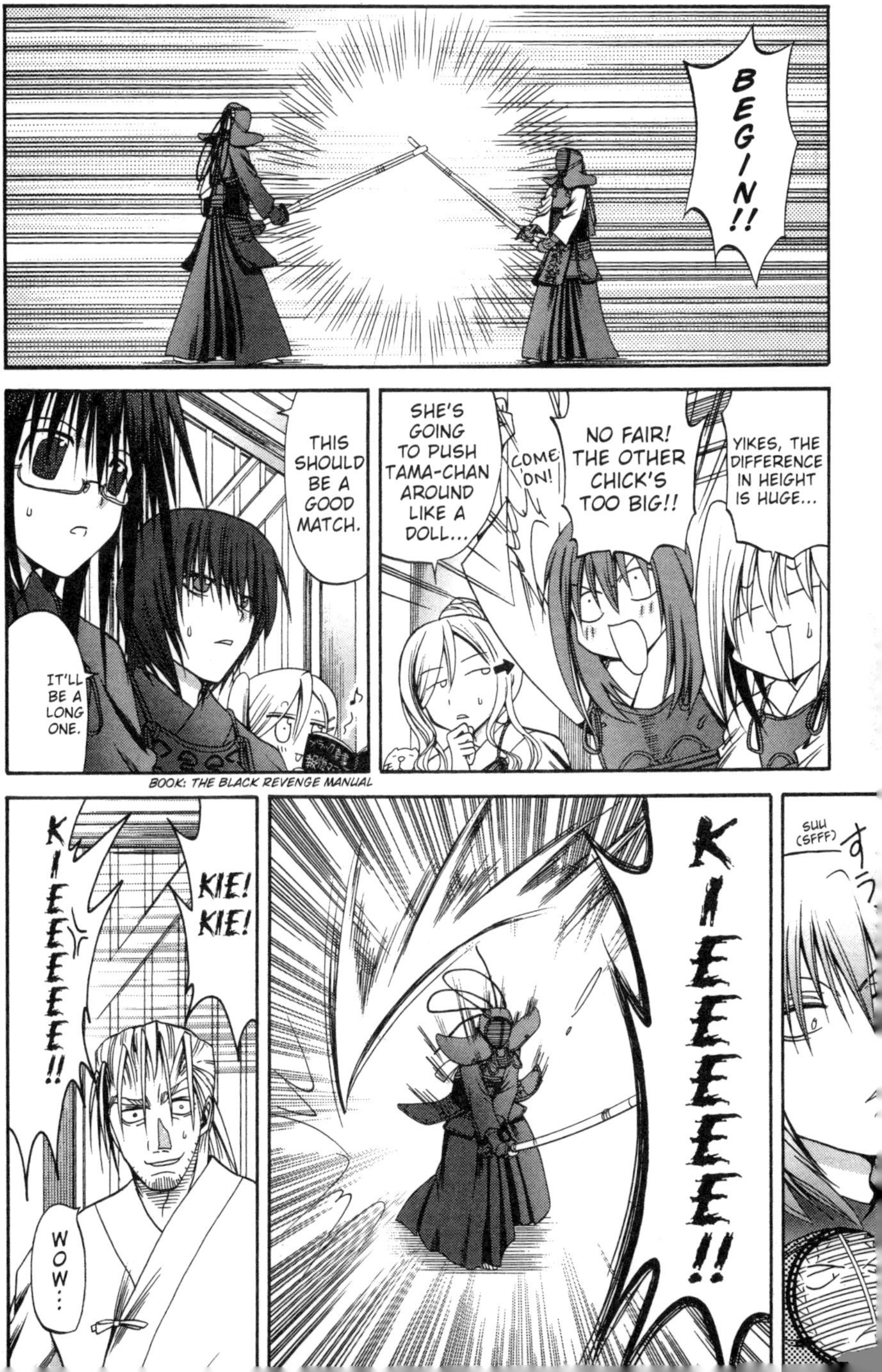
BEGIN!!
YIKES, THE DIFFERENCE IN HEIGHT IS HUGE...
NO FAIR! THE OTHER CHICK'S TOO BIG!!
COME ON!
SHE'S GOING TO PUSH TAMA-CHAN AROUND LIKE A DOLL...
THIS SHOULD BE A GOOD MATCH.
IT'LL BE A LONG ONE.
BOOK: THE BLACK REVENGE MANUAL
SUU (SFFF)
KIEEEEEEEE!!
KIEEEEEEEE!!
KIE! KIE!
WOW...

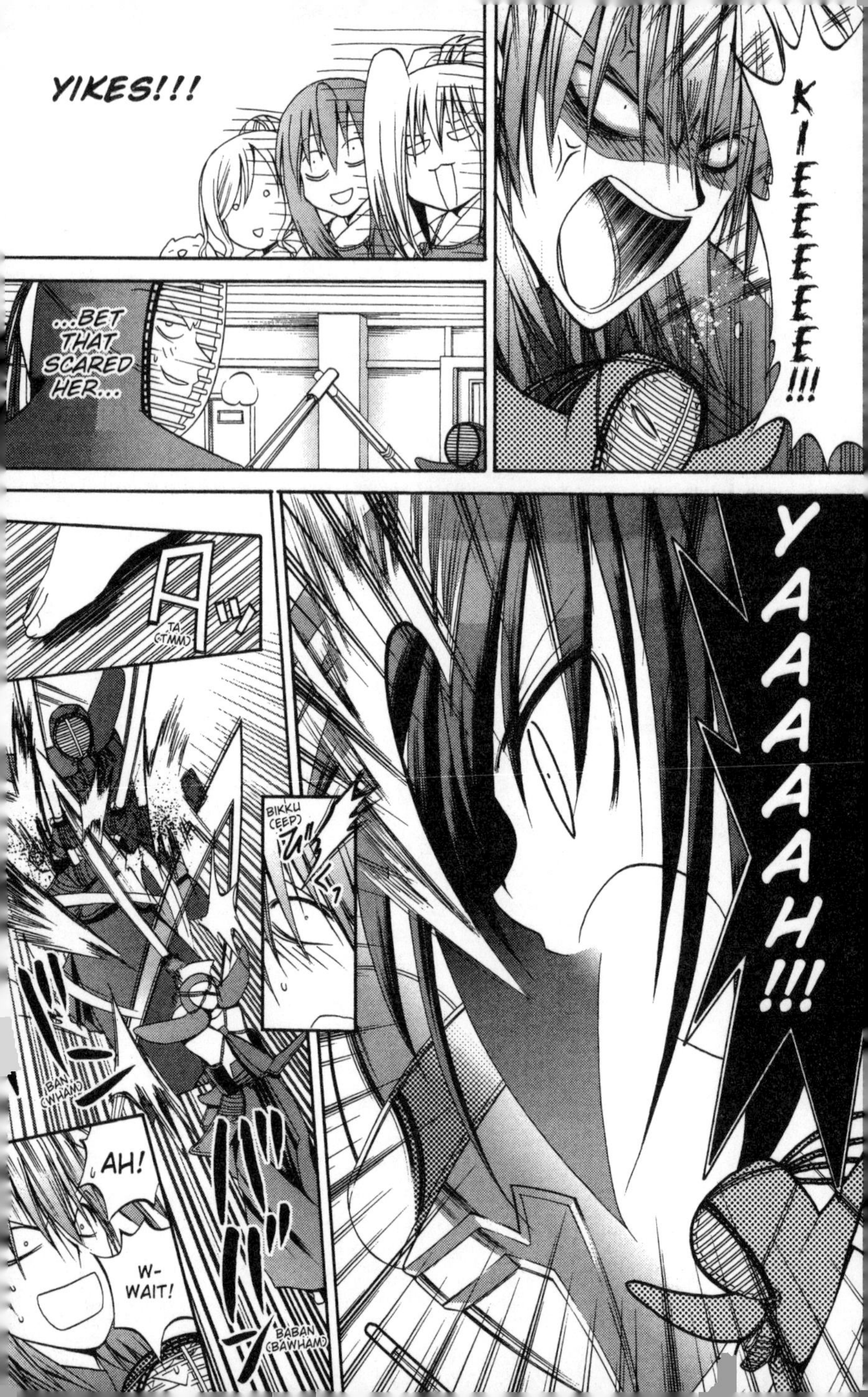
KIEEEEEEE!!!
YIKES!!!
...BET THAT SCARED HER...
YAAAAAAH!!!
TA (TMM)
BIKKU (EEP)
BAN (WHAM)
AH!
W- WAIT!
BABAN (BAWHAM)

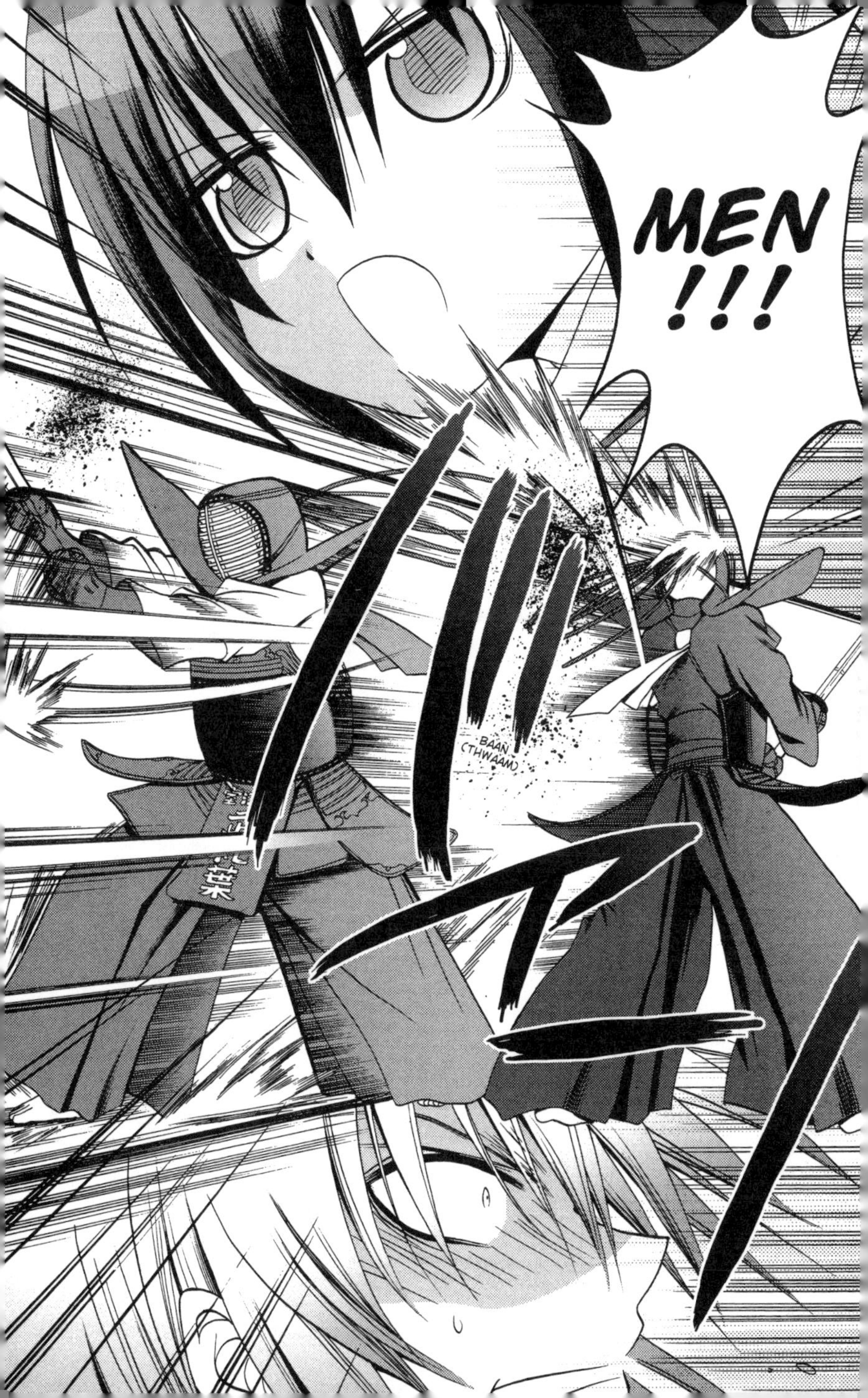
MEN!!!
BAAN (THWAAM)

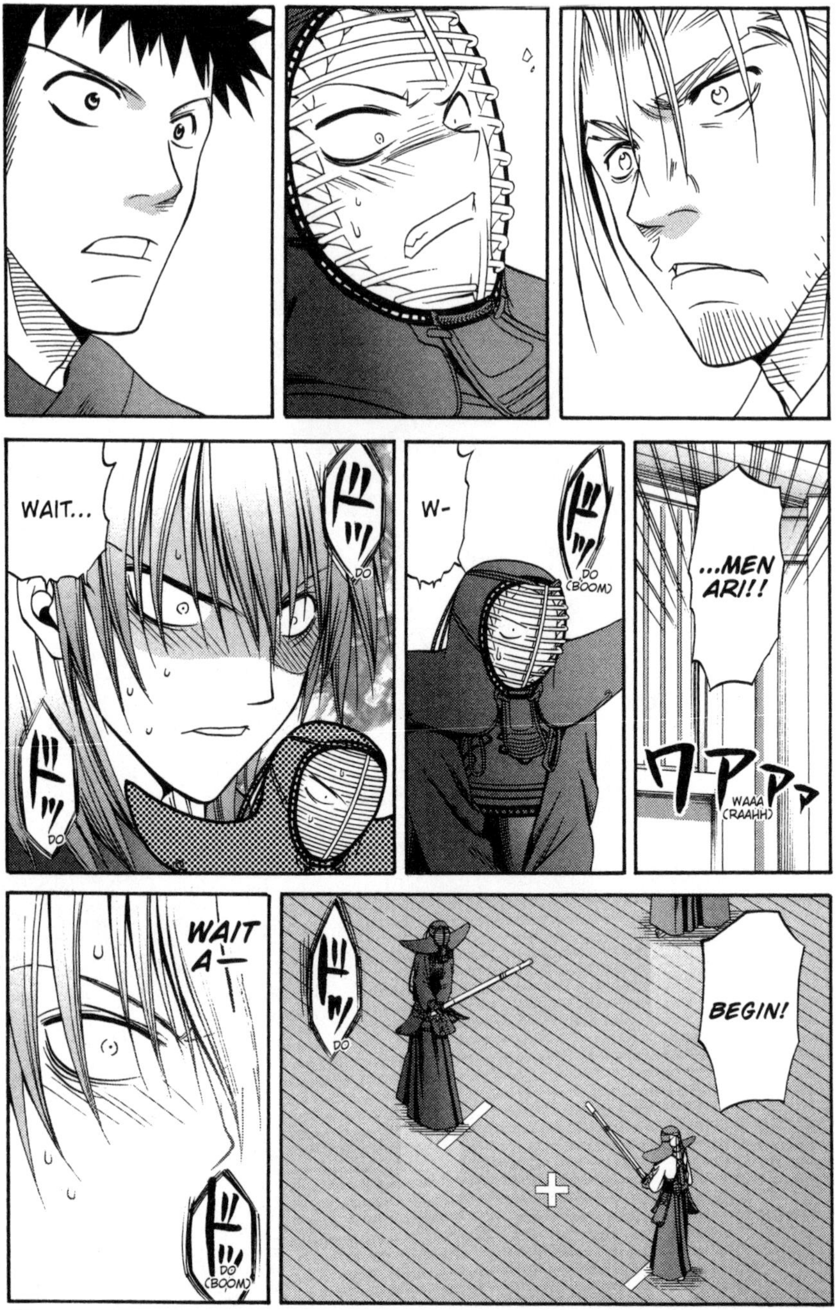
...MEN ARI!!
ワアァァ
WAAA (RAAHH)
W-
ドッ
DO (BOOM)
WAIT...
ドッ
DO
ドッ
DO
BEGIN!
ドッ
DO
WAIT A—
ドッ
DO (BOOM)

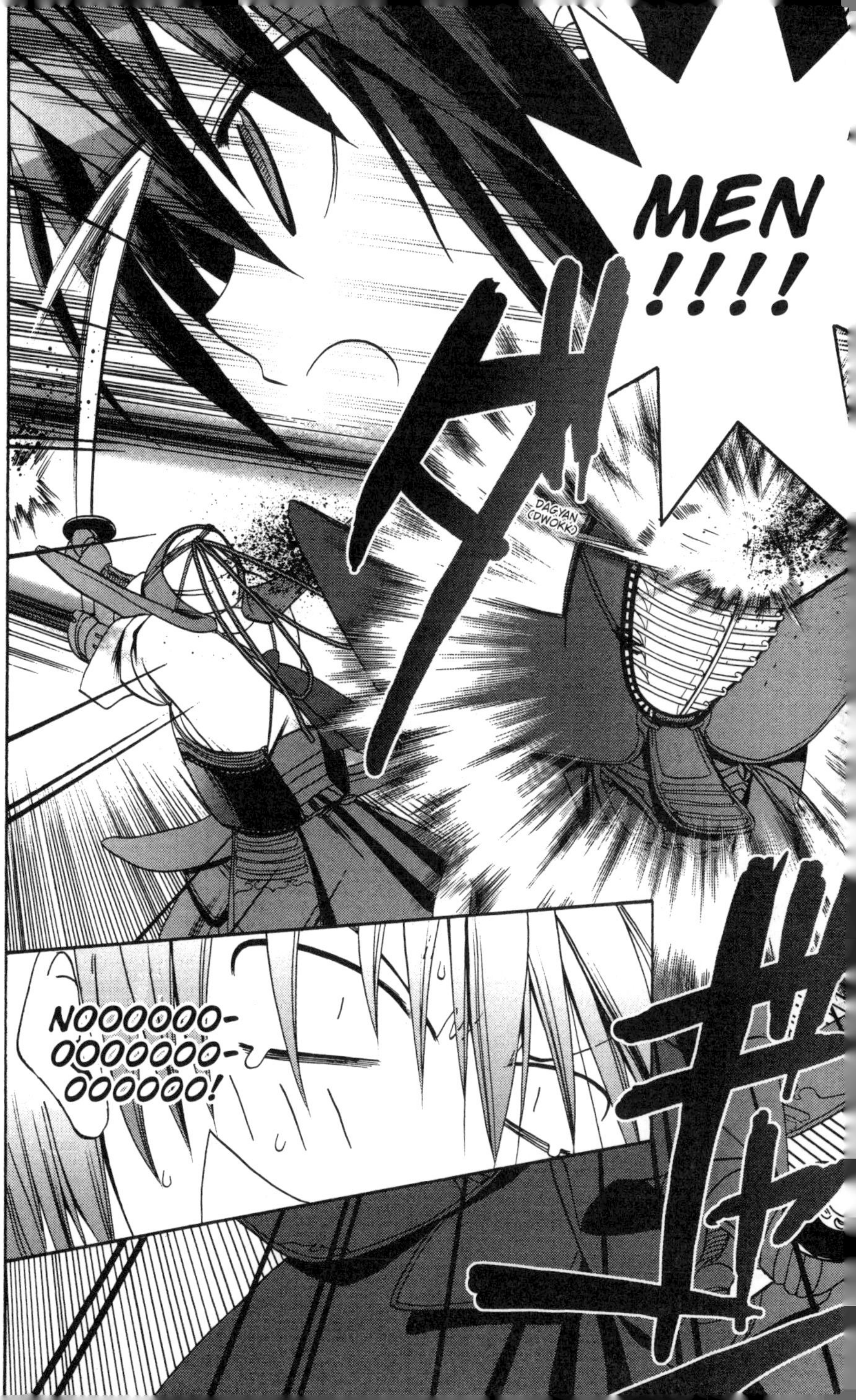
MEN !!!!
DAGYAN (DWOKK)
NOOOOOO-OOOOOOO-OOOOOO!

BAMBOO BLADE

ANDOU-SAN'S KENDO INSTRUCTION DOJO

BLACK

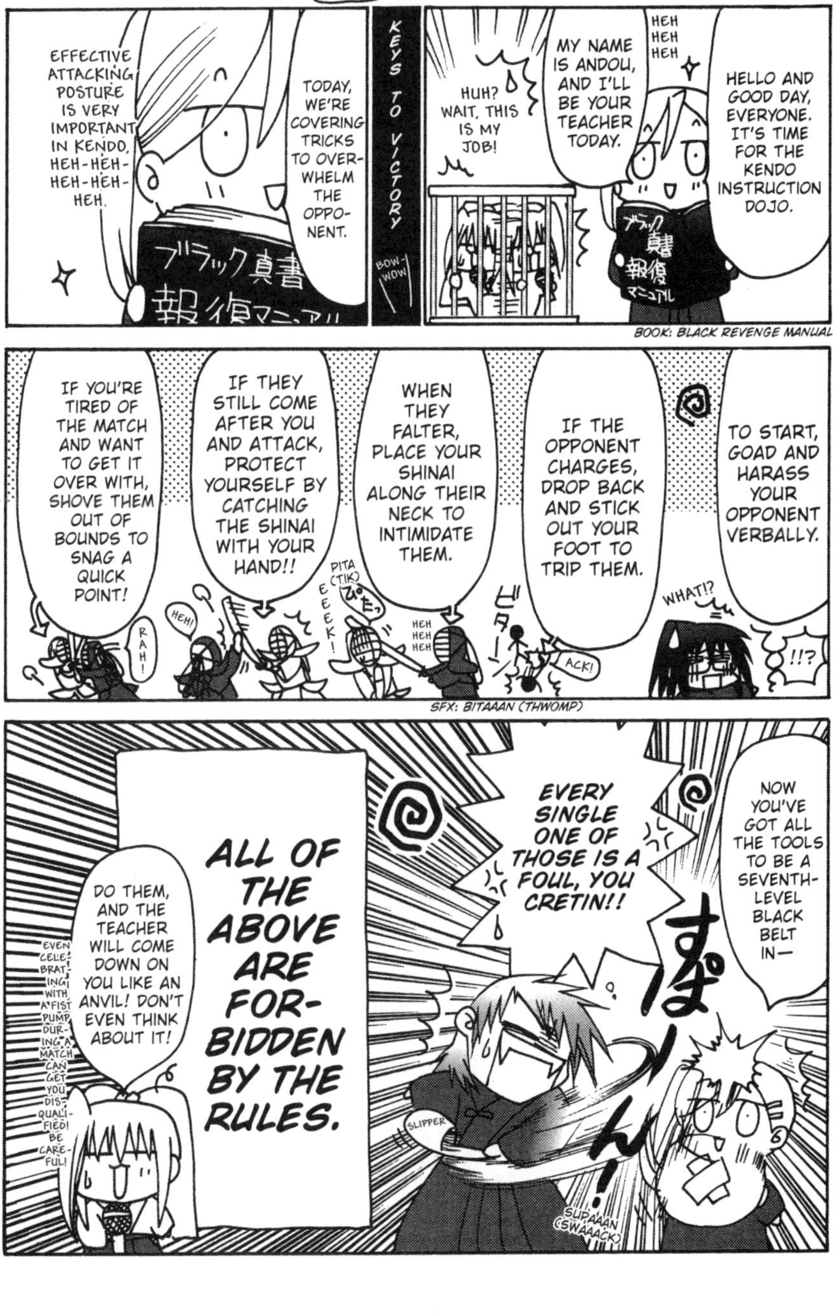
HEH HEH HEH
HELLO AND GOOD DAY, EVERYONE. IT'S TIME FOR THE KENDO INSTRUCTION DOJO.
MY NAME IS ANDOU, AND I'LL BE YOUR TEACHER TODAY.
HUH? WAIT, THIS IS MY JOB!
ブラック真書 報復マニュアル
KEYS TO VICTORY
BOW-WOW
TODAY, WE'RE COVERING TRICKS TO OVER-WHELM THE OPPO-NENT.
EFFECTIVE ATTACKING POSTURE IS VERY IMPORTANT IN KENDO, HEH-HEH-HEH-HEH-HEH.
ブラック真書 報復マニュアル
TO START, GOAD AND HARASS YOUR OPPONENT VERBALLY.
WHAT!?
!!?
IF THE OPPONENT CHARGES, DROP BACK AND STICK OUT YOUR FOOT TO TRIP THEM.
ACK!
WHEN THEY FALTER, PLACE YOUR SHINAI ALONG THEIR NECK TO INTIMIDATE THEM.
HEH HEH HEH
PITA (TIK)
EEEEK!
IF THEY STILL COME AFTER YOU AND ATTACK, PROTECT YOURSELF BY CATCHING THE SHINAI WITH YOUR HAND!!
HEH!
RAH!
IF YOU'RE TIRED OF THE MATCH AND WANT TO GET IT OVER WITH, SHOVE THEM OUT OF BOUNDS TO SNAG A QUICK POINT!
NOW YOU'VE GOT ALL THE TOOLS TO BE A SEVENTH-LEVEL BLACK BELT IN—
EVERY SINGLE ONE OF THOSE IS A FOUL, YOU CRETIN!!
SLIPPER
SUPAAAN (SWAAACK)
ALL OF THE ABOVE ARE FOR-BIDDEN BY THE RULES.
DO THEM, AND THE TEACHER WILL COME DOWN ON YOU LIKE AN ANVIL! DON'T EVEN THINK ABOUT IT!
EVEN CELE-BRAT-ING WITH A FIST PUMP DUR-ING A MATCH CAN GET YOU DIS-QUALI-FIED! BE CARE-FUL!

BOOK: BLACK REVENGE MANUAL

SFX: BITAAAN (THWOMP)

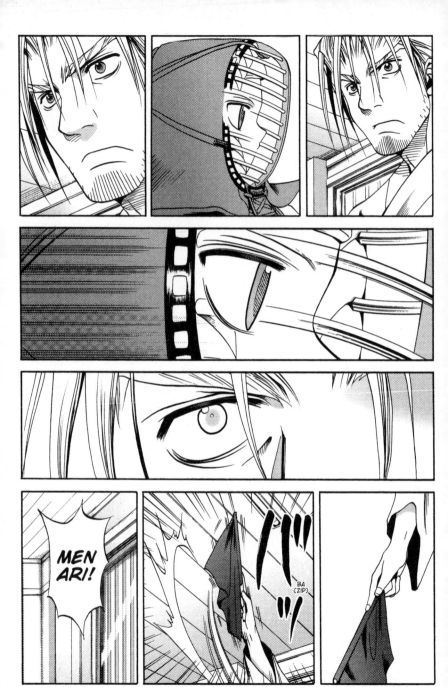

MEN ARI!

BA
(ZIP)

47

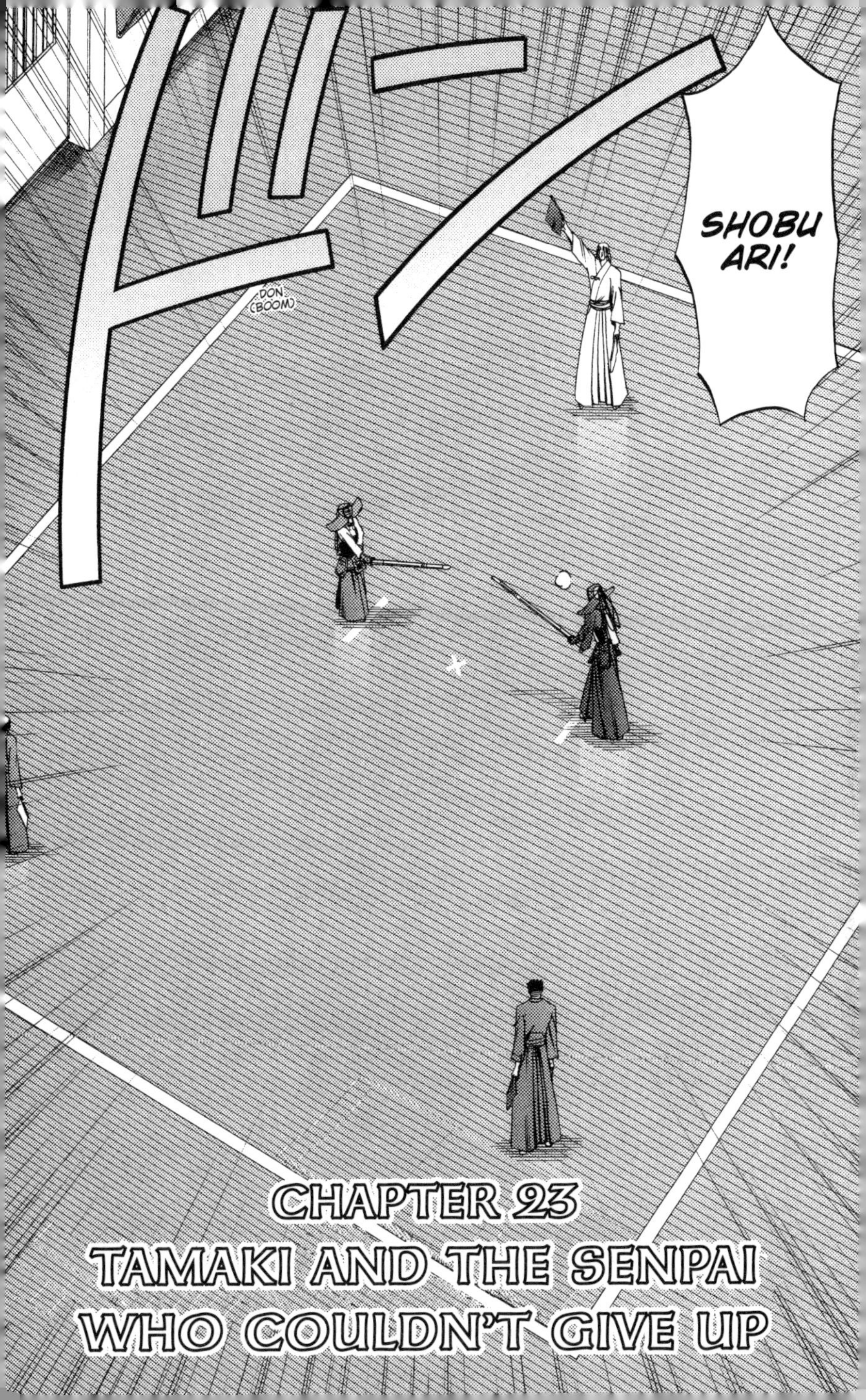
SHOBU ARI!
DON (BOOM)
CHAPTER 23
TAMAKI AND THE SENPAI WHO COULDN'T GIVE UP

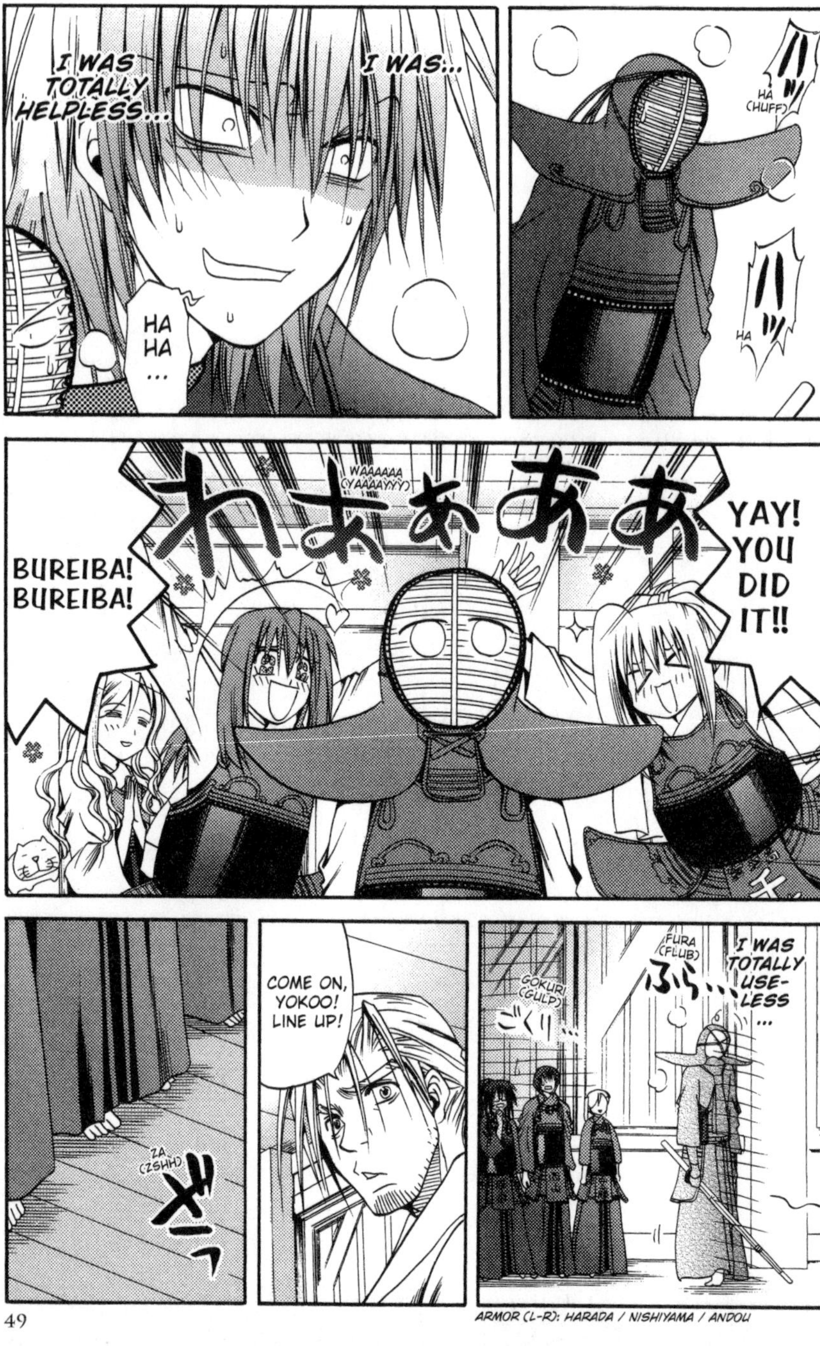
HA (HUFF)
HA
I WAS...
I WAS TOTALLY HELPLESS...
HA HA ...
YAY! YOU DID IT!!
WAAAAAA (YAAAAYYY)
BUREIBA! BUREIBA!
I WAS TOTALLY USE-LESS ...
FURA (FLUB)
ふら…
GOKURI (GULP)
ごくり…
COME ON, YOKOO! LINE UP!
ZA (ZSHH)
ARMOR (L-R): HARADA / NISHIYAMA / ANDOU

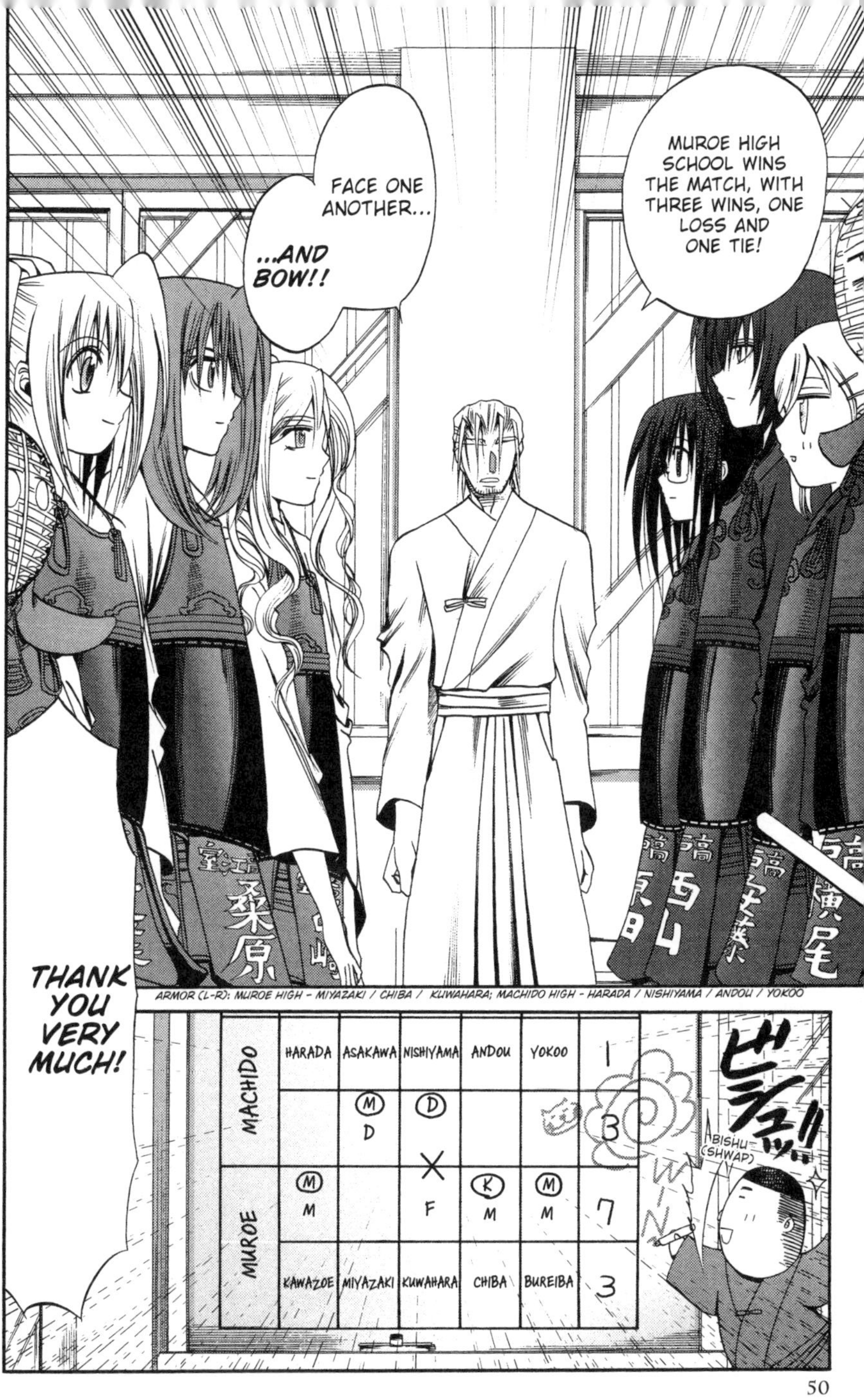
MUROE HIGH SCHOOL WINS THE MATCH, WITH THREE WINS, ONE LOSS AND ONE TIE!
FACE ONE ANOTHER...
...AND BOW!!
THANK YOU VERY MUCH!
ARMOR (L-R): MUROE HIGH - MIYAZAKI / CHIBA / KUWAHARA; MACHIDO HIGH - HARADA / NISHIYAMA / ANDOU / YOKOO
ビシュッ!!
BISHU (SHWAP)
MACHIDO
HARADA ASAKAWA NISHIYAMA ANDOU YOKOO 1
M D D 3
X
M M K M F M M 7
MUROE
KAWAZOE MIYAZAKI KUWAHARA CHIBA BUREIBA 3

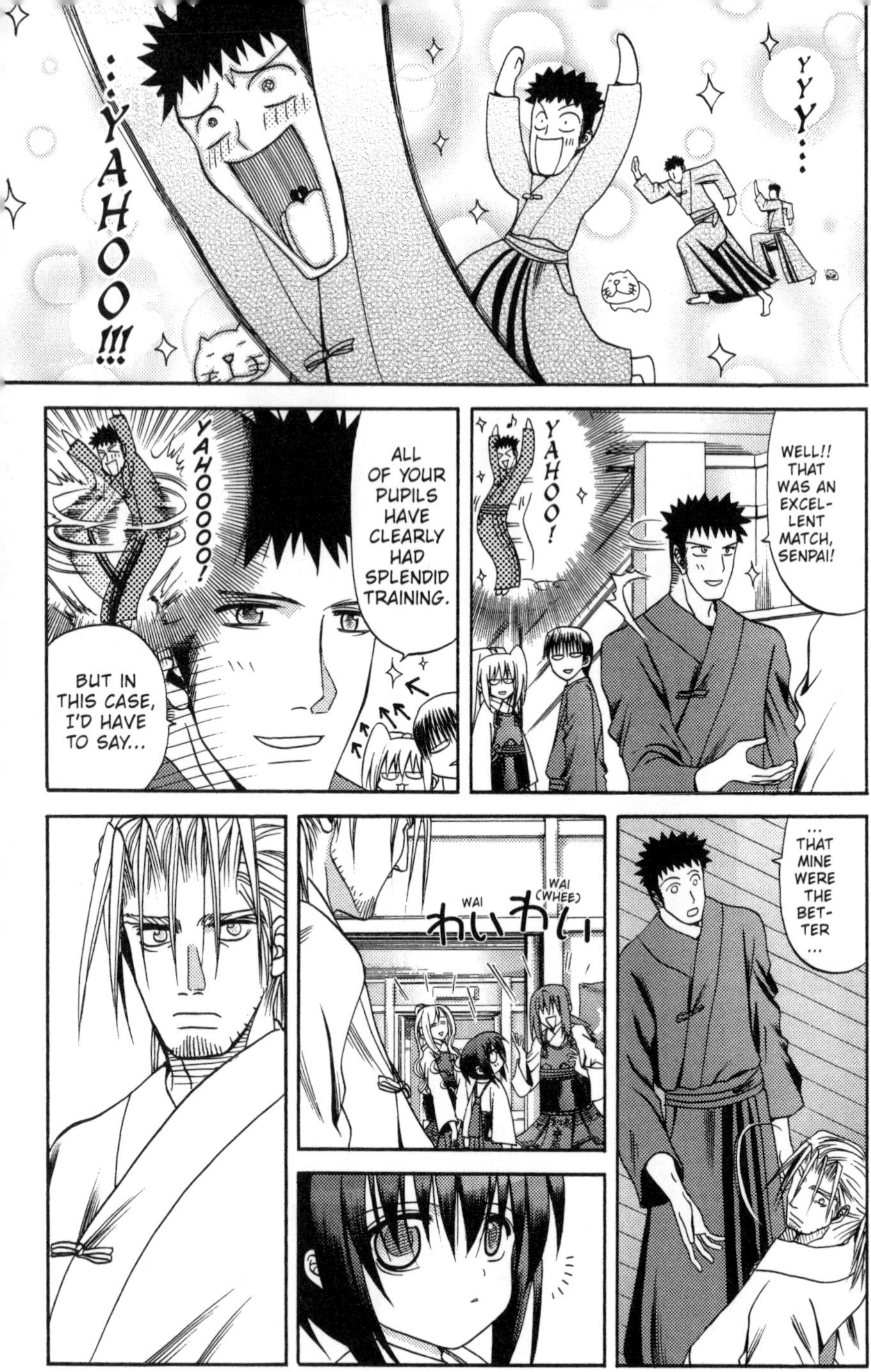
YYY...
...YAHOO!!!
WELL!! THAT WAS AN EXCEL-LENT MATCH, SENPAI!
YAHOO!
ALL OF YOUR PUPILS HAVE CLEARLY HAD SPLENDID TRAINING.
YAHOOOOOO!
BUT IN THIS CASE, I'D HAVE TO SAY...
...THAT MINE WERE THE BET-TER...
わいわい
WAI WAI (WHEE)

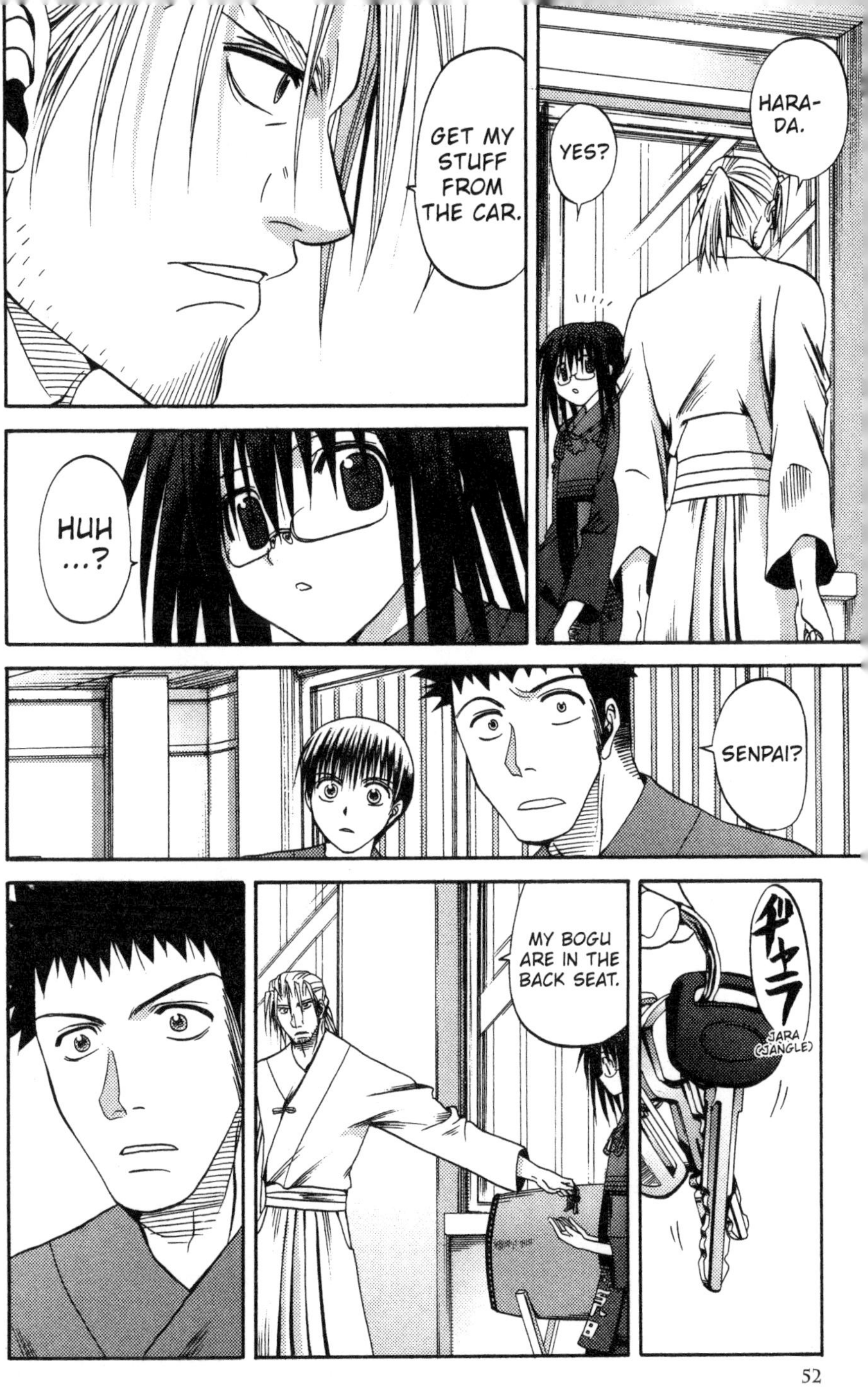
HARA-DA.
YES?
GET MY STUFF FROM THE CAR.
HUH ...?
SENPAI?
ジャラ
JARA (JANGLE)
MY BOGU ARE IN THE BACK SEAT.

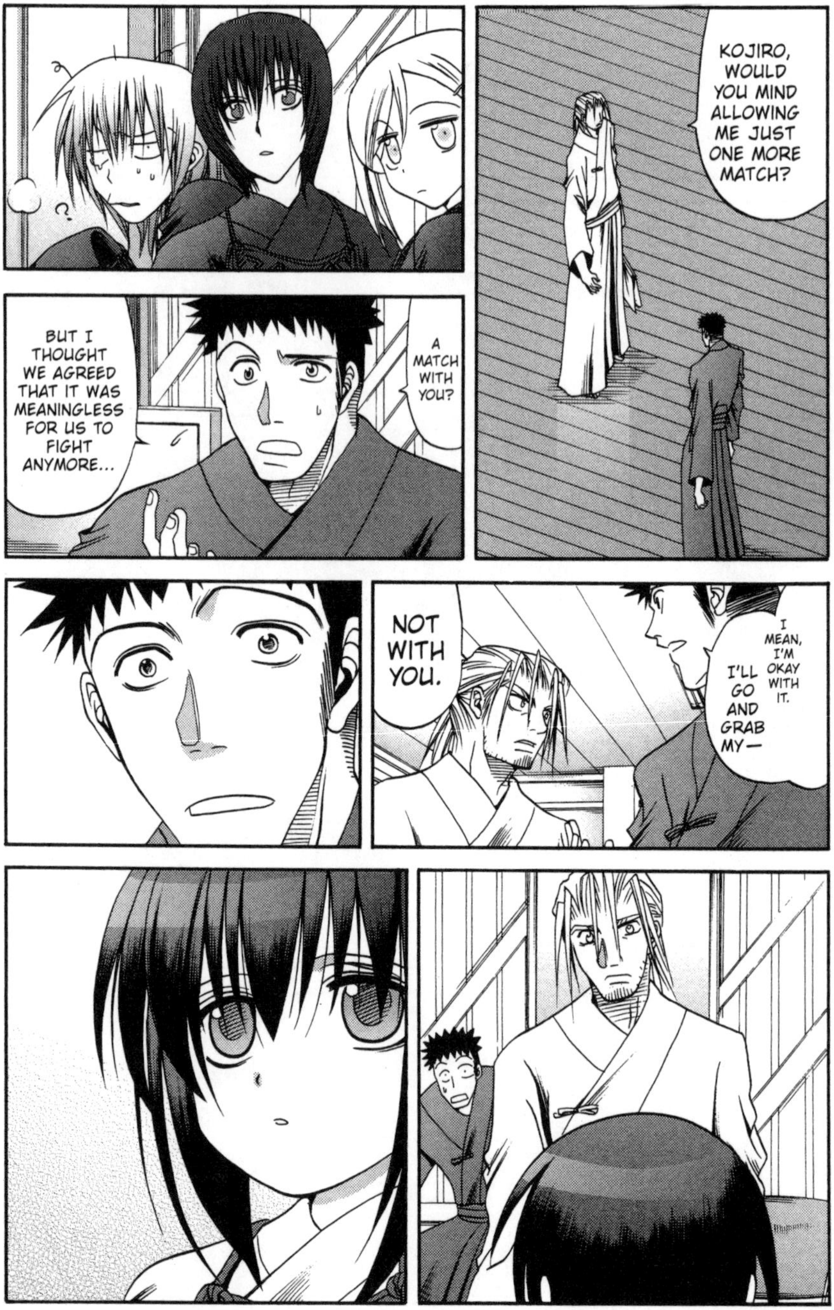
KOJIRO, WOULD YOU MIND ALLOWING ME JUST ONE MORE MATCH?
A MATCH WITH YOU?
BUT I THOUGHT WE AGREED THAT IT WAS MEANINGLESS FOR US TO FIGHT ANYMORE...
I MEAN, I'M OKAY WITH IT.
I'LL GO AND GRAB MY—
NOT WITH YOU.

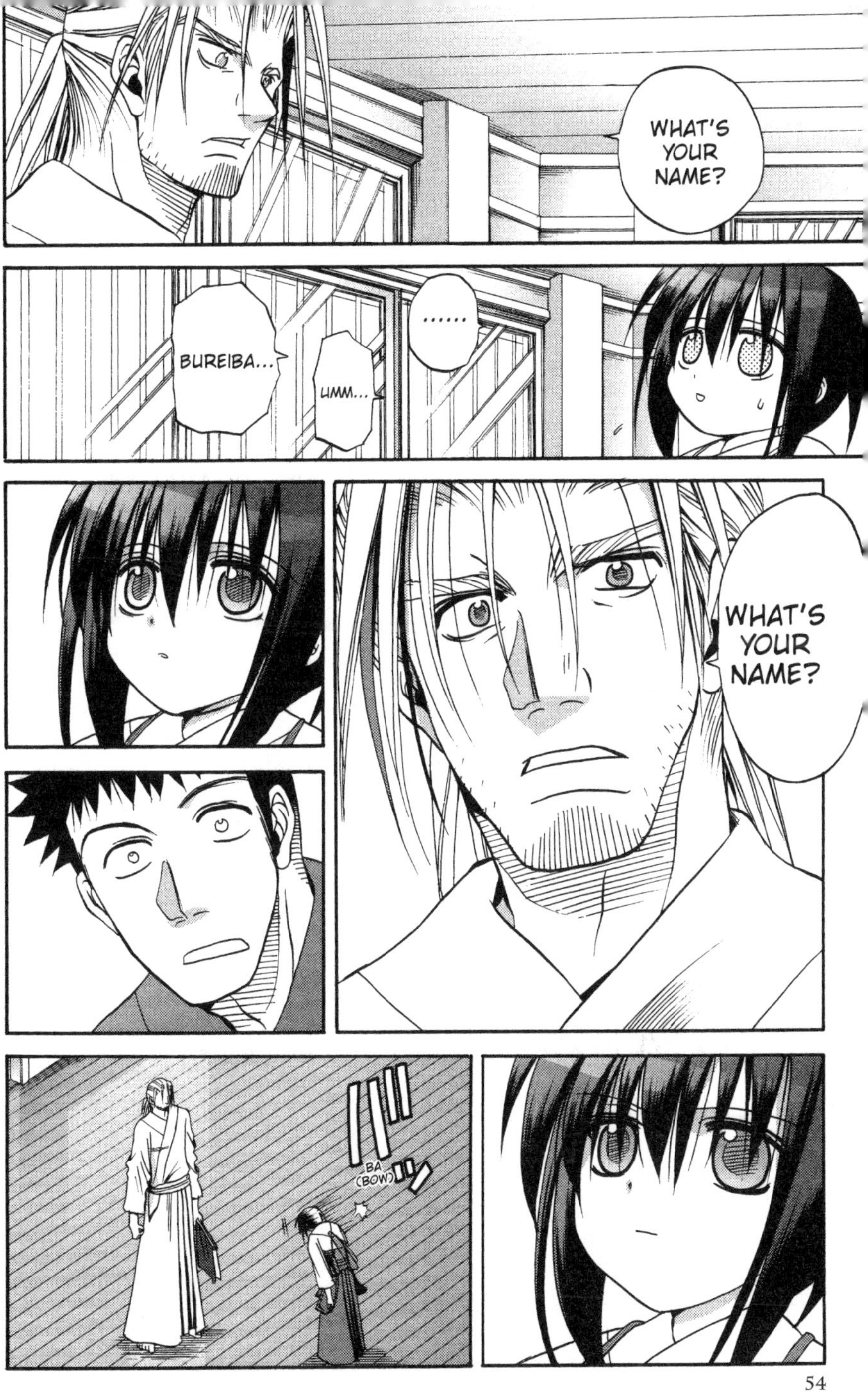
WHAT'S YOUR NAME?
......
UMM...
BUREIBA...
WHAT'S YOUR NAME?
BA (BOW)

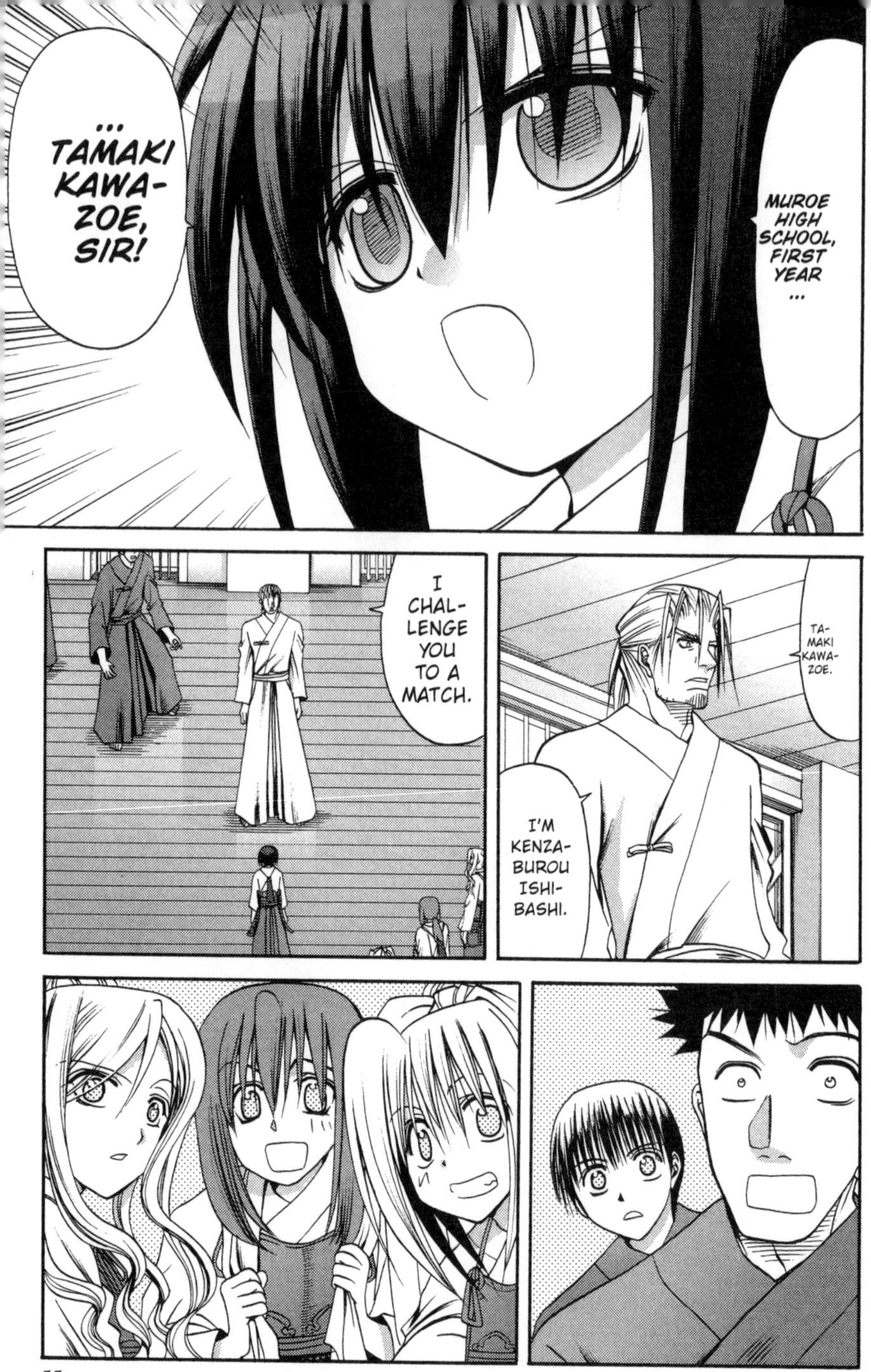
MUROE HIGH SCHOOL, FIRST YEAR ...
... TAMAKI KAWAZOE, SIR!
TAMAKI KAWAZOE.
I'M KENZABUROU ISHIBASHI.
I CHALLENGE YOU TO A MATCH.

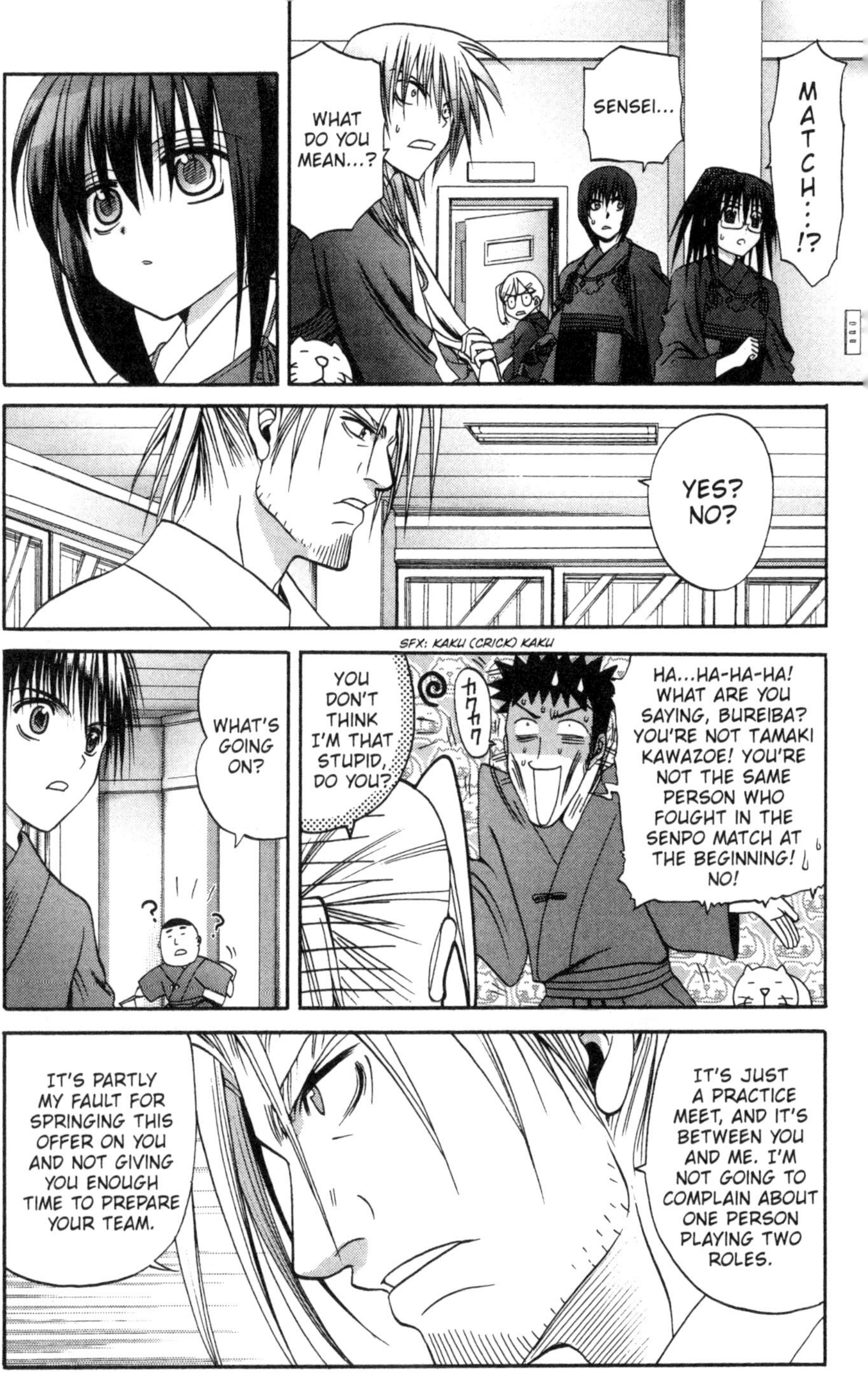
MATCH...!?
SENSEI...
WHAT DO YOU MEAN...?
YES? NO?
SFX: KAKU (CRICK) KAKU
HA...HA-HA-HA! WHAT ARE YOU SAYING, BUREIBA? YOU'RE NOT TAMAKI KAWAZOE! YOU'RE NOT THE SAME PERSON WHO FOUGHT IN THE SENPO MATCH AT THE BEGINNING! NO!
カクカク
YOU DON'T THINK I'M THAT STUPID, DO YOU?
WHAT'S GOING ON?
IT'S JUST A PRACTICE MEET, AND IT'S BETWEEN YOU AND ME. I'M NOT GOING TO COMPLAIN ABOUT ONE PERSON PLAYING TWO ROLES.
IT'S PARTLY MY FAULT FOR SPRINGING THIS OFFER ON YOU AND NOT GIVING YOU ENOUGH TIME TO PREPARE YOUR TEAM.

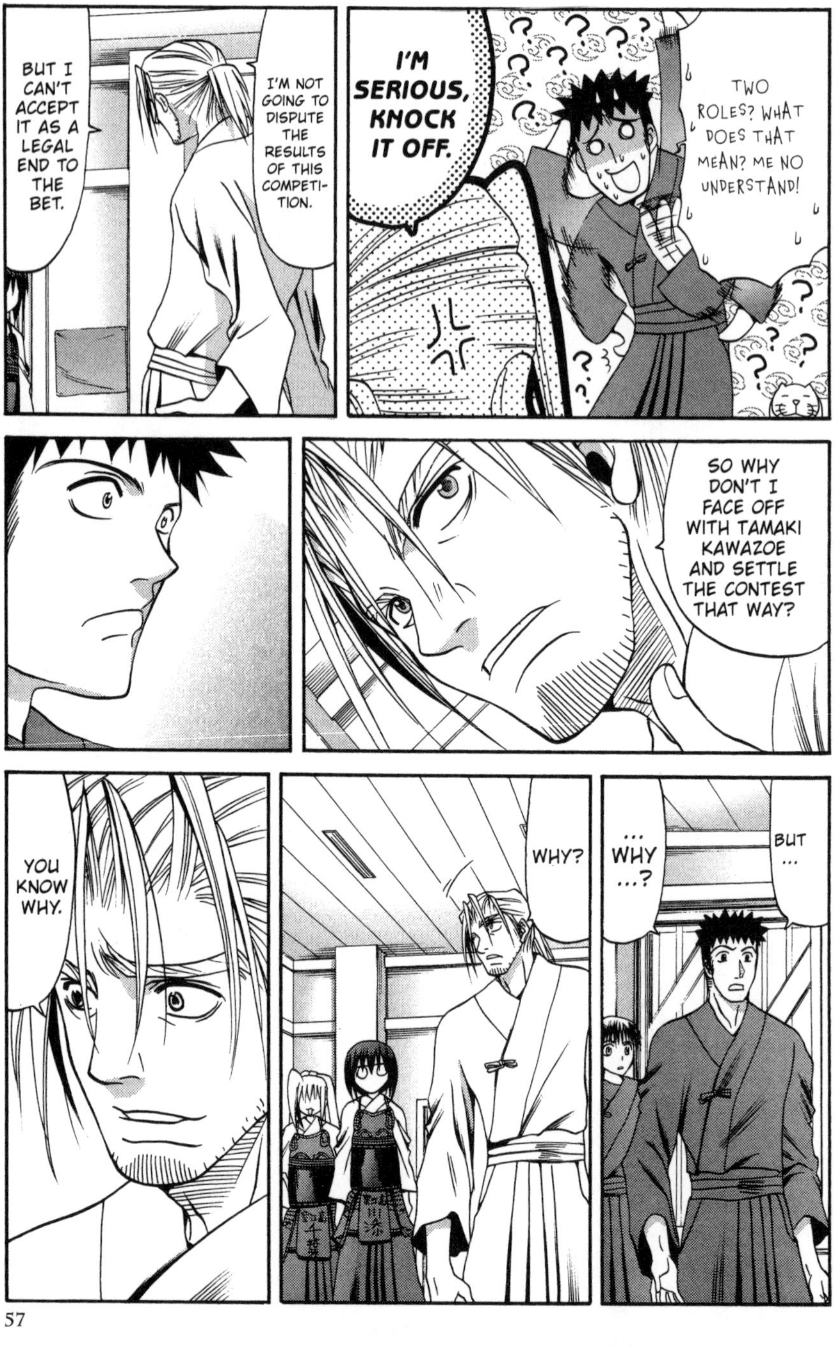

TWO ROLES? WHAT DOES THAT MEAN? ME NO UNDERSTAND!
I'M SERIOUS, KNOCK IT OFF.
I'M NOT GOING TO DISPUTE THE RESULTS OF THIS COMPETITION.
BUT I CAN'T ACCEPT IT AS A LEGAL END TO THE BET.
SO WHY DON'T I FACE OFF WITH TAMAKI KAWAZOE AND SETTLE THE CONTEST THAT WAY?
BUT ...
... WHY ...?
WHY?
YOU KNOW WHY.

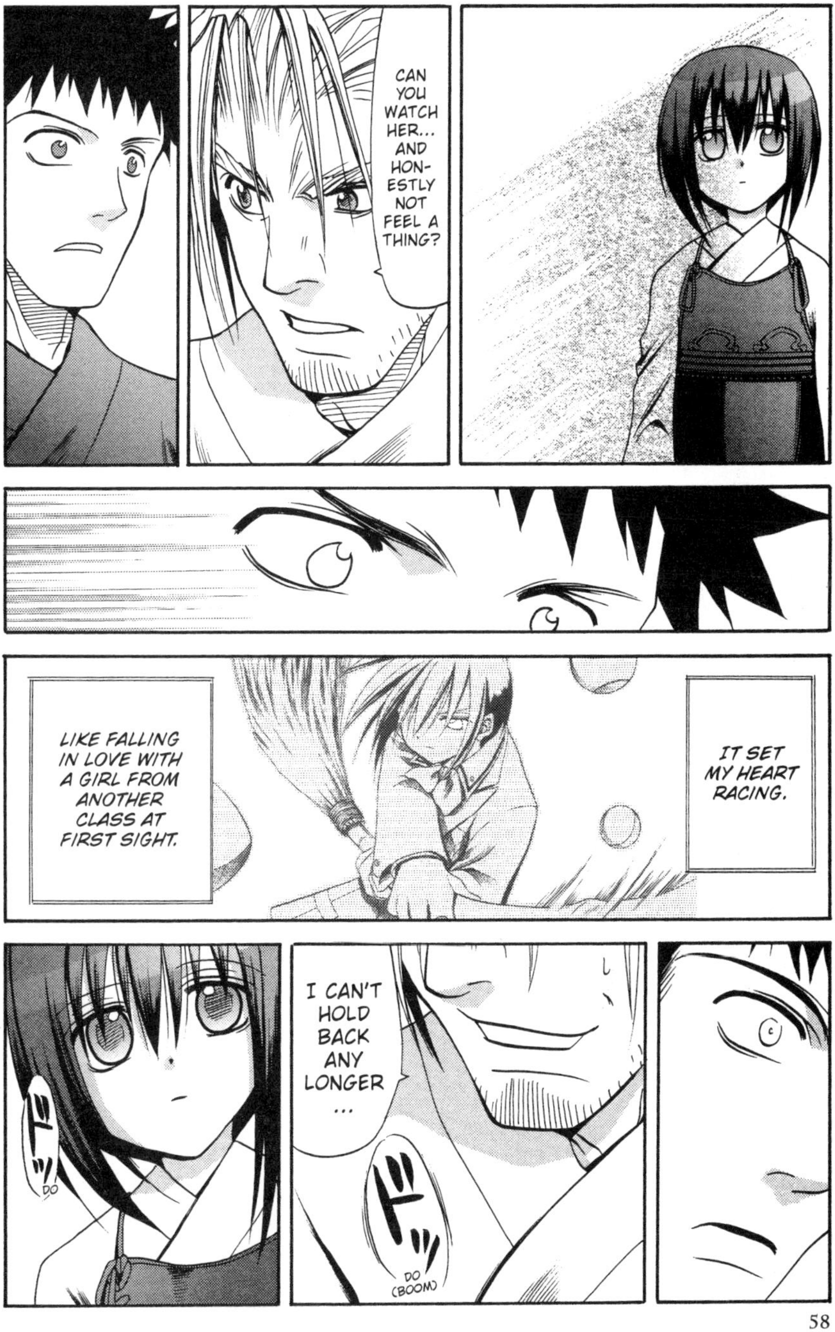
CAN YOU WATCH HER... AND HON-ESTLY NOT FEEL A THING?
IT SET MY HEART RACING.
LIKE FALLING IN LOVE WITH A GIRL FROM ANOTHER CLASS AT FIRST SIGHT.
I CAN'T HOLD BACK ANY LONGER ...
ドッ
DO (BOOM)
ドッ
DO

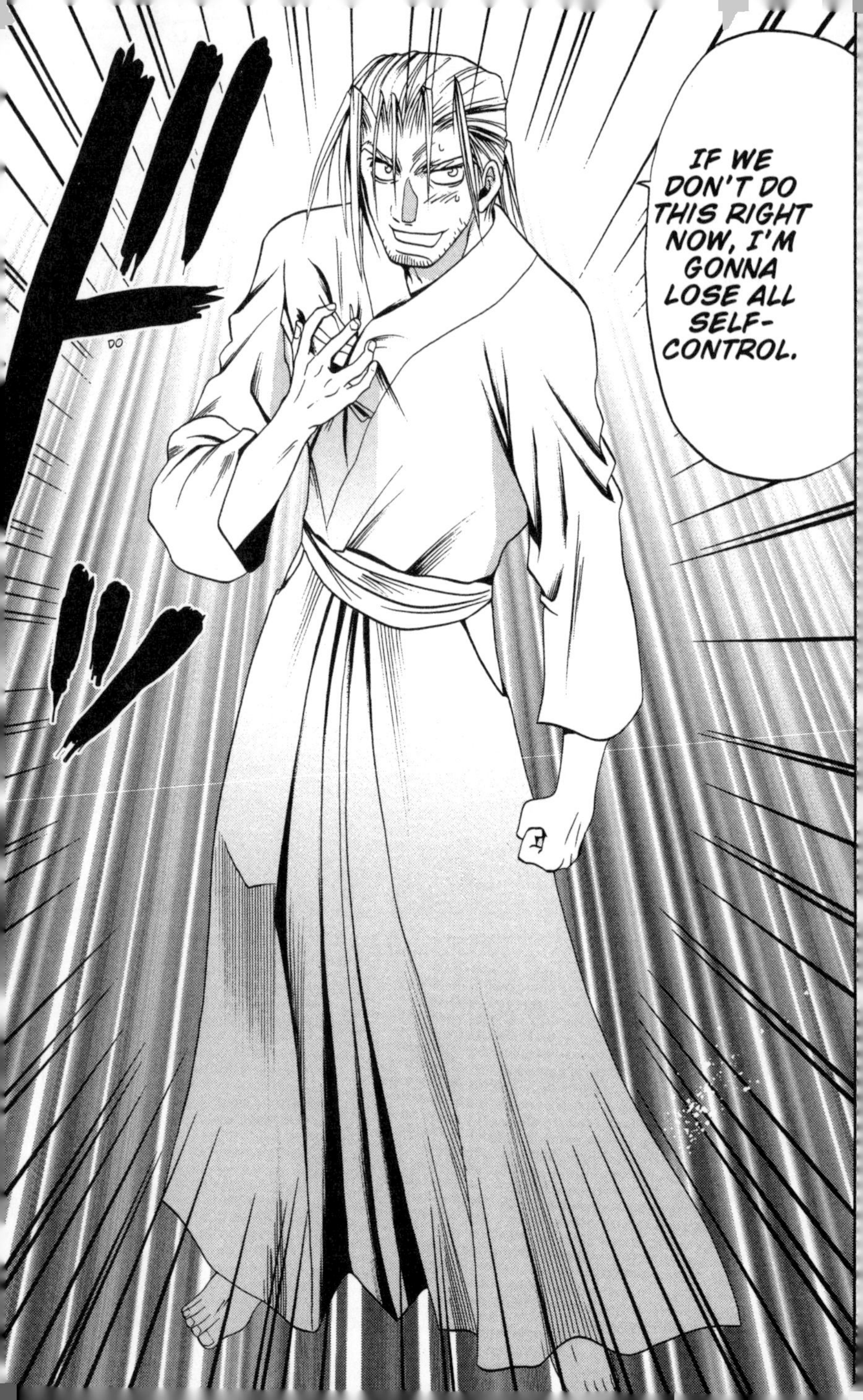
IF WE DON'T DO THIS RIGHT NOW, I'M GONNA LOSE ALL SELF-CONTROL.
DO

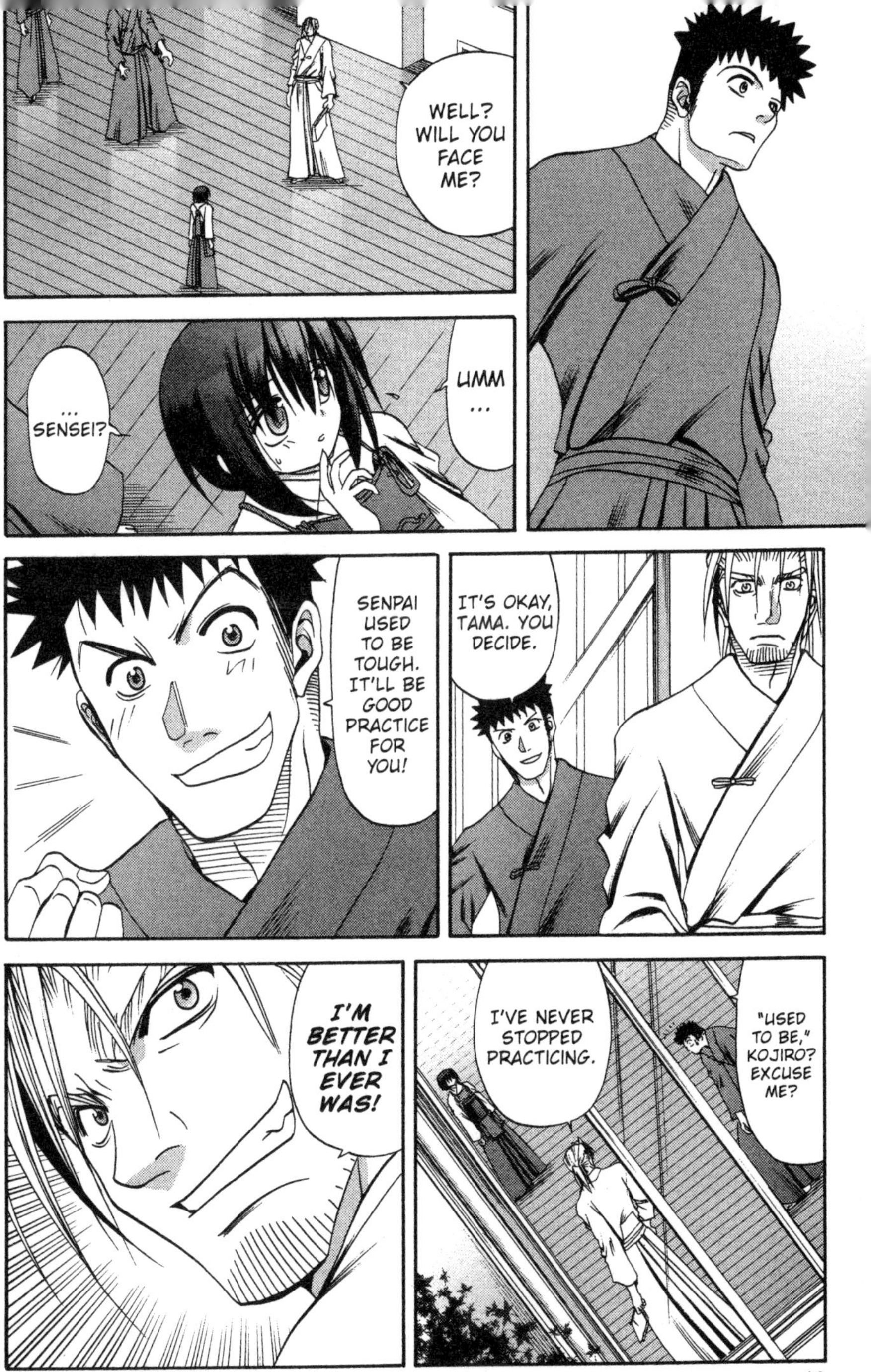
WELL? WILL YOU FACE ME?
UMM ...
... SENSEI?
IT'S OKAY, TAMA. YOU DECIDE.
SENPAI USED TO BE TOUGH. IT'LL BE GOOD PRACTICE FOR YOU!
"USED TO BE," KOJIRO? EXCUSE ME?
I'VE NEVER STOPPED PRACTICING.
I'M BETTER THAN I EVER WAS!

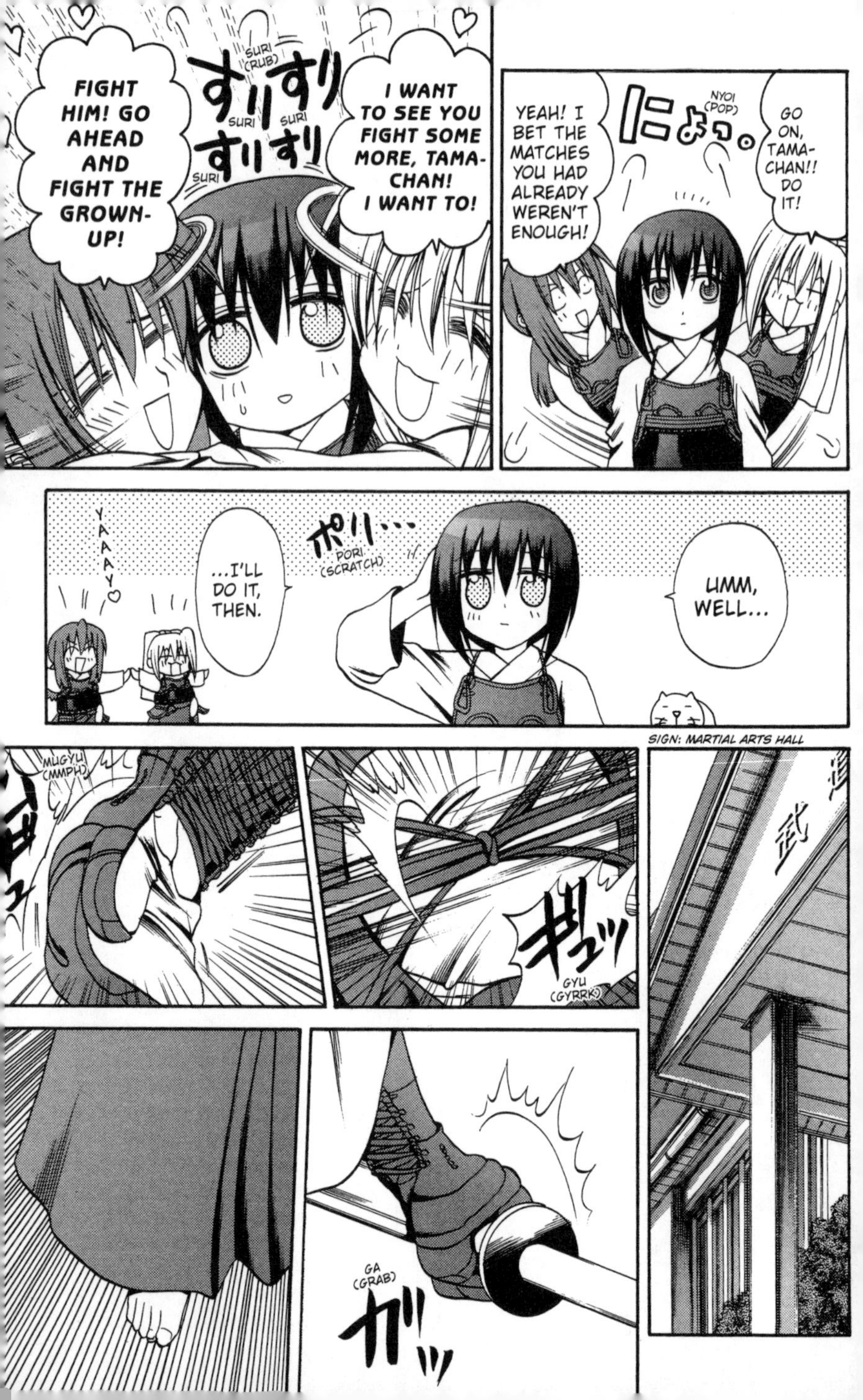
GO ON, TAMA-CHAN!! DO IT!
NYOI (POP)
YEAH! I BET THE MATCHES YOU HAD ALREADY WEREN'T ENOUGH!
I WANT TO SEE YOU FIGHT SOME MORE, TAMA-CHAN! I WANT TO!
SURI (RUB) SURI SURI SURI
FIGHT HIM! GO AHEAD AND FIGHT THE GROWN-UP!
UMM, WELL...
PORI (SCRATCH)
...I'LL DO IT, THEN.
YAAAAY♡
SIGN: MARTIAL ARTS HALL
GYU (GYRRK)
MUGYU (MMPH)
GA (GRAB)

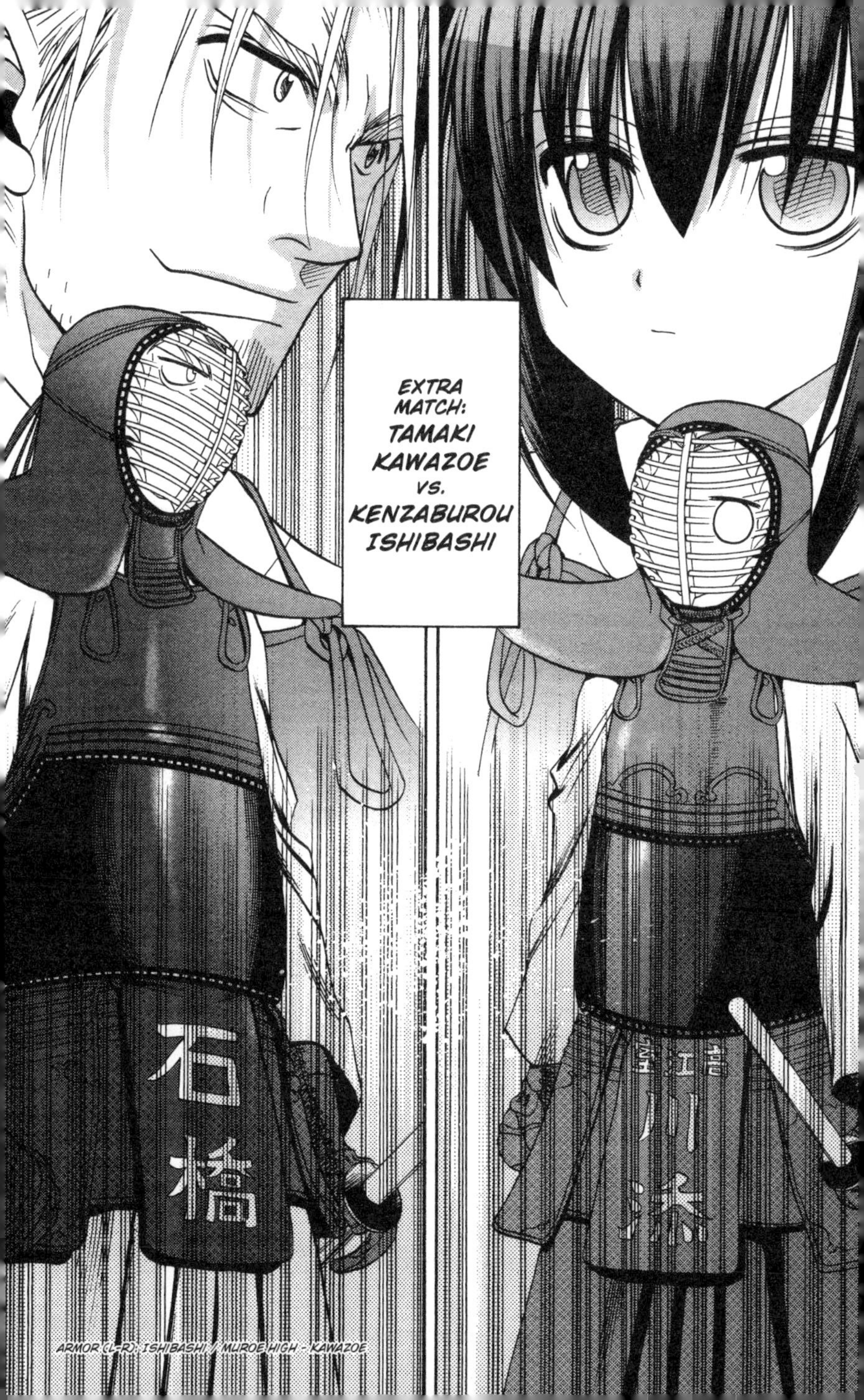
EXTRA MATCH: TAMAKI KAWAZOE VS. KENZABUROU ISHIBASHI
石橋
川添
ARMOR (L-R): ISHIBASHI / MUROE HIGH - KAWAZOE

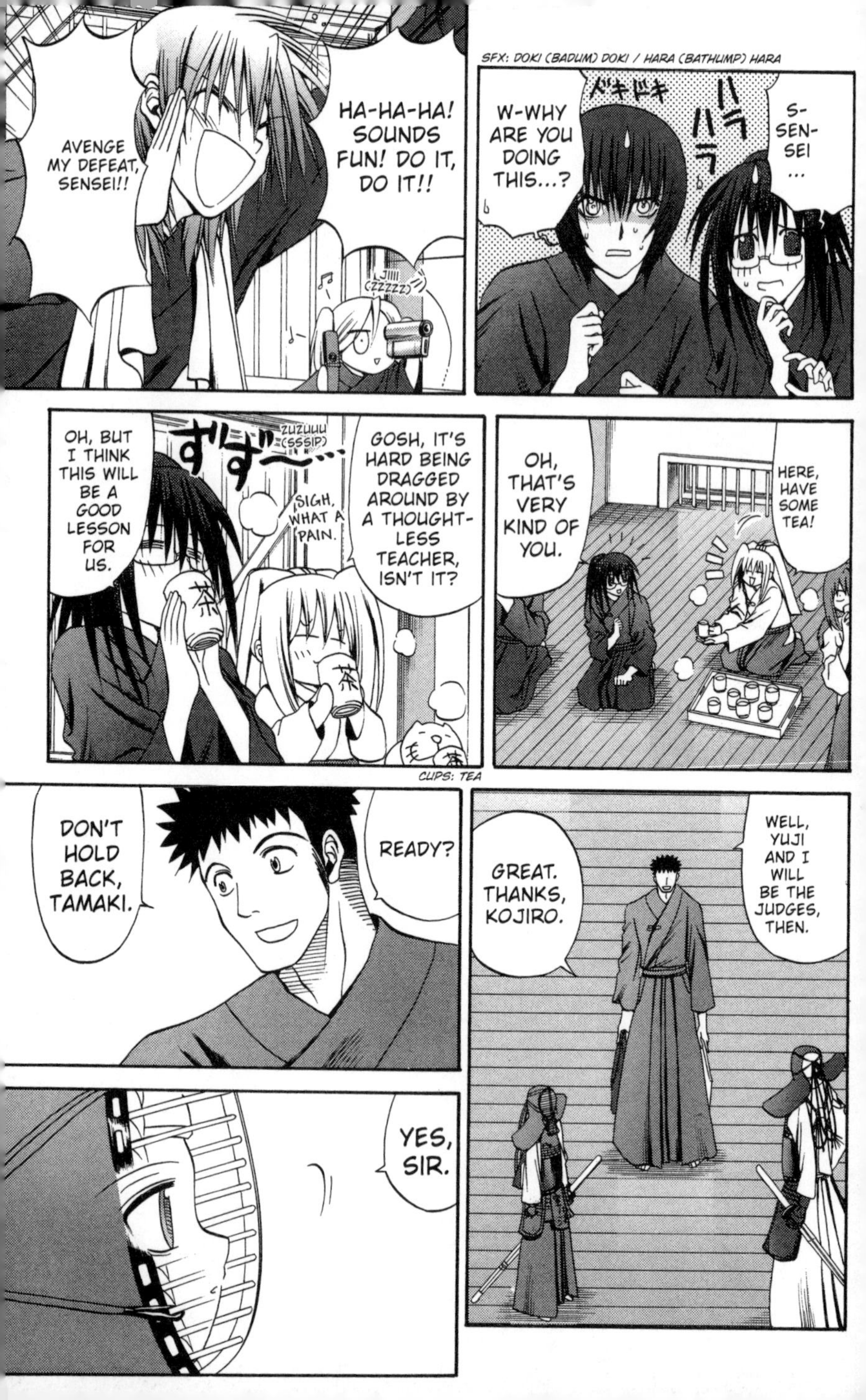
SFX: DOKI (BADUM) DOKI / HARA (BATHUMP) HARA
S-SENSEI...
W-WHY ARE YOU DOING THIS...?
HA-HA-HA! SOUNDS FUN! DO IT, DO IT!!
AVENGE MY DEFEAT, SENSEI!!
JIIII (ZZZZZ)
HERE, HAVE SOME TEA!
OH, THAT'S VERY KIND OF YOU.
GOSH, IT'S HARD BEING DRAGGED AROUND BY A THOUGHTLESS TEACHER, ISN'T IT?
SIGH, WHAT A PAIN.
ZUZUUU (SSSIP)
OH, BUT I THINK THIS WILL BE A GOOD LESSON FOR US.
CUPS: TEA
WELL, YUJI AND I WILL BE THE JUDGES, THEN.
GREAT. THANKS, KOJIRO.
READY?
DON'T HOLD BACK, TAMAKI.
YES, SIR.

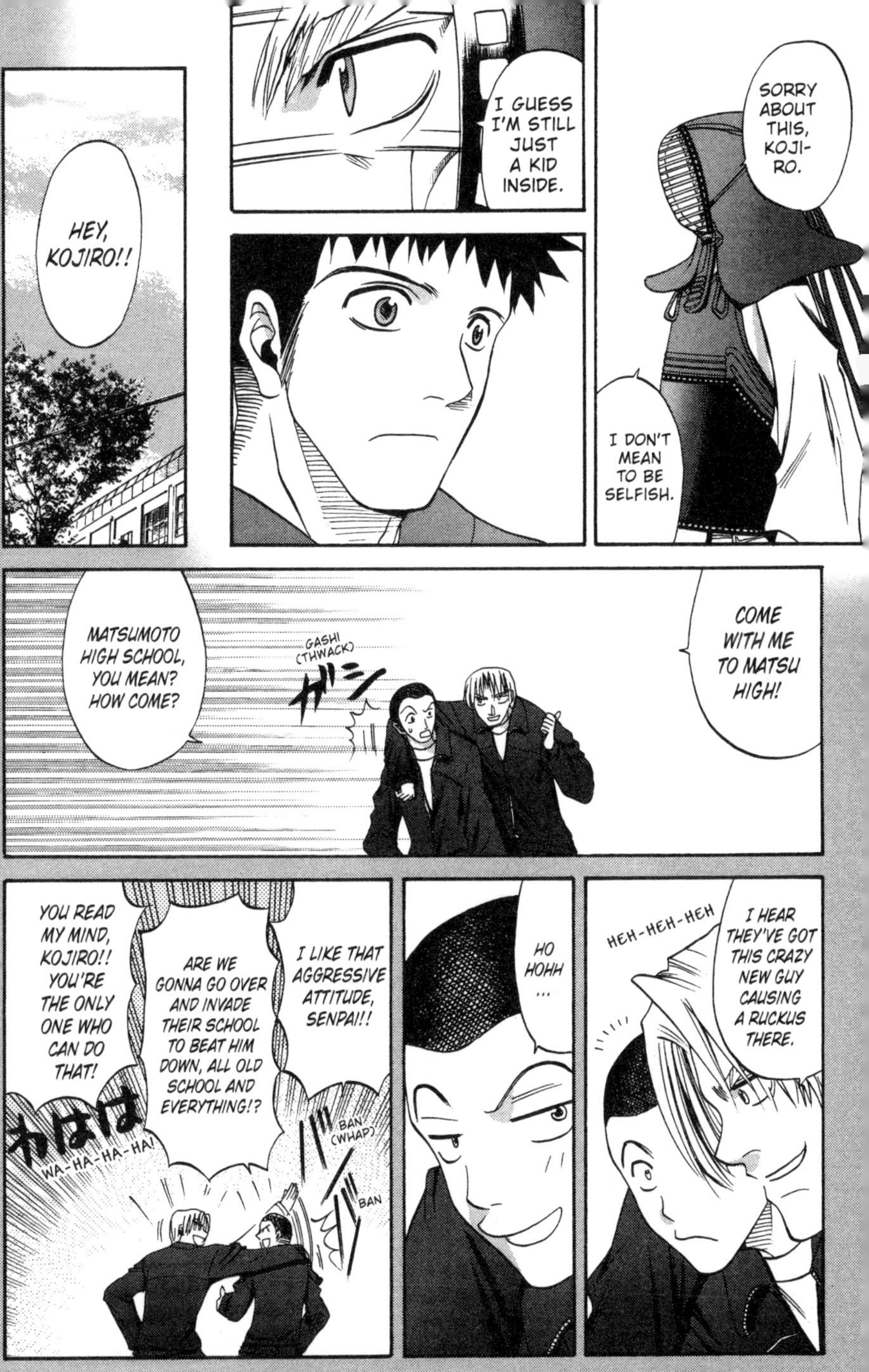
SORRY ABOUT THIS, KOJIRO.
I DON'T MEAN TO BE SELFISH.
I GUESS I'M STILL JUST A KID INSIDE.
HEY, KOJIRO!!
COME WITH ME TO MATSU HIGH!
GASHI (THWACK)
MATSUMOTO HIGH SCHOOL, YOU MEAN? HOW COME?
HEH-HEH-HEH
I HEAR THEY'VE GOT THIS CRAZY NEW GUY CAUSING A RUCKUS THERE.
HO HOHH ...
I LIKE THAT AGGRESSIVE ATTITUDE, SENPAI!!
ARE WE GONNA GO OVER AND INVADE THEIR SCHOOL TO BEAT HIM DOWN, ALL OLD SCHOOL AND EVERYTHING!?
YOU READ MY MIND, KOJIRO!! YOU'RE THE ONLY ONE WHO CAN DO THAT!
BAN (WHAP)
BAN
わはは
WA-HA-HA-HA!

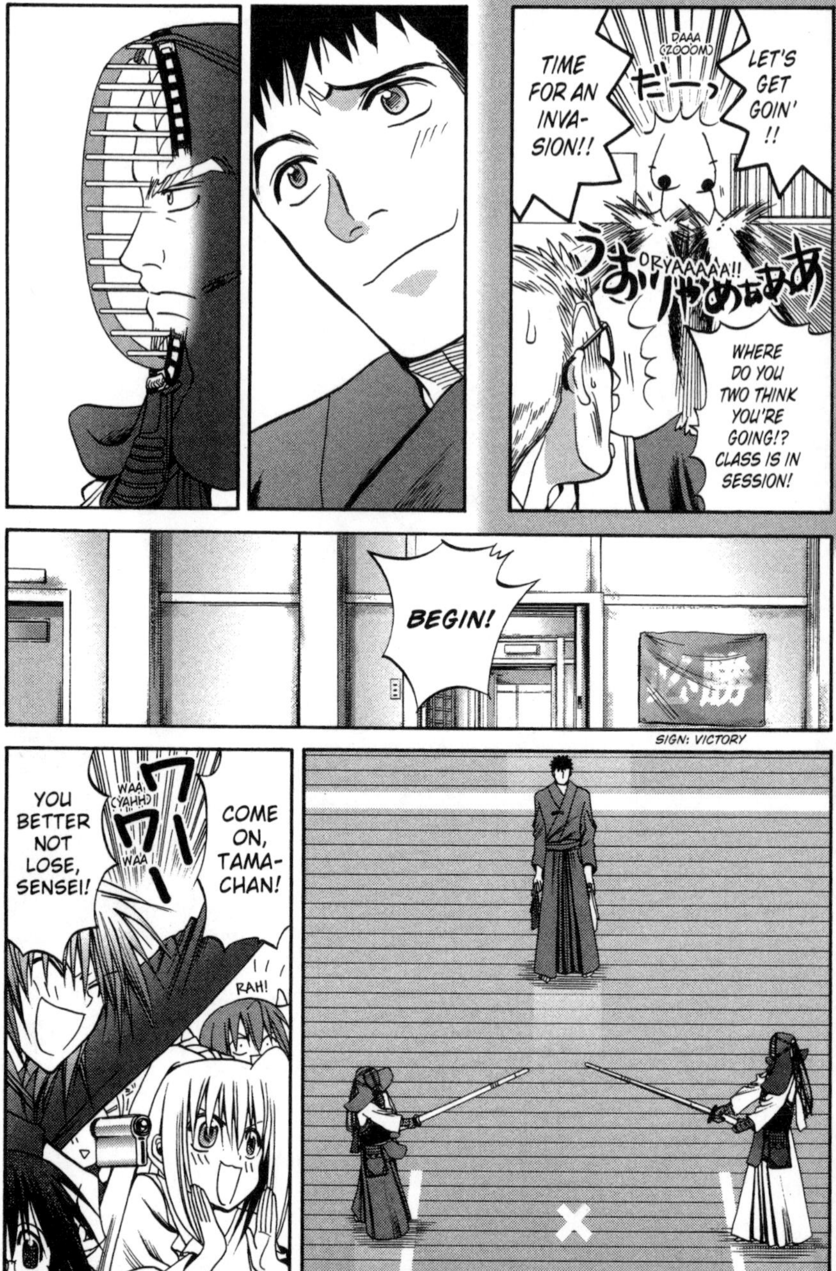
LET'S GET GOIN' !!
DAAA (ZOOOM)
だーっ
TIME FOR AN INVA-SION!!
うぉりゃあぁぁあ
ORYAAAAA!!
WHERE DO YOU TWO THINK YOU'RE GOING!? CLASS IS IN SESSION!
BEGIN!
SIGN: VICTORY
COME ON, TAMA-CHAN!
WAA (YAHH)
ワーワー
WAA
YOU BETTER NOT LOSE, SENSEI!
RAH!
SFX: JIII (VRR)

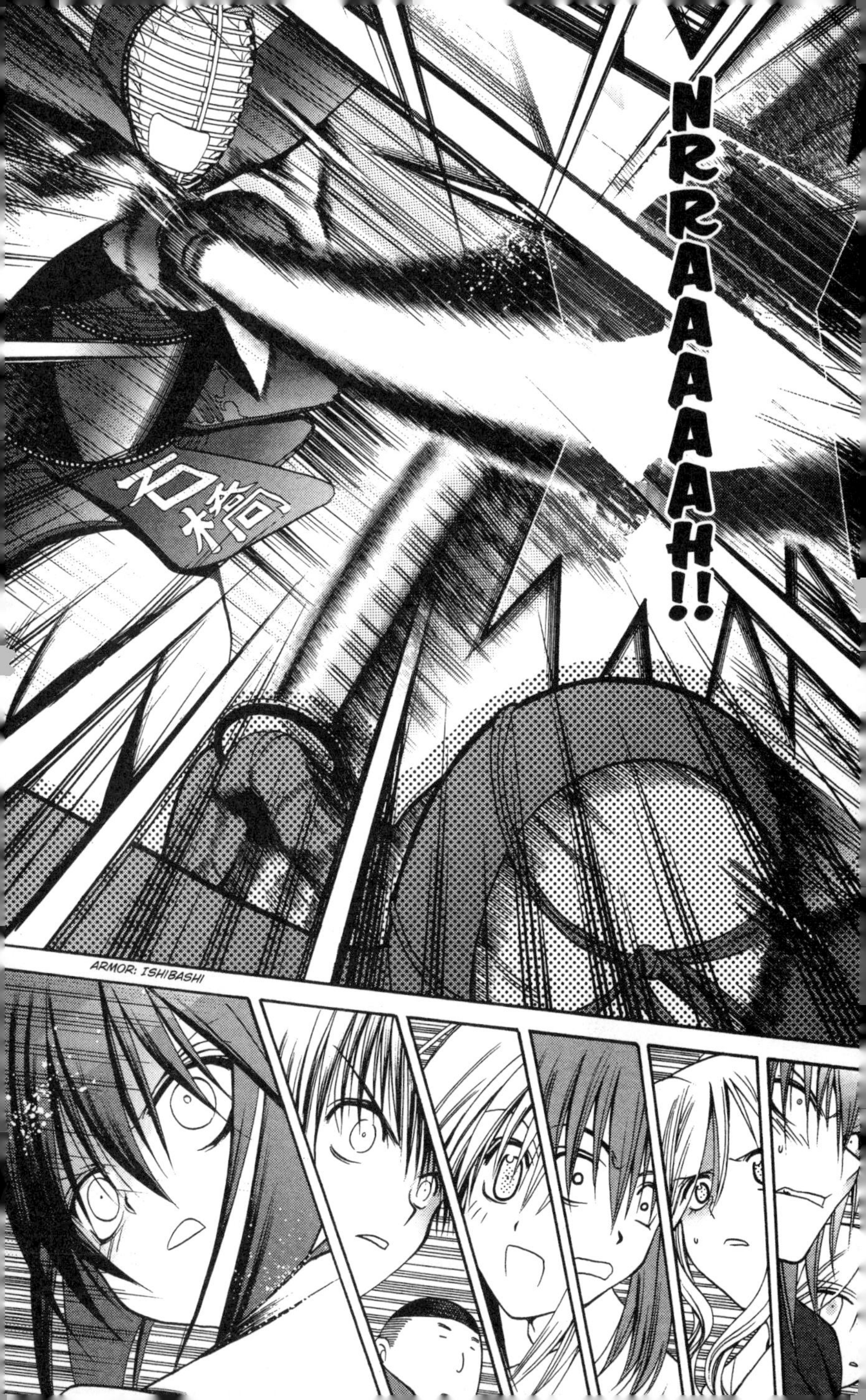
NRRAAAAAH!!
ARMOR: ISHIBASHI

BAMBOO BLADE

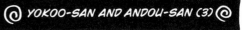

YOKOO-SAN AND ANDOU-SAN (3)

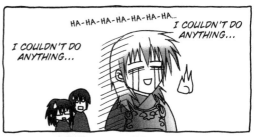

I COULDN'T DO ANYTHING...
HA-HA-HA-HA-HA-HA-HA...
I COULDN'T DO ANYTHING...
POOR YOKOO-SAN IS TOTALLY OUT OF HER MIND.
HA HA HA HA HA HA
SHE SEEMS OBLIVIOUS TO ANYTHING WE DO.
さっさっ
SASA (SWISH)
SEEMS OBLIVIOUS TO ANYTHING WE DO...
SEEMS OBLIVIOUS TO ANYTHING WE DO...
SEEMS OBLIVIOUS TO ANYTHING WE DO...
I'M GONNA DRAW SOME NOSE HAIRS ON HER...
ぱあんっ
PAAN (THWAP)
HA HA HA HA HA HA HA
EVEN UNCONSCIOUS, SHE STILL KNOWS WHEN TO SMACK ANDOU-SAN FOR HER BAD JOKES.
THAT'S PRETTY COOL.
MARKER
SLIPPER

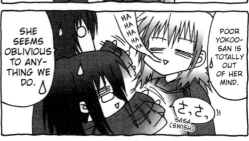

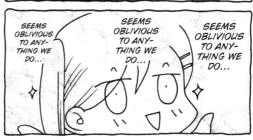

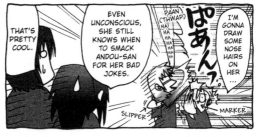

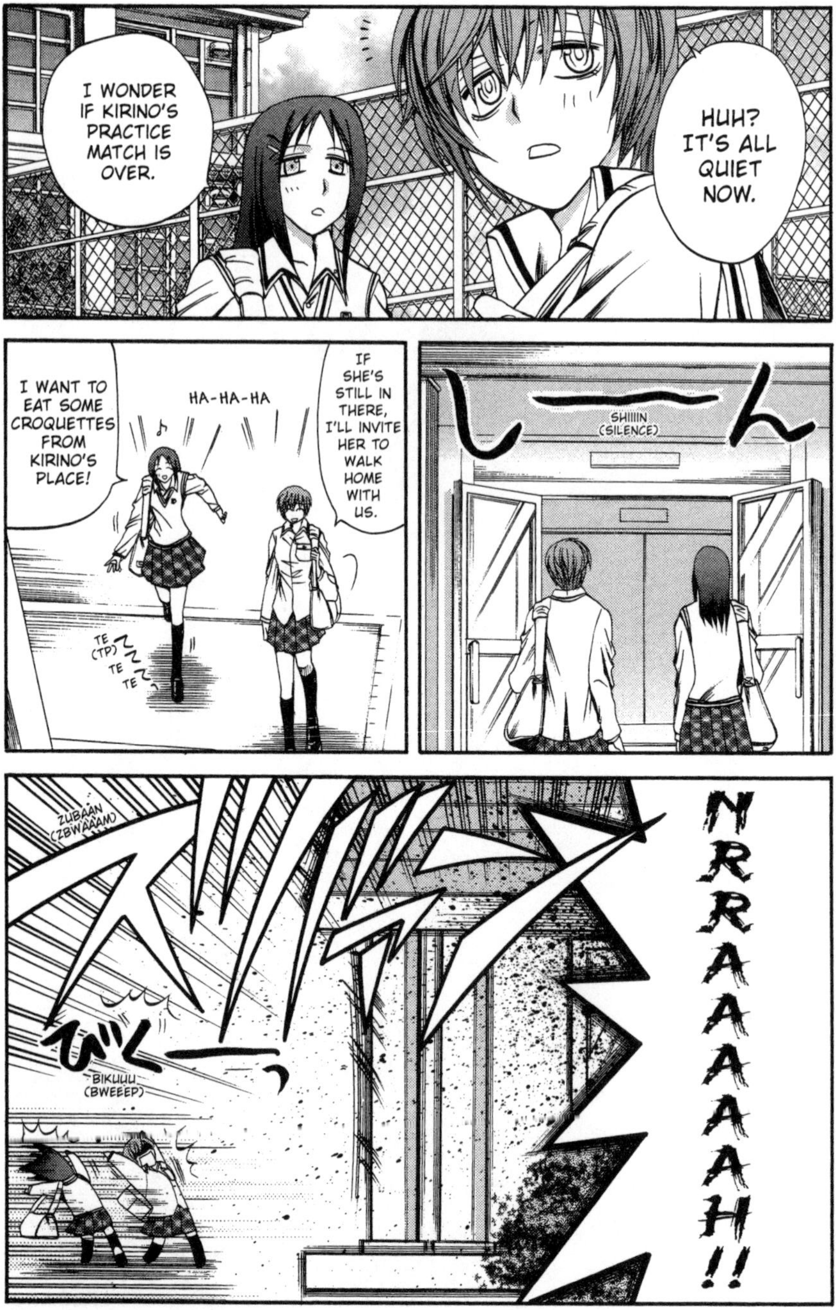
HUH? IT'S ALL QUIET NOW.
I WONDER IF KIRINO'S PRACTICE MATCH IS OVER.
しーん
SHIIIN (SILENCE)
IF SHE'S STILL IN THERE, I'LL INVITE HER TO WALK HOME WITH US.
HA-HA-HA
I WANT TO EAT SOME CROQUETTES FROM KIRINO'S PLACE!
TE (TP) TE TE
NRRAAAAAAAH!!
ZUBAAN (ZBWAAAM)
びくーっ
BIKUUU (BWEEEP)

CHAPTER 24
HOME AND PRACTICE

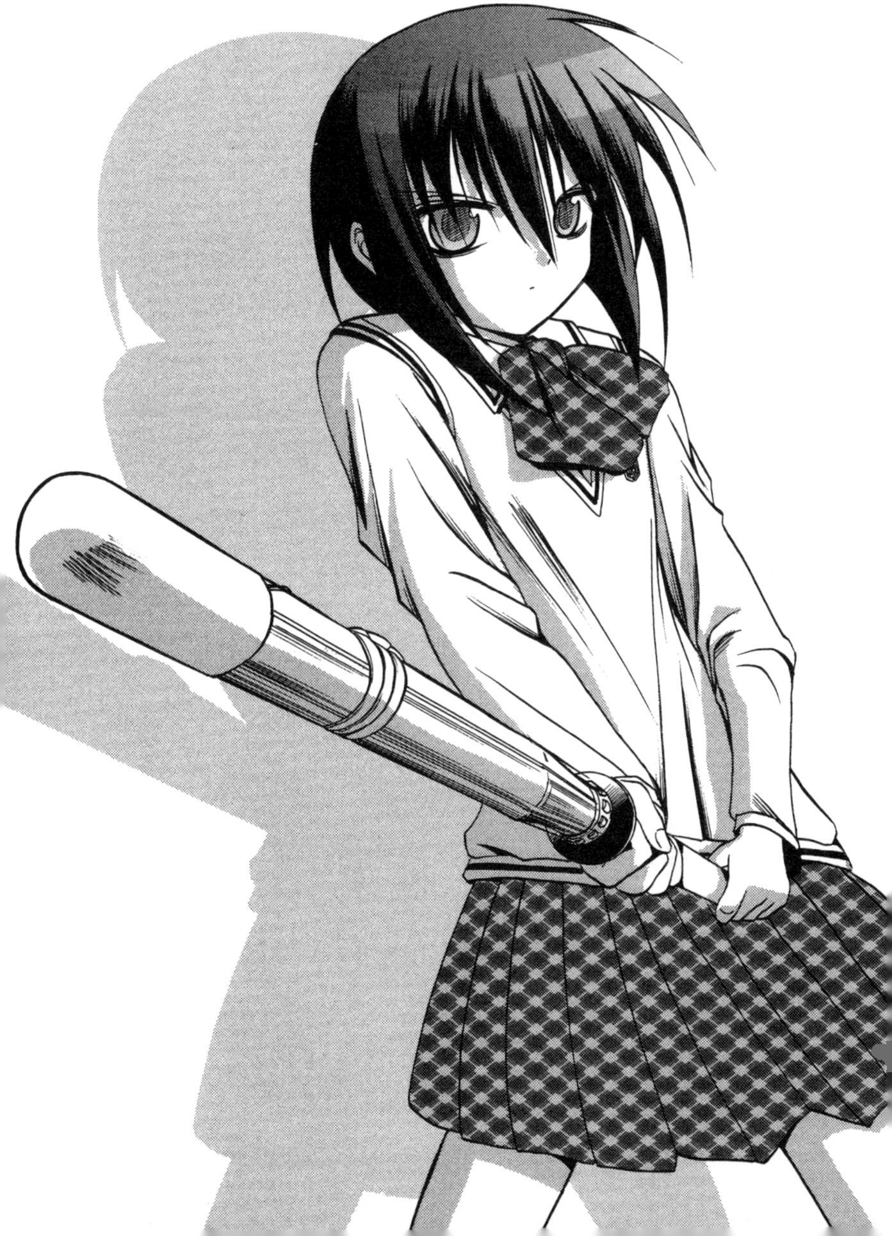

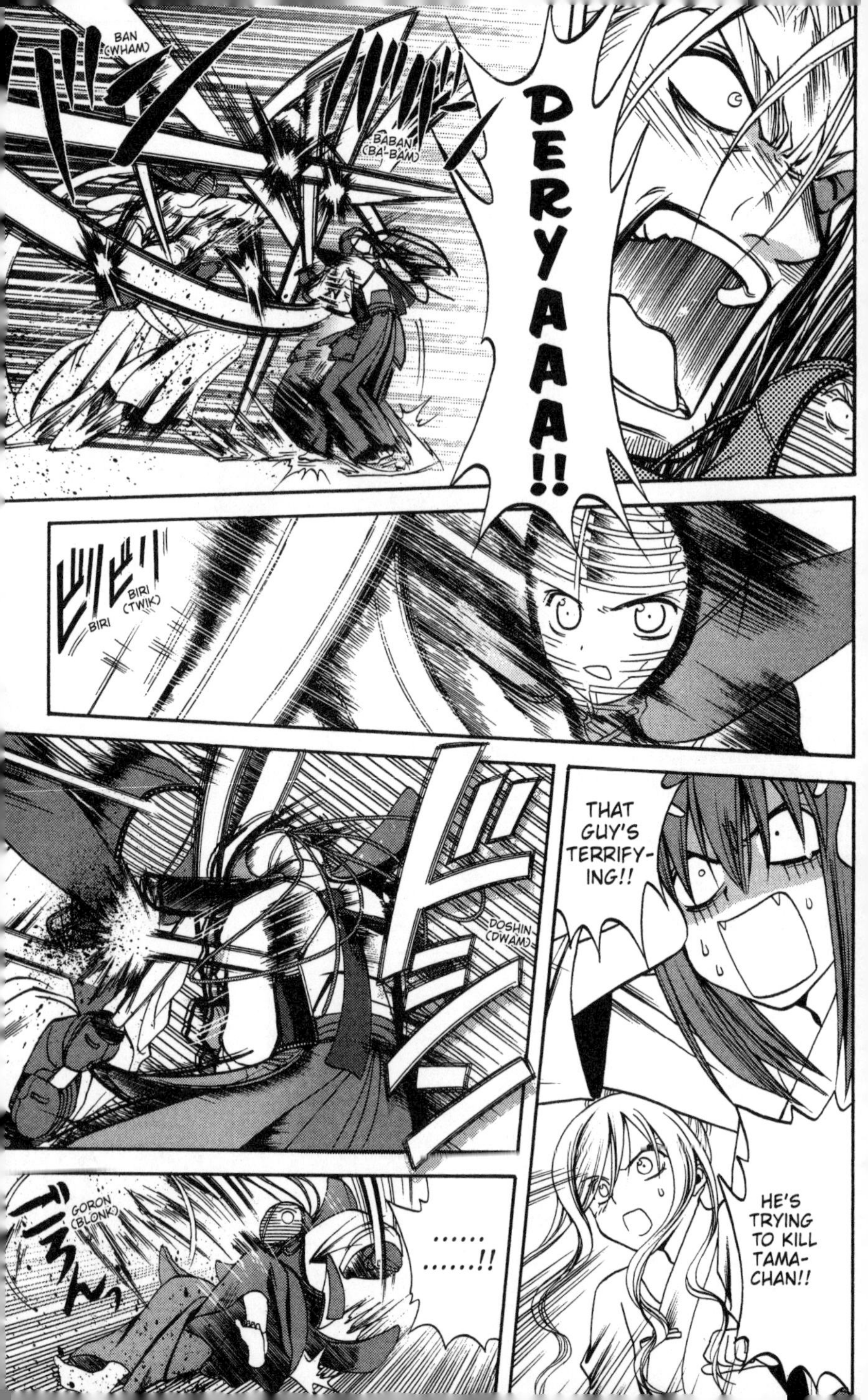
DERYAAA!!
BABAN (BA-BAM)
BAN (WHAM)
BIRI BIRI (TWIK)
THAT GUY'S TERRIFY-ING!!
DOSHIN (DWAM)
HE'S TRYING TO KILL TAMA-CHAN!!
....!!
GORON (BLONK)

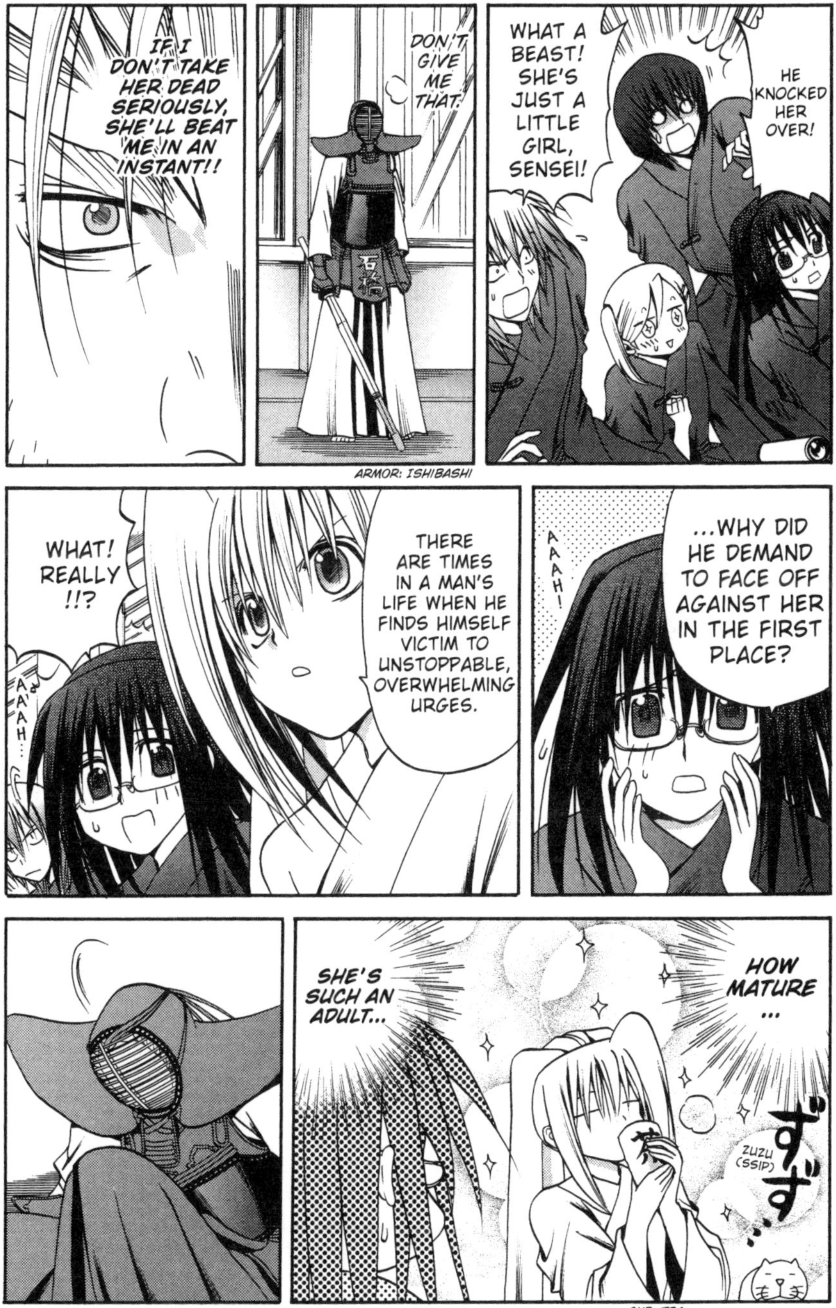
HE KNOCKED HER OVER!
WHAT A BEAST! SHE'S JUST A LITTLE GIRL, SENSEI!
DON'T GIVE ME THAT.
IF I DON'T TAKE HER DEAD SERIOUSLY, SHE'LL BEAT ME IN AN INSTANT!!
ARMOR: ISHIBASHI
...WHY DID HE DEMAND TO FACE OFF AGAINST HER IN THE FIRST PLACE?
AAAH!
THERE ARE TIMES IN A MAN'S LIFE WHEN HE FINDS HIMSELF VICTIM TO UNSTOPPABLE, OVERWHELMING URGES.
WHAT! REALLY!!?
AAAAH...
HOW MATURE...
SHE'S SUCH AN ADULT...
ずず
ZUZU (SSIP)
CUP: TEA

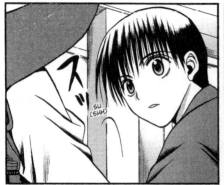

SU
(SHH)

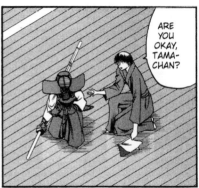

ARE YOU OKAY, TAMA-CHAN?

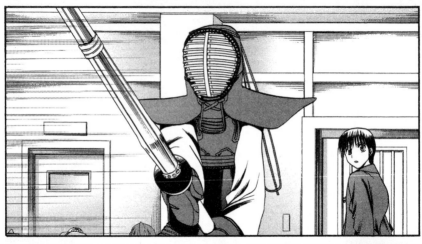

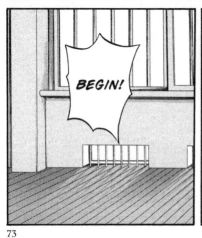

BEGIN!

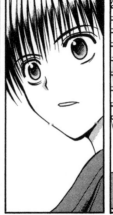

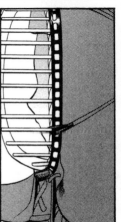

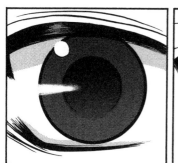
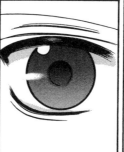
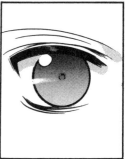
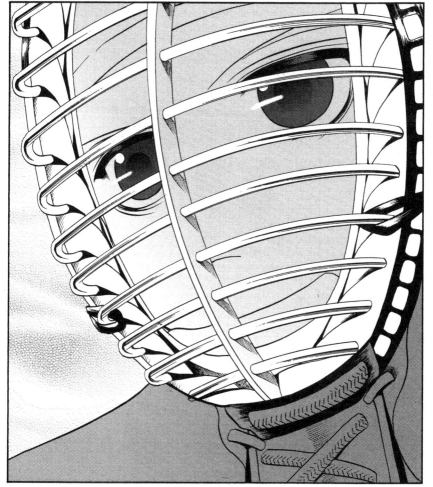

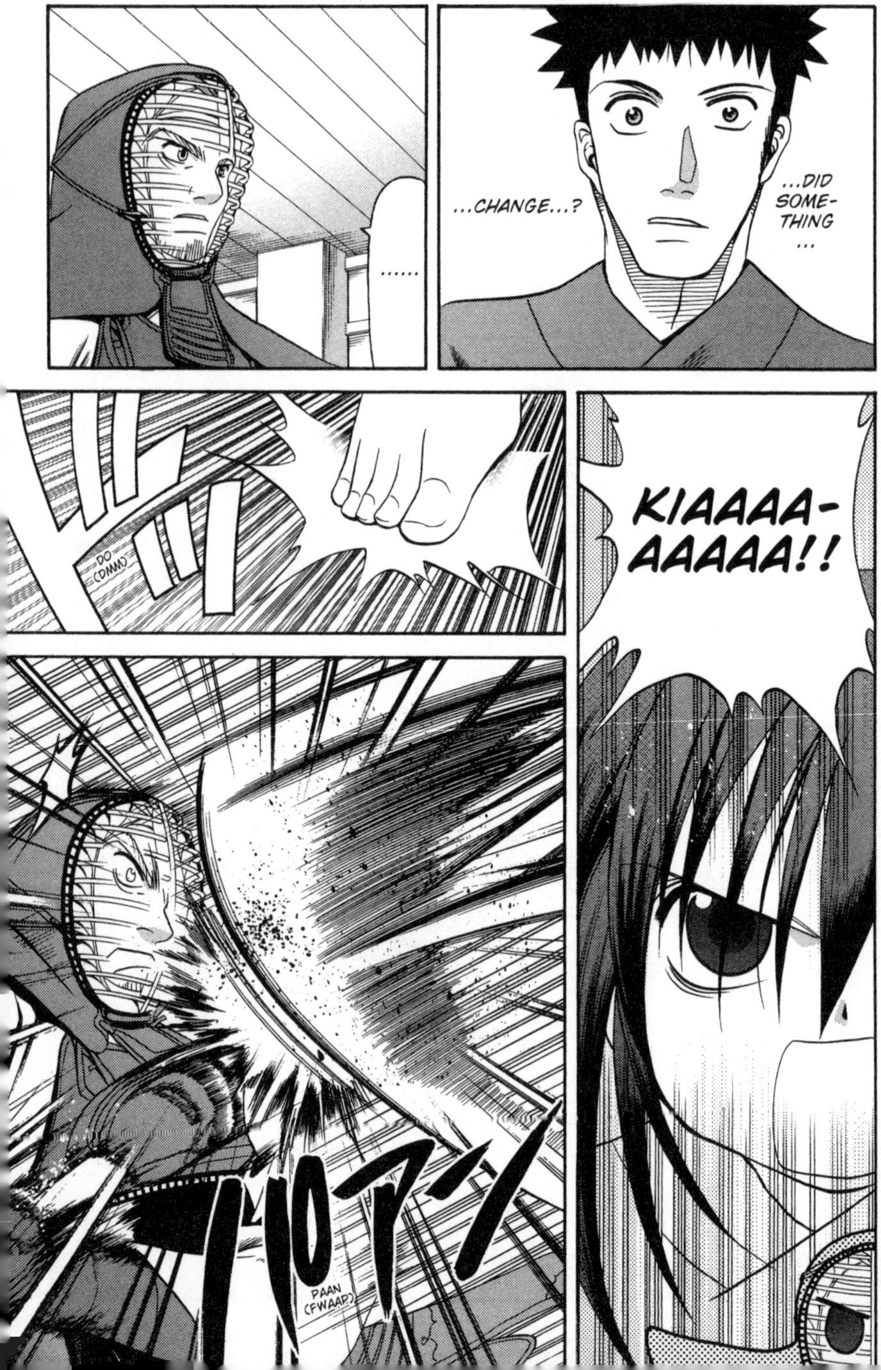
...DID SOMETHING ...
...CHANGE...?
......
KIAAAAAAAAAA!!
DO (DMM)
PAAN (FWAAP)

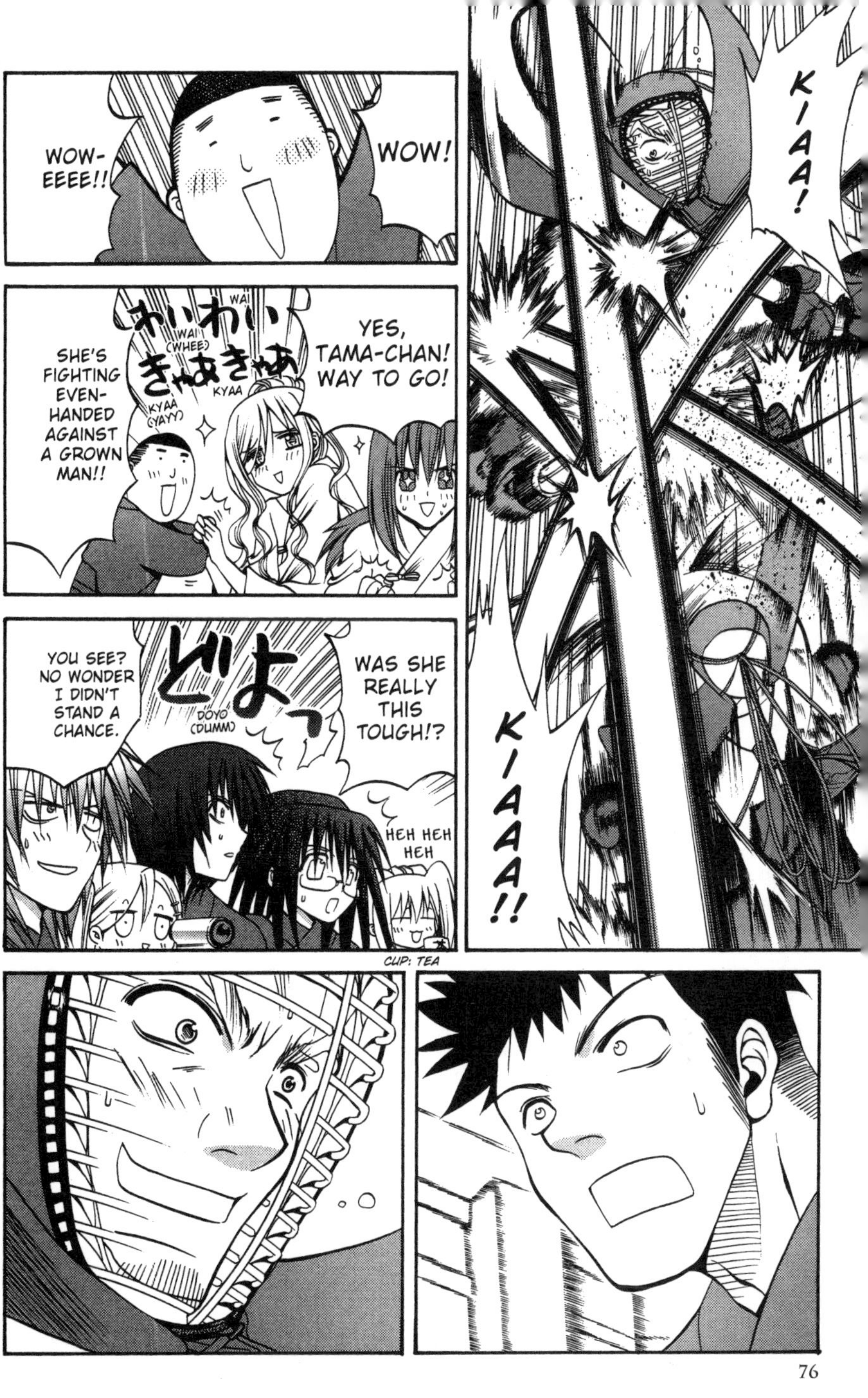
KIAA!
KIAAAA!!
WOW!
WOW-EEEE!!
YES, TAMA-CHAN! WAY TO GO!
わいわい
WAI WAI (WHEE)
きゃあきゃあ
KYAA KYAA (YAYY)
SHE'S FIGHTING EVEN-HANDED AGAINST A GROWN MAN!!
WAS SHE REALLY THIS TOUGH!?
どよっ
DOYO (DUMM)
YOU SEE? NO WONDER I DIDN'T STAND A CHANCE.
HEH HEH HEH
CUP: TEA

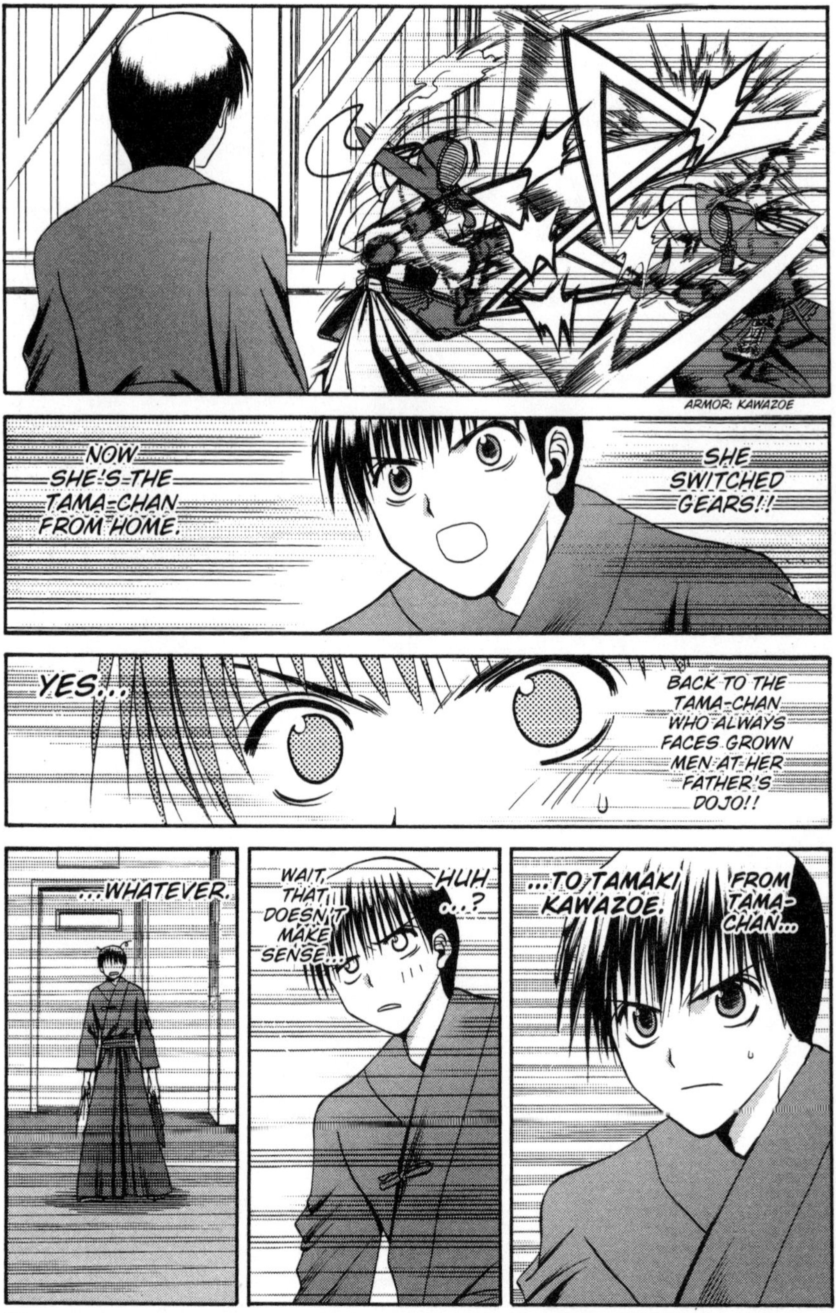
ARMOR: KAWAZOE
SHE SWITCHED GEARS!!
NOW SHE'S THE TAMA-CHAN FROM HOME.
BACK TO THE TAMA-CHAN WHO ALWAYS FACES GROWN MEN AT HER FATHER'S DOJO!!
YES...
FROM TAMA-CHAN...
...TO TAMAKI KAWAZOE.
HUH...?
WAIT, THAT DOESN'T MAKE SENSE...
...WHATEVER.

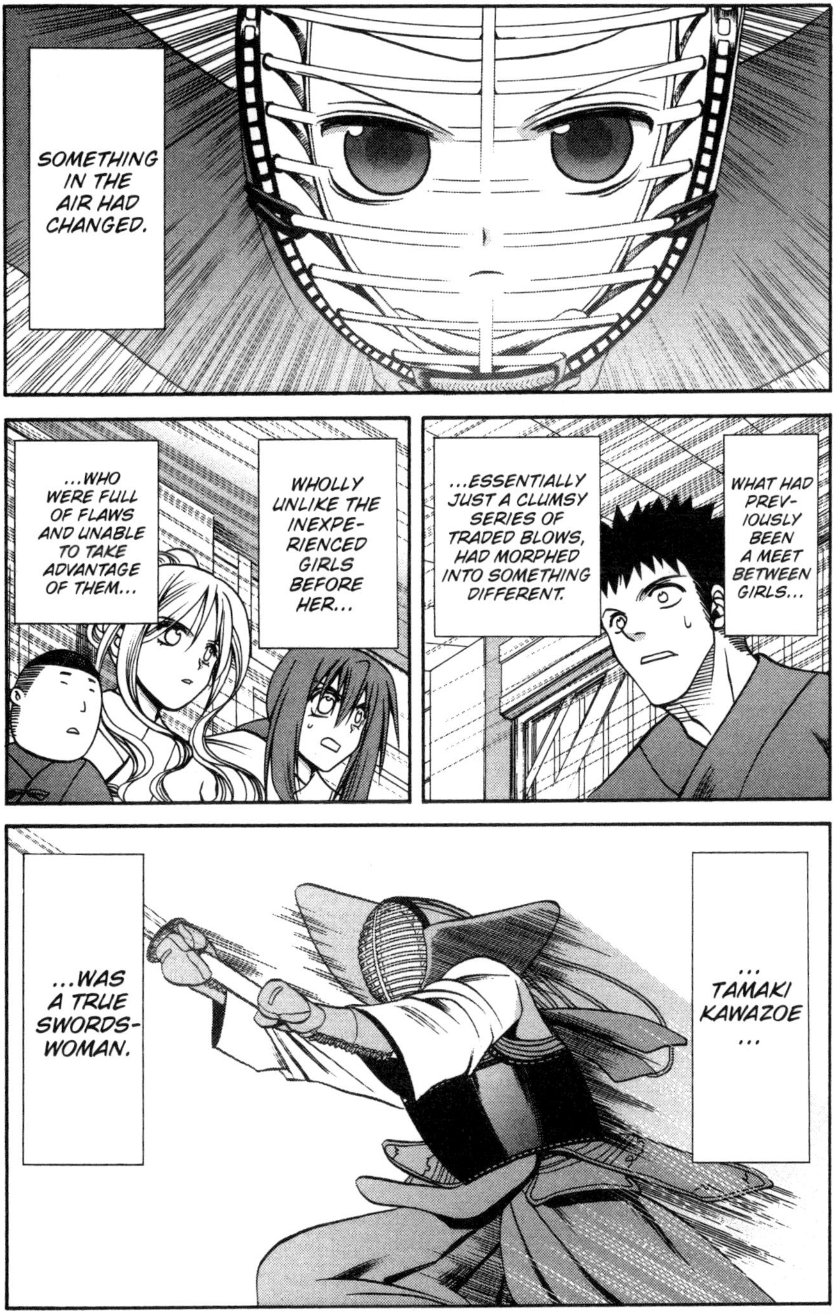
SOMETHING IN THE AIR HAD CHANGED.
WHAT HAD PREVIOUSLY BEEN A MEET BETWEEN GIRLS...
...ESSENTIALLY JUST A CLUMSY SERIES OF TRADED BLOWS, HAD MORPHED INTO SOMETHING DIFFERENT.
WHOLLY UNLIKE THE INEXPERIENCED GIRLS BEFORE HER...
...WHO WERE FULL OF FLAWS AND UNABLE TO TAKE ADVANTAGE OF THEM...
...TAMAKI KAWAZOE...
...WAS A TRUE SWORDSWOMAN.

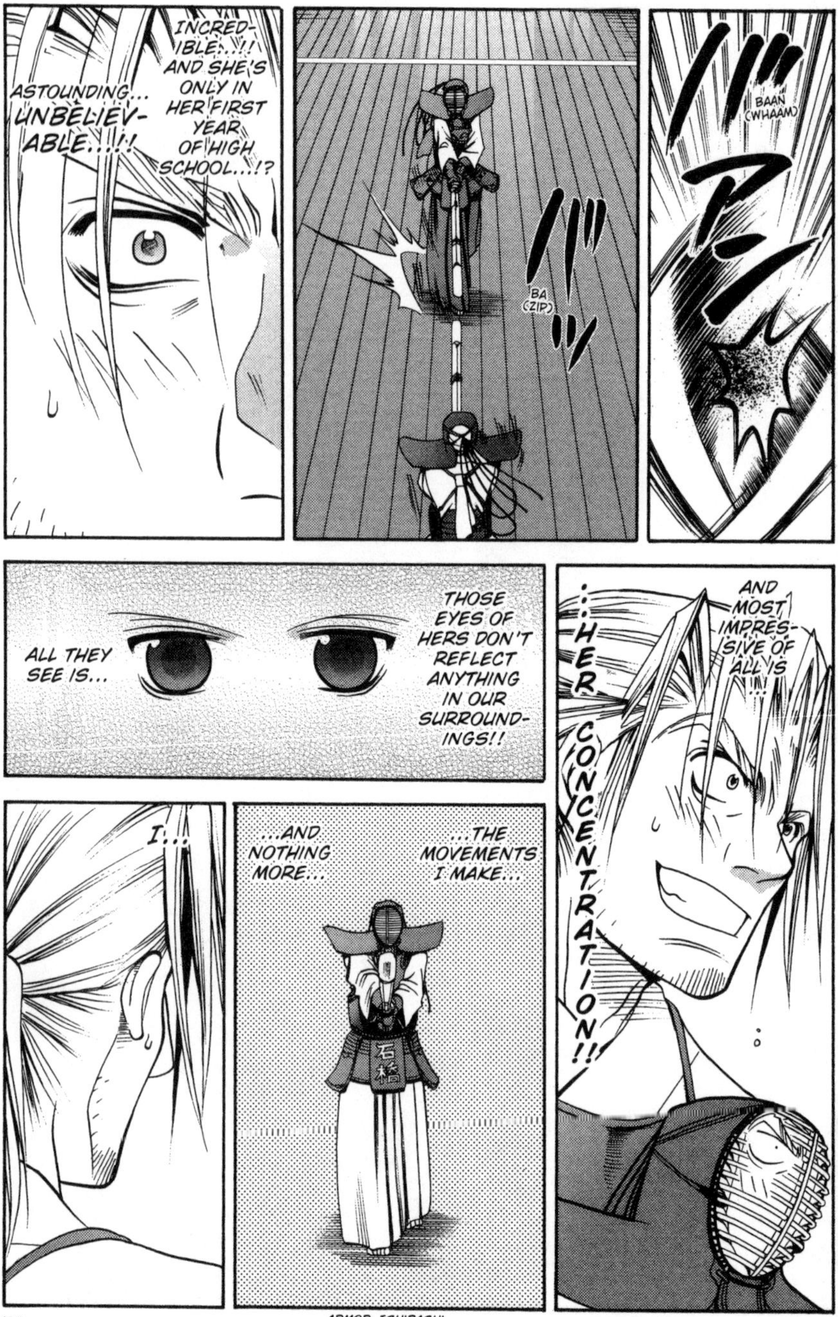
BAAN (WHAAM)
BA (ZIP)
INCRED-IBLE...!! AND SHE'S ONLY IN HER FIRST YEAR OF HIGH SCHOOL...!?
ASTOUNDING... UNBELIEV-ABLE...!!!
AND MOST IMPRES-SIVE OF ALL IS...
...HER CONCENTRATION!!
THOSE EYES OF HERS DON'T REFLECT ANYTHING IN OUR SURROUND-INGS!!
ALL THEY SEE IS...
...THE MOVEMENTS I MAKE...
...AND NOTHING MORE...
I...

ARMOR: ISHIBASHI

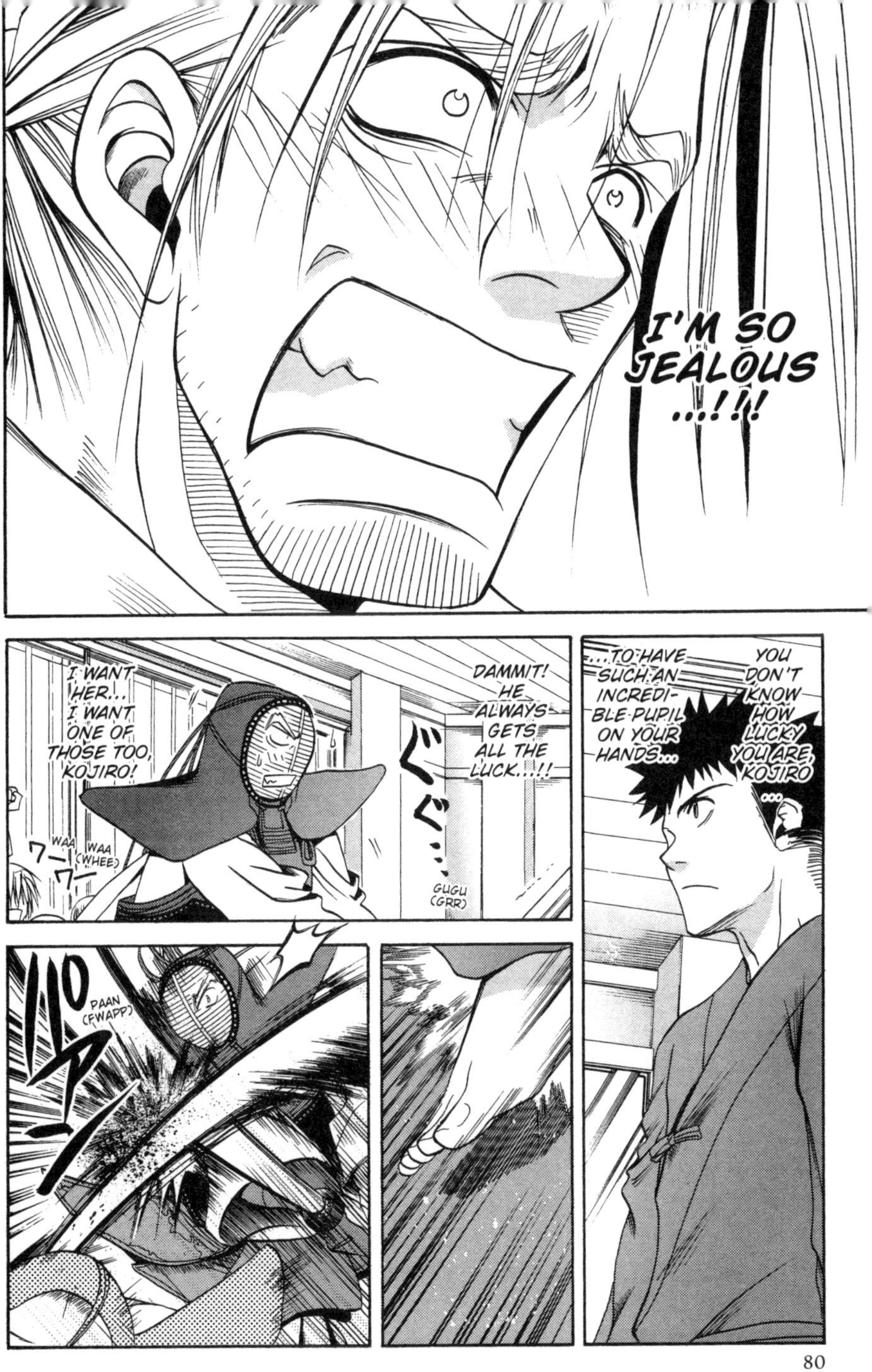
I'M SO JEALOUS ...!!!
YOU DON'T KNOW HOW LUCKY YOU ARE, KOJIRO ...
...TO HAVE SUCH AN INCREDIBLE PUPIL ON YOUR HANDS...
DAMMIT! HE ALWAYS GETS ALL THE LUCK...!!
GUGU (GRR)
I WANT HER... I WANT ONE OF THOSE TOO, KOJIRO!
WAA WAA (WHEE)
PAAN (FWAPP)

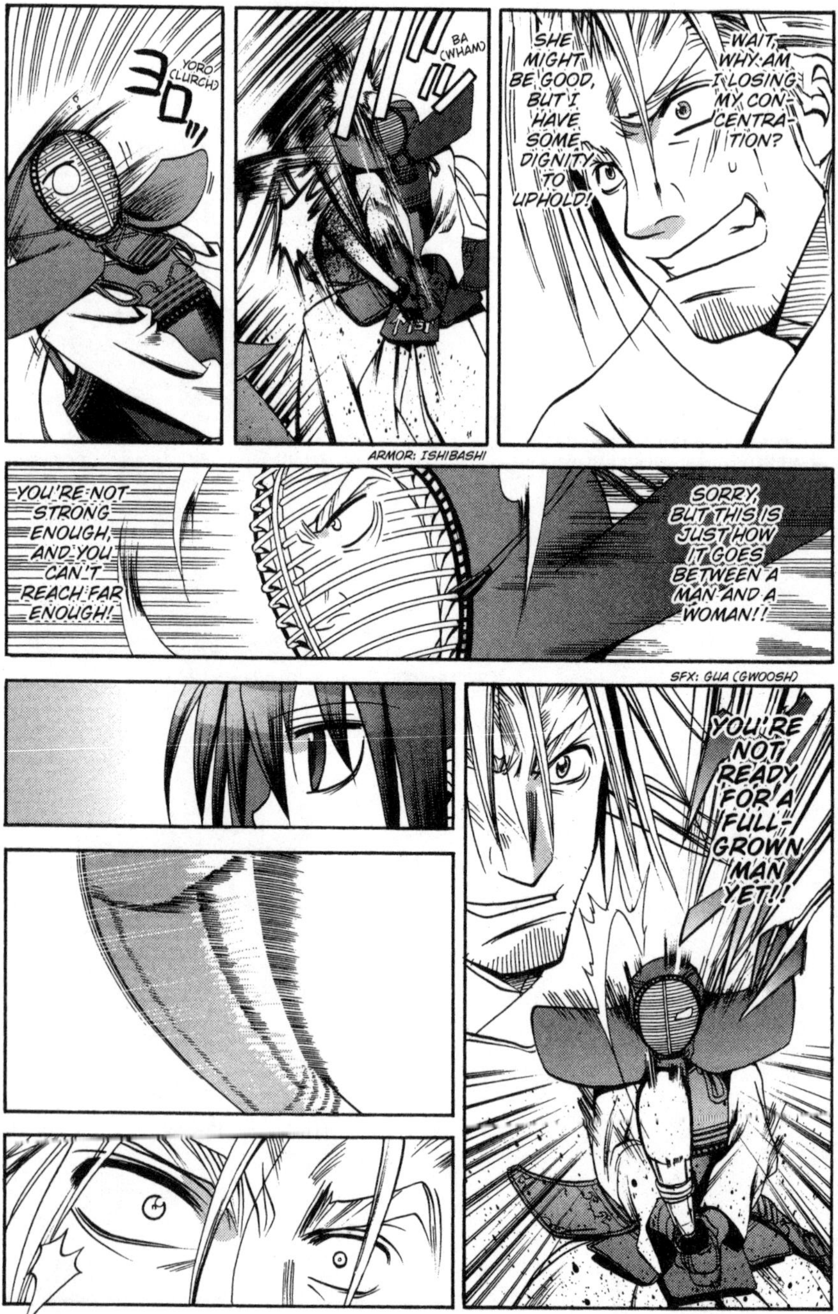
WAIT, WHY AM I LOSING MY CONCENTRATION?
SHE MIGHT BE GOOD, BUT I HAVE SOME DIGNITY TO UPHOLD!
BA (WHAM)
YORO (LURCH)
ARMOR: ISHIBASHI
SORRY, BUT THIS IS JUST HOW IT GOES BETWEEN A MAN AND A WOMAN!!
YOU'RE NOT STRONG ENOUGH, AND YOU CAN'T REACH FAR ENOUGH!
SFX: GUA (GWOOSH)
YOU'RE NOT READY FOR A FULL-GROWN MAN YET!!

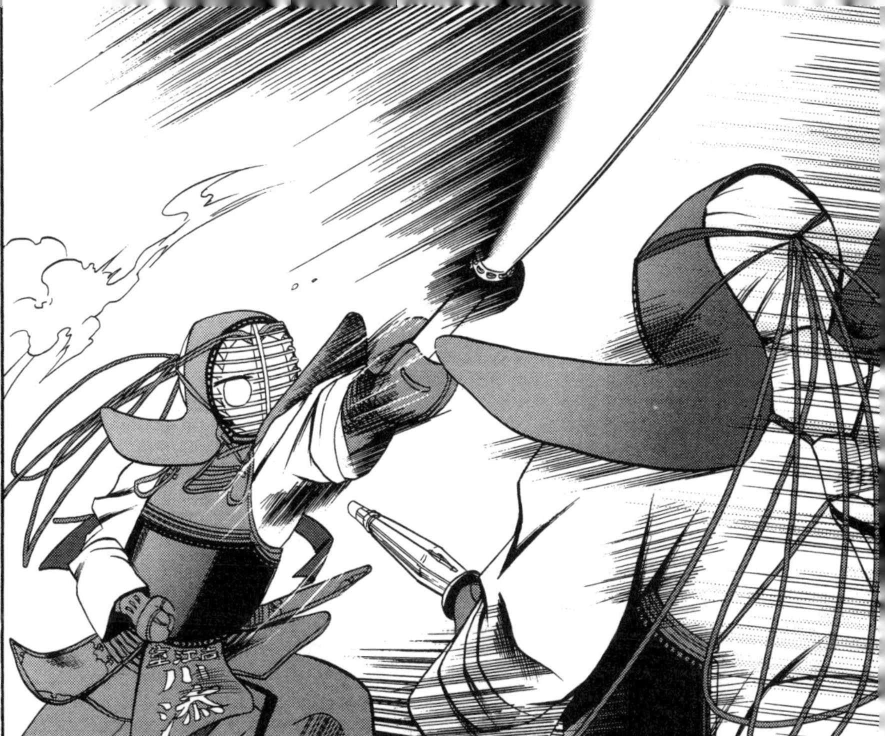

ARMOR: MUROE HIGH - KAWAZOE

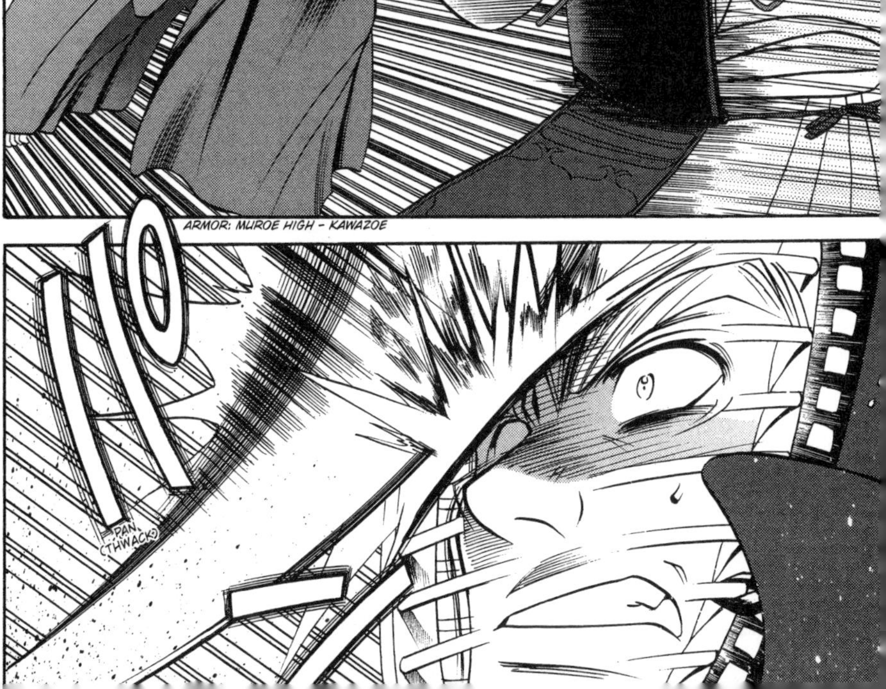
PAN (THWACK)

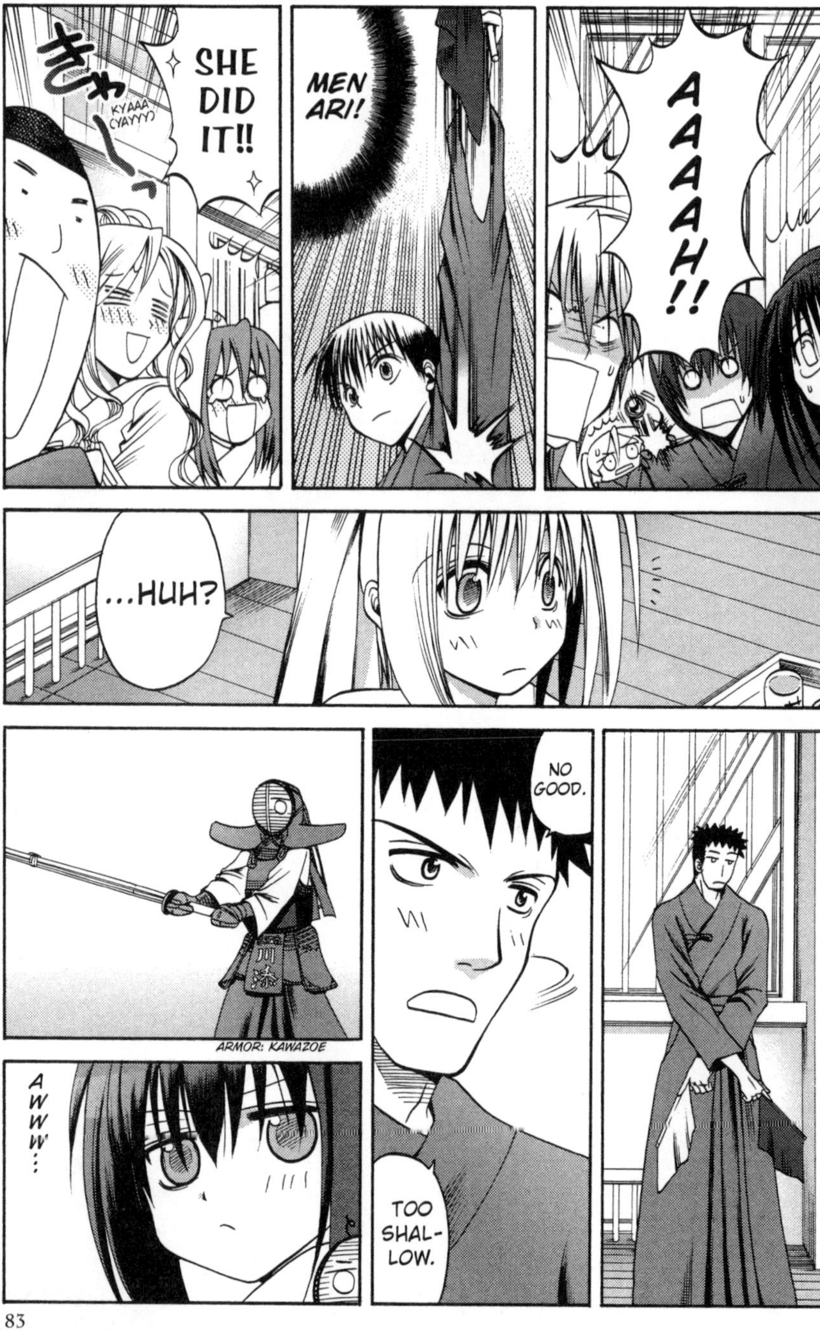
AAAAAH!!
MEN ARI!
SHE DID IT!!
きゃ〜っ
KYAAA (YAYYY)
...HUH?
NO GOOD.
TOO SHAL-LOW.
ARMOR: KAWAZOE
AWWW...

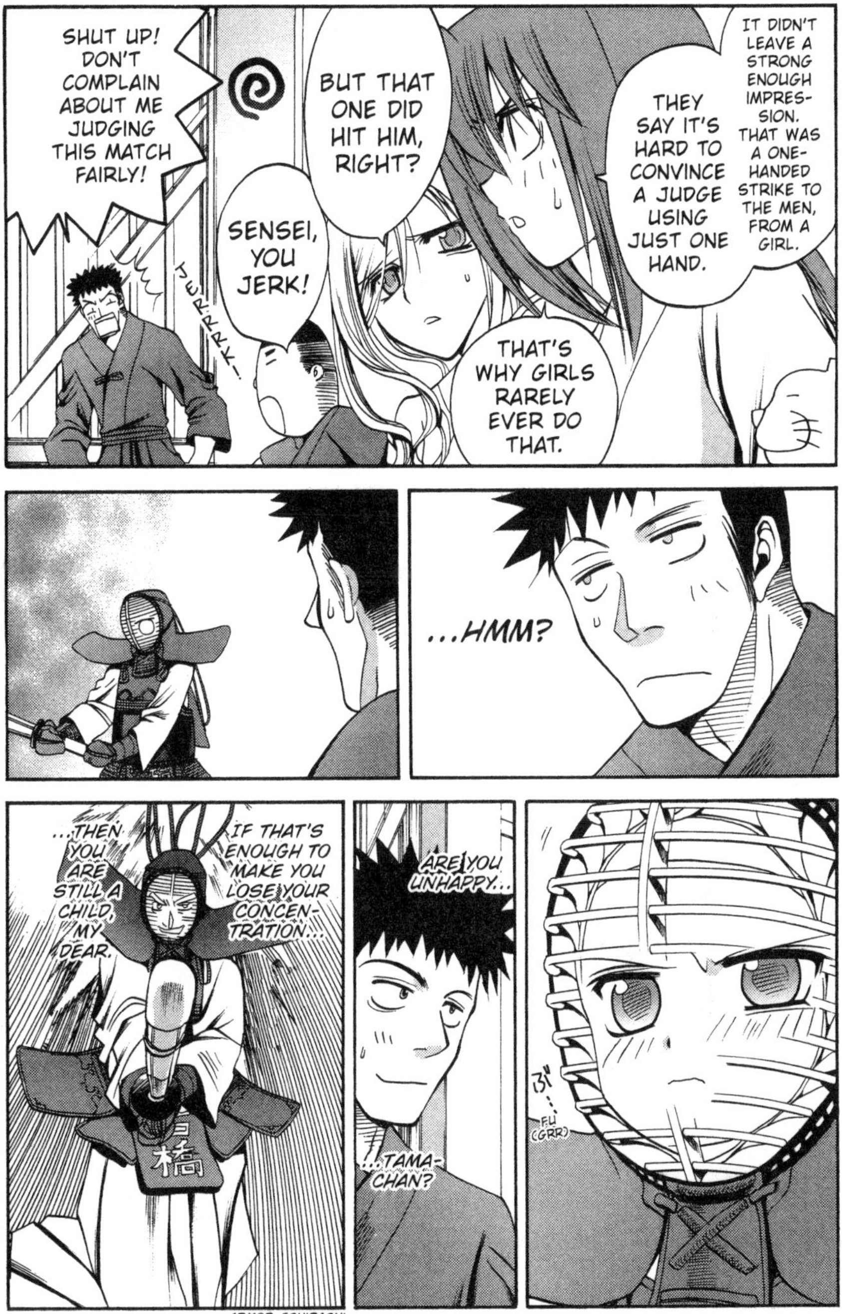
SENSEI, YOU JERK!
JERRRRK!
SHUT UP! DON'T COMPLAIN ABOUT ME JUDGING THIS MATCH FAIRLY!
BUT THAT ONE DID HIT HIM, RIGHT?
THEY SAY IT'S HARD TO CONVINCE A JUDGE USING JUST ONE HAND.
IT DIDN'T LEAVE A STRONG ENOUGH IMPRESSION. THAT WAS A ONE-HANDED STRIKE TO THE MEN, FROM A GIRL.
THAT'S WHY GIRLS RARELY EVER DO THAT.
...HMM?
ぶ…
FU (GRR)
ARE YOU UNHAPPY...
...TAMA-CHAN?
IF THAT'S ENOUGH TO MAKE YOU LOSE YOUR CONCENTRATION...
...THEN YOU ARE STILL A CHILD, MY DEAR.

ARMOR: ISHIBASHI

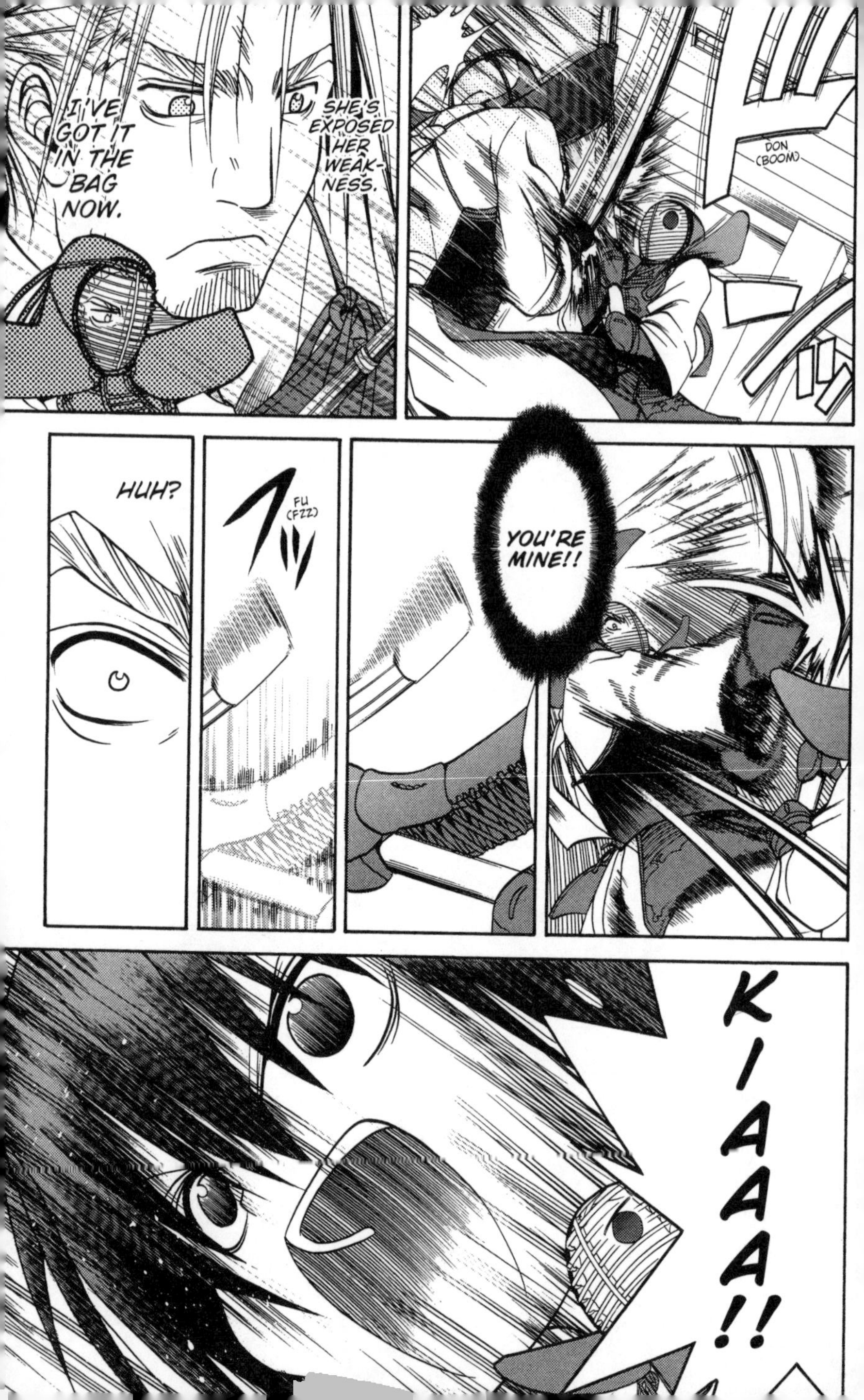
DON (BOOM)
SHE'S EXPOSED HER WEAKNESS.
I'VE GOT IT IN THE BAG NOW.
YOU'RE MINE!!
FU (FZZ)
HUH?
KIAAAA!!

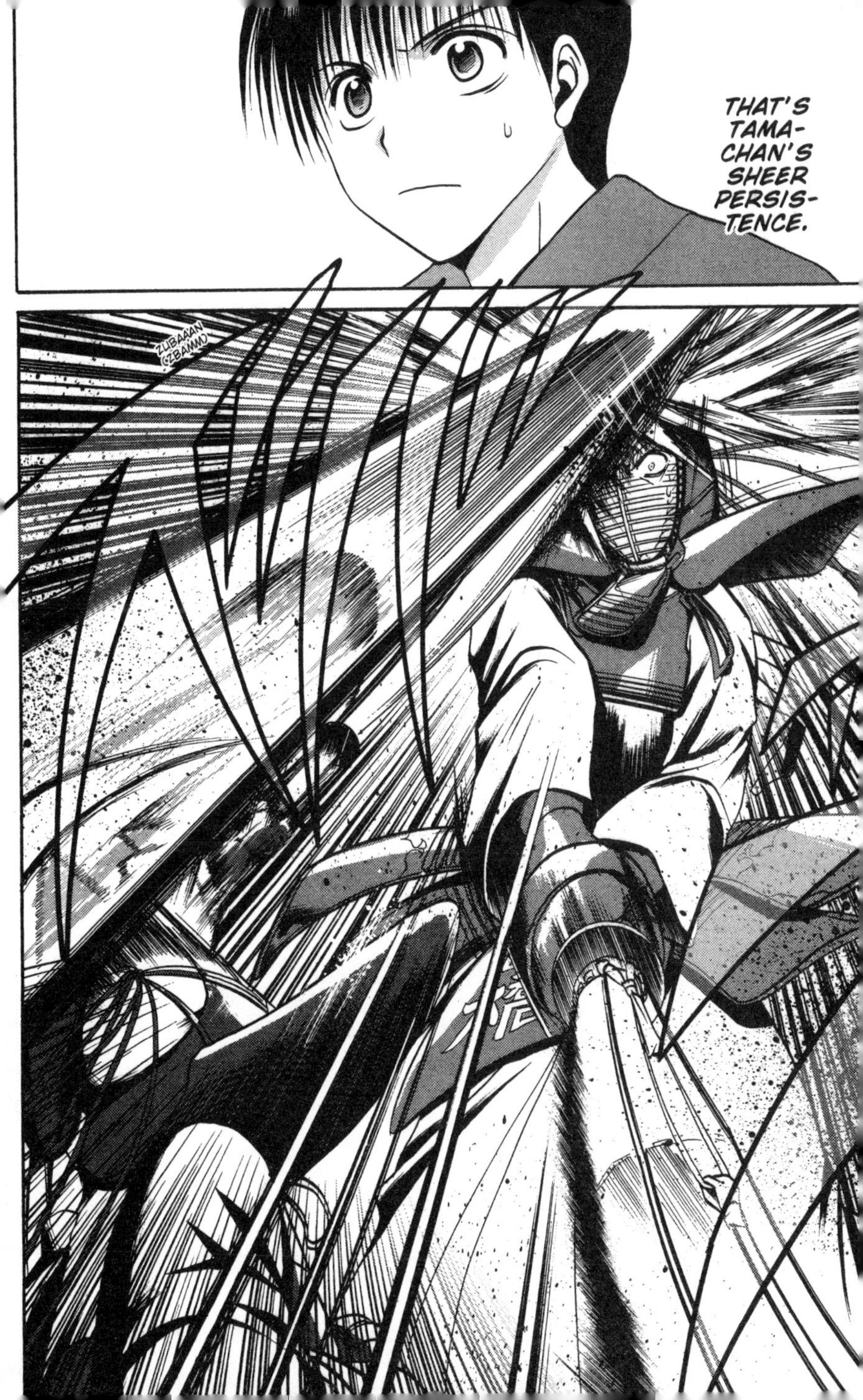
THAT'S TAMA-CHAN'S SHEER PERSIS-TENCE.
ZUBAAAN (ZBAMM)

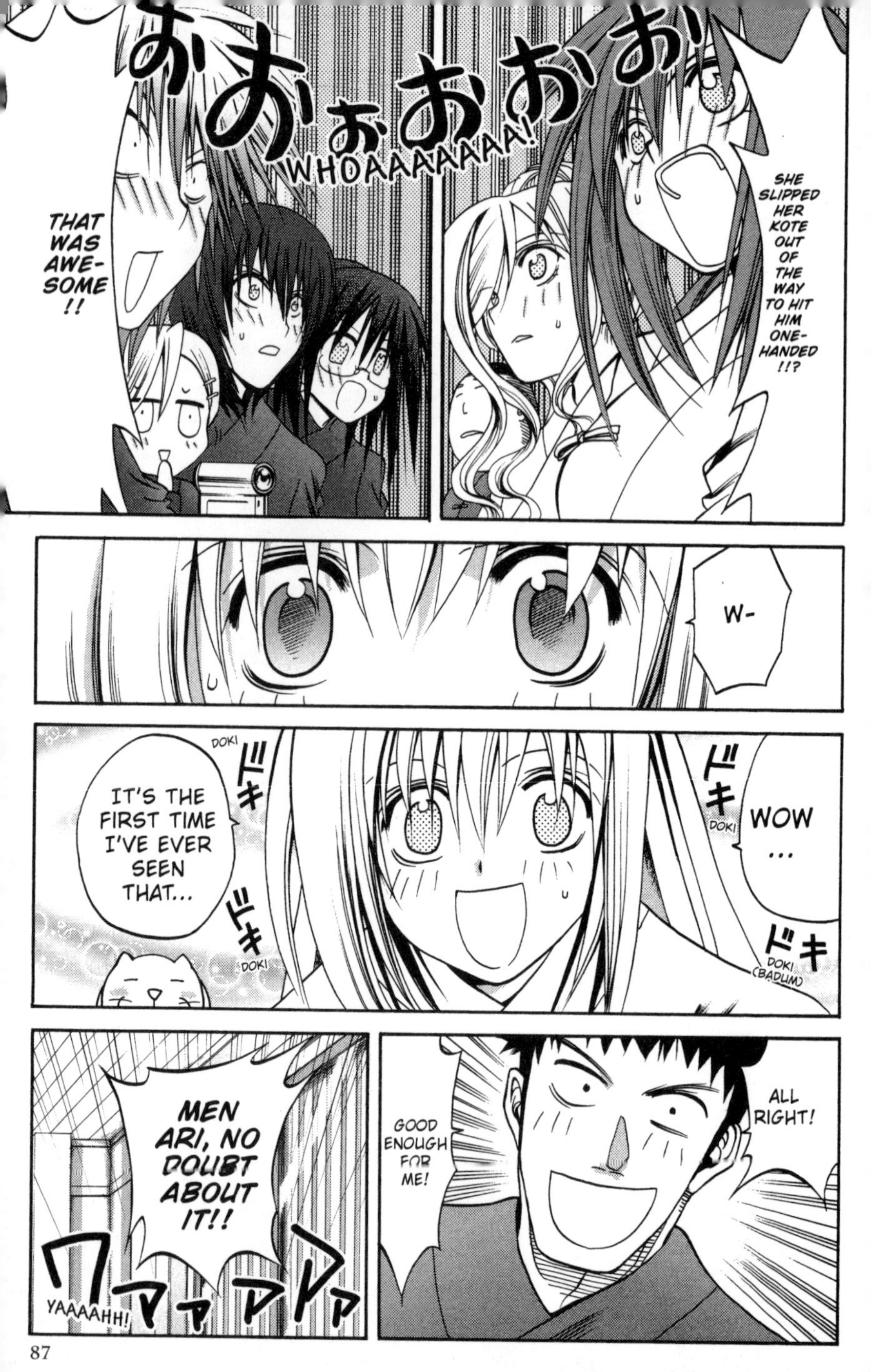
おおぉおおお!
WHOAAAAAAA!
SHE SLIPPED HER KOTE OUT OF THE WAY TO HIT HIM ONE-HANDED!!?
THAT WAS AWE-SOME!!
W-
ドキ
DOKI
WOW...
ドキ
DOKI (BADUM)
IT'S THE FIRST TIME I'VE EVER SEEN THAT...
ドキ
DOKI
ALL RIGHT!
GOOD ENOUGH FOR ME!
MEN ARI, NO DOUBT ABOUT IT!!
ワァァアァア
YAAAAHH!

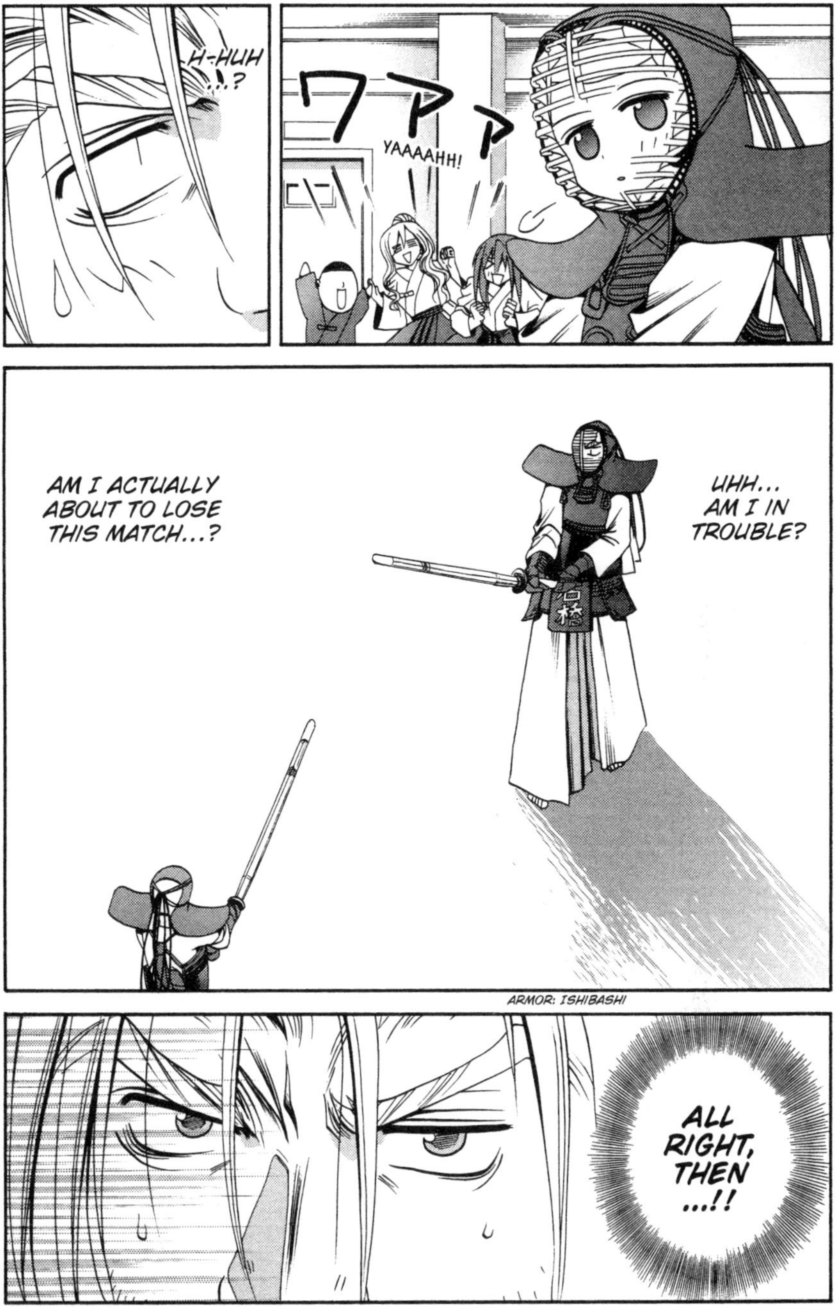
ワアア
YAAAAHH!
H-HUH ...!?
UHH... AM I IN TROUBLE?
AM I ACTUALLY ABOUT TO LOSE THIS MATCH...?
ARMOR: ISHIBASHI
ALL RIGHT, THEN ...!!

BAMBOO BLADE

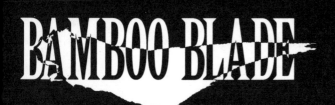

BAMBOO BLADE

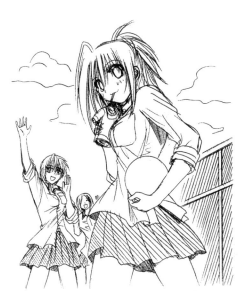

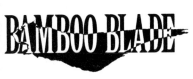

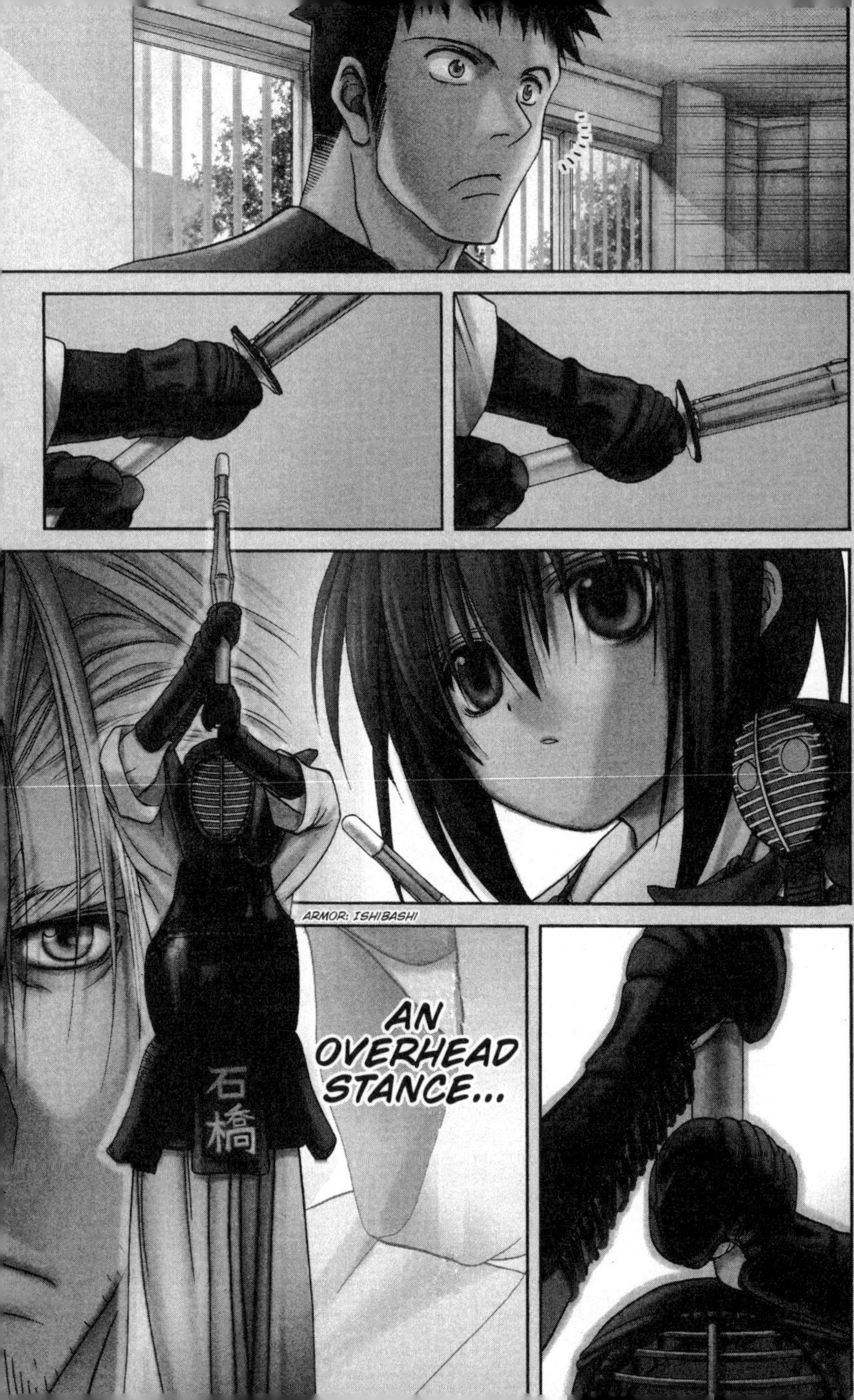
ARMOR: ISHIBASHI
石橋
AN OVERHEAD STANCE...

SIGN: SALE

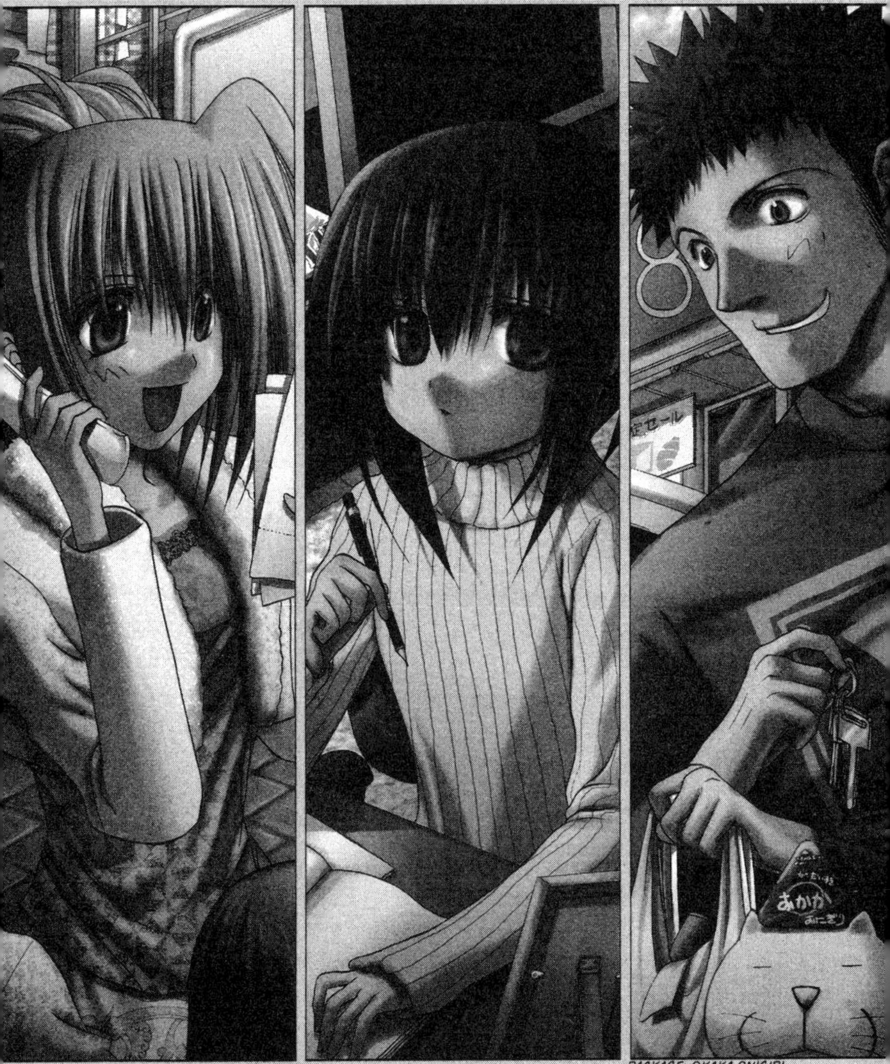

PACKAGE: OKAKA ONIGIRI

CHAPTER 25
TAMAKI AND THE OVERHEAD STANCE

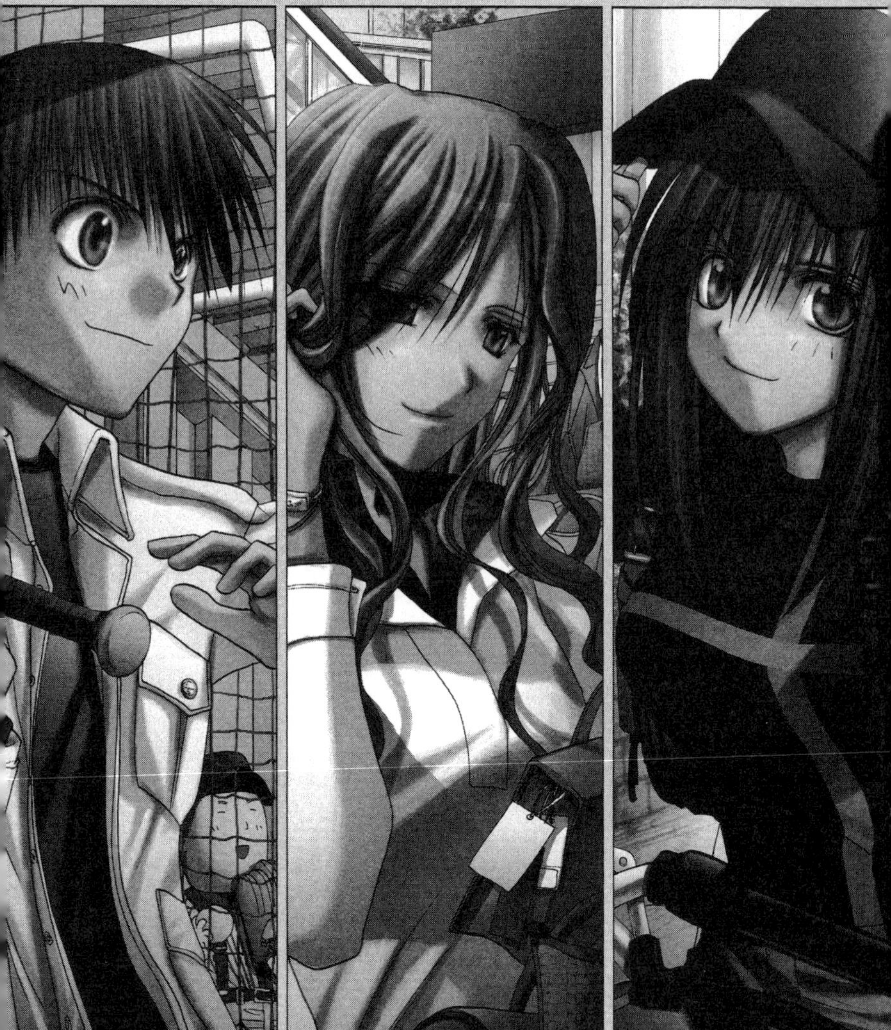

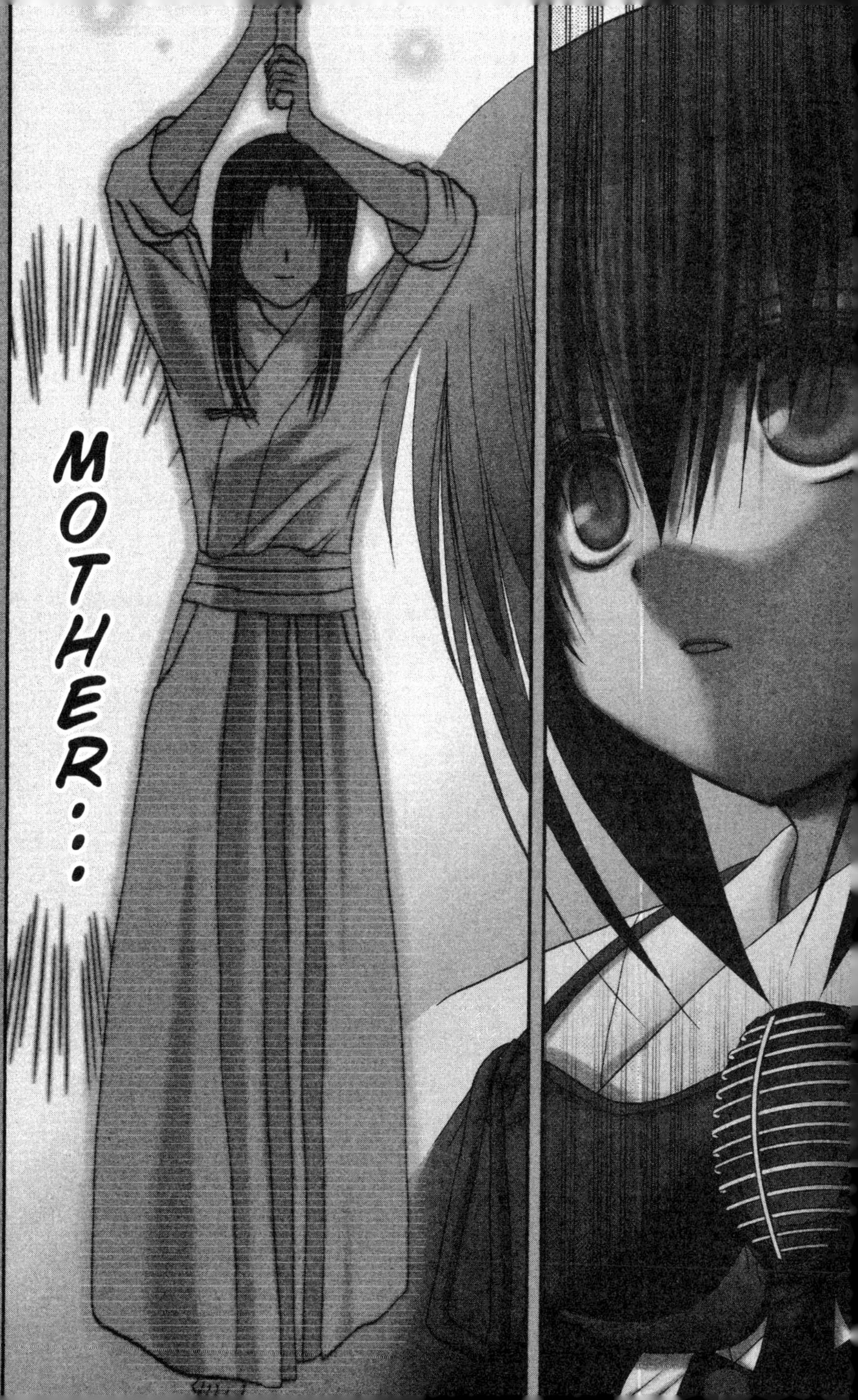
MOTHER...

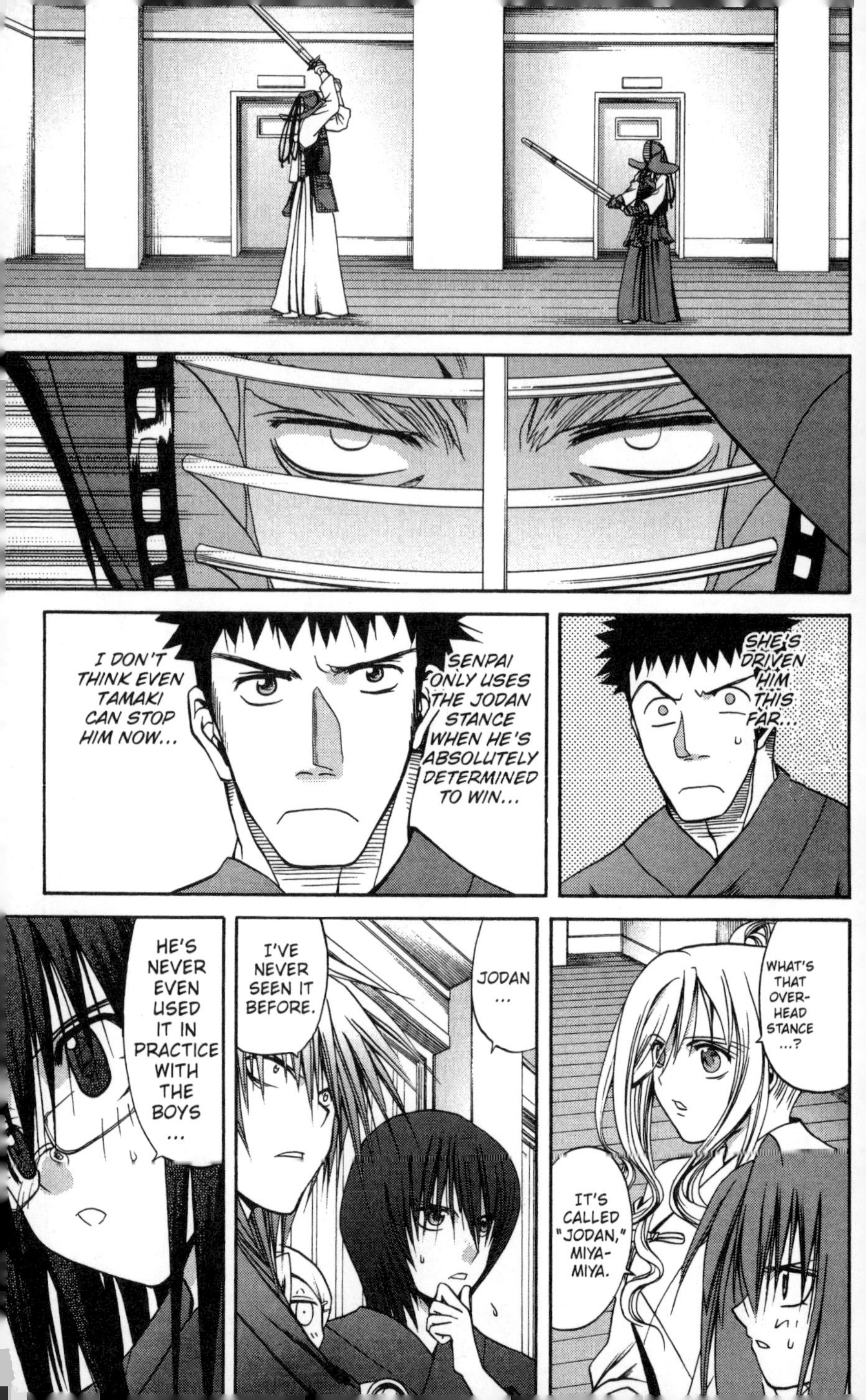
SHE'S DRIVEN HIM THIS FAR...
SENPAI ONLY USES THE JODAN STANCE WHEN HE'S ABSOLUTELY DETERMINED TO WIN...
I DON'T THINK EVEN TAMAKI CAN STOP HIM NOW...
WHAT'S THAT OVER-HEAD STANCE ...?
IT'S CALLED "JODAN," MIYA-MIYA.
JODAN ...
I'VE NEVER SEEN IT BEFORE.
HE'S NEVER EVEN USED IT IN PRACTICE WITH THE BOYS ...

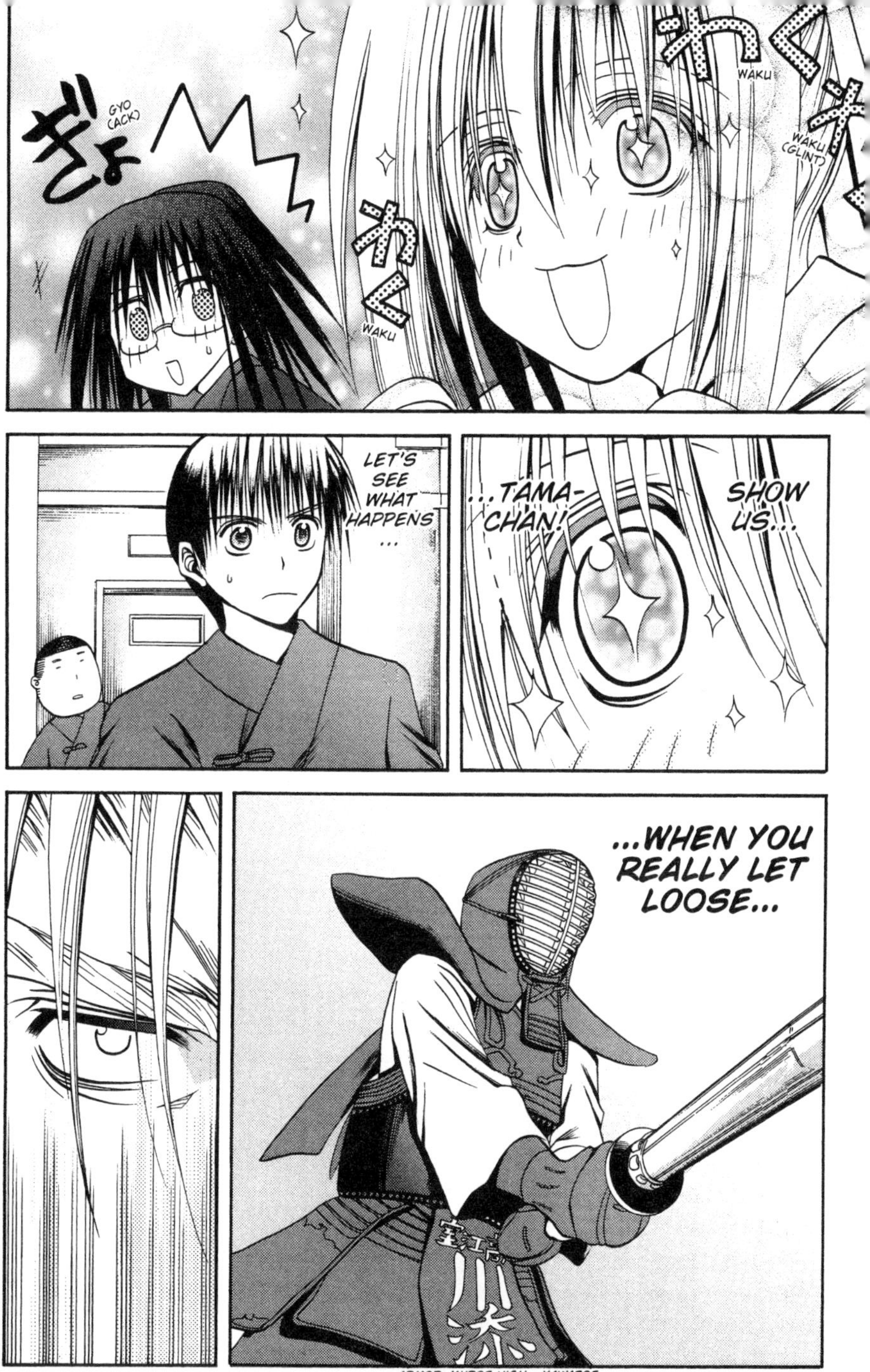
わく
WAKU
WAKU (GLINT)
わく
WAKU
ぎょ
GYO (ACK)
SHOW US...
...TAMA-CHAN!
LET'S SEE WHAT HAPPENS ...
...WHEN YOU REALLY LET LOOSE...

ARMOR: MUROE HIGH - KAWAZOE

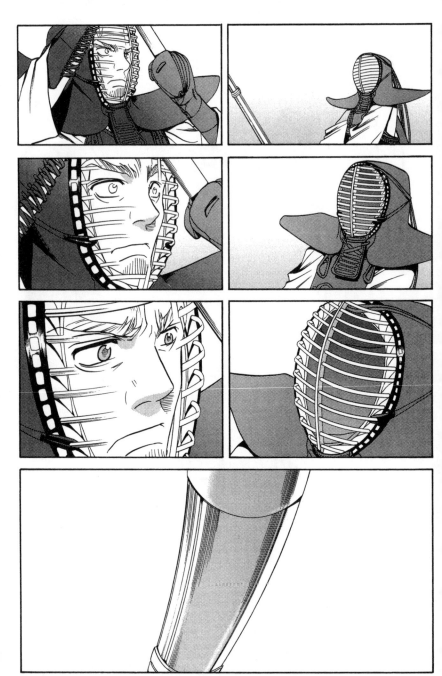

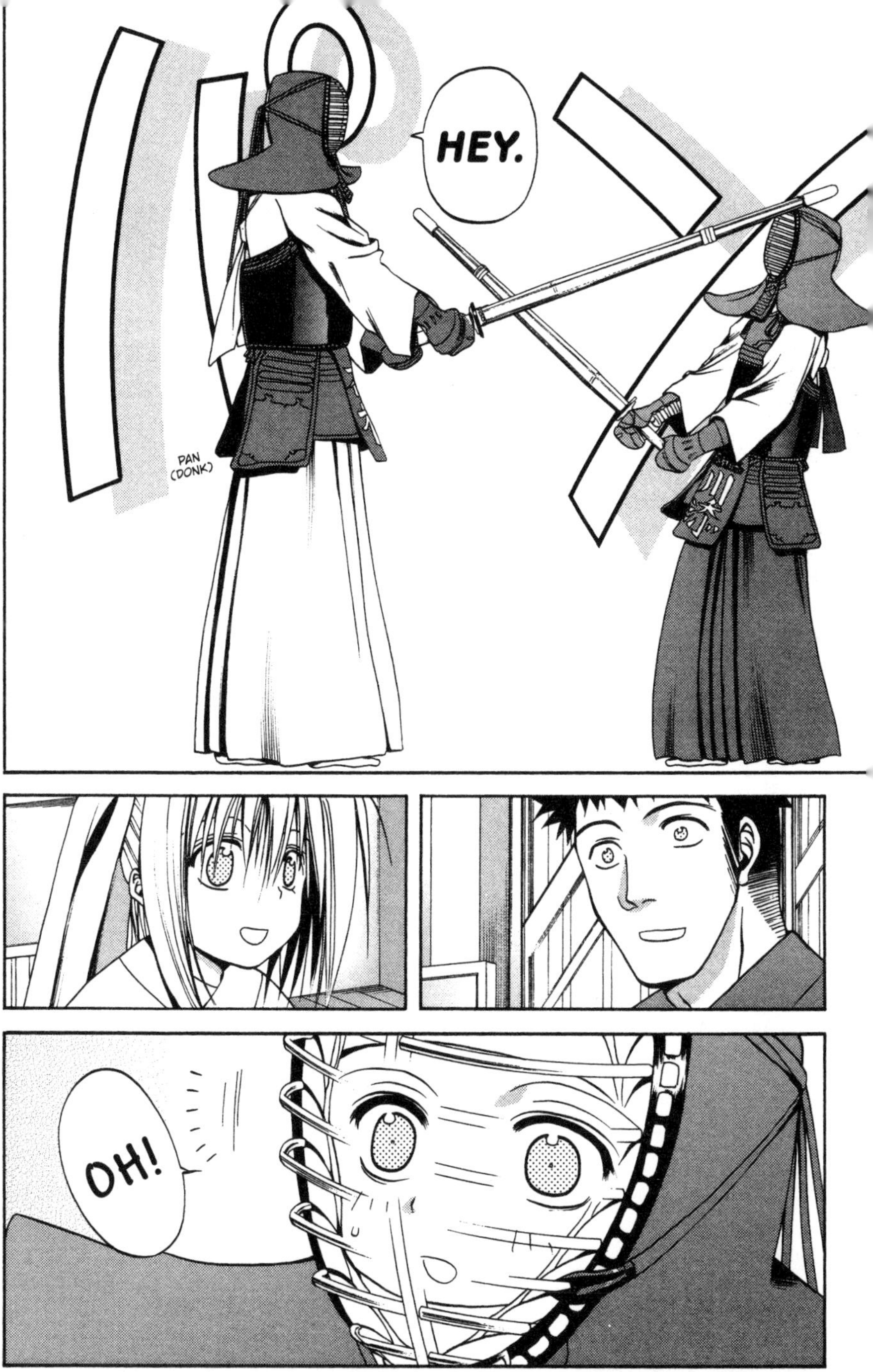
HEY.
PAN (DONK)
OH!

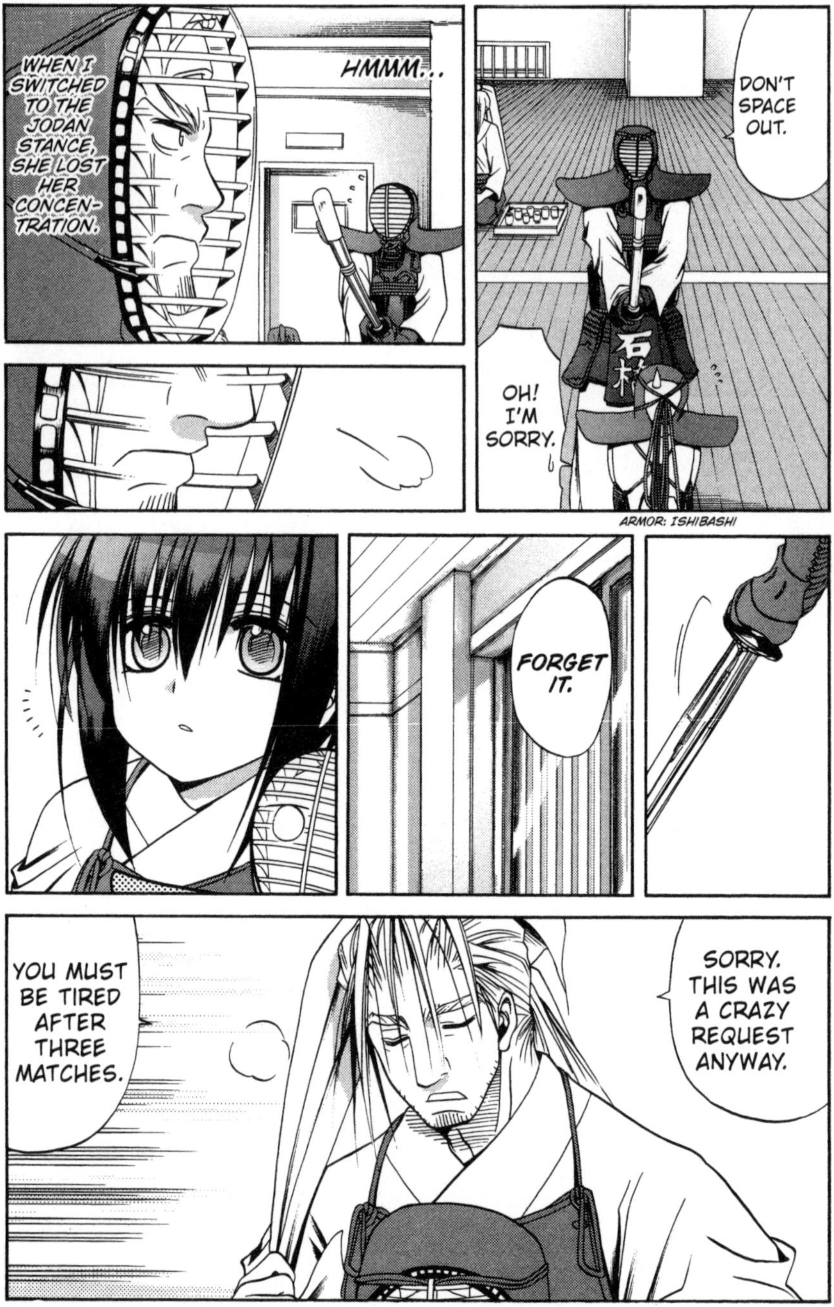
DON'T SPACE OUT.
OH! I'M SORRY.
ARMOR: ISHIBASHI
HMMM...
WHEN I SWITCHED TO THE JODAN STANCE, SHE LOST HER CONCEN-TRATION.
FORGET IT.
SORRY. THIS WAS A CRAZY REQUEST ANYWAY.
YOU MUST BE TIRED AFTER THREE MATCHES.

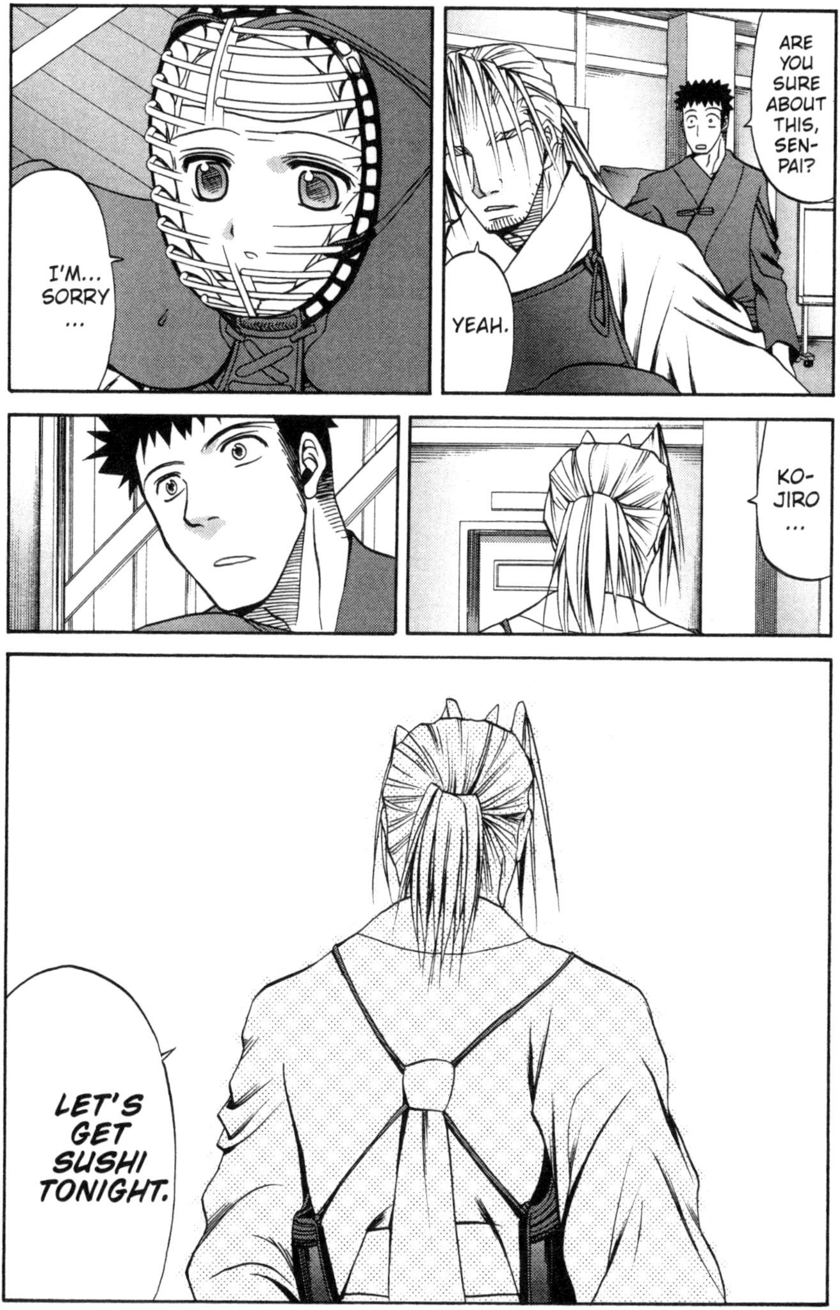
ARE YOU SURE ABOUT THIS, SEN-PAI?
YEAH.
I'M... SORRY ...
KO-JIRO ...
LET'S GET SUSHI TONIGHT.

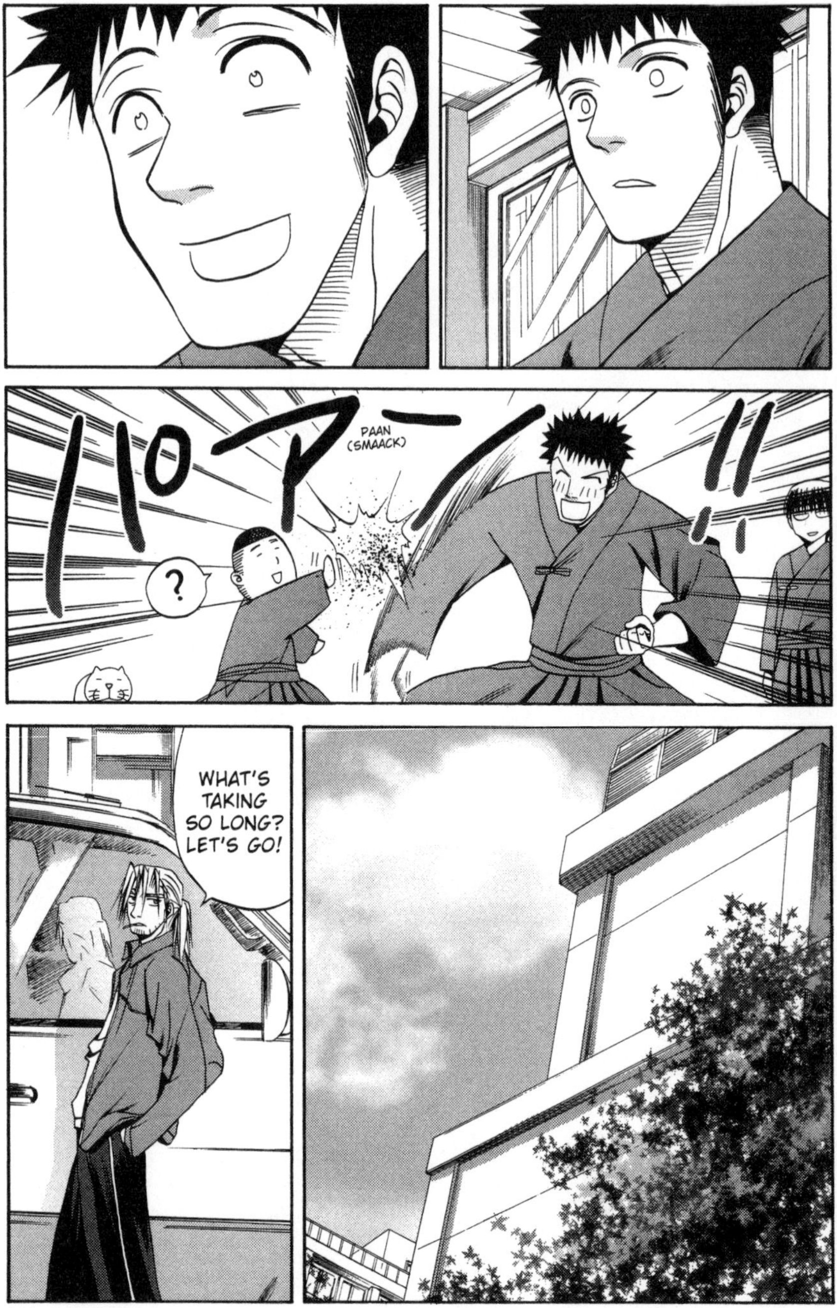
パアーー!!
PAAN (SMAACK)
?
WHAT'S TAKING SO LONG? LET'S GO!

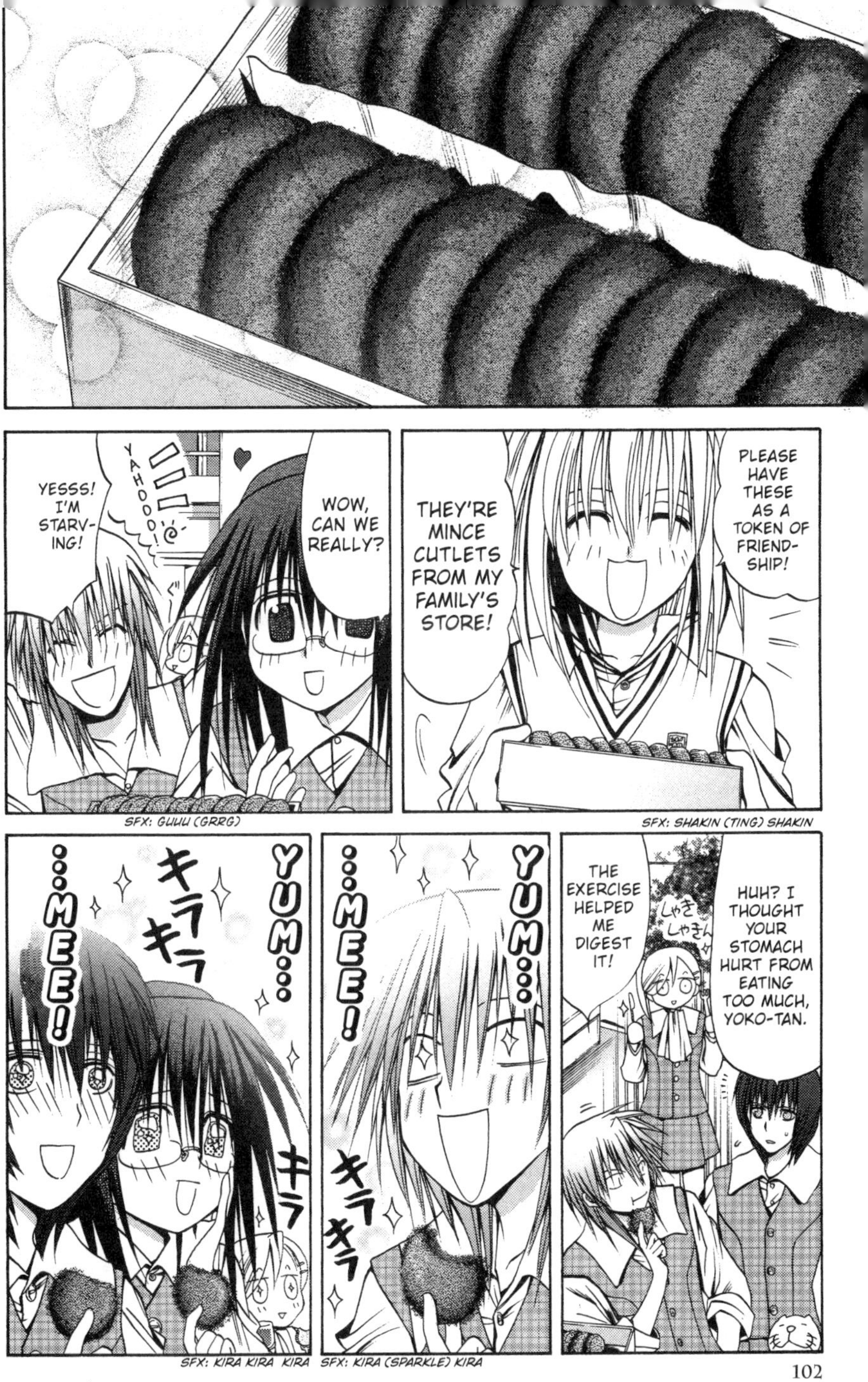
PLEASE HAVE THESE AS A TOKEN OF FRIEND-SHIP!
THEY'RE MINCE CUTLETS FROM MY FAMILY'S STORE!
SFX: SHAKIN (TING) SHAKIN
WOW, CAN WE REALLY?
YAHOOO!
YESSS! I'M STARV-ING!
SFX: GUUU (GRRG)
HUH? I THOUGHT YOUR STOMACH HURT FROM EATING TOO MUCH, YOKO-TAN.
THE EXERCISE HELPED ME DIGEST IT!
しゃきしゃきん
YUM...
...MEE!
キラキラ
SFX: KIRA (SPARKLE) KIRA
YUM...
...MEE!
キラキラ
キラ
SFX: KIRA KIRA KIRA

SFX: GIKU (GERK)

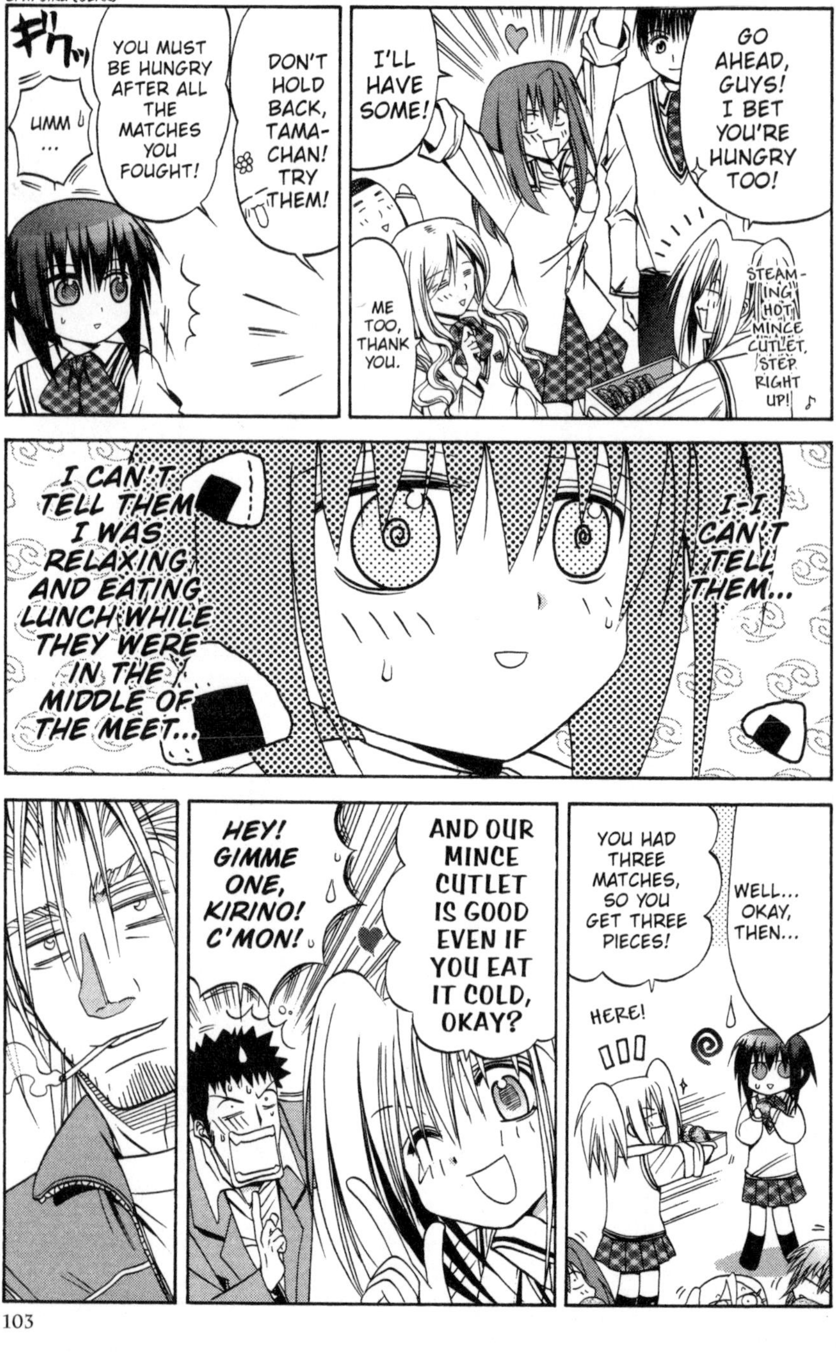
GO AHEAD, GUYS! I BET YOU'RE HUNGRY TOO!
I'LL HAVE SOME!
STEAMING HOT MINCE CUTLET, STEP RIGHT UP! ♪
ME TOO, THANK YOU.
DON'T HOLD BACK, TAMA-CHAN! TRY THEM!
YOU MUST BE HUNGRY AFTER ALL THE MATCHES YOU FOUGHT!
UMM...
I-I CAN'T TELL THEM...
I CAN'T TELL THEM I WAS RELAXING AND EATING LUNCH WHILE THEY WERE IN THE MIDDLE OF THE MEET...
YOU HAD THREE MATCHES, SO YOU GET THREE PIECES!
WELL... OKAY, THEN...
HERE!
AND OUR MINCE CUTLET IS GOOD EVEN IF YOU EAT IT COLD, OKAY?
HEY! GIMME ONE, KIRINO! C'MON!

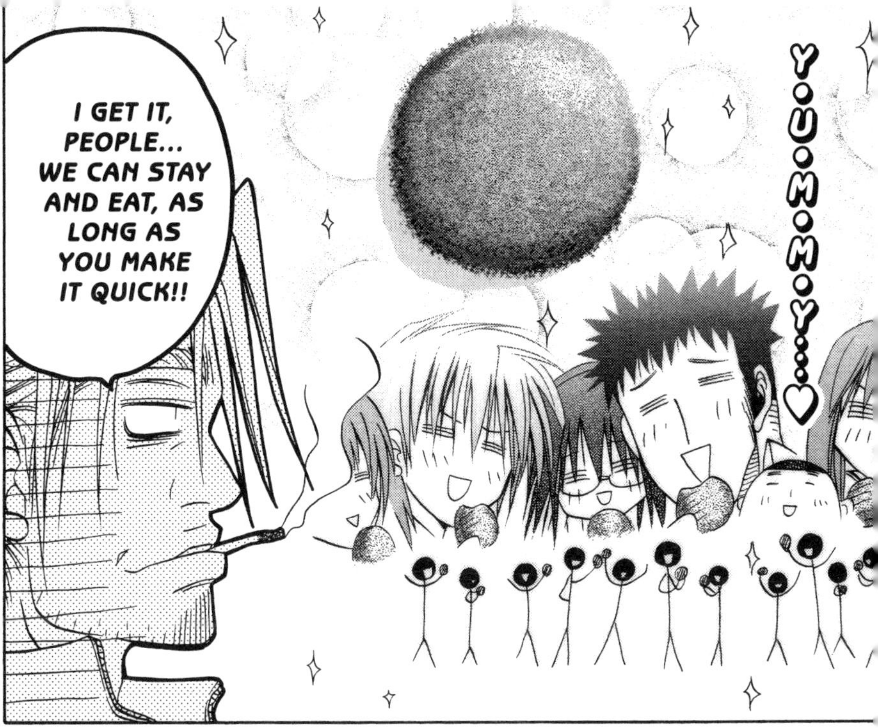
YUMMY...♥
I GET IT, PEOPLE... WE CAN STAY AND EAT, AS LONG AS YOU MAKE IT QUICK!!

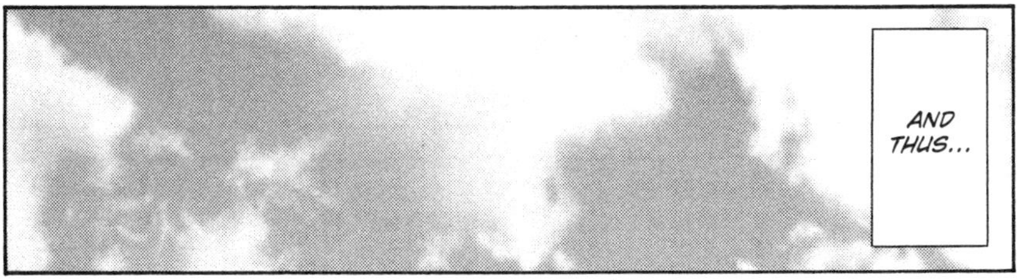
AND THUS...

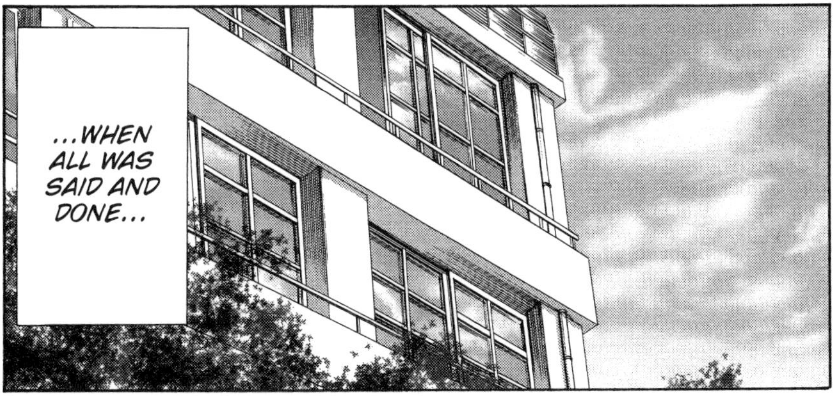
...WHEN ALL WAS SAID AND DONE...

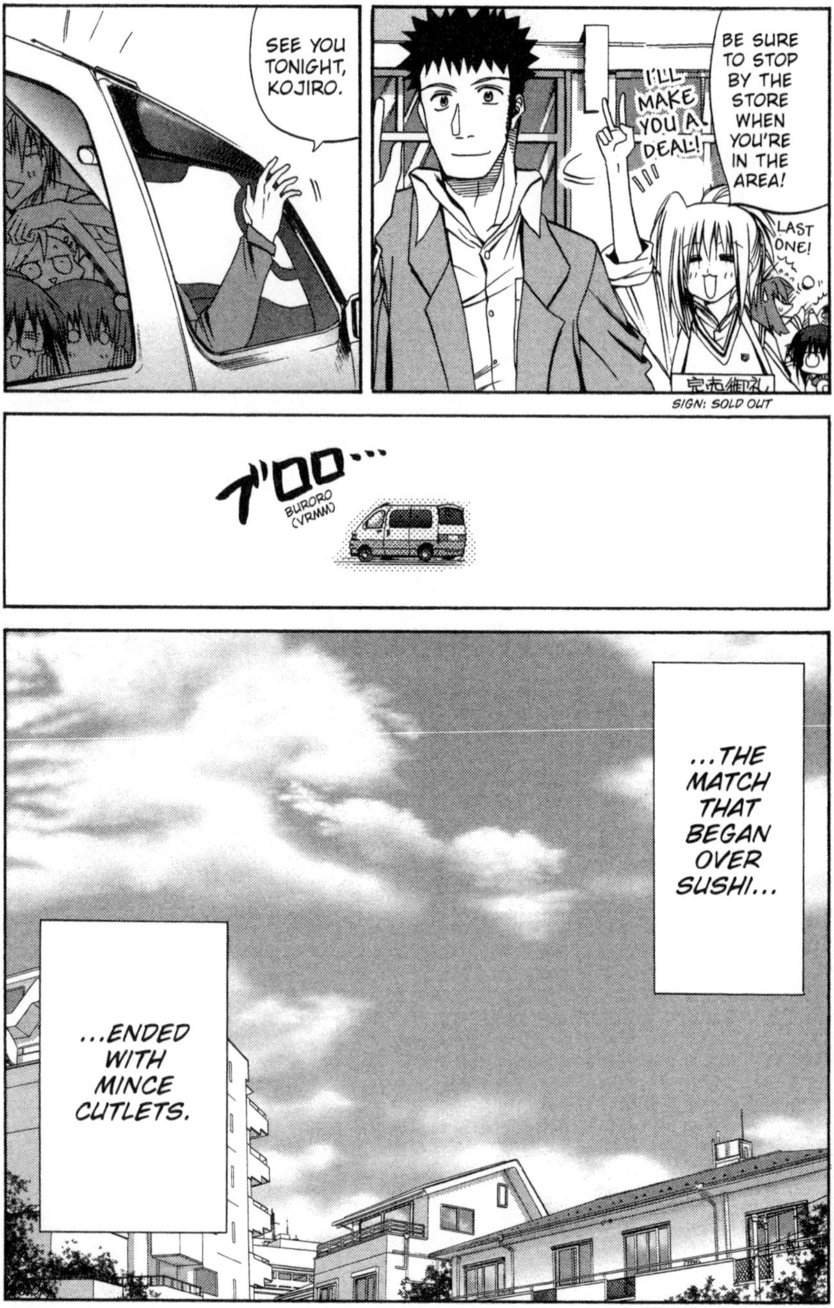
BE SURE TO STOP BY THE STORE WHEN YOU'RE IN THE AREA!
I'LL MAKE YOU A DEAL!
LAST ONE!
完売御礼
SIGN: SOLD OUT
SEE YOU TONIGHT, KOJIRO.
ブロロ…
BURORO (VRMM)
...THE MATCH THAT BEGAN OVER SUSHI...
...ENDED WITH MINCE CUTLETS.

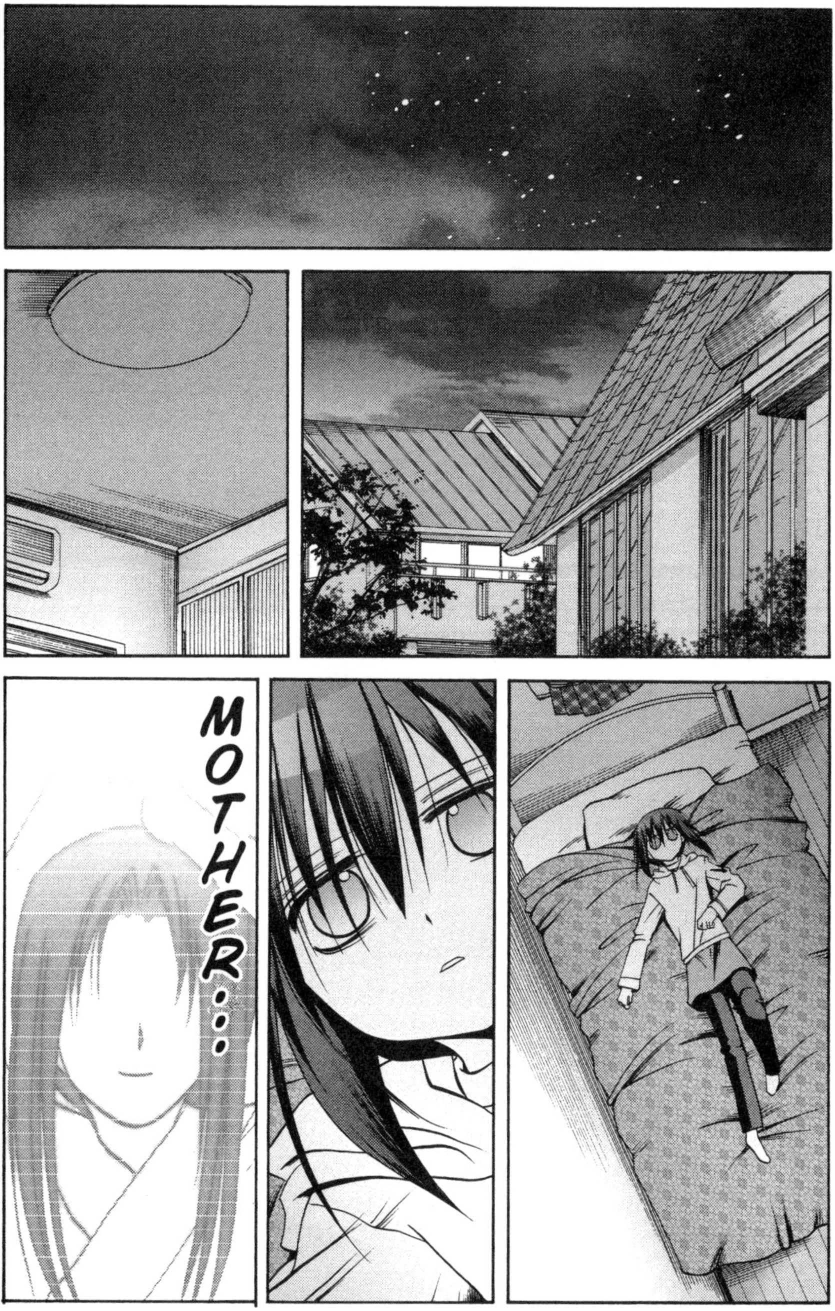
MOTHER...

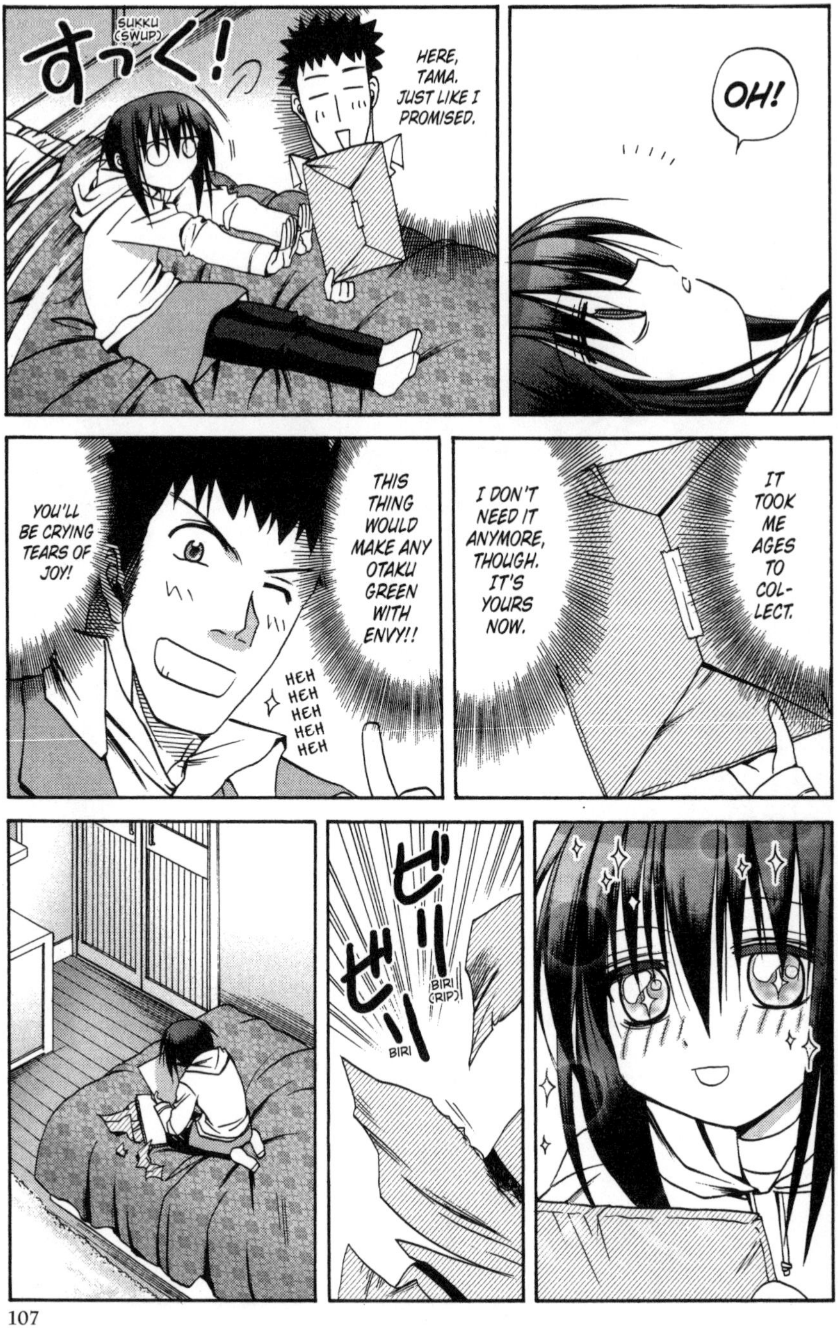
OH!
HERE, TAMA. JUST LIKE I PROMISED.
すっく!
SUKKU (SWUP)
IT TOOK ME AGES TO COL- LECT.
I DON'T NEED IT ANYMORE, THOUGH. IT'S YOURS NOW.
THIS THING WOULD MAKE ANY OTAKU GREEN WITH ENVY!!
YOU'LL BE CRYING TEARS OF JOY!
HEH HEH HEH HEH HEH
ビリー
ビリ
BIRI (RIP)
BIRI

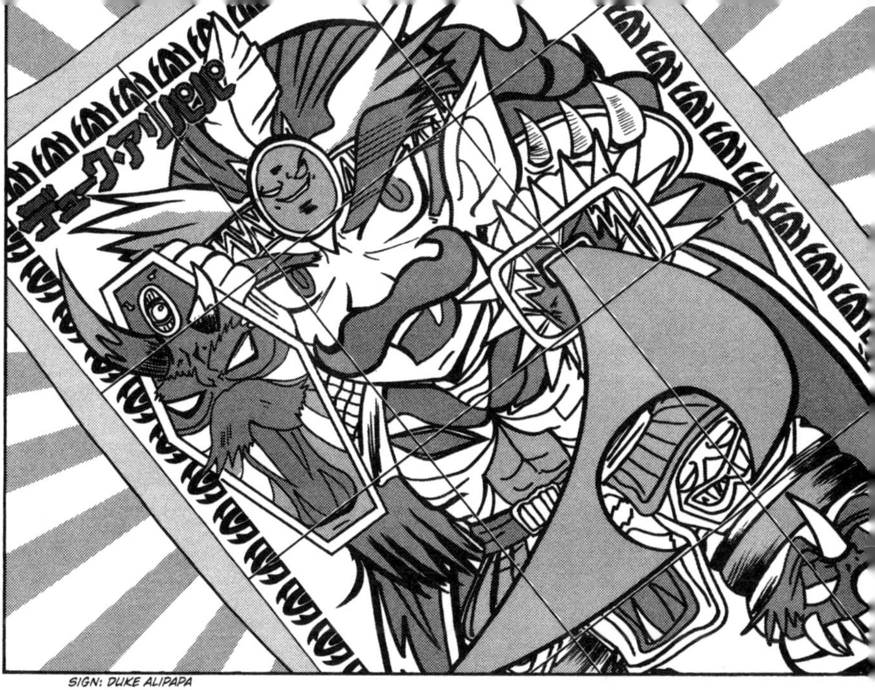
デューク・アリパパ

SIGN: DUKE ALIPAPA

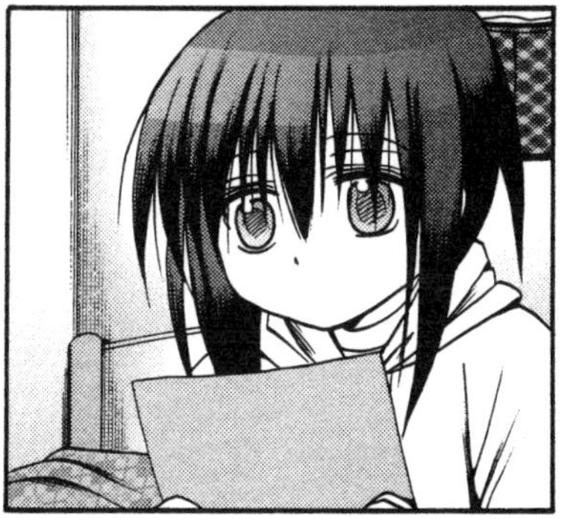

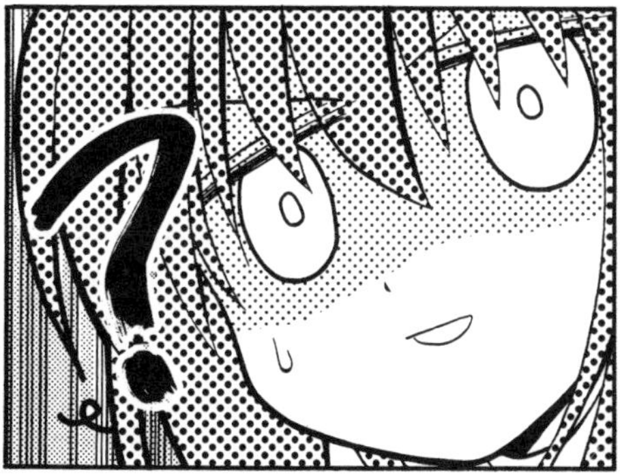
?

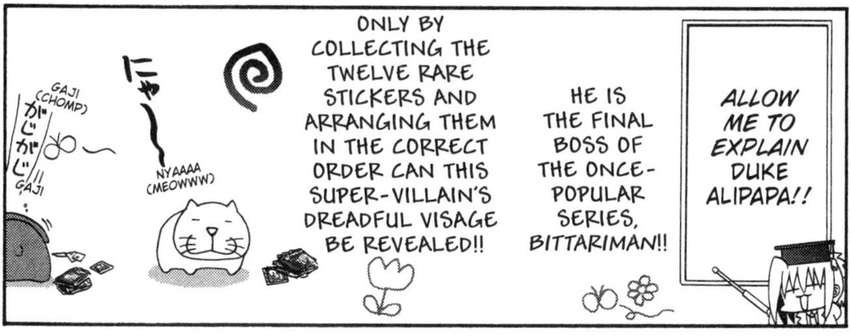
ALLOW ME TO EXPLAIN DUKE ALIPAPA!!
HE IS THE FINAL BOSS OF THE ONCE-POPULAR SERIES, BITTARIMAN!!
ONLY BY COLLECTING THE TWELVE RARE STICKERS AND ARRANGING THEM IN THE CORRECT ORDER CAN THIS SUPER-VILLAIN'S DREADFUL VISAGE BE REVEALED!!
にゃ〜〜
NYAAAA (MEOWWW)
がじがじ
GAJI (CHOMP) GAJI

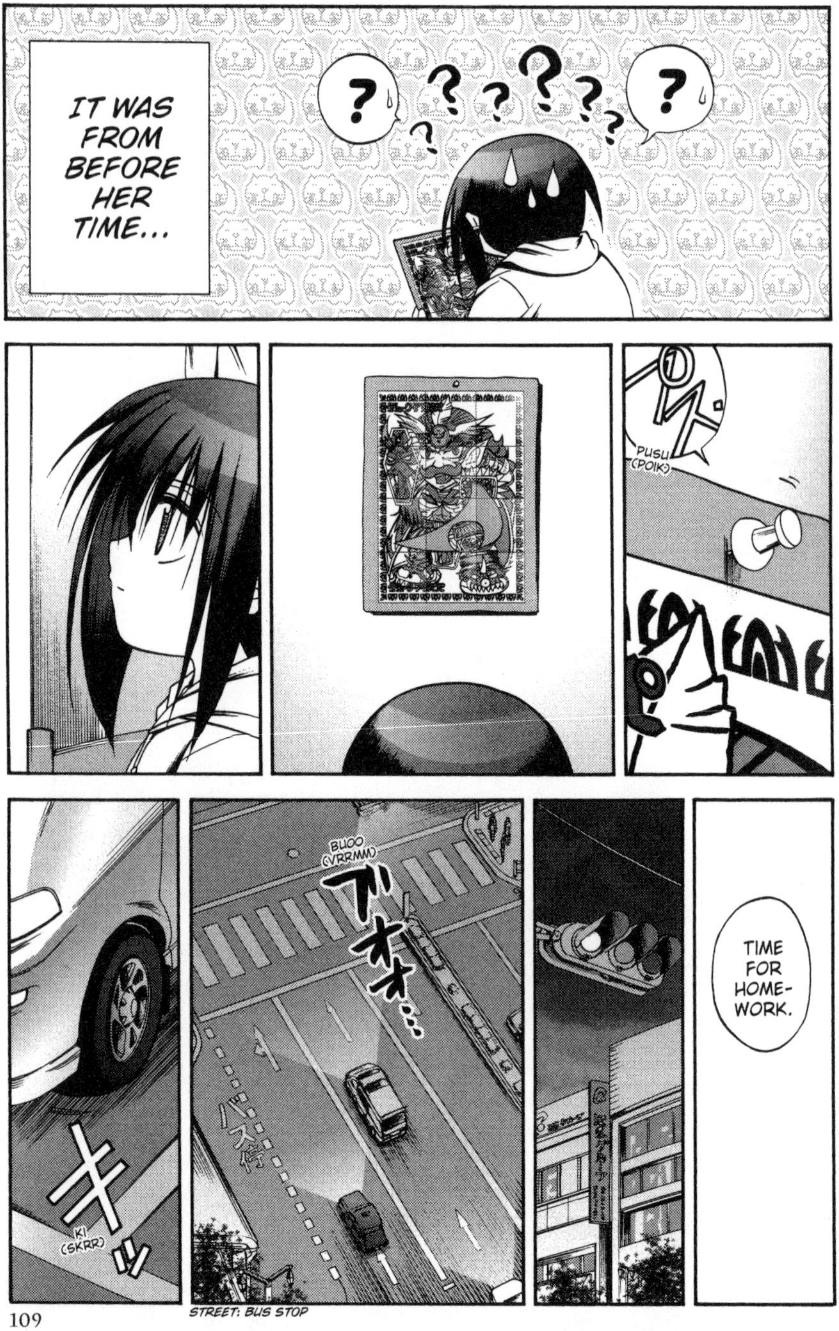
?
?
IT WAS FROM BEFORE HER TIME...
PUSU (POIK)
TIME FOR HOMEWORK.
BUOO (VRRMM)
KI (SKRR)
STREET: BUS STOP

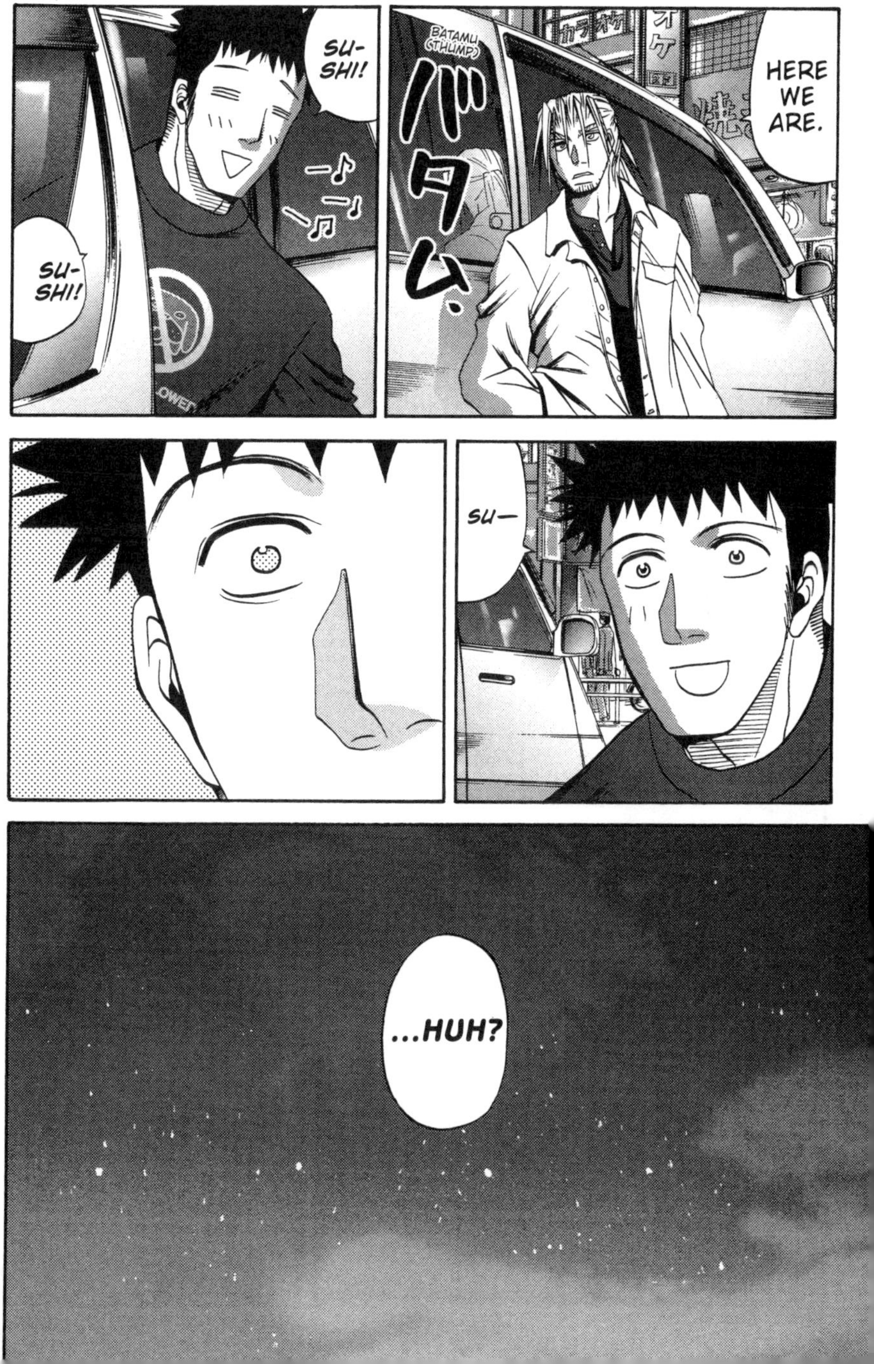
BATAMU (THUMP)
バタム
HERE WE ARE.
SU-SHI!
SU-SHI!
SU—
...HUH?

BAMBOO BLADE

BAMBOO BLADE

バンブーブレード

SAKE

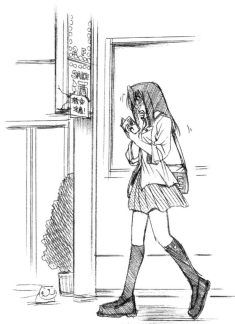

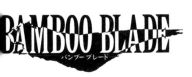

SIGN: WATCH YOUR HEAD!

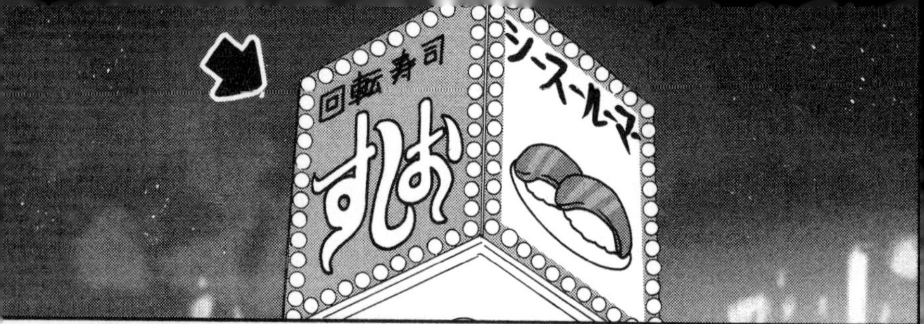
回転寿司
すしお

SIGN (ABOVE): REVOLVING SUSHI - SUSHIO; SOOSHEE / BANNER: REVOLVING SUSHIO - SUSHIO / DOORS: SUSHI

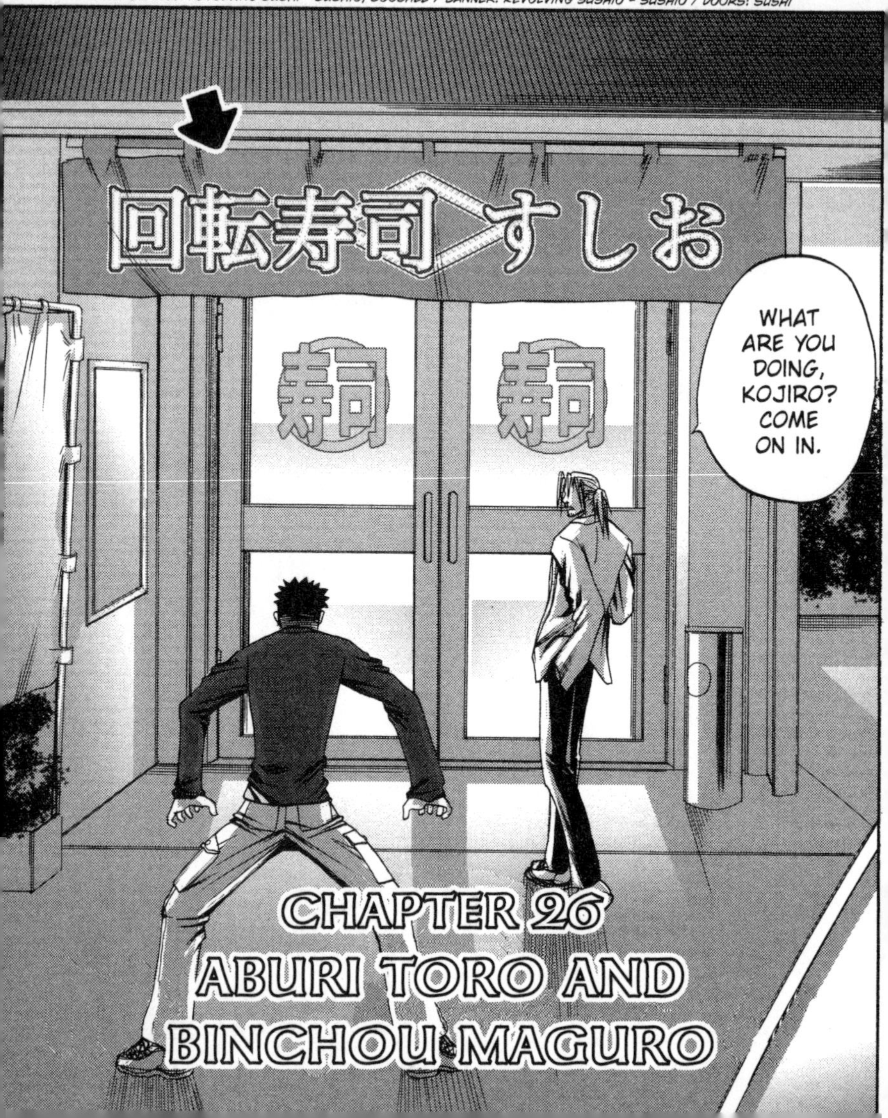
回転寿司 すしお
寿司
寿司
WHAT ARE YOU DOING, KOJIRO? COME ON IN.
CHAPTER 26
ABURI TORO AND BINCHOU MAGURO

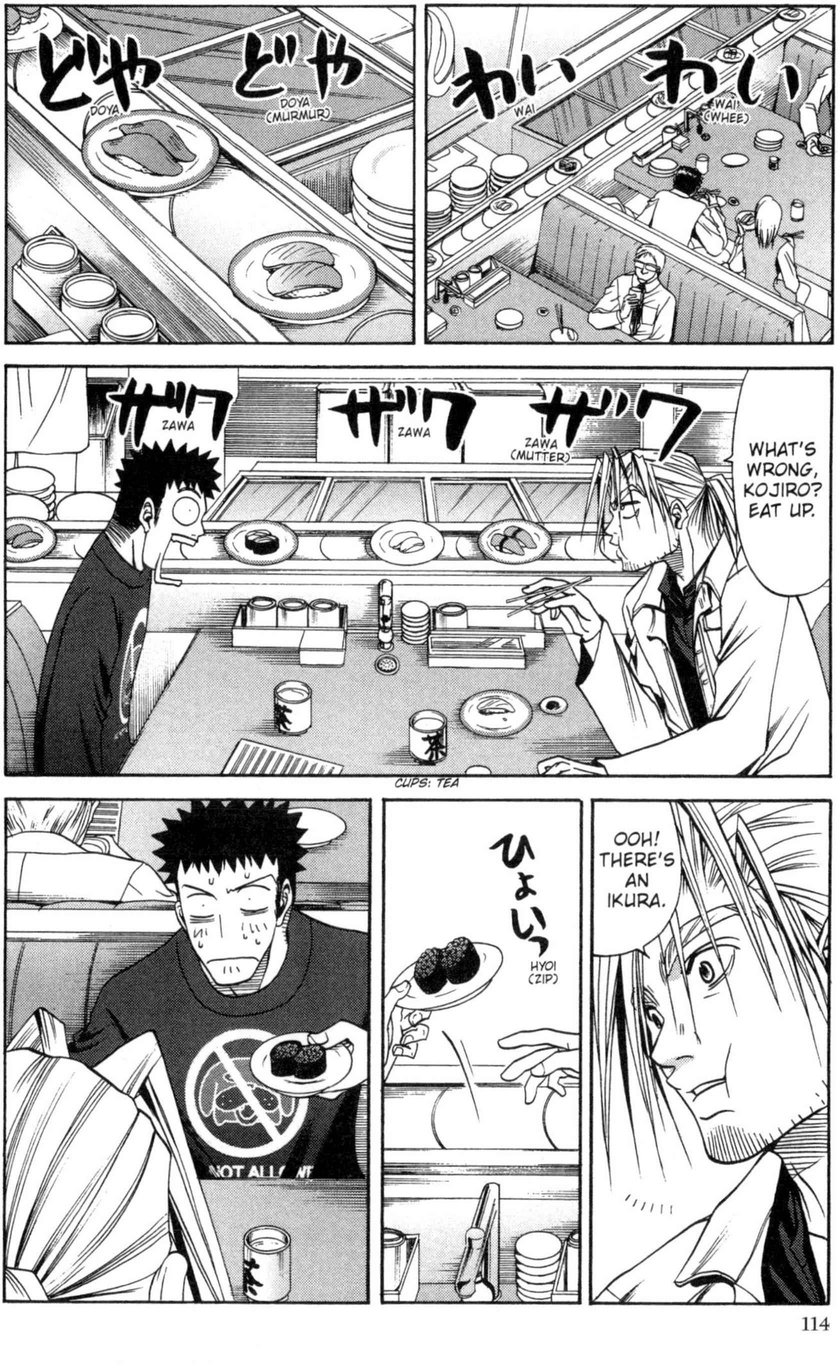
わい わい
WAI
WAI (WHEE)
どや どや
DOYA
DOYA (MURMUR)
ザワ ザワ ザワ
ZAWA
ZAWA
ZAWA (MUTTER)
WHAT'S WRONG, KOJIRO? EAT UP.
CUPS: TEA
OOH! THERE'S AN IKURA.
ひょいっ
HYOI (ZIP)

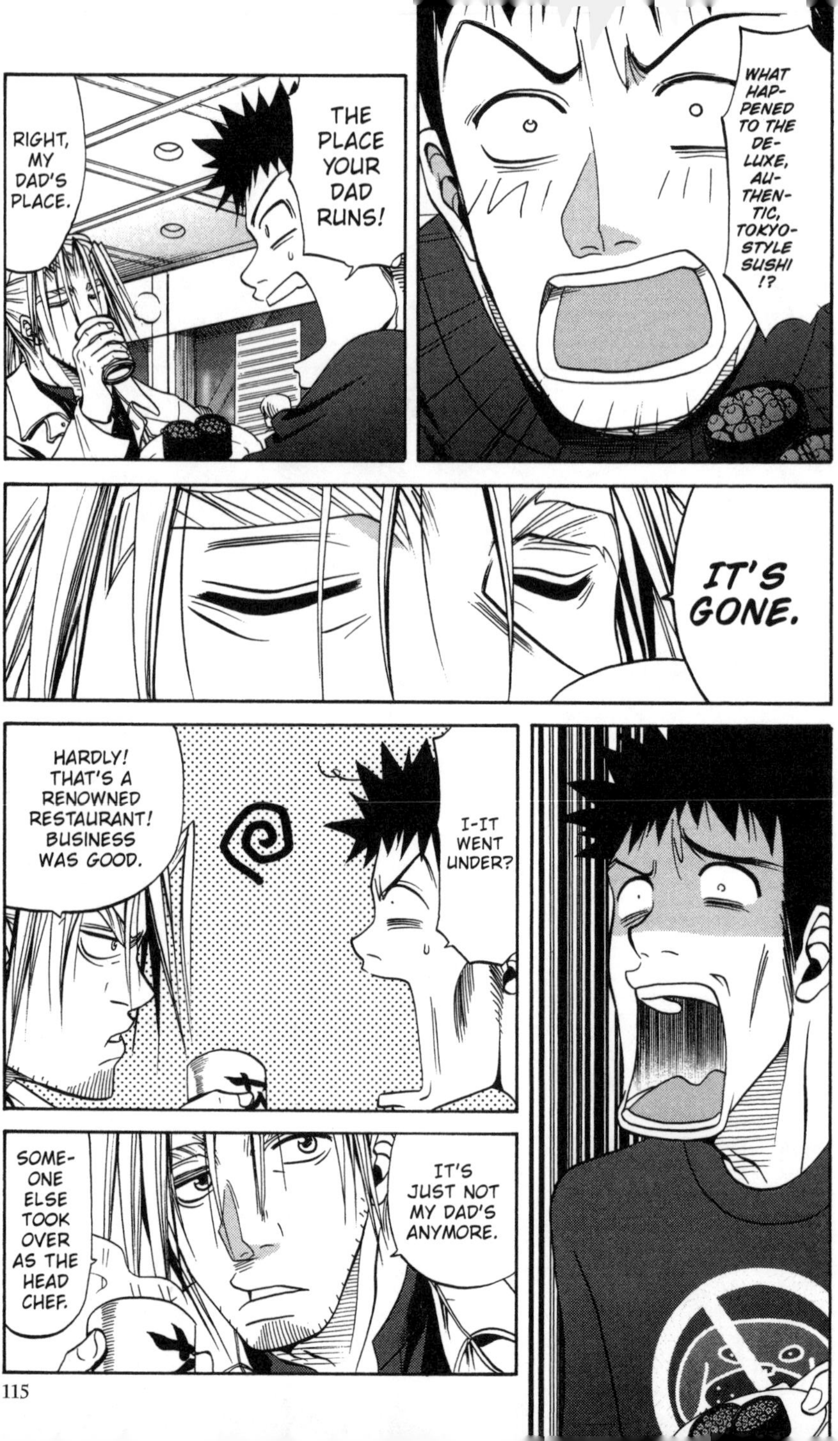
WHAT HAP-PENED TO THE DE-LUXE, AU-THEN-TIC, TOKYO-STYLE SUSHI !?
THE PLACE YOUR DAD RUNS!
RIGHT, MY DAD'S PLACE.
IT'S GONE.
I-IT WENT UNDER?
HARDLY! THAT'S A RENOWNED RESTAURANT! BUSINESS WAS GOOD.
IT'S JUST NOT MY DAD'S ANYMORE.
SOME-ONE ELSE TOOK OVER AS THE HEAD CHEF.

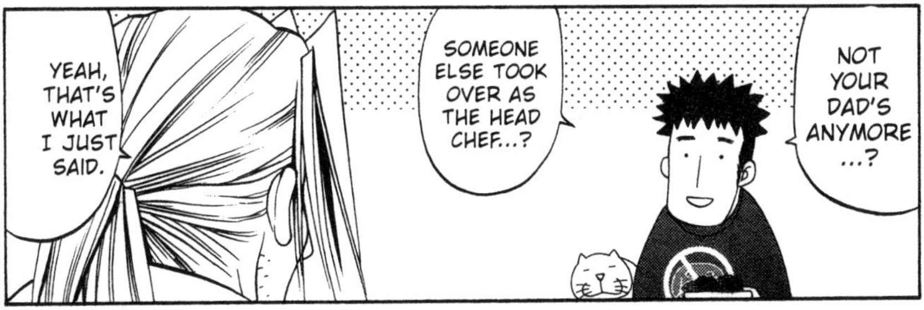
NOT YOUR DAD'S ANYMORE ...?
SOMEONE ELSE TOOK OVER AS THE HEAD CHEF...?
YEAH, THAT'S WHAT I JUST SAID.

SIGNS: ENI SUSHI

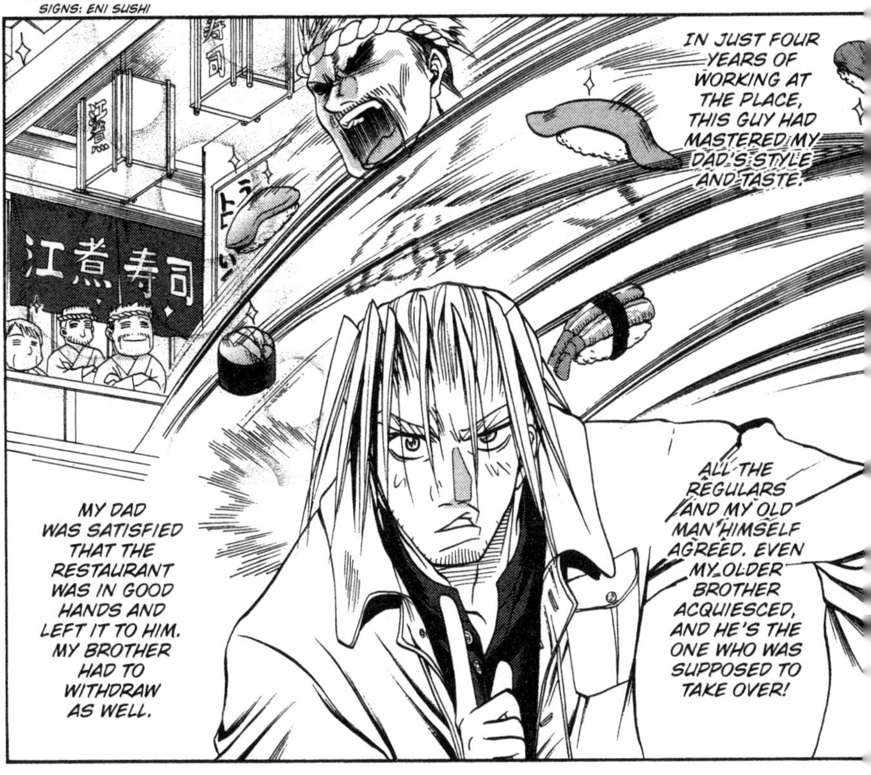
IN JUST FOUR YEARS OF WORKING AT THE PLACE, THIS GUY HAD MASTERED MY DAD'S STYLE AND TASTE.
江煮寿司
ALL THE REGULARS AND MY OLD MAN HIMSELF AGREED. EVEN MY OLDER BROTHER ACQUIESCED, AND HE'S THE ONE WHO WAS SUPPOSED TO TAKE OVER!
MY DAD WAS SATISFIED THAT THE RESTAURANT WAS IN GOOD HANDS AND LEFT IT TO HIM. MY BROTHER HAD TO WITHDRAW AS WELL.

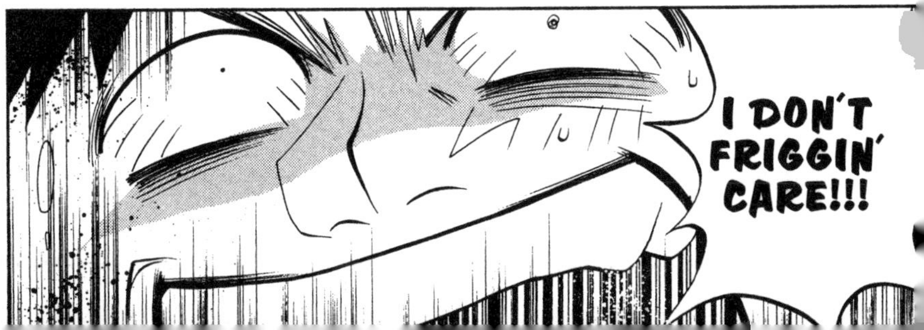
I DON'T FRIGGIN' CARE!!!

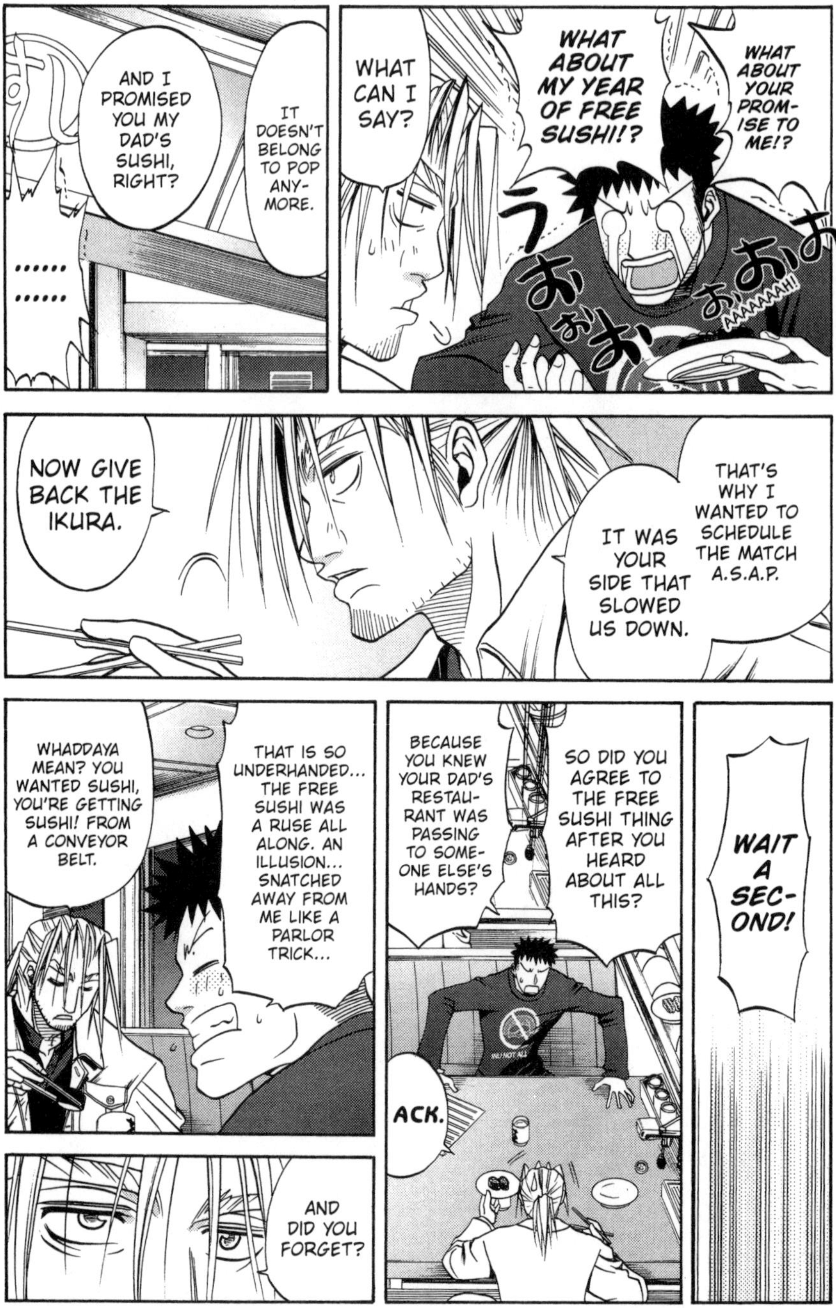
WHAT ABOUT YOUR PROMISE TO ME!?
WHAT ABOUT MY YEAR OF FREE SUSHI!?
うおおおおおお
AAAAAAAH!
WHAT CAN I SAY?
IT DOESN'T BELONG TO POP ANYMORE.
AND I PROMISED YOU MY DAD'S SUSHI, RIGHT?
......
......
THAT'S WHY I WANTED TO SCHEDULE THE MATCH A.S.A.P.
IT WAS YOUR SIDE THAT SLOWED US DOWN.
NOW GIVE BACK THE IKURA.
WAIT A SECOND!
SO DID YOU AGREE TO THE FREE SUSHI THING AFTER YOU HEARD ABOUT ALL THIS?
BECAUSE YOU KNEW YOUR DAD'S RESTAURANT WAS PASSING TO SOMEONE ELSE'S HANDS?
ACK.
THAT IS SO UNDERHANDED... THE FREE SUSHI WAS A RUSE ALL ALONG. AN ILLUSION... SNATCHED AWAY FROM ME LIKE A PARLOR TRICK...
WHADDAYA MEAN? YOU WANTED SUSHI, YOU'RE GETTING SUSHI! FROM A CONVEYOR BELT.
AND DID YOU FORGET?

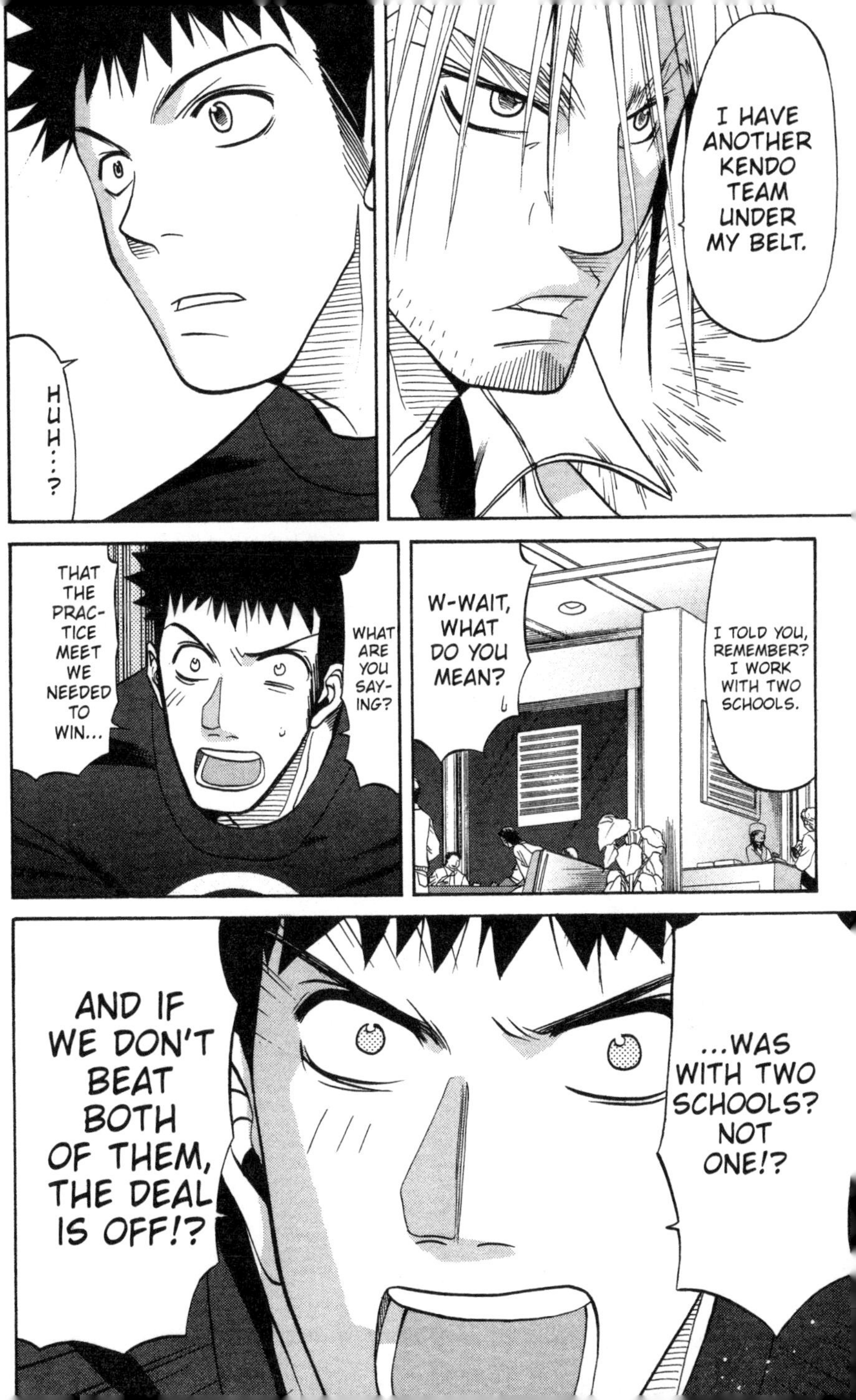
I HAVE ANOTHER KENDO TEAM UNDER MY BELT.
HUH...?
W-WAIT, WHAT DO YOU MEAN?
I TOLD YOU, REMEMBER? I WORK WITH TWO SCHOOLS.
WHAT ARE YOU SAYING?
THAT THE PRAC-TICE MEET WE NEEDED TO WIN...
...WAS WITH TWO SCHOOLS? NOT ONE!?
AND IF WE DON'T BEAT BOTH OF THEM, THE DEAL IS OFF!?

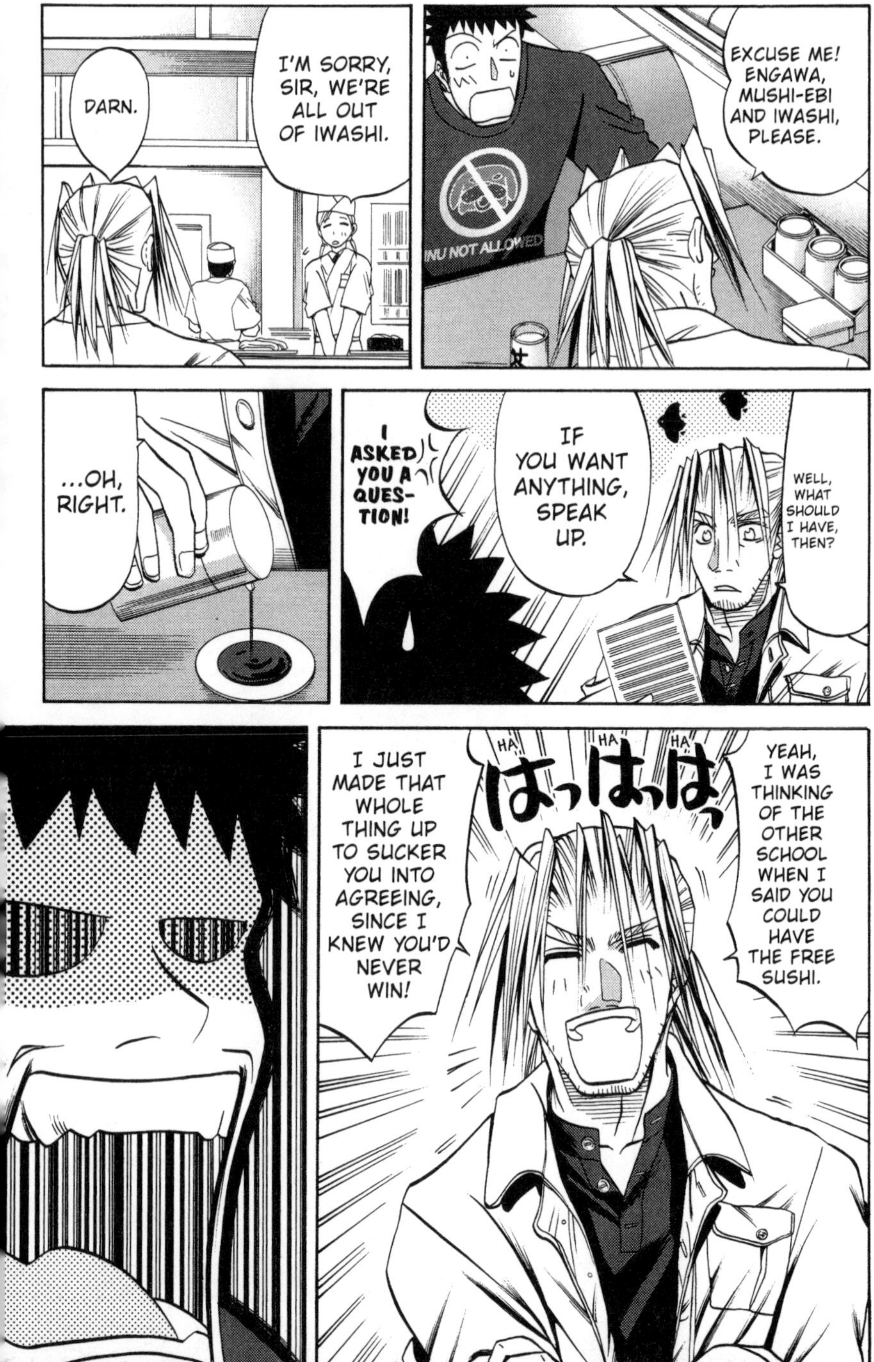
EXCUSE ME! ENGAWA, MUSHI-EBI AND IWASHI, PLEASE.
INU NOT ALLOWED
I'M SORRY, SIR, WE'RE ALL OUT OF IWASHI.
DARN.
WELL, WHAT SHOULD I HAVE, THEN?
IF YOU WANT ANYTHING, SPEAK UP.
I ASKED YOU A QUES-TION!
...OH, RIGHT.
YEAH, I WAS THINKING OF THE OTHER SCHOOL WHEN I SAID YOU COULD HAVE THE FREE SUSHI.
HA HA HA
はっはっはっ
I JUST MADE THAT WHOLE THING UP TO SUCKER YOU INTO AGREEING, SINCE I KNEW YOU'D NEVER WIN!

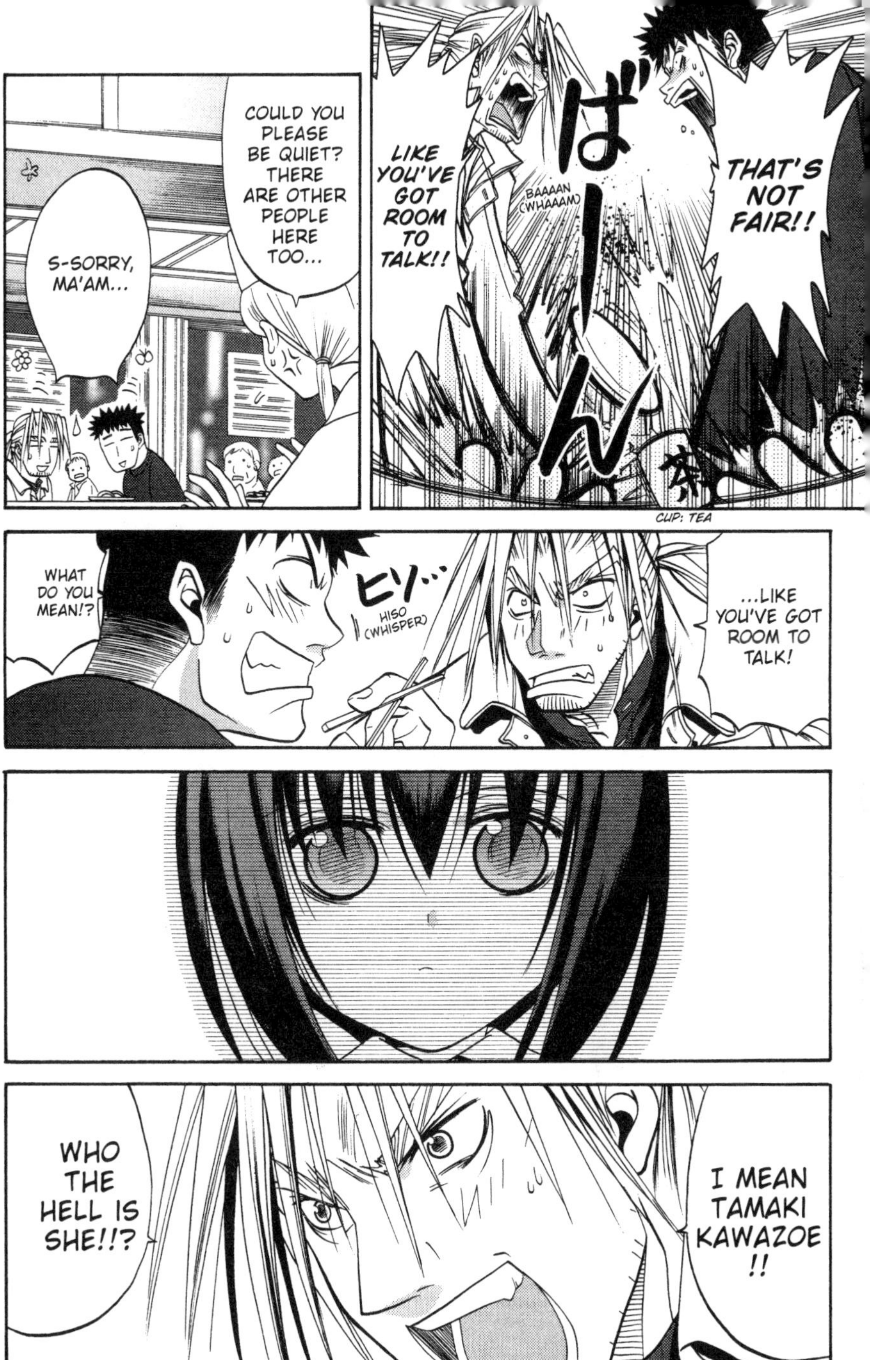
THAT'S NOT FAIR!!
ばーん
BAAAAN (WHAAAM)
LIKE YOU'VE GOT ROOM TO TALK!!
茶
CUP: TEA
COULD YOU PLEASE BE QUIET? THERE ARE OTHER PEOPLE HERE TOO...
S-SORRY, MA'AM...
...LIKE YOU'VE GOT ROOM TO TALK!
ヒソ…
HISO (WHISPER)
WHAT DO YOU MEAN!?
I MEAN TAMAKI KAWAZOE!!
WHO THE HELL IS SHE!!?

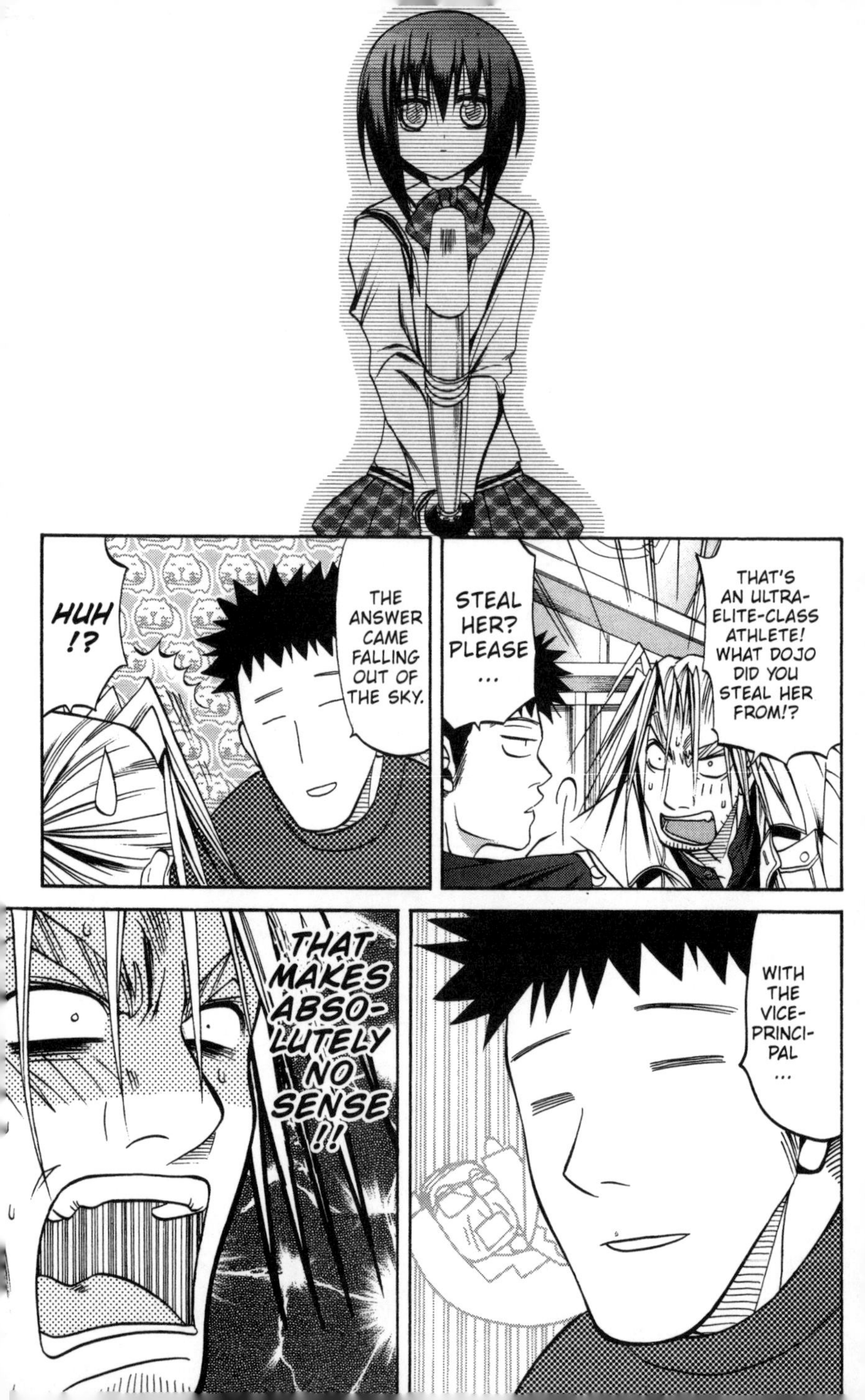
THAT'S AN ULTRA-ELITE-CLASS ATHLETE! WHAT DOJO DID YOU STEAL HER FROM!?
STEAL HER? PLEASE ...
THE ANSWER CAME FALLING OUT OF THE SKY.
HUH !?
WITH THE VICE-PRINCIPAL ...
THAT MAKES ABSOLUTELY NO SENSE!!

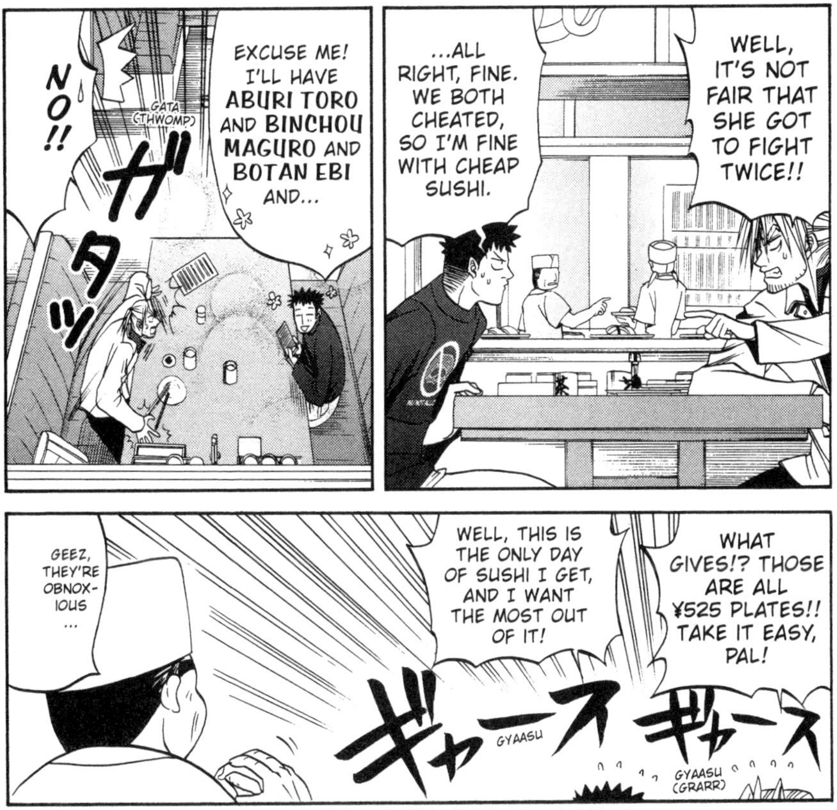
WELL, IT'S NOT FAIR THAT SHE GOT TO FIGHT TWICE!!
...ALL RIGHT, FINE. WE BOTH CHEATED, SO I'M FINE WITH CHEAP SUSHI.
EXCUSE ME! I'LL HAVE ABURI TORO AND BINCHOU MAGURO AND BOTAN EBI AND...
GATA (THWOMP)
NO!!
WHAT GIVES!? THOSE ARE ALL ¥525 PLATES!! TAKE IT EASY, PAL!
WELL, THIS IS THE ONLY DAY OF SUSHI I GET, AND I WANT THE MOST OUT OF IT!
GEEZ, THEY'RE OBNOXIOUS...
GYAASU
GYAASU (GRARR)

SIGN: REVOLVING SUSHI - SUSHIO; SOOSHEE CUPS: TEA

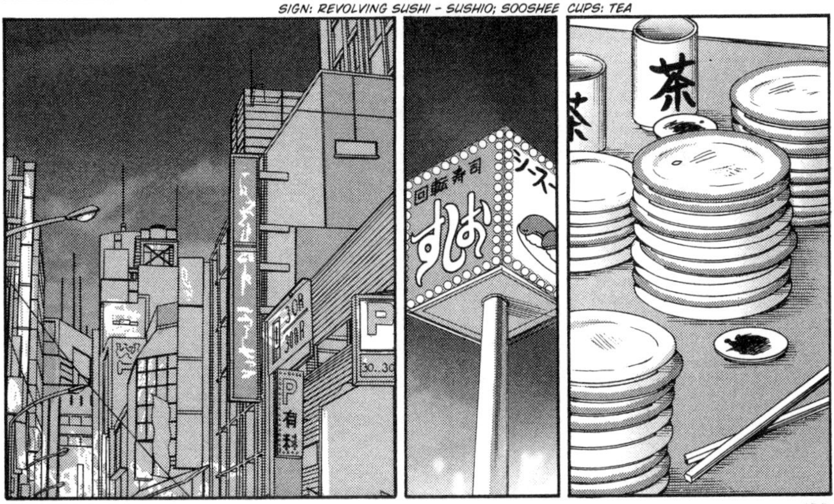
回転寿司
すしお
シースー
茶

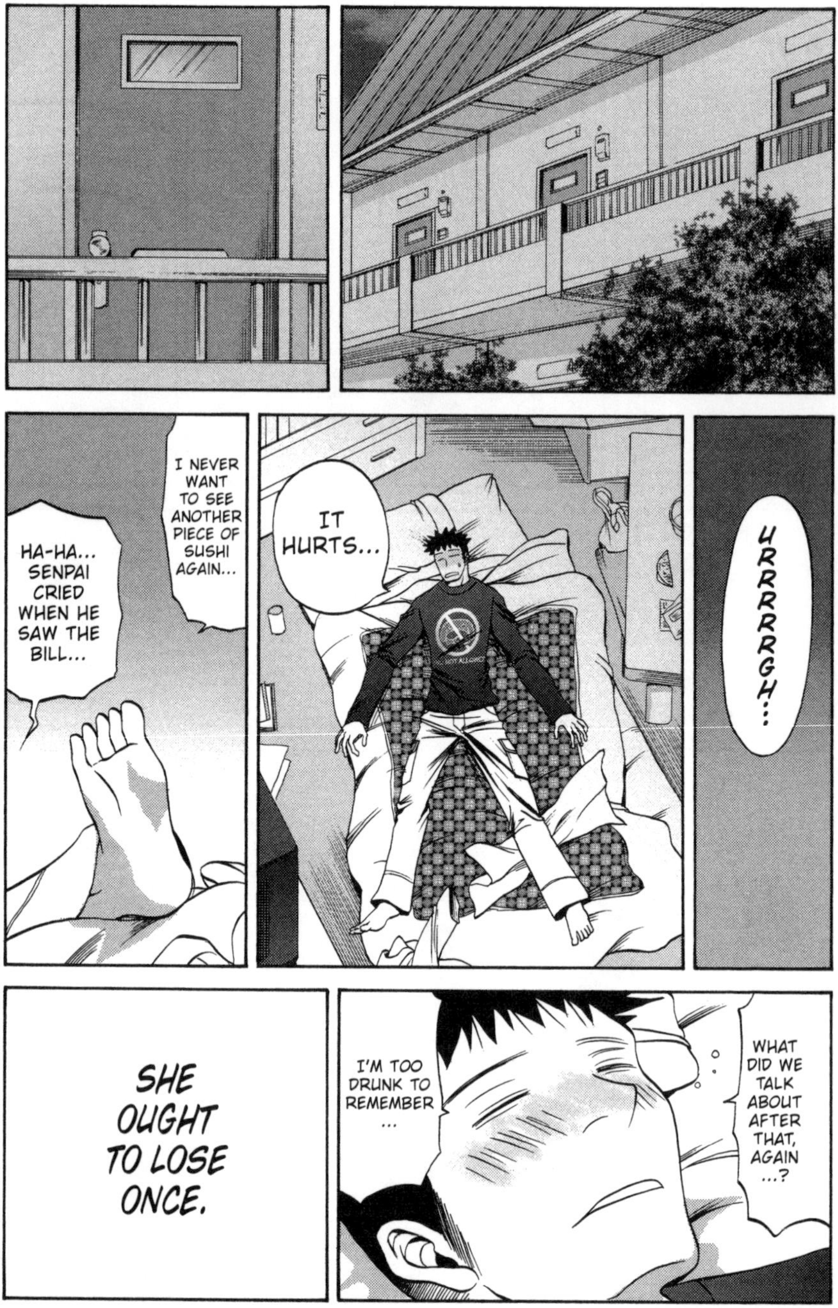
URRRRRGH...
IT HURTS...
I NEVER WANT TO SEE ANOTHER PIECE OF SUSHI AGAIN...
HA-HA... SENPAI CRIED WHEN HE SAW THE BILL...
WHAT DID WE TALK ABOUT AFTER THAT, AGAIN...?
I'M TOO DRUNK TO REMEMBER...
SHE OUGHT TO LOSE ONCE.

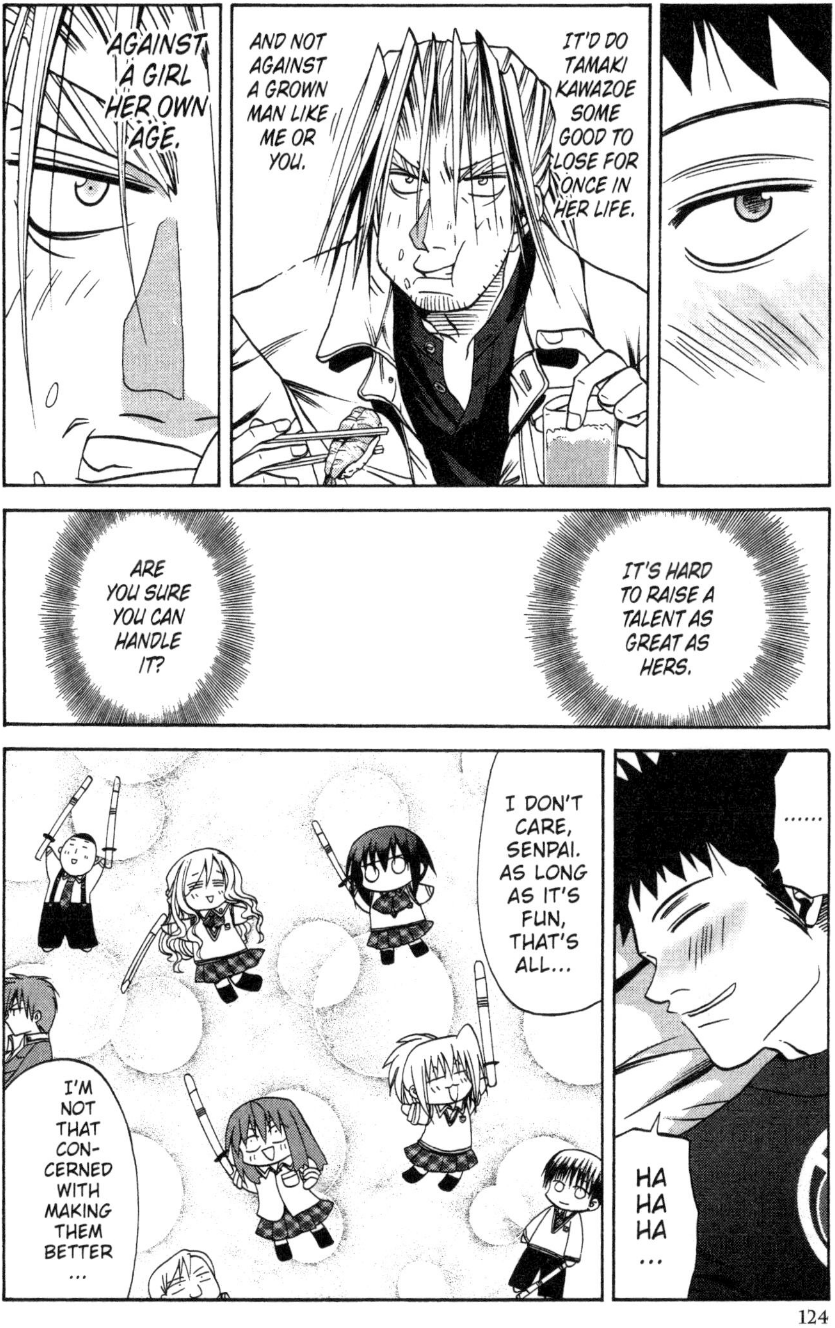
IT'D DO TAMAKI KAWAZOE SOME GOOD TO LOSE FOR ONCE IN HER LIFE.
AND NOT AGAINST A GROWN MAN LIKE ME OR YOU.
AGAINST A GIRL HER OWN AGE.
IT'S HARD TO RAISE A TALENT AS GREAT AS HERS.
ARE YOU SURE YOU CAN HANDLE IT?
......
HA HA HA ...
I DON'T CARE, SENPAI. AS LONG AS IT'S FUN, THAT'S ALL...
I'M NOT THAT CON-CERNED WITH MAKING THEM BETTER ...

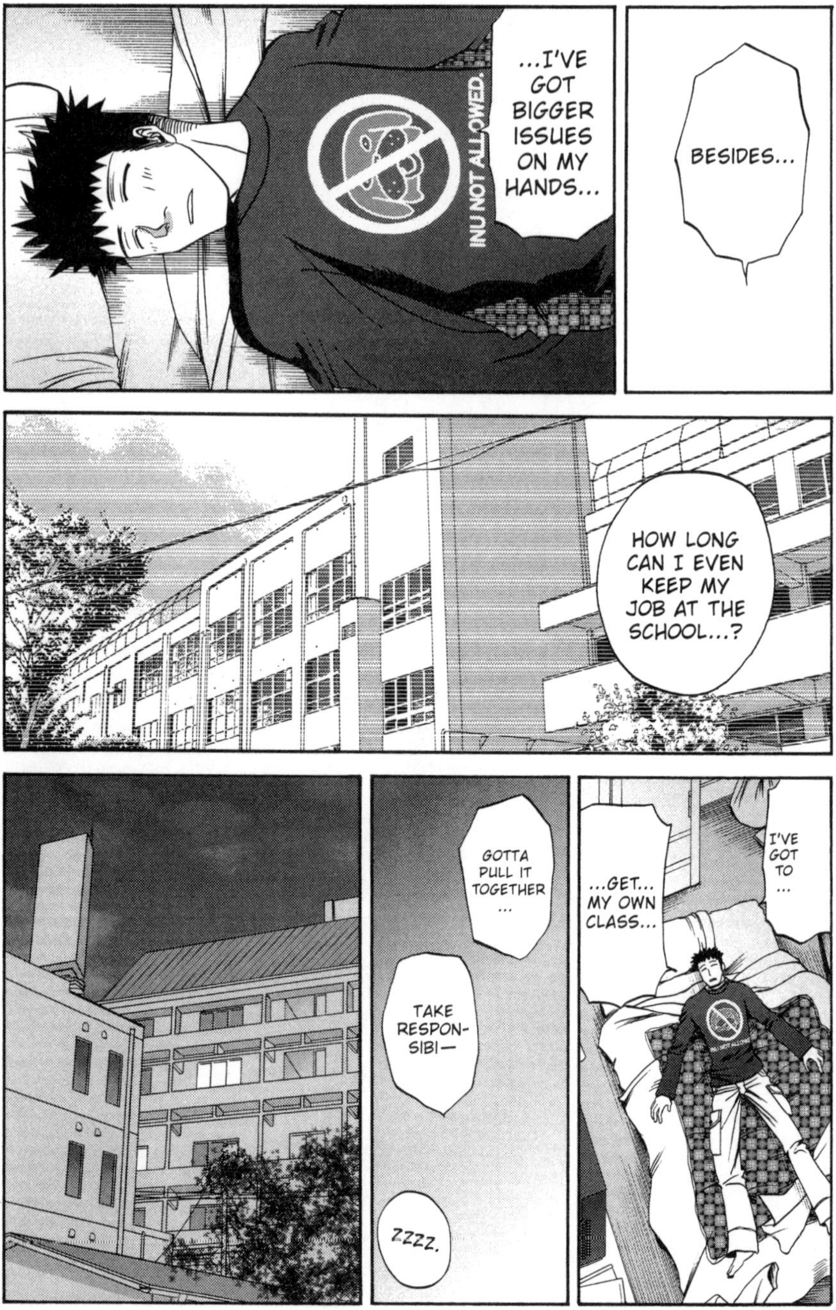
BESIDES...
...I'VE GOT BIGGER ISSUES ON MY HANDS...
INU NOT ALLOWED.
HOW LONG CAN I EVEN KEEP MY JOB AT THE SCHOOL...?
I'VE GOT TO ...
...GET... MY OWN CLASS...
GOTTA PULL IT TOGETHER ...
TAKE RESPON-SIBI—
ZZZZ.

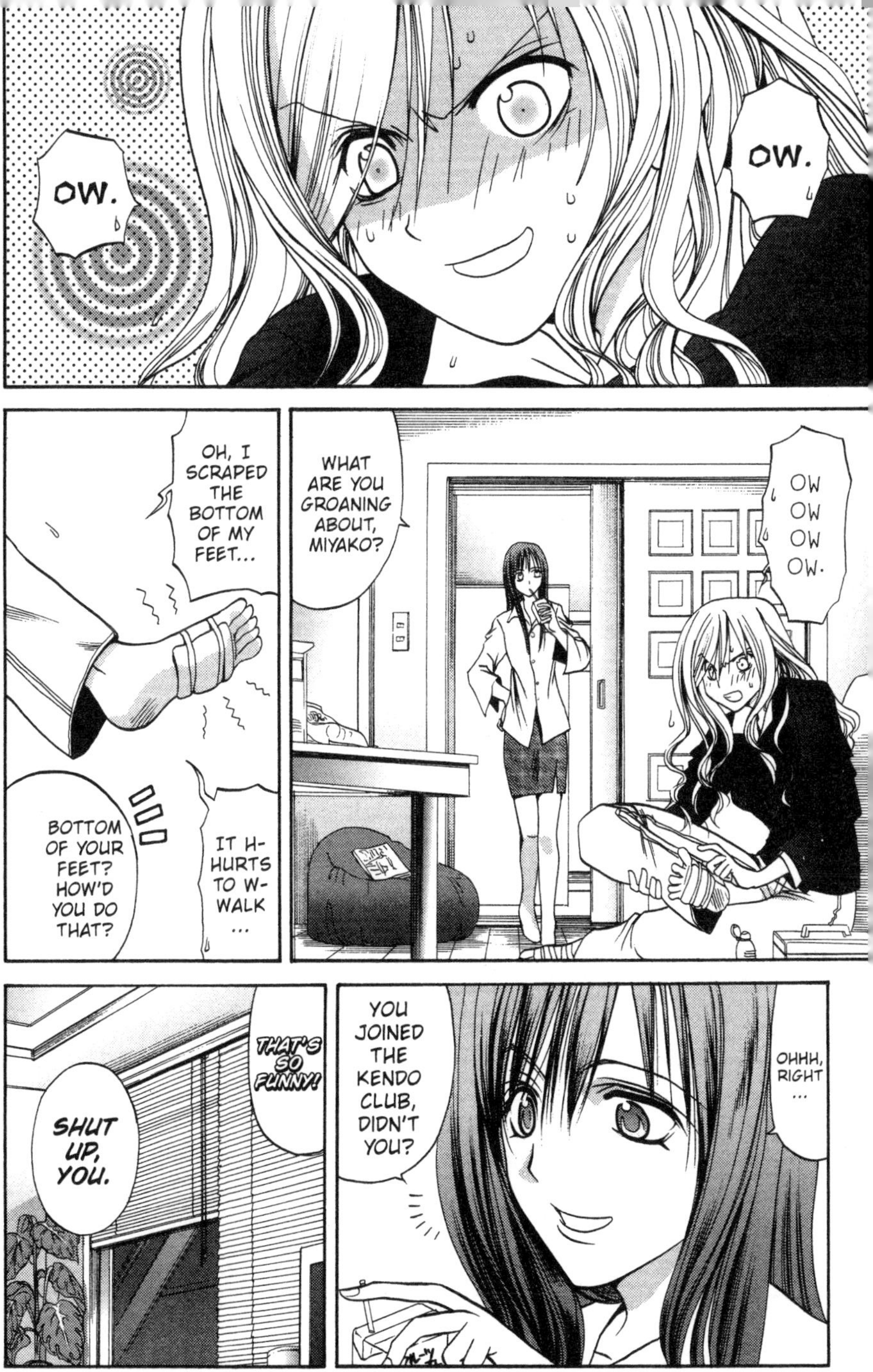
OW.
OW.
OW OW OW OW.
WHAT ARE YOU GROANING ABOUT, MIYAKO?
OH, I SCRAPED THE BOTTOM OF MY FEET...
IT H-HURTS TO W-WALK ...
BOTTOM OF YOUR FEET? HOW'D YOU DO THAT?
OHHH, RIGHT ...
YOU JOINED THE KENDO CLUB, DIDN'T YOU?
THAT'S SO FUNNY!
SHUT UP, YOU.

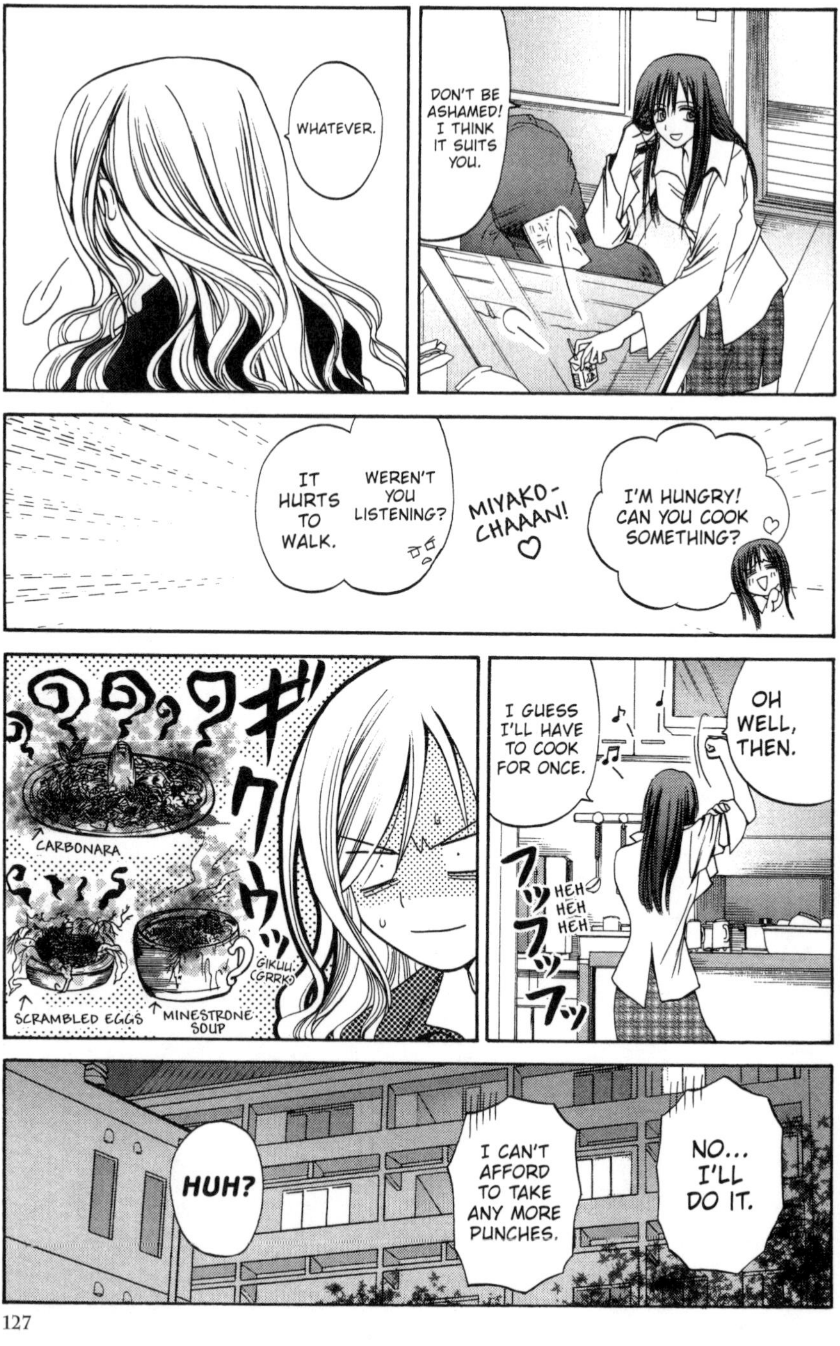
DON'T BE ASHAMED! I THINK IT SUITS YOU.
WHATEVER.
I'M HUNGRY! CAN YOU COOK SOMETHING? ♡
MIYAKO-CHAAAN! ♡
WEREN'T YOU LISTENING?
IT HURTS TO WALK.
OH WELL, THEN.
I GUESS I'LL HAVE TO COOK FOR ONCE.
フッフッフッ
HEH HEH HEH
ギクウッ
GIKUU (GRRK)
CARBONARA
SCRAMBLED EGGS
MINESTRONE SOUP
NO... I'LL DO IT.
I CAN'T AFFORD TO TAKE ANY MORE PUNCHES.
HUH?

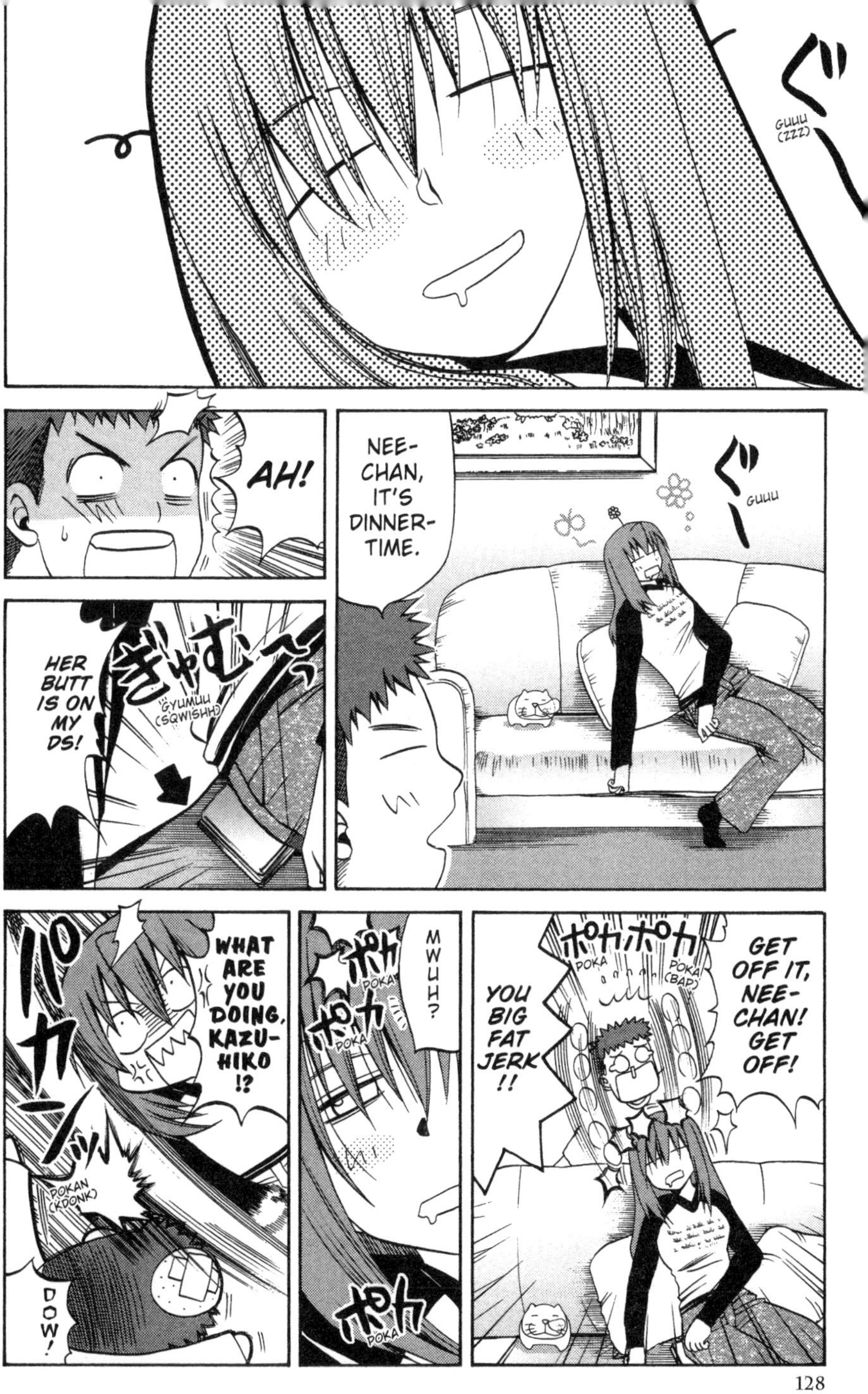
GUUU (ZZZ)
NEE-CHAN, IT'S DINNER-TIME.
GUUU
AH!
HER BUTT IS ON MY DS!
GYUMUU (SQWISHH)
GET OFF IT, NEE-CHAN! GET OFF!
POKA POKA (BAP)
YOU BIG FAT JERK!!
MWUH?
POKA
POKA
POKA
WHAT ARE YOU DOING, KAZUHIKO!?
POKAN (KDONK)
DOW!

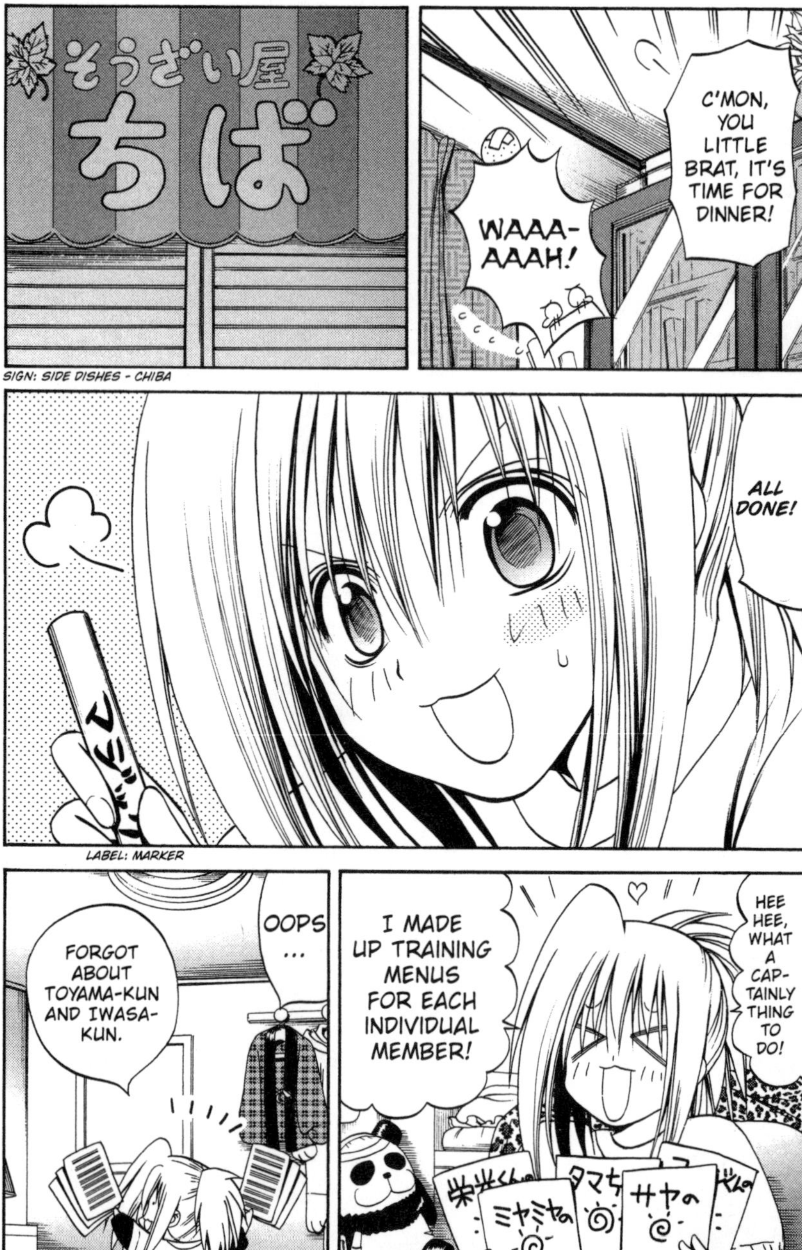
C'MON, YOU LITTLE BRAT, IT'S TIME FOR DINNER!
WAAAAAAH!
そうざい屋
ちば
SIGN: SIDE DISHES - CHIBA
ALL DONE!
LABEL: MARKER
HEE HEE, WHAT A CAPTAINLY THING TO DO!
I MADE UP TRAINING MENUS FOR EACH INDIVIDUAL MEMBER!
OOPS...
FORGOT ABOUT TOYAMA-KUN AND IWASA-KUN.
PAPERS (L-R): EIKOU-KUN'S / MIYA-MIYA'S / TAMA-CHAN'S / SAYA'S / YUJI-KUN'S

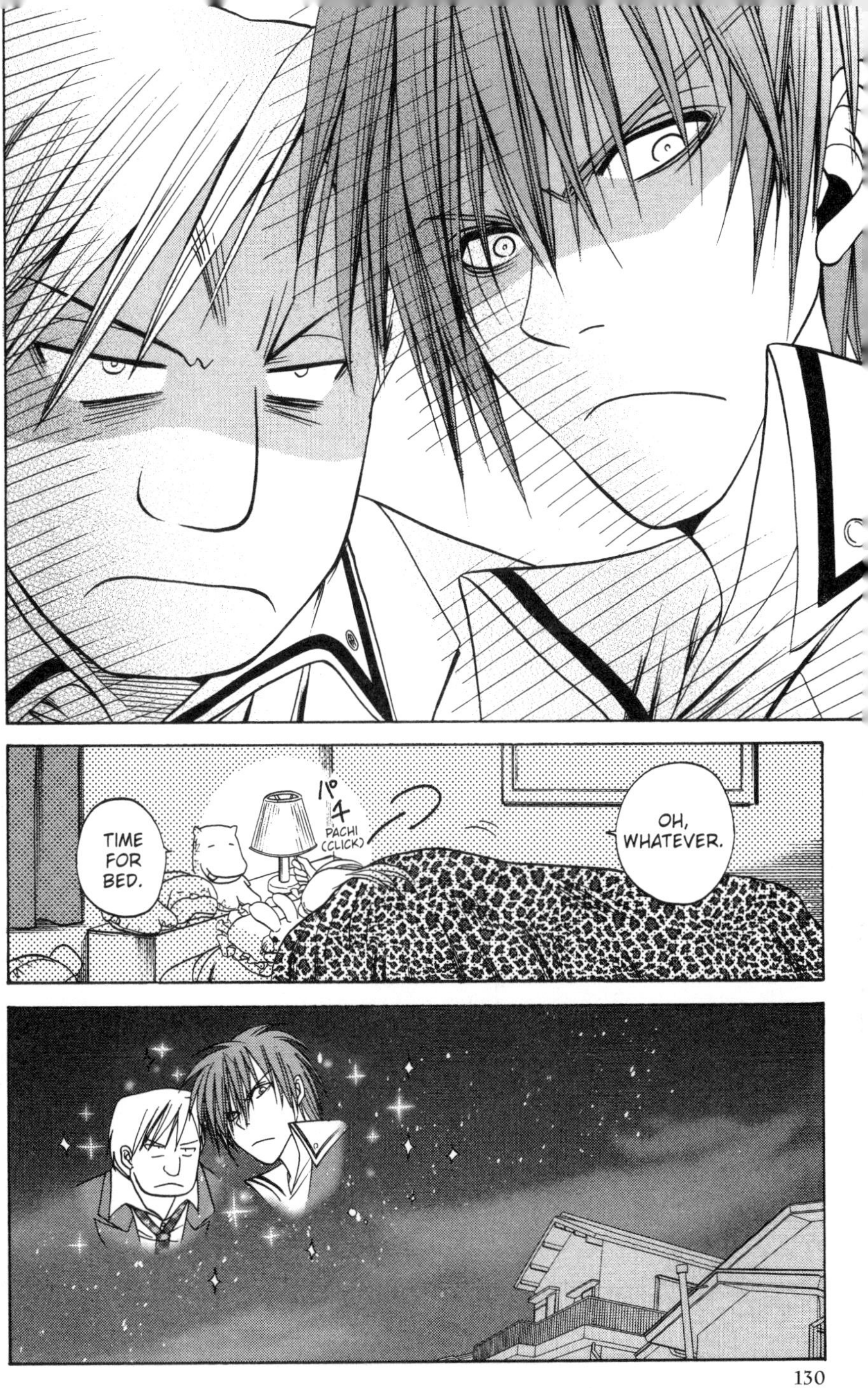
OH, WHATEVER.
パチ
PACHI (CLICK)
TIME FOR BED.

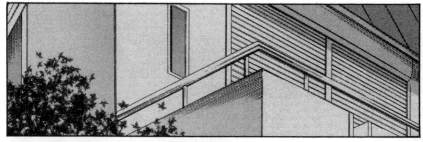

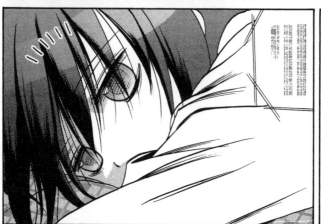

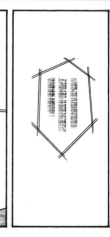

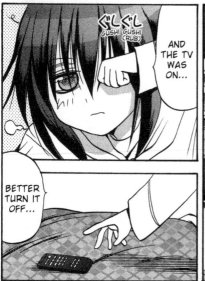

GUSHI GUSHI (RUB)

AND THE TV WAS ON...

BETTER TURN IT OFF...

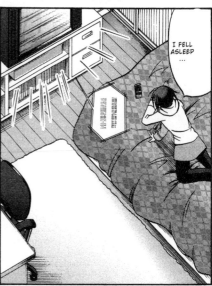

I FELL ASLEEP...

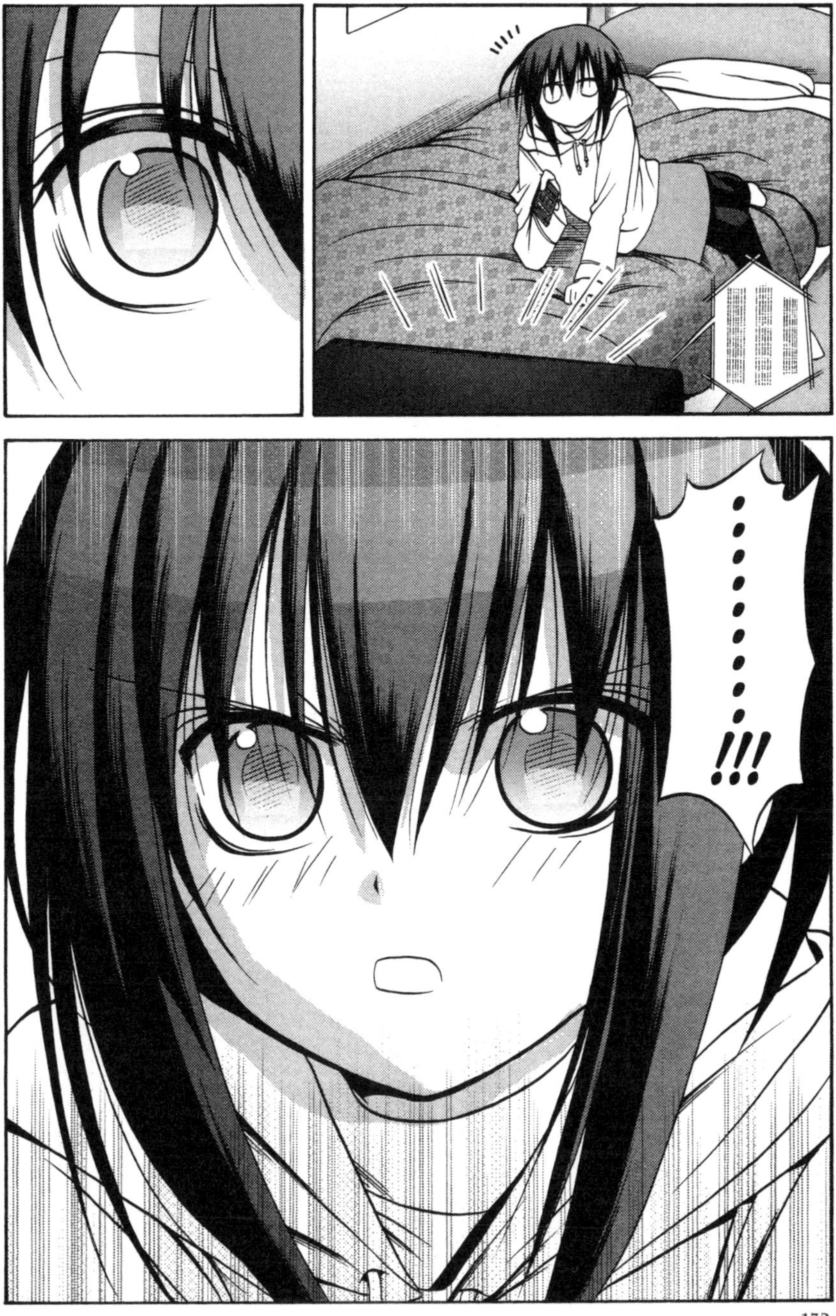
...........!!!

BAMBOO BLADE

IWASA-KUN'S GLASS HEART

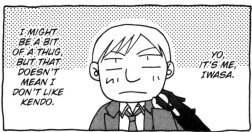

YO, IT'S ME, IWASA.
I MIGHT BE A BIT OF A THUG, BUT THAT DOESN'T MEAN I DON'T LIKE KENDO.
I LIKE HEARING ABOUT PEOPLE WHO ARE REAL GOOD AT KENDO, FOR INSTANCE.
PAAN (WHACK)
IF I TURN ON THE TV WHEN I'M BORED AND THERE'S A KENDO MATCH ON, I'LL WATCH IT.
SOMETIMES I EVEN FEEL LIKE HOLDING A SHINAI.
BUN (SWOOM)
BUN
SHOES OFF, OF COURSE.
WHEN THE KENDO CLUB MEMBERS AREN'T AROUND, I MIGHT EVEN FEEL LIKE SNEAKING INTO THE DOJO TO SWING ONE AROUND A BIT.
BUT NOT OF-TEN!
AND SOME-TIMES ...
HEY ...
KILLER TRAINING MENUS
TAMA-CHAN
SAYA
MIYA-MIYA
EIKOU-KUN
... THERE ISN'T ONE FOR ME OR TOYA-MA!!
...I EVEN GET MY FEELINGS HURT JUST A BIT.

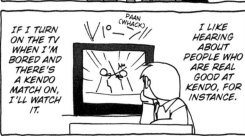

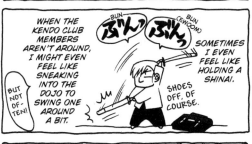

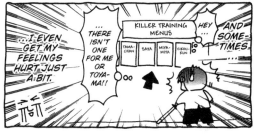

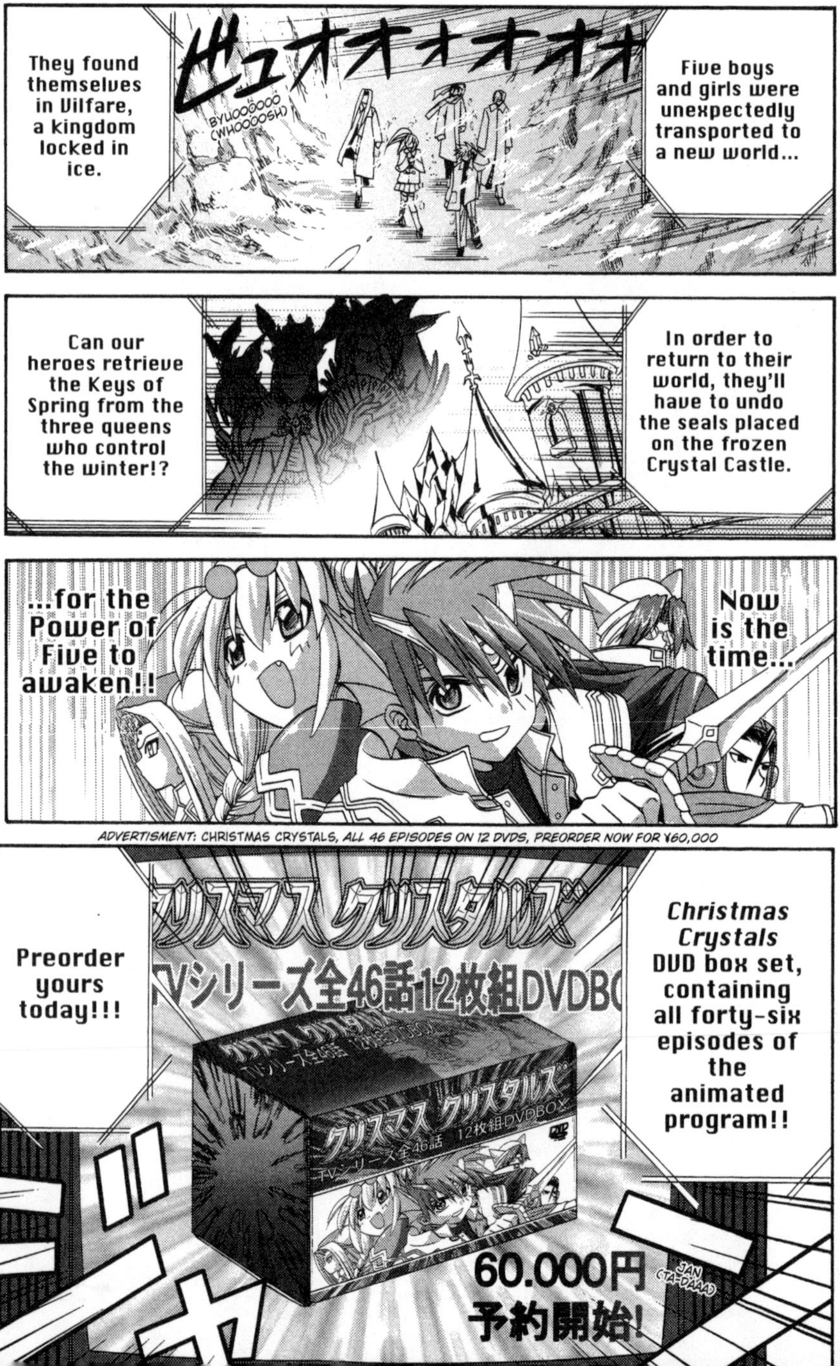
Five boys and girls were unexpectedly transported to a new world...
ビュオオオオオオオ
BYUOOOOOO (WHOOOOOSH)
They found themselves in Vilfare, a kingdom locked in ice.
In order to return to their world, they'll have to undo the seals placed on the frozen Crystal Castle.
Can our heroes retrieve the Keys of Spring from the three queens who control the winter!?
Now is the time...
...for the Power of Five to awaken!!
ADVERTISMENT: CHRISTMAS CRYSTALS, ALL 46 EPISODES ON 12 DVDS, PREORDER NOW FOR ¥60,000
Christmas Crystals DVD box set, containing all forty-six episodes of the animated program!!
クリスマスクリスタルズ
TVシリーズ全46話 12枚組DVDBO
クリスマス クリスタルズ
TVシリーズ全46話 12枚組DVDBOX
60.000円
予約開始!
JAN (TA-DAAA)
Preorder yours today!!!

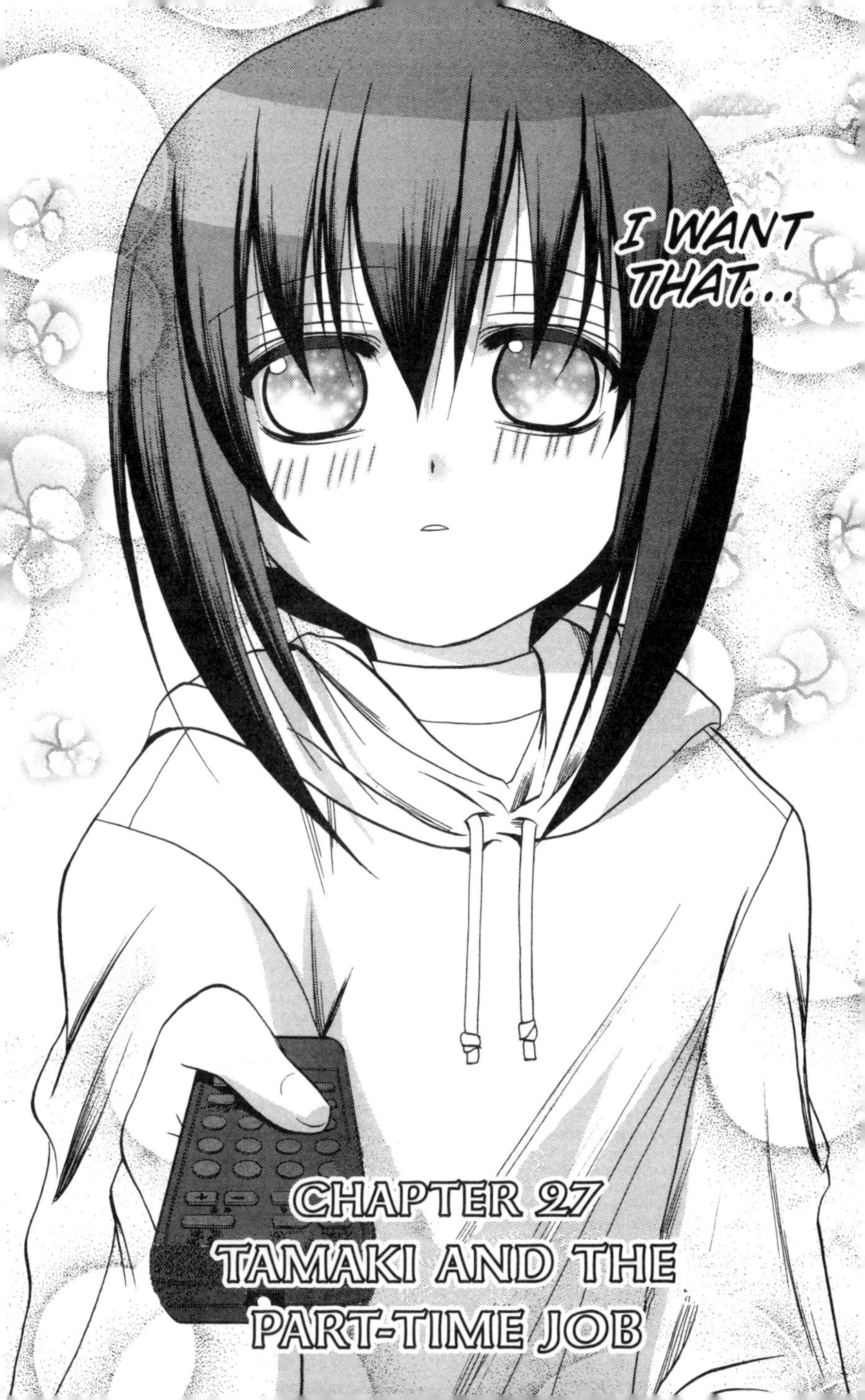
I WANT THAT...
CHAPTER 27
TAMAKI AND THE PART-TIME JOB

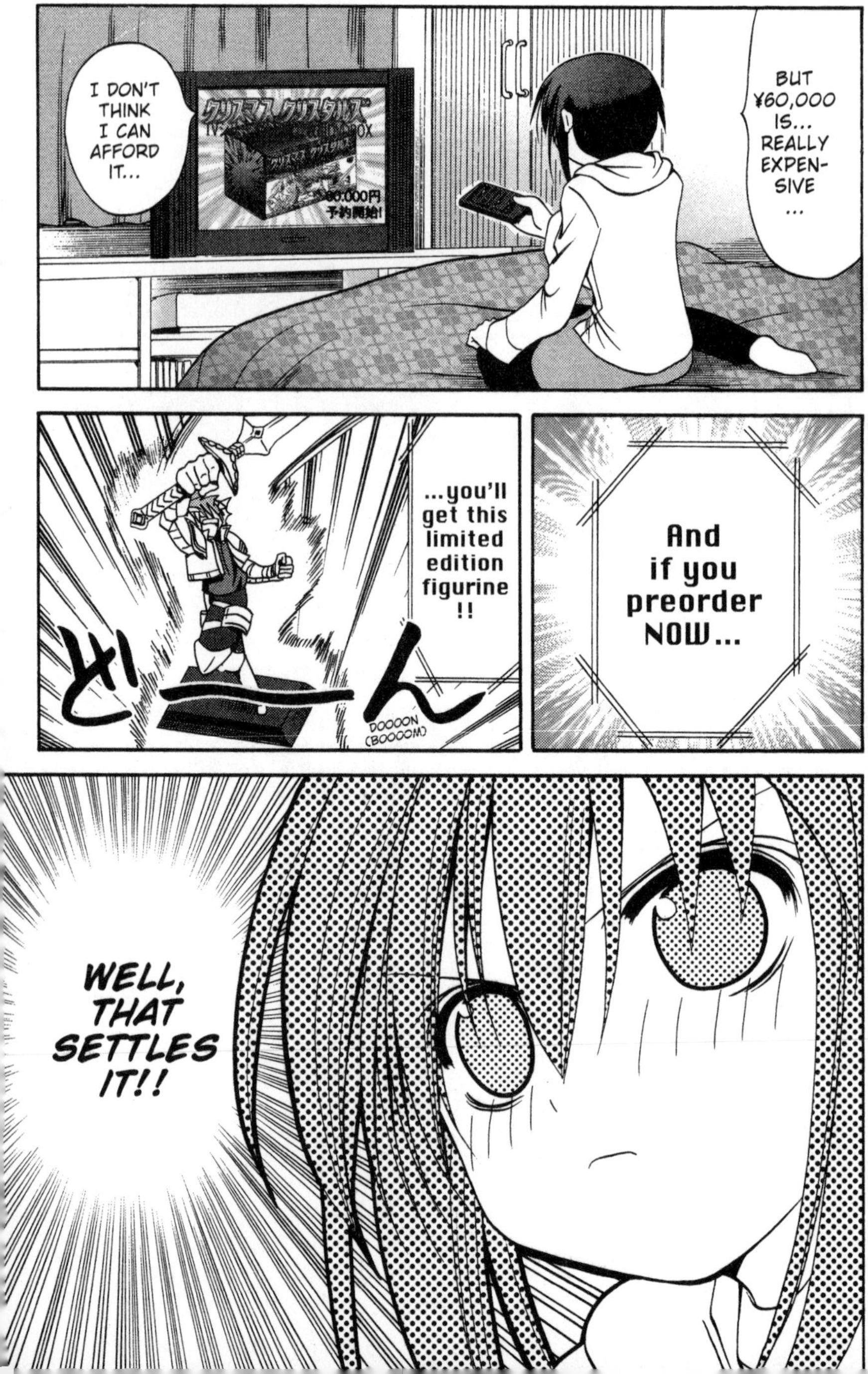
BUT ¥60,000 IS... REALLY EXPENSIVE...
I DON'T THINK I CAN AFFORD IT...
And if you preorder NOW...
...you'll get this limited edition figurine!!
DOOOON (BOOOOM)
WELL, THAT SETTLES IT!!

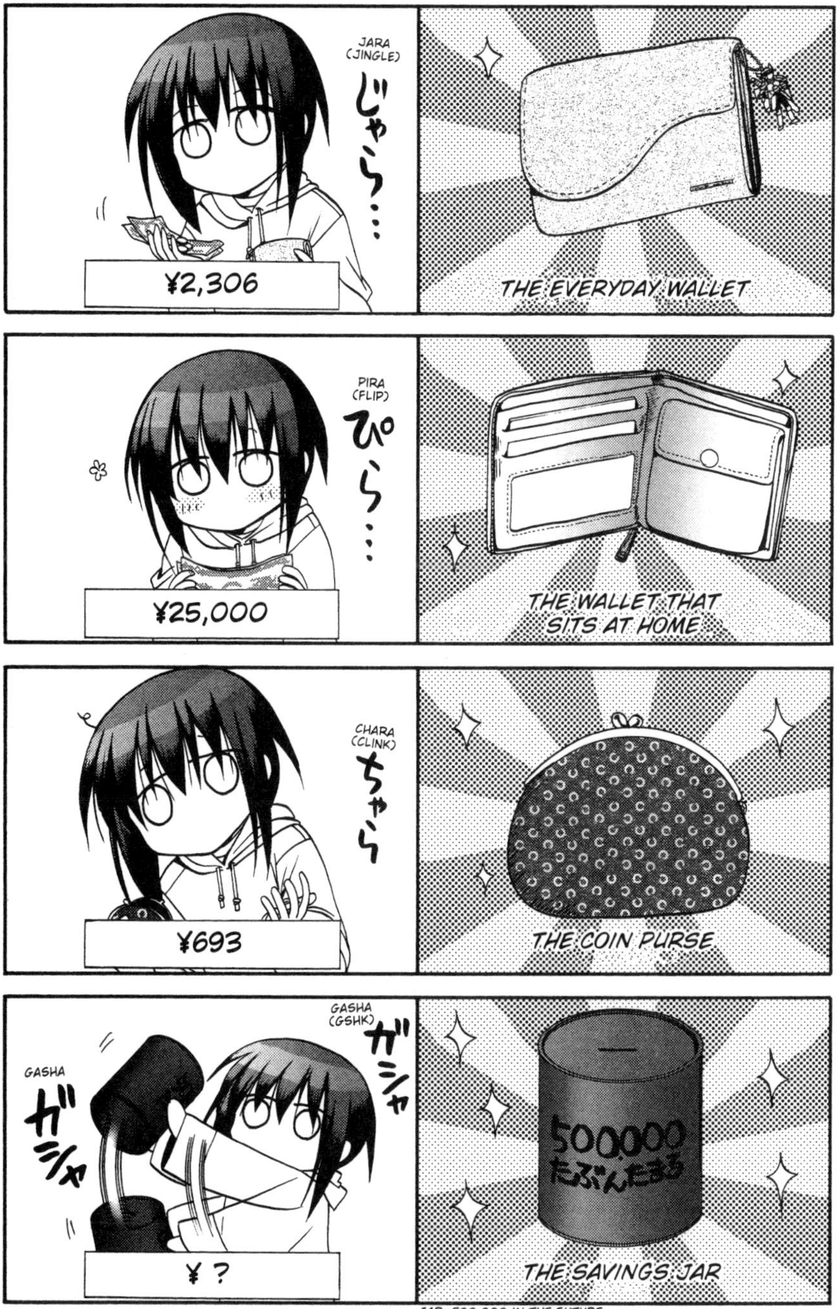
THE EVERYDAY WALLET
JARA (JINGLE)
じゃら…
¥2,306
THE WALLET THAT SITS AT HOME
PIRA (FLIP)
ぴら…
¥25,000
THE COIN PURSE
CHARA (CLINK)
ちゃら
¥693
500,000 たぶんたまる
THE SAVINGS JAR
GASHA (GSHK)
ガシャ
GASHA
ガシャ
¥ ?

JAR: 500,000 IN THE FUTURE

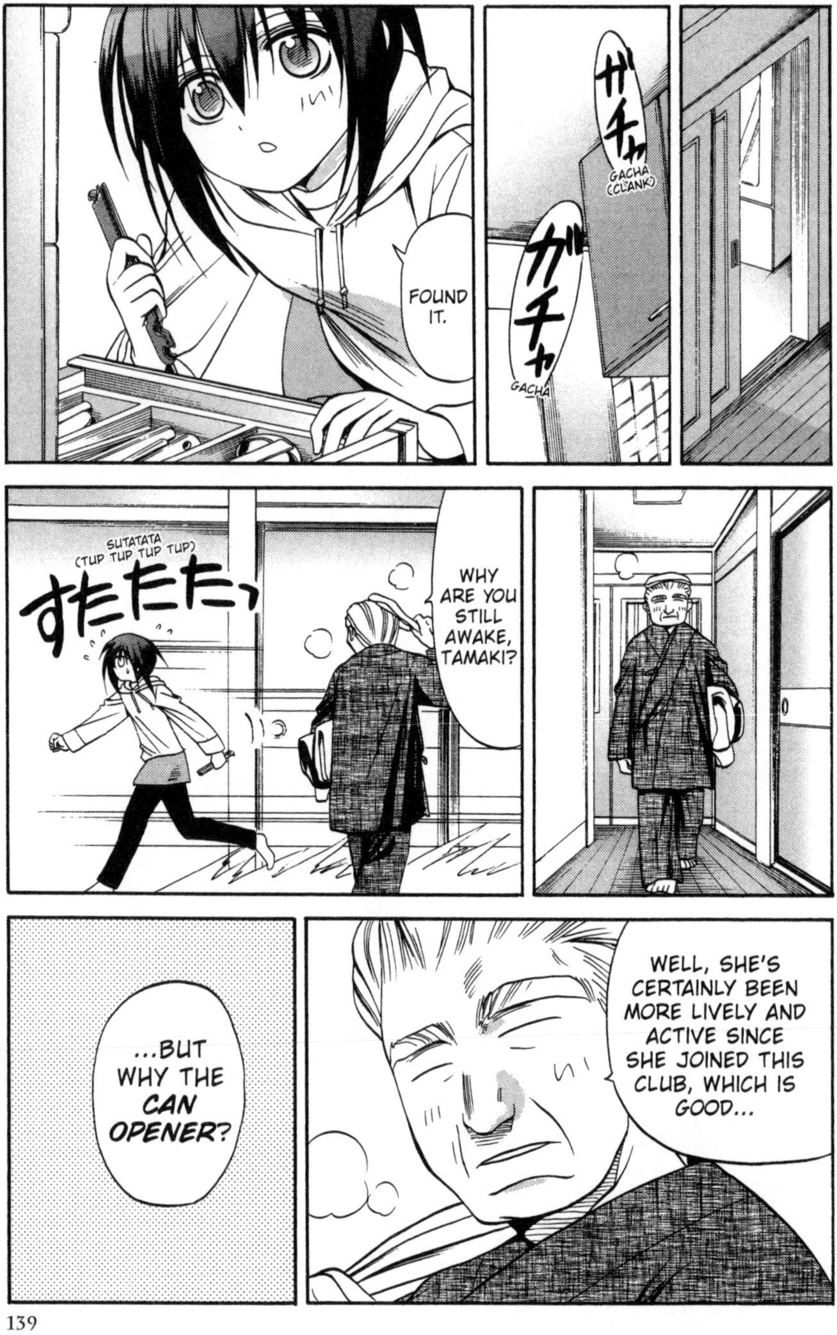
ガチャ
GACHA (CLANK)
ガチャ
GACHA
FOUND IT.
WHY ARE YOU STILL AWAKE, TAMAKI?
すたたたっ
SUTATATA (TUP TUP TUP TUP)
WELL, SHE'S CERTAINLY BEEN MORE LIVELY AND ACTIVE SINCE SHE JOINED THIS CLUB, WHICH IS GOOD...
...BUT WHY THE *CAN OPENER*?

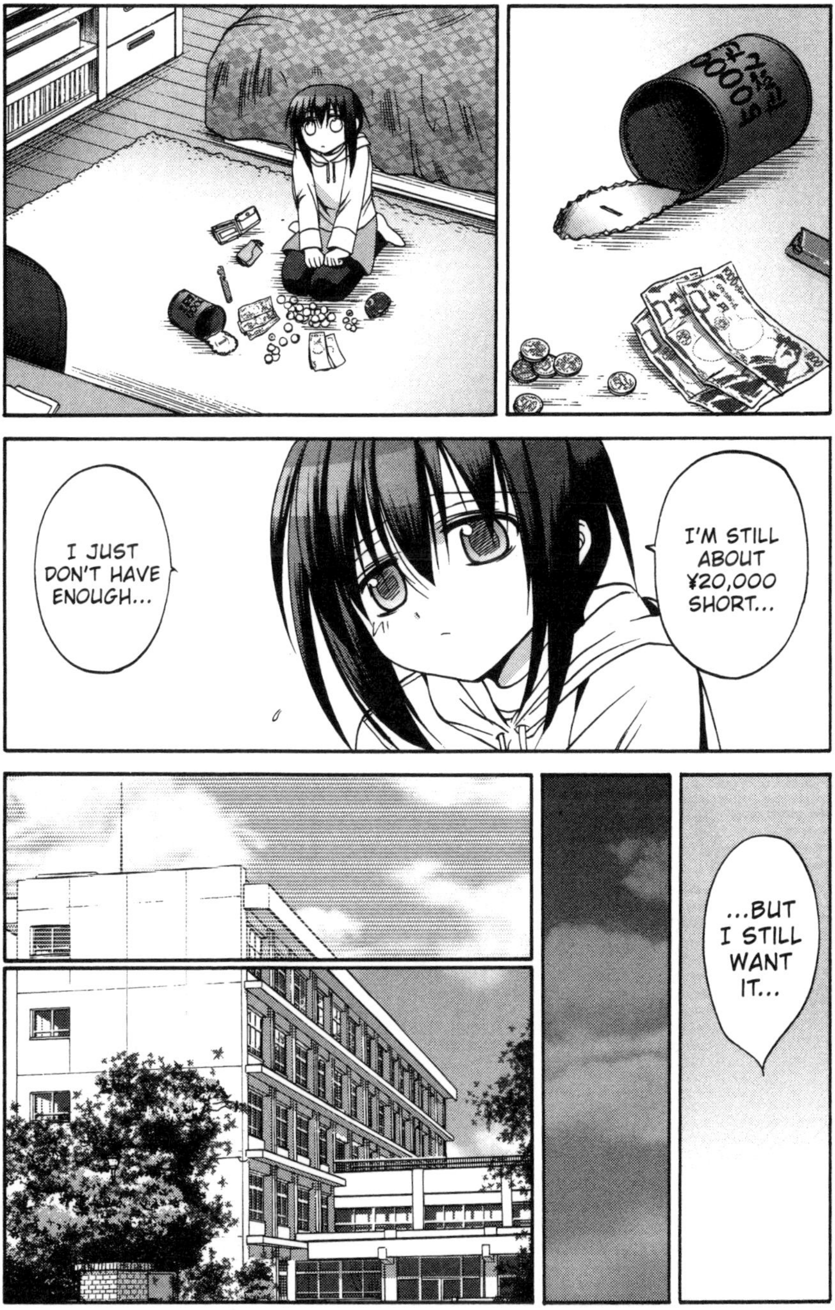
I'M STILL ABOUT ¥20,000 SHORT...
I JUST DON'T HAVE ENOUGH...
...BUT I STILL WANT IT...

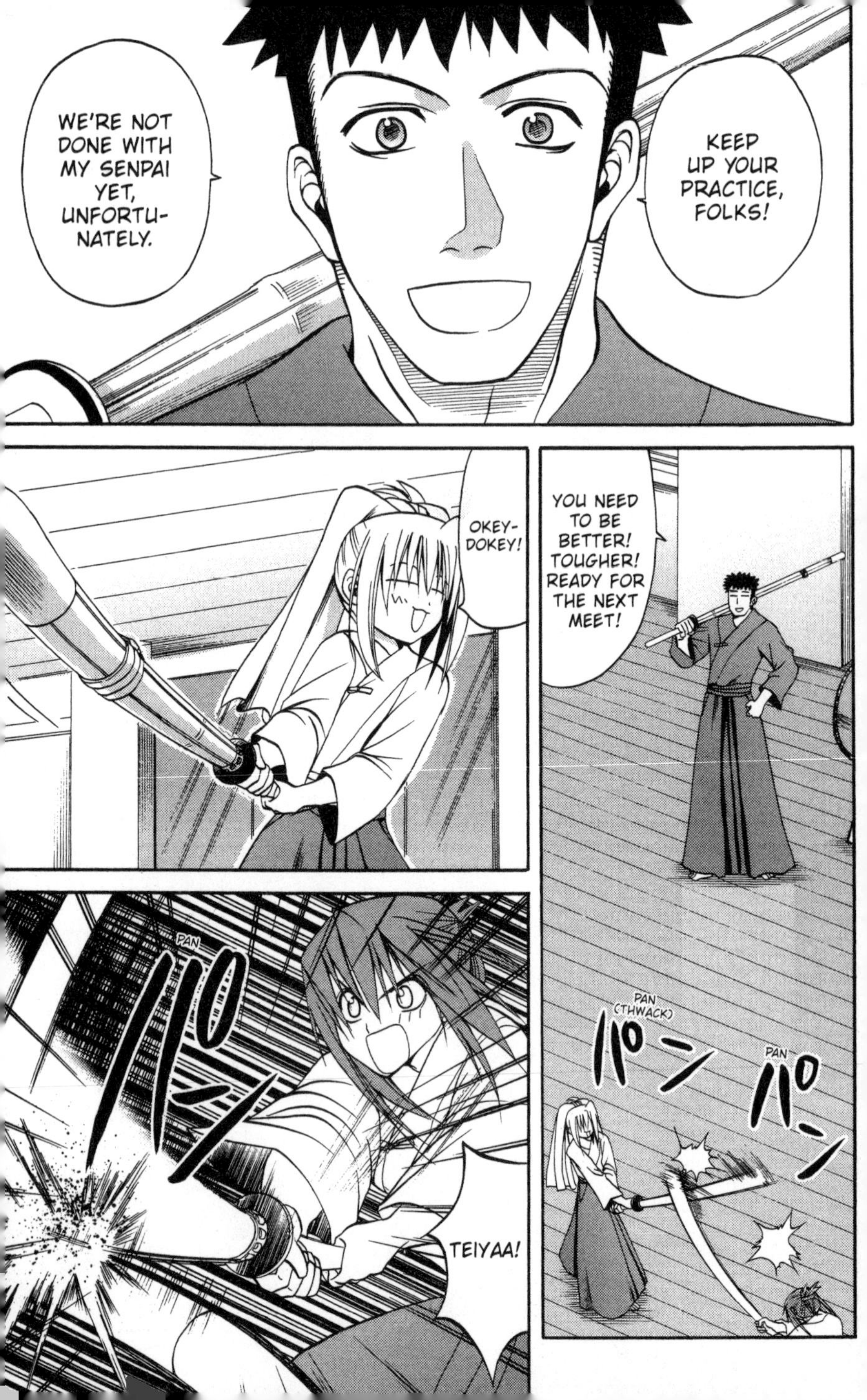
KEEP UP YOUR PRACTICE, FOLKS!
WE'RE NOT DONE WITH MY SENPAI YET, UNFORTUNATELY.
YOU NEED TO BE BETTER! TOUGHER! READY FOR THE NEXT MEET!
OKEY-DOKEY!
PAN (THWACK)
パン
PAN
パン
PAN
パン
TEIYAA!

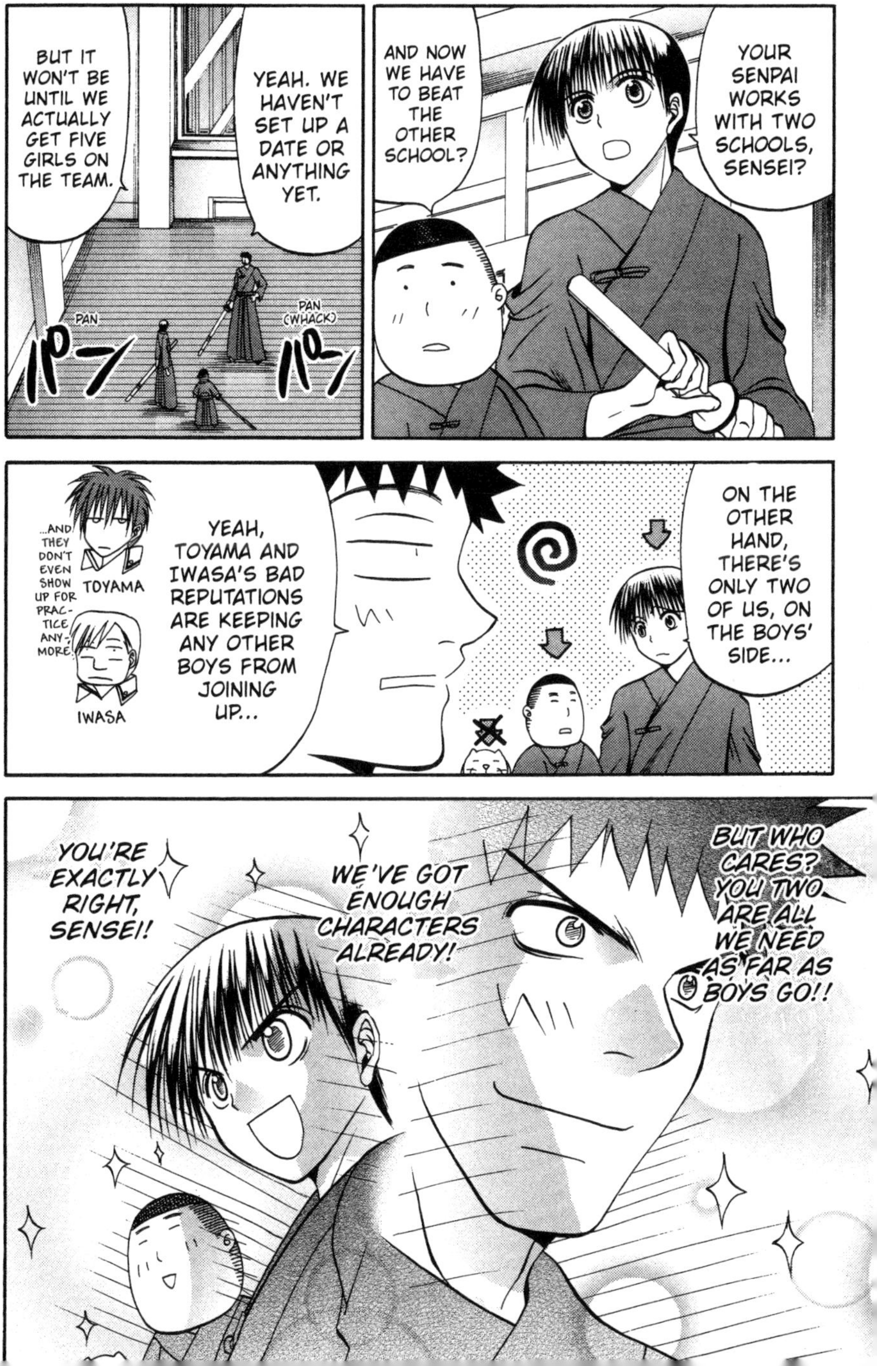
YOUR SENPAI WORKS WITH TWO SCHOOLS, SENSEI?
AND NOW WE HAVE TO BEAT THE OTHER SCHOOL?
YEAH. WE HAVEN'T SET UP A DATE OR ANYTHING YET.
BUT IT WON'T BE UNTIL WE ACTUALLY GET FIVE GIRLS ON THE TEAM.
PAN (WHACK)
PAN
ON THE OTHER HAND, THERE'S ONLY TWO OF US, ON THE BOYS' SIDE...
YEAH, TOYAMA AND IWASA'S BAD REPUTATIONS ARE KEEPING ANY OTHER BOYS FROM JOINING UP...
...AND THEY DON'T EVEN SHOW UP FOR PRAC-TICE ANY-MORE.
TOYAMA
IWASA
BUT WHO CARES? YOU TWO ARE ALL WE NEED AS FAR AS BOYS GO!!
WE'VE GOT ENOUGH CHARACTERS ALREADY!
YOU'RE EXACTLY RIGHT, SENSEI!

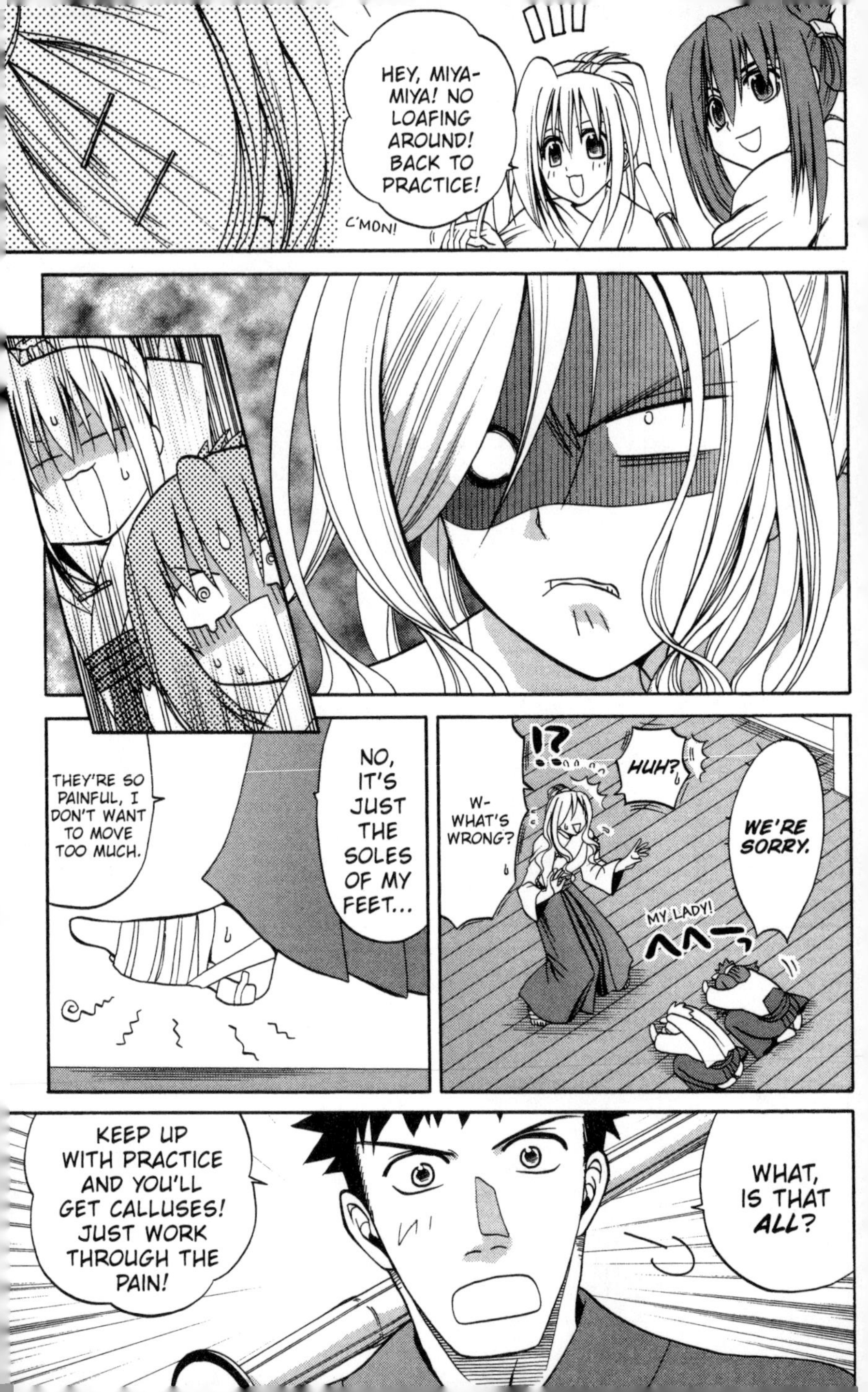
HEY, MIYA-MIYA! NO LOAFING AROUND! BACK TO PRACTICE!
C'MON!
NO, IT'S JUST THE SOLES OF MY FEET...
THEY'RE SO PAINFUL, I DON'T WANT TO MOVE TOO MUCH.
WE'RE SORRY.
HUH?
!?
W-WHAT'S WRONG?
MY LADY!
WHAT, IS THAT ALL?
KEEP UP WITH PRACTICE AND YOU'LL GET CALLUSES! JUST WORK THROUGH THE PAIN!

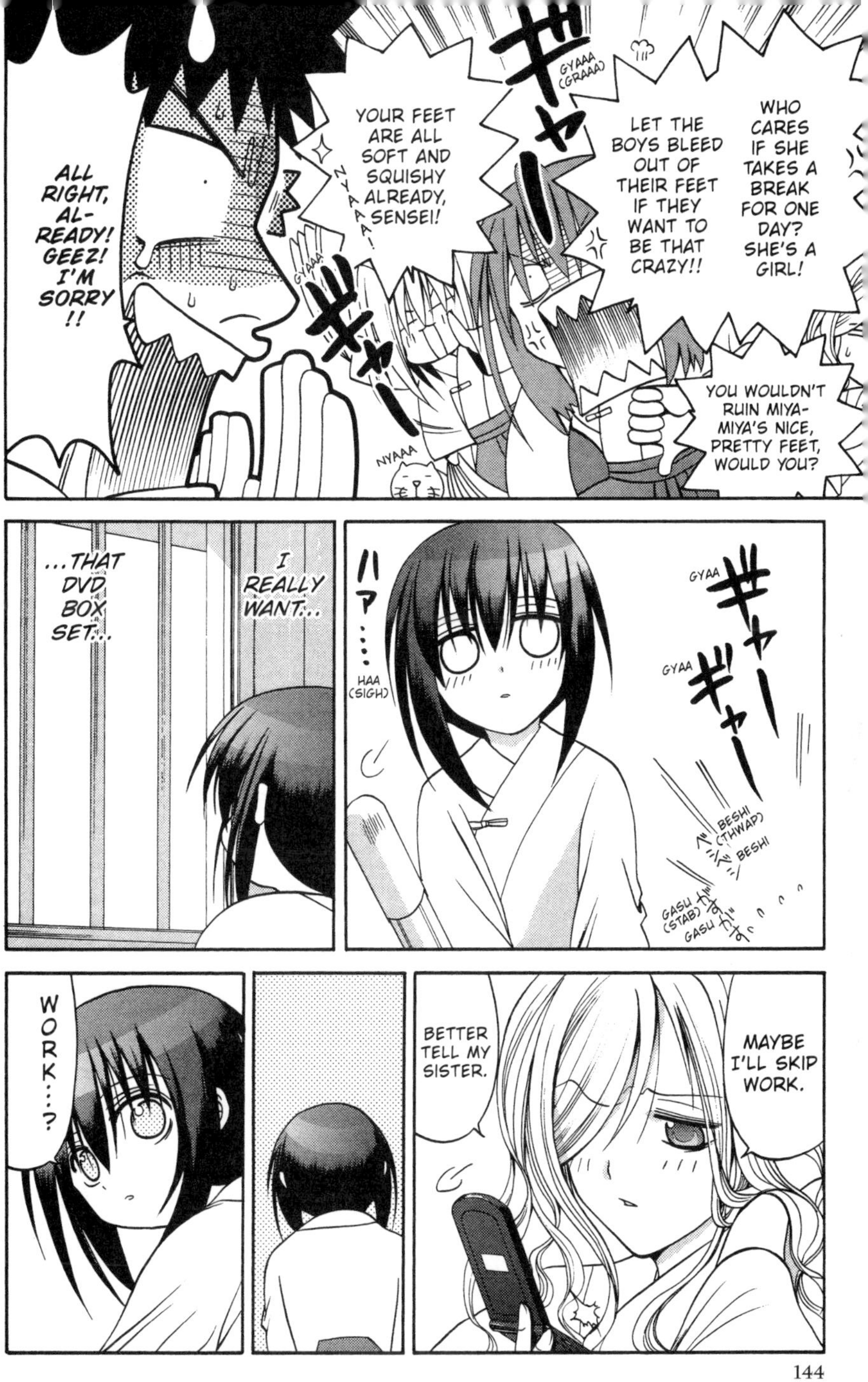
WHO CARES IF SHE TAKES A BREAK FOR ONE DAY? SHE'S A GIRL!
GYAAA (GRAAA)
LET THE BOYS BLEED OUT OF THEIR FEET IF THEY WANT TO BE THAT CRAZY!!
YOUR FEET ARE ALL SOFT AND SQUISHY ALREADY, SENSEI!
NYAAAA!
GYAAA
YOU WOULDN'T RUIN MIYA-MIYA'S NICE, PRETTY FEET, WOULD YOU?
NYAAA
ALL RIGHT, AL-READY! GEEZ! I'M SORRY!!
GYAA
GYAA
BESHI (THWAP)
BESHI
GASU (STAB)
GASU
HAA (SIGH)
I REALLY WANT...
...THAT DVD BOX SET...
MAYBE I'LL SKIP WORK.
BETTER TELL MY SISTER.
WORK...?

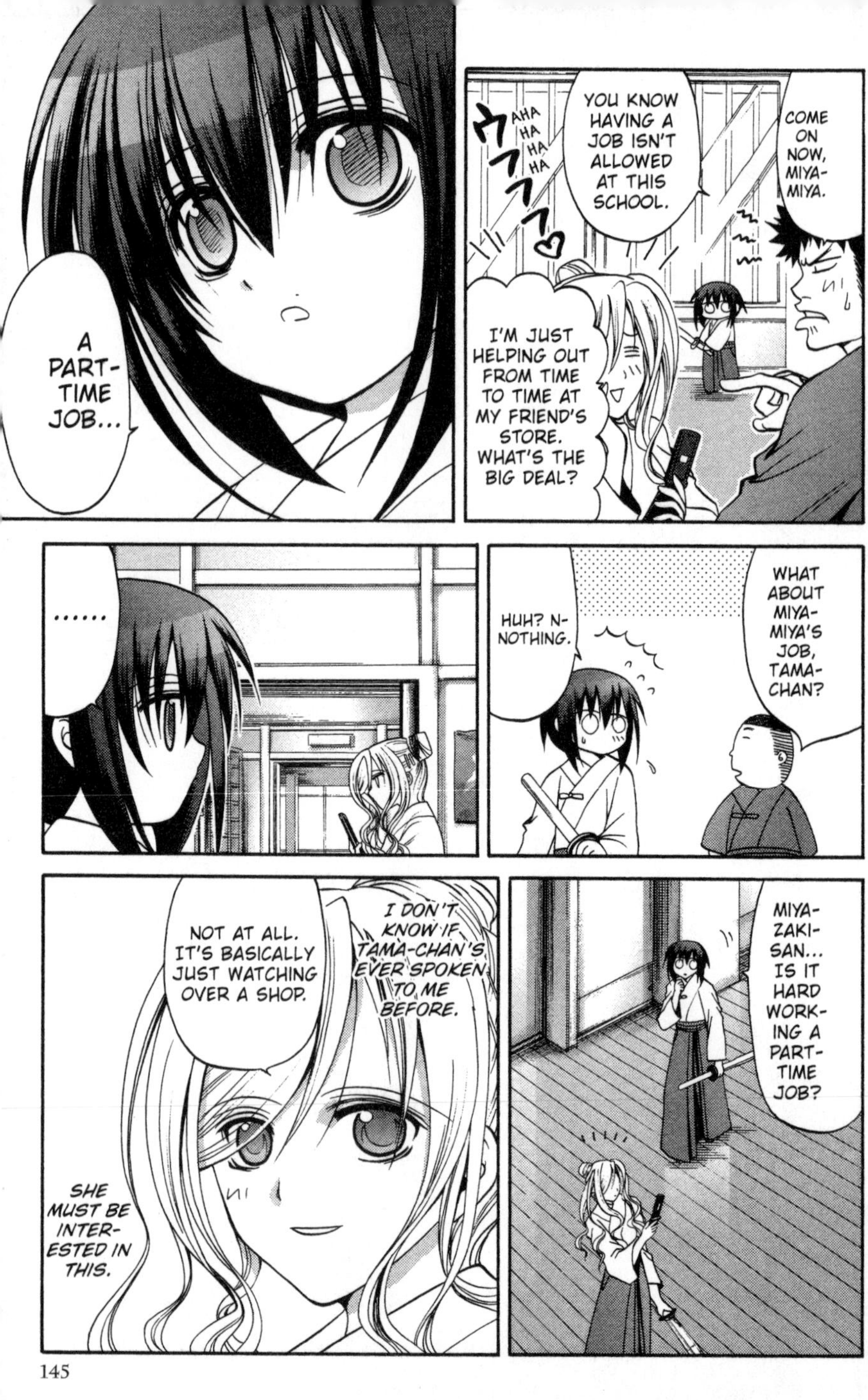
COME ON NOW, MIYA-MIYA.
YOU KNOW HAVING A JOB ISN'T ALLOWED AT THIS SCHOOL.
AHA HA HA HA
I'M JUST HELPING OUT FROM TIME TO TIME AT MY FRIEND'S STORE. WHAT'S THE BIG DEAL?
A PART-TIME JOB...
WHAT ABOUT MIYA-MIYA'S JOB, TAMA-CHAN?
HUH? N-NOTHING.
......
MIYA-ZAKI-SAN... IS IT HARD WORK-ING A PART-TIME JOB?
I DON'T KNOW IF TAMA-CHAN'S EVER SPOKEN TO ME BEFORE.
NOT AT ALL. IT'S BASICALLY JUST WATCHING OVER A SHOP.
SHE MUST BE INTER-ESTED IN THIS.

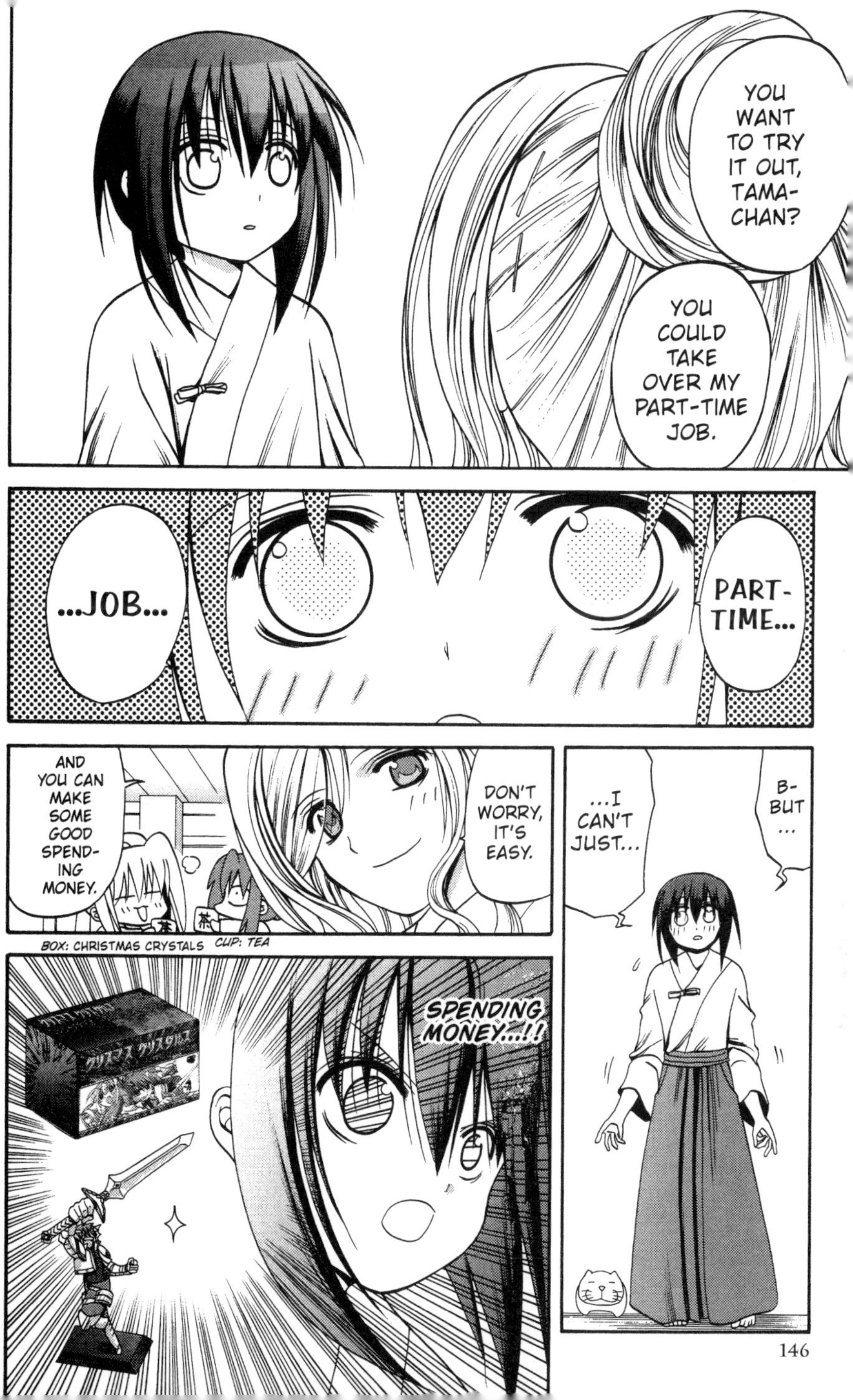
YOU WANT TO TRY IT OUT, TAMA-CHAN?
YOU COULD TAKE OVER MY PART-TIME JOB.
PART-TIME...
...JOB...
B-BUT...
...I CAN'T JUST...
DON'T WORRY, IT'S EASY.
AND YOU CAN MAKE SOME GOOD SPENDING MONEY.
BOX: CHRISTMAS CRYSTALS CUP: TEA
SPENDING MONEY...!!

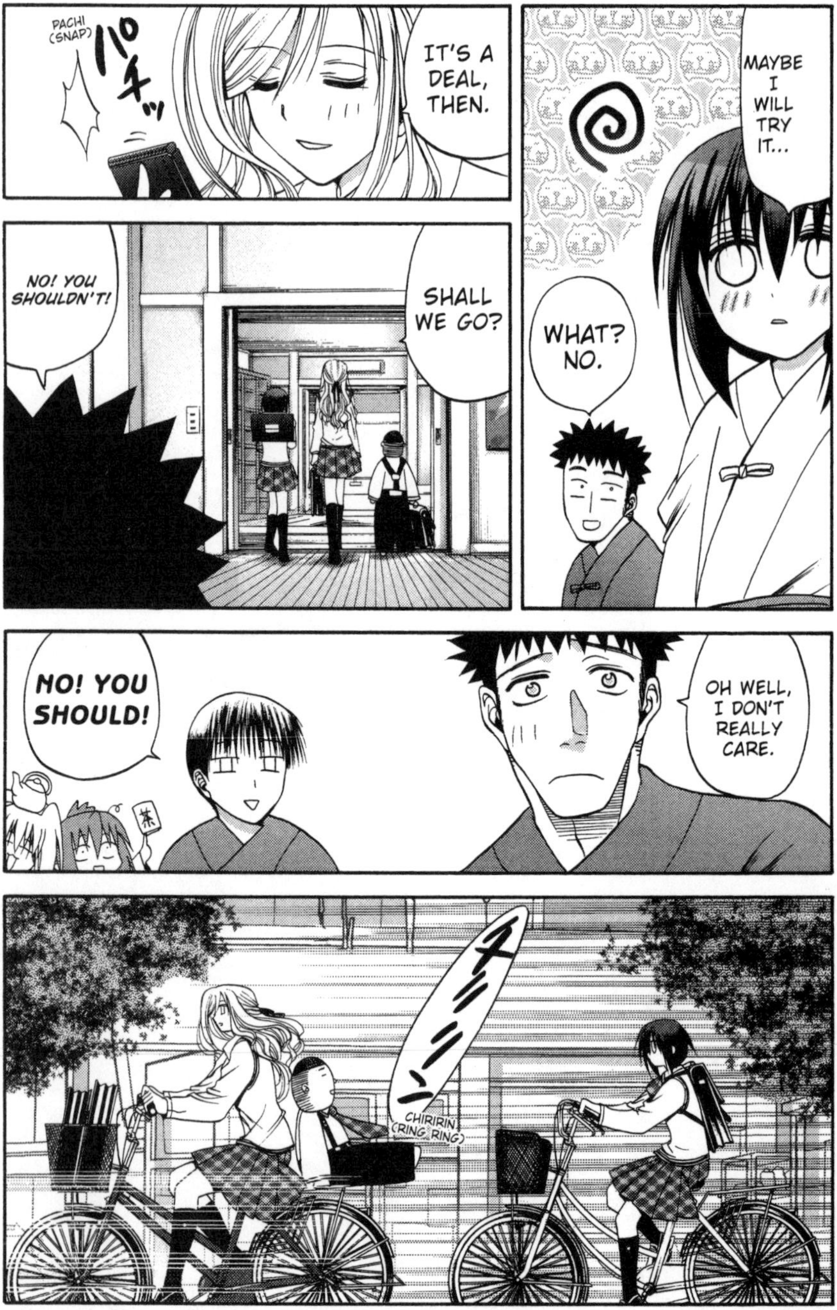
MAYBE I WILL TRY IT...
WHAT? NO.
PACHI (SNAP)
IT'S A DEAL, THEN.
SHALL WE GO?
NO! YOU SHOULDN'T!
OH WELL, I DON'T REALLY CARE.
NO! YOU SHOULD!
CHIRIRIN (RING RING)

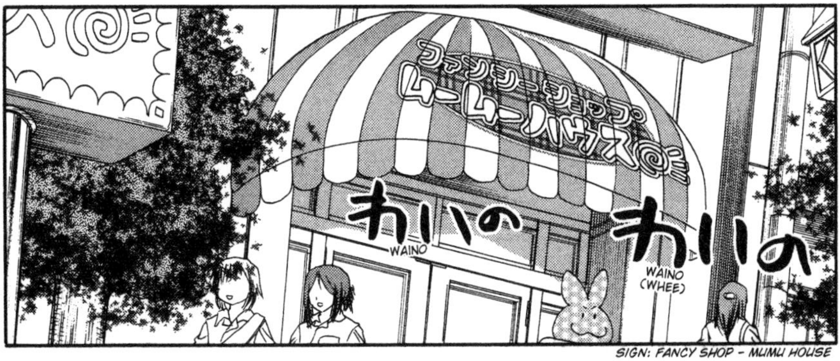
ファンシーショップ ムームーハウス
わいの
WAINO (WHEE)
わいの
WAINO
SIGN: FANCY SHOP - MUMU HOUSE

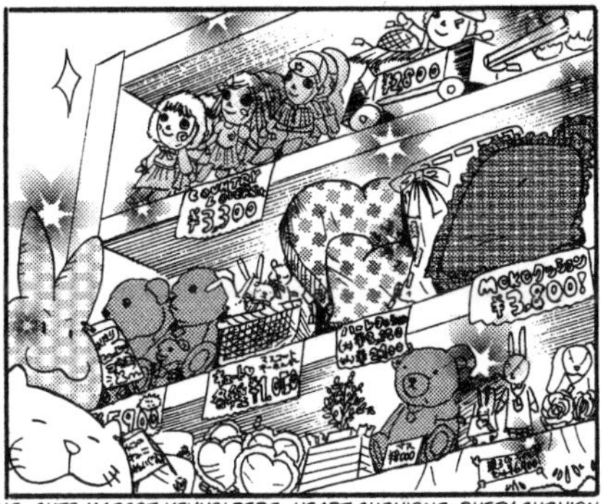
SIGNS: CUTE MASCOT KEYHOLDERS; HEART CUSHIONS, PUFFY CUSHION

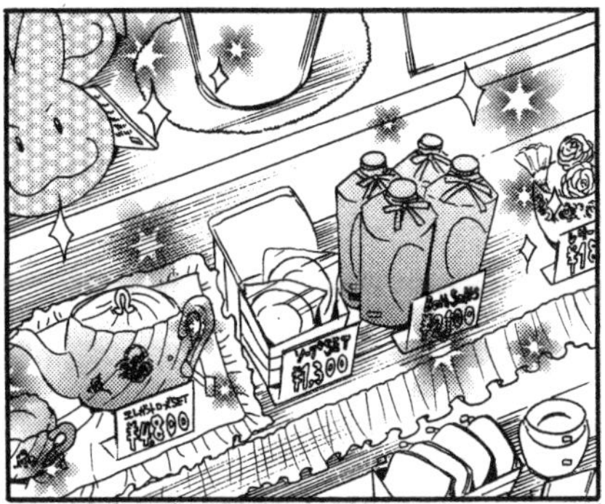
SIGNS: ELEGANT ROSE TEA SET; SOAP SET

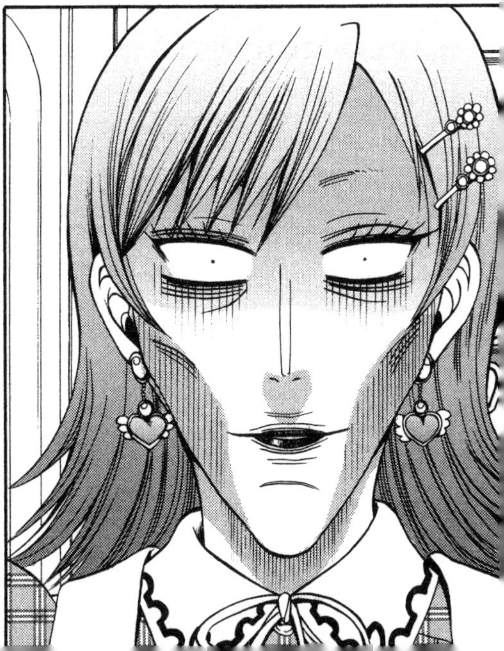

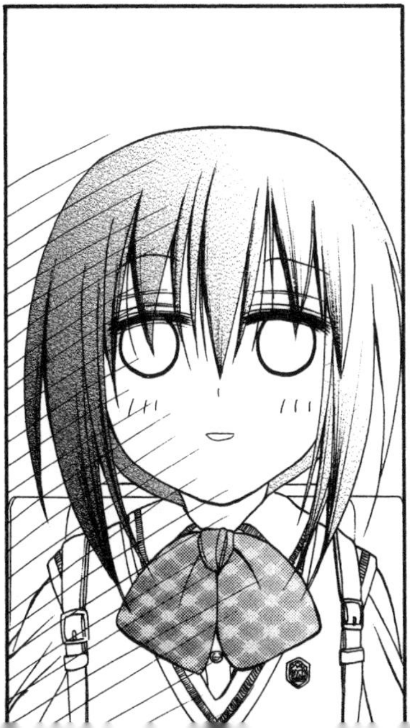

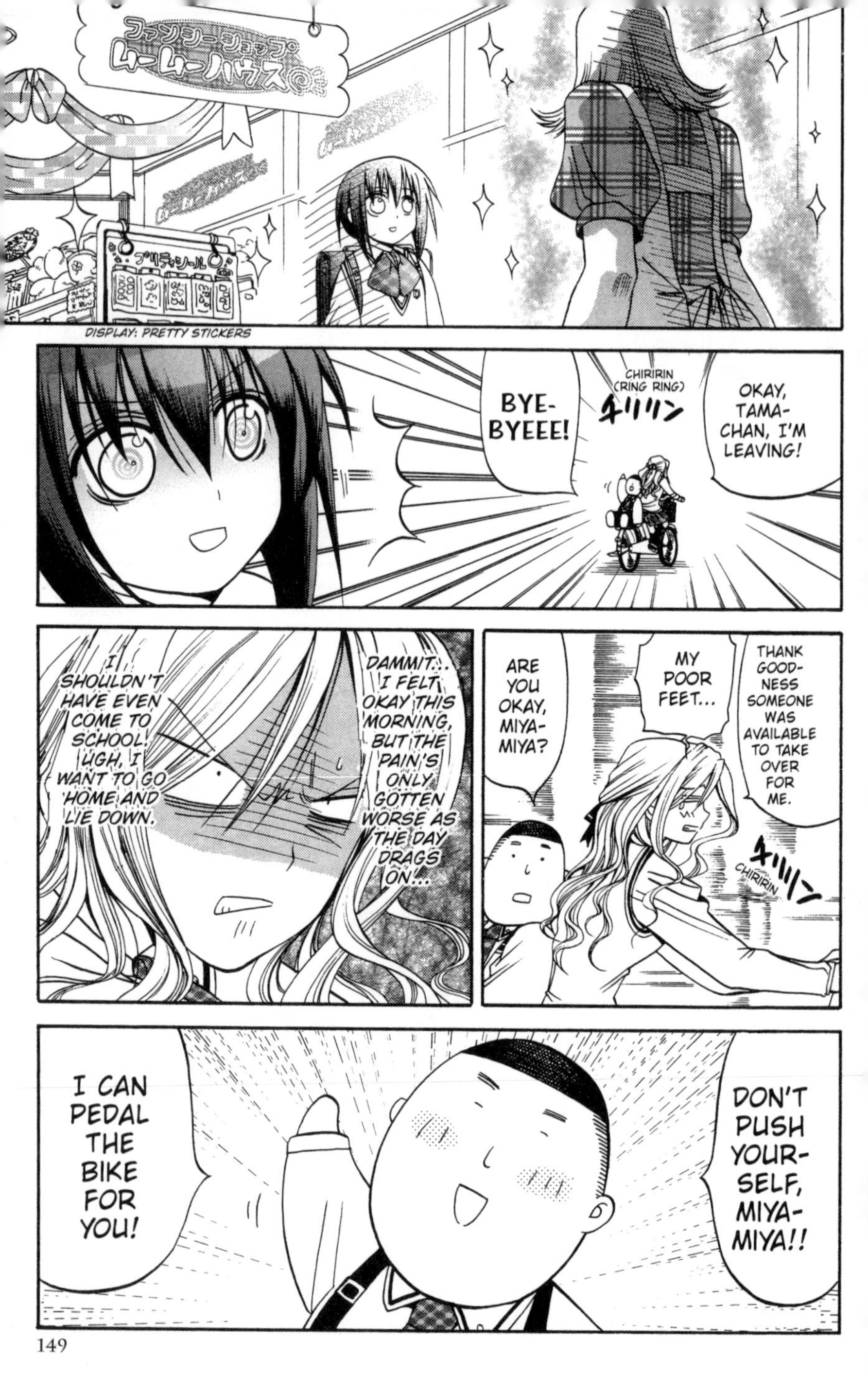
ファンシーショップ
ムームーハウス
プリティシール
DISPLAY: PRETTY STICKERS
OKAY, TAMA-CHAN, I'M LEAVING!
CHIRIRIN (RING RING)
チリリン
BYE-BYEEE!
THANK GOODNESS SOMEONE WAS AVAILABLE TO TAKE OVER FOR ME.
MY POOR FEET...
ARE YOU OKAY, MIYA-MIYA?
チリリン
CHIRIRIN
DAMMIT... I FELT OKAY THIS MORNING, BUT THE PAIN'S ONLY GOTTEN WORSE AS THE DAY DRAGS ON...
I SHOULDN'T HAVE EVEN COME TO SCHOOL. UGH, I WANT TO GO HOME AND LIE DOWN.
DON'T PUSH YOURSELF, MIYA-MIYA!!
I CAN PEDAL THE BIKE FOR YOU!

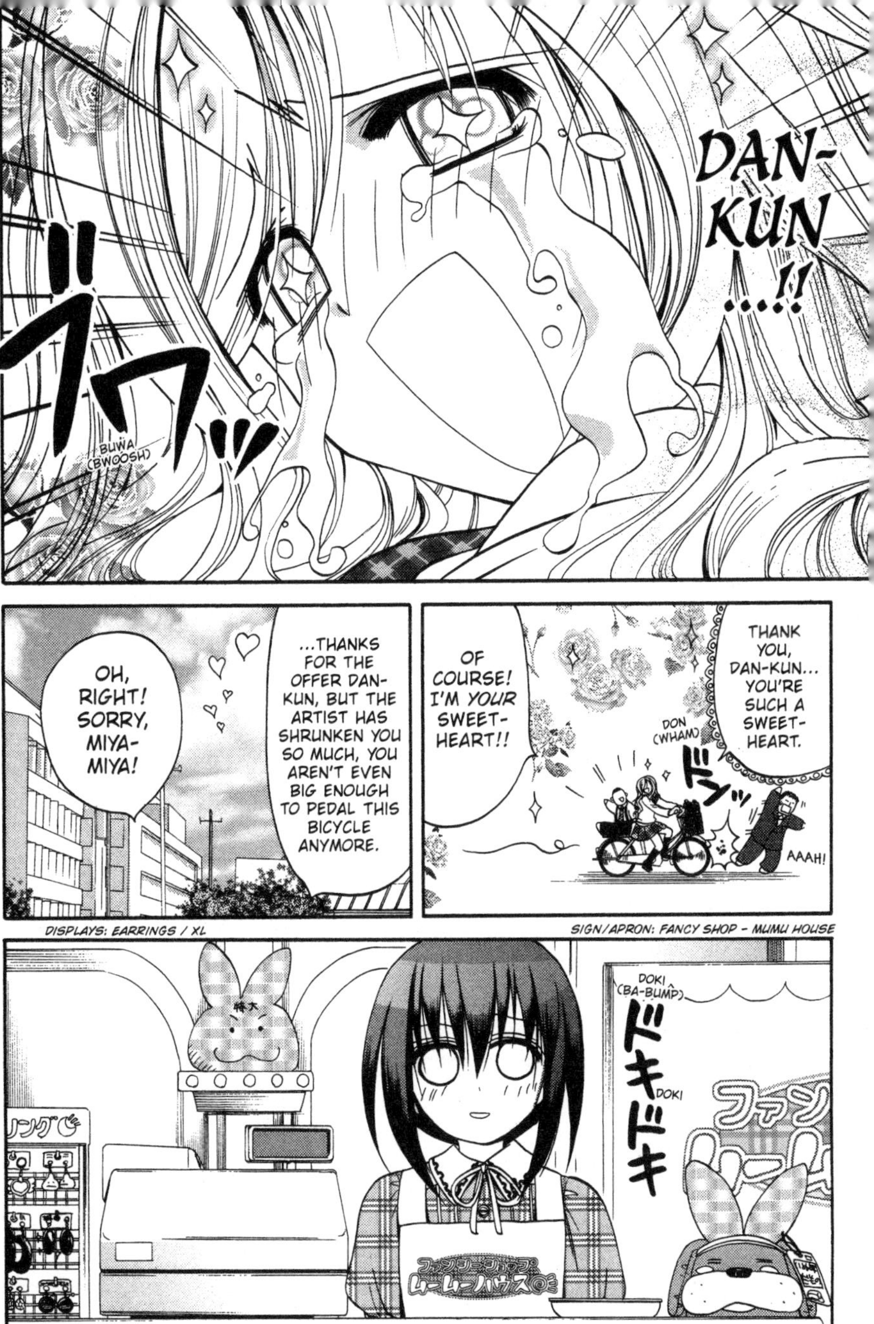

DAN-KUN...!!
BUWA (BWOOSH)
THANK YOU, DAN-KUN... YOU'RE SUCH A SWEET-HEART.
OF COURSE! I'M *YOUR* SWEET-HEART!!
DON (WHAM)
AAAH!
...THANKS FOR THE OFFER DAN-KUN, BUT THE ARTIST HAS SHRUNKEN YOU SO MUCH, YOU AREN'T EVEN BIG ENOUGH TO PEDAL THIS BICYCLE ANYMORE.
OH, RIGHT! SORRY, MIYA-MIYA!
SIGN/APRON: FANCY SHOP - MUMU HOUSE
DISPLAYS: EARRINGS / XL
DOKI (BA-BUMP)
DOKI

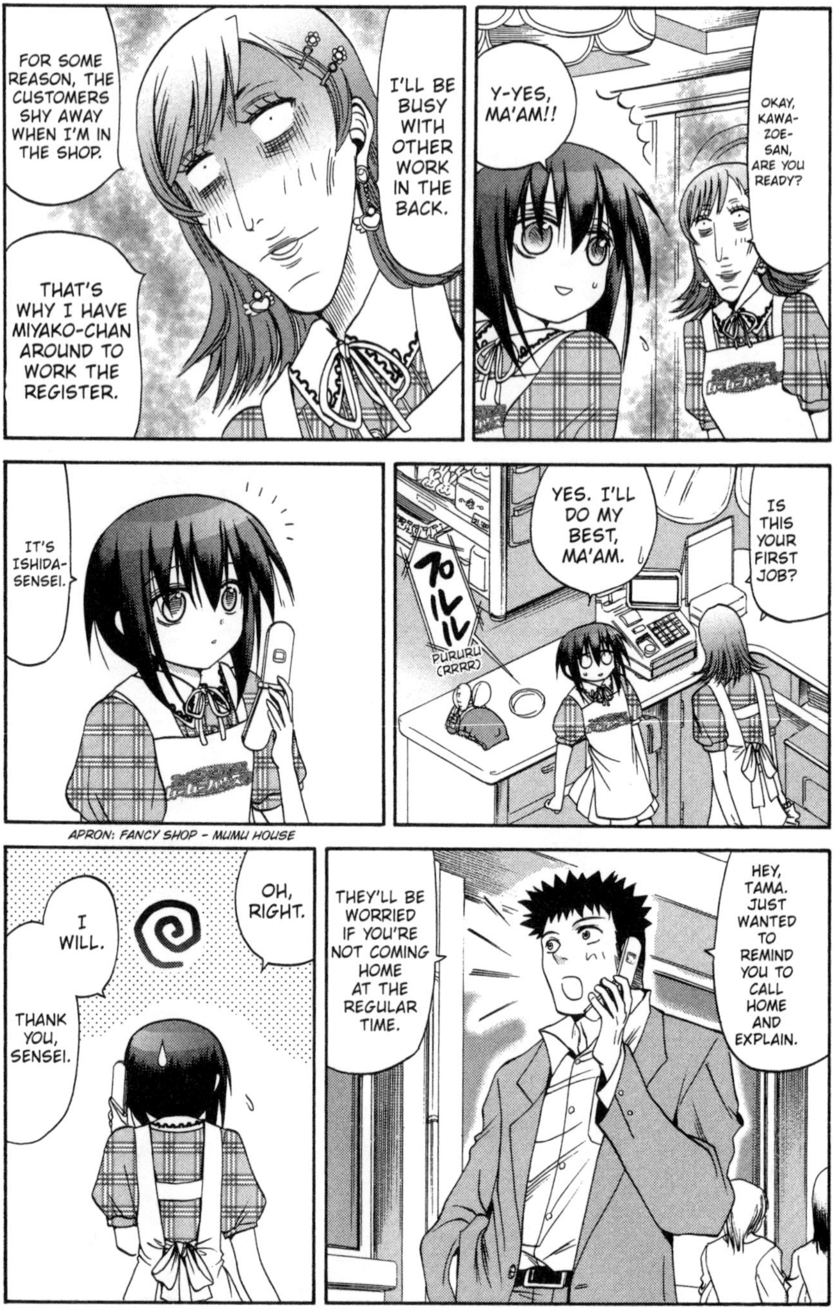
OKAY, KAWAZOE-SAN, ARE YOU READY?
Y-YES, MA'AM!!
I'LL BE BUSY WITH OTHER WORK IN THE BACK.
FOR SOME REASON, THE CUSTOMERS SHY AWAY WHEN I'M IN THE SHOP.
THAT'S WHY I HAVE MIYAKO-CHAN AROUND TO WORK THE REGISTER.
IS THIS YOUR FIRST JOB?
YES. I'LL DO MY BEST, MA'AM.
PURURU (RRRR)
IT'S ISHIDA-SENSEI.
APRON: FANCY SHOP - MUMU HOUSE
HEY, TAMA. JUST WANTED TO REMIND YOU TO CALL HOME AND EXPLAIN.
THEY'LL BE WORRIED IF YOU'RE NOT COMING HOME AT THE REGULAR TIME.
OH, RIGHT.
I WILL.
THANK YOU, SENSEI.

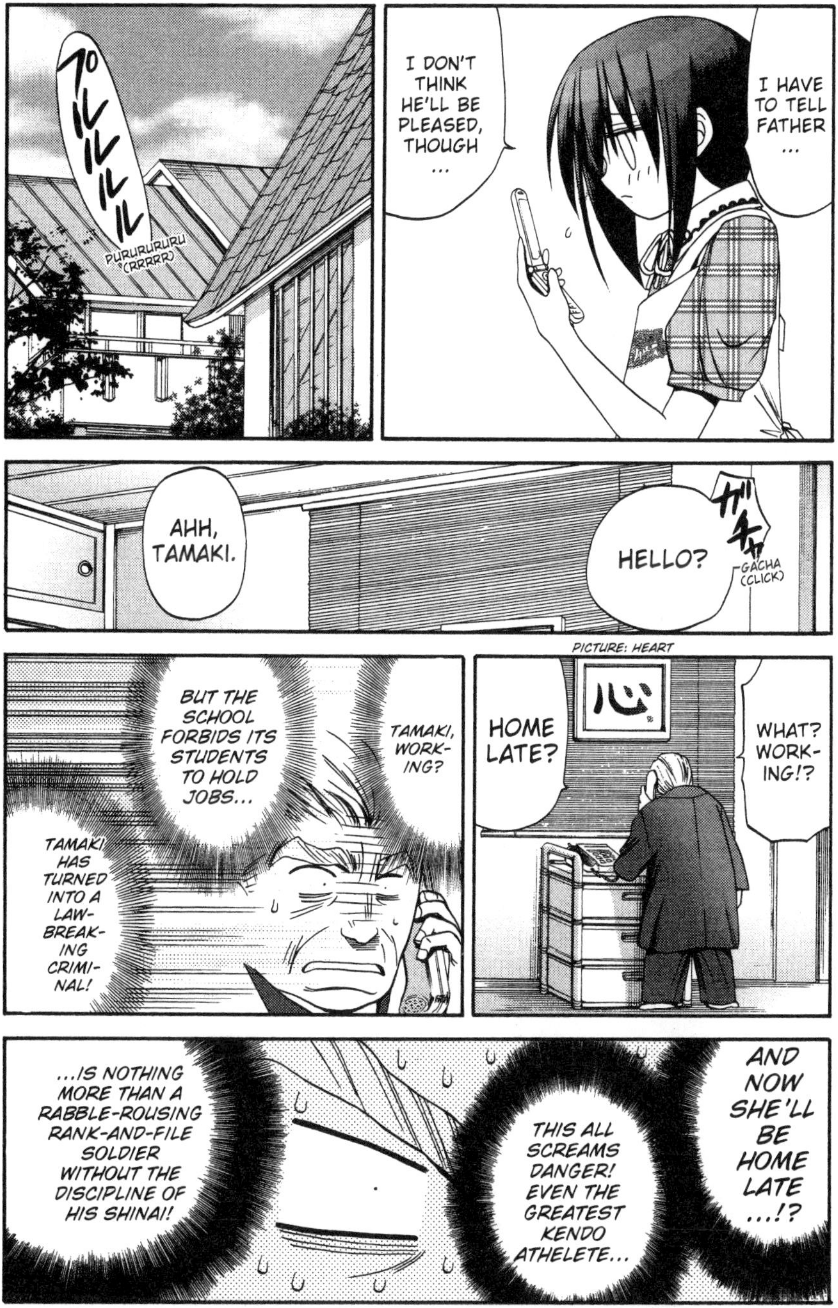
I HAVE TO TELL FATHER ...
I DON'T THINK HE'LL BE PLEASED, THOUGH ...
プルルルル
PURURURURU (RRRRR)
ガチャ
GACHA (CLICK)
HELLO?
AHH, TAMAKI.
PICTURE: HEART
心
WHAT? WORKING!?
HOME LATE?
TAMAKI, WORKING?
BUT THE SCHOOL FORBIDS ITS STUDENTS TO HOLD JOBS...
TAMAKI HAS TURNED INTO A LAW-BREAKING CRIMINAL!
AND NOW SHE'LL BE HOME LATE...!?
THIS ALL SCREAMS DANGER! EVEN THE GREATEST KENDO ATHELETE...
...IS NOTHING MORE THAN A RABBLE-ROUSING RANK-AND-FILE SOLDIER WITHOUT THE DISCIPLINE OF HIS SHINAI!

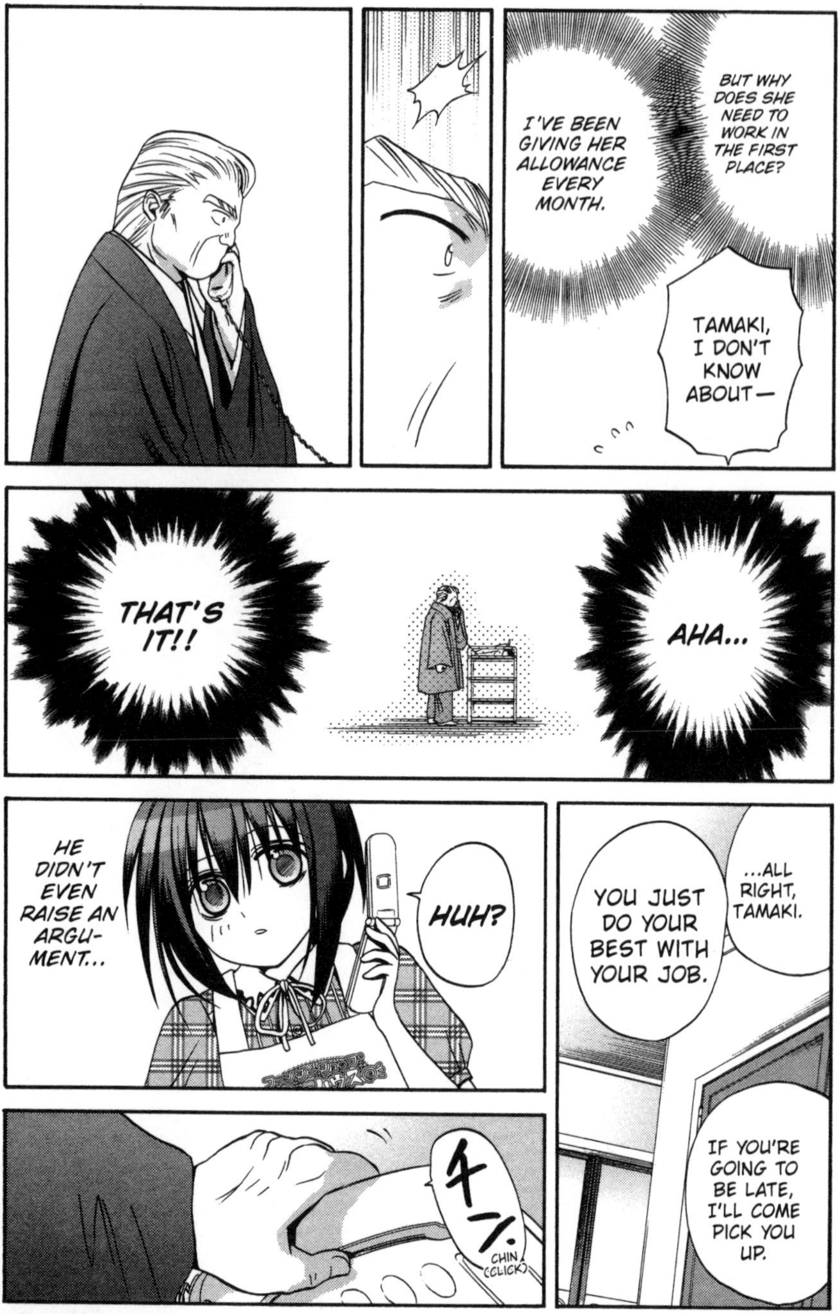
BUT WHY DOES SHE NEED TO WORK IN THE FIRST PLACE?
I'VE BEEN GIVING HER ALLOWANCE EVERY MONTH.
TAMAKI, I DON'T KNOW ABOUT—
AHA...
THAT'S IT!!
...ALL RIGHT, TAMAKI.
YOU JUST DO YOUR BEST WITH YOUR JOB.
IF YOU'RE GOING TO BE LATE, I'LL COME PICK YOU UP.
HUH?
HE DIDN'T EVEN RAISE AN ARGUMENT...
チン
CHIN (CLICK)

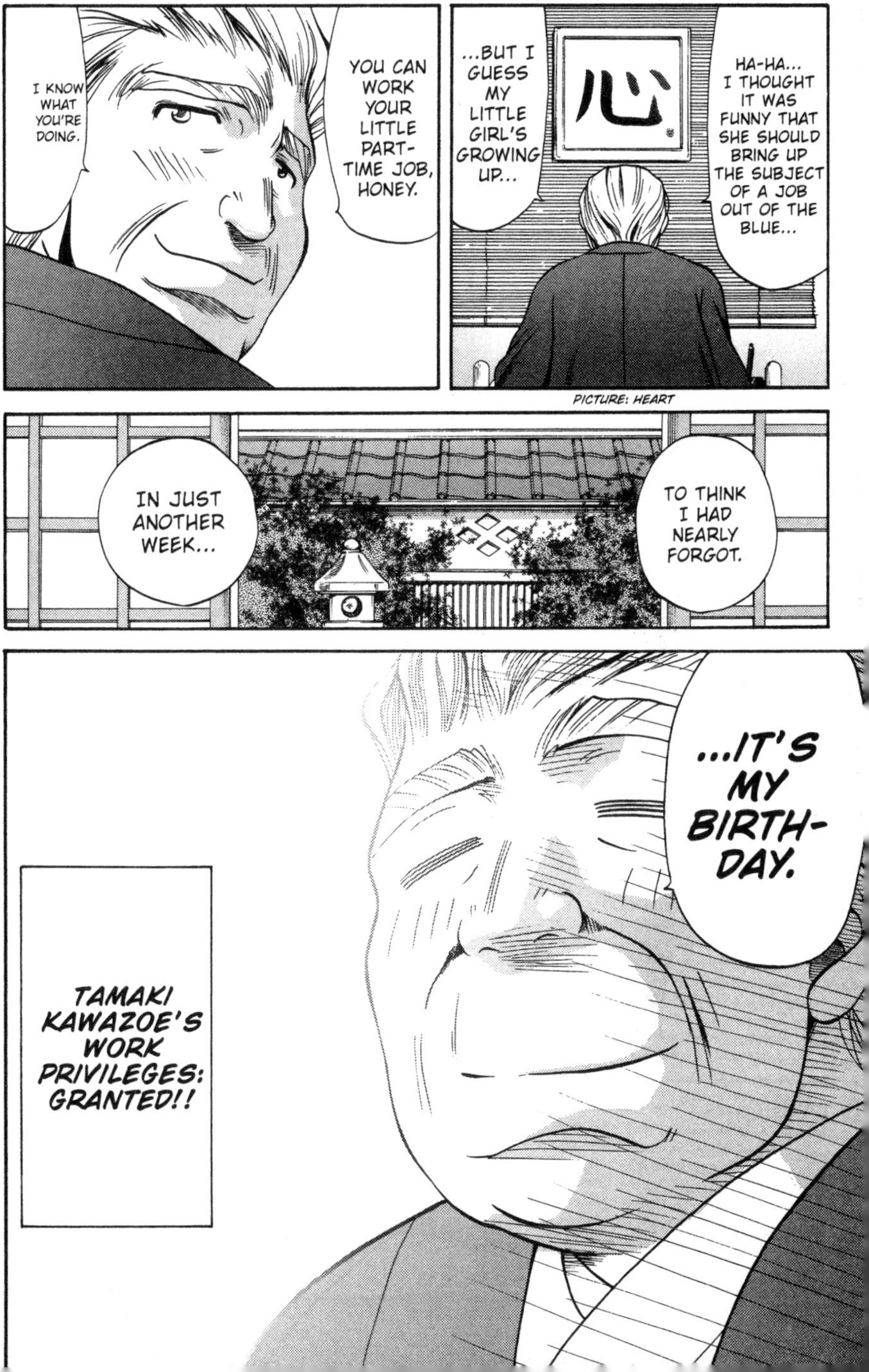
HA-HA... I THOUGHT IT WAS FUNNY THAT SHE SHOULD BRING UP THE SUBJECT OF A JOB OUT OF THE BLUE...
...BUT I GUESS MY LITTLE GIRL'S GROWING UP...
心
PICTURE: HEART
YOU CAN WORK YOUR LITTLE PART-TIME JOB, HONEY.
I KNOW WHAT YOU'RE DOING.
TO THINK I HAD NEARLY FORGOT.
IN JUST ANOTHER WEEK...
...IT'S MY BIRTH-DAY.
TAMAKI KAWAZOE'S WORK PRIVILEGES: GRANTED!!

BAMBOO BLADE

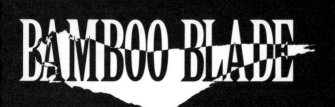

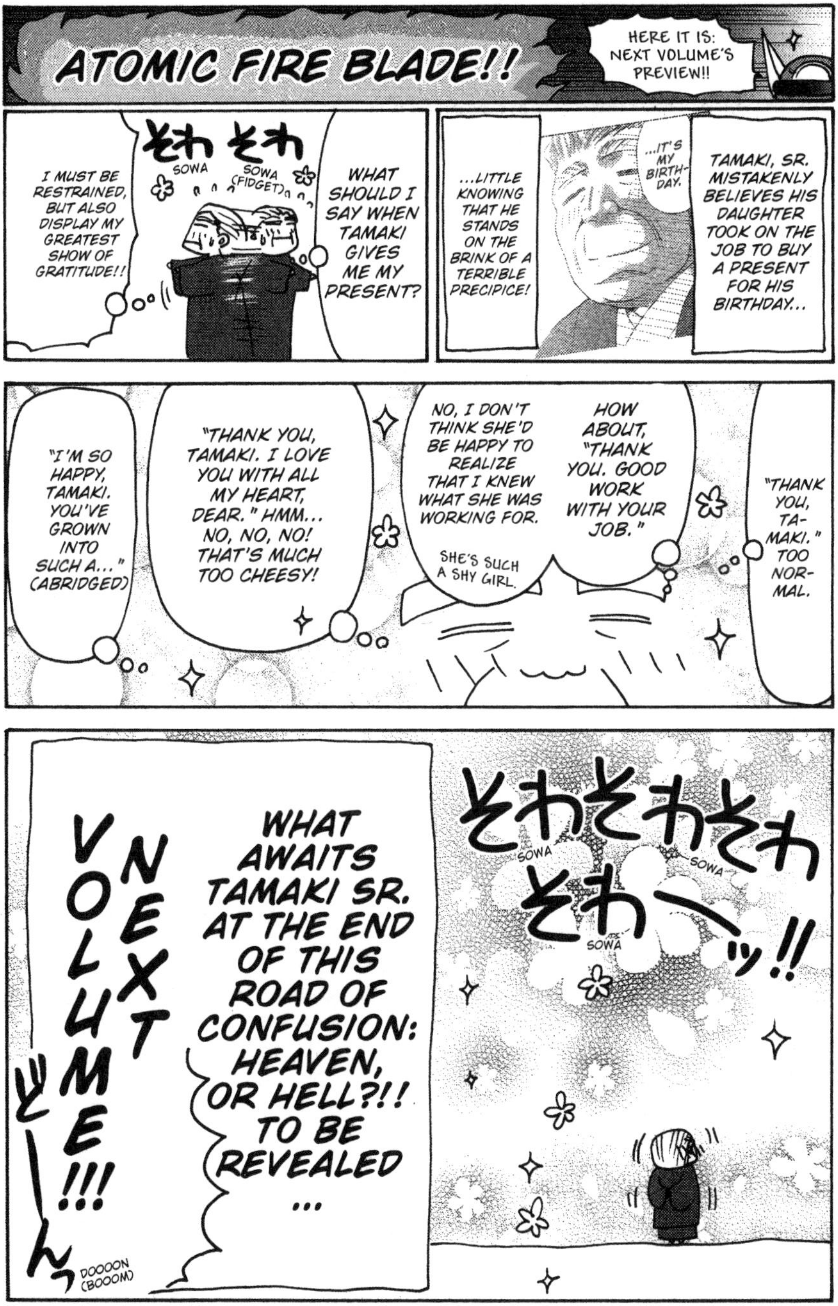
HERE IT IS: NEXT VOLUME'S PREVIEW!!
ATOMIC FIRE BLADE!!
TAMAKI, SR. MISTAKENLY BELIEVES HIS DAUGHTER TOOK ON THE JOB TO BUY A PRESENT FOR HIS BIRTHDAY...
...IT'S MY BIRTH-DAY.
...LITTLE KNOWING THAT HE STANDS ON THE BRINK OF A TERRIBLE PRECIPICE!
WHAT SHOULD I SAY WHEN TAMAKI GIVES ME MY PRESENT?
そわ そわ
SOWA SOWA (FIDGET)
I MUST BE RESTRAINED, BUT ALSO DISPLAY MY GREATEST SHOW OF GRATITUDE!!
"THANK YOU, TA-MAKI." TOO NOR-MAL.
HOW ABOUT, "THANK YOU. GOOD WORK WITH YOUR JOB."
NO, I DON'T THINK SHE'D BE HAPPY TO REALIZE THAT I KNEW WHAT SHE WAS WORKING FOR.
SHE'S SUCH A SHY GIRL.
"THANK YOU, TAMAKI. I LOVE YOU WITH ALL MY HEART, DEAR." HMM... NO, NO, NO! THAT'S MUCH TOO CHEESY!
"I'M SO HAPPY, TAMAKI. YOU'VE GROWN INTO SUCH A..." (ABRIDGED)
そわそわそわそわーッ!!
SOWA SOWA SOWA
WHAT AWAITS TAMAKI SR. AT THE END OF THIS ROAD OF CONFUSION: HEAVEN, OR HELL?!! TO BE REVEALED ...
NEXT VOLUME!!!
どーんっ
DOOOON (BOOOM)

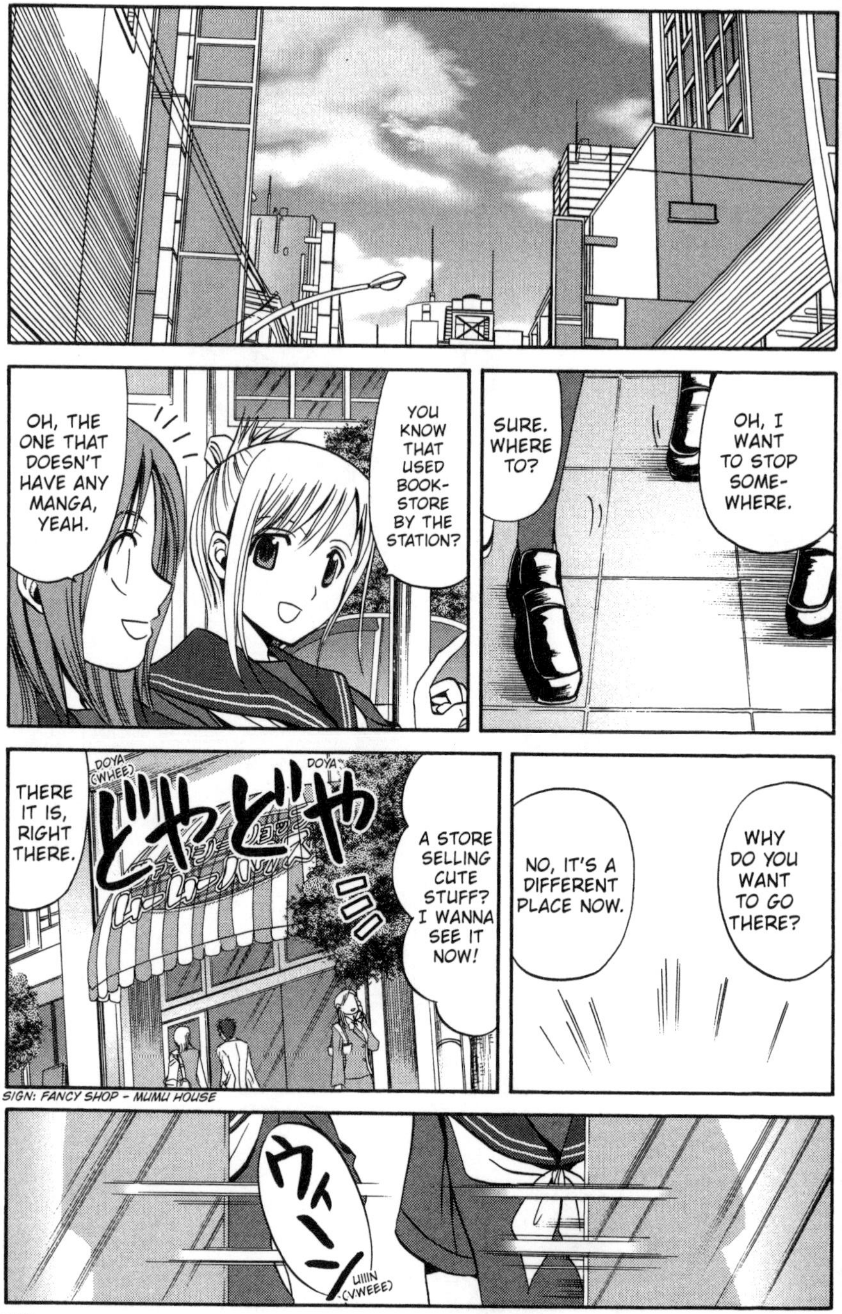
OH, I WANT TO STOP SOME-WHERE.
SURE. WHERE TO?
YOU KNOW THAT USED BOOK-STORE BY THE STATION?
OH, THE ONE THAT DOESN'T HAVE ANY MANGA, YEAH.
WHY DO YOU WANT TO GO THERE?
NO, IT'S A DIFFERENT PLACE NOW.
DOYA (WHEE) DOYA
THERE IT IS, RIGHT THERE.
A STORE SELLING CUTE STUFF? I WANNA SEE IT NOW!
UIIIN (V:WEEE)
SIGN: FANCY SHOP - MUMU HOUSE

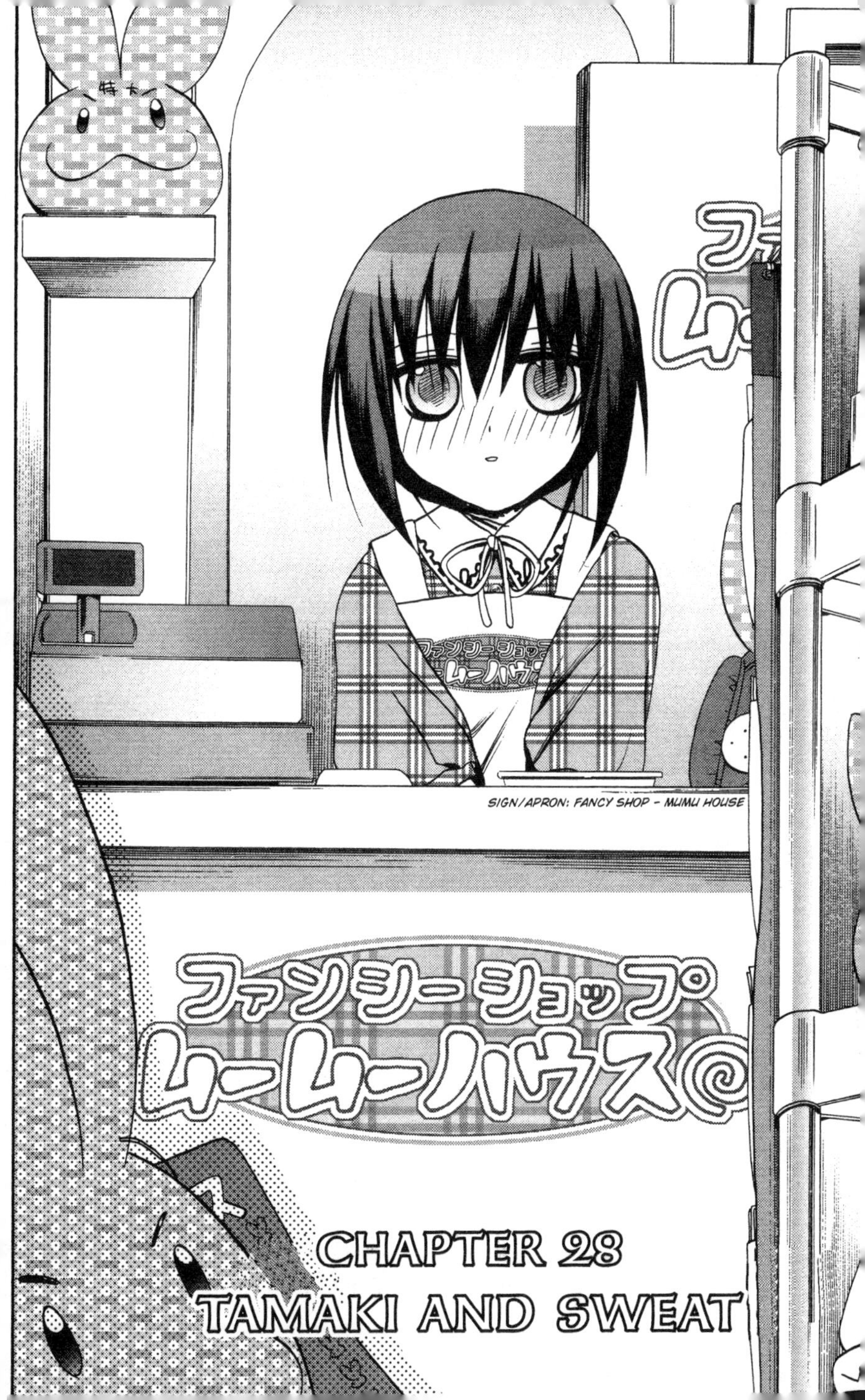
SIGN/APRON: FANCY SHOP - MUMU HOUSE
ファンシーショップ
ムームーハウス@
CHAPTER 28
TAMAKI AND SWEAT

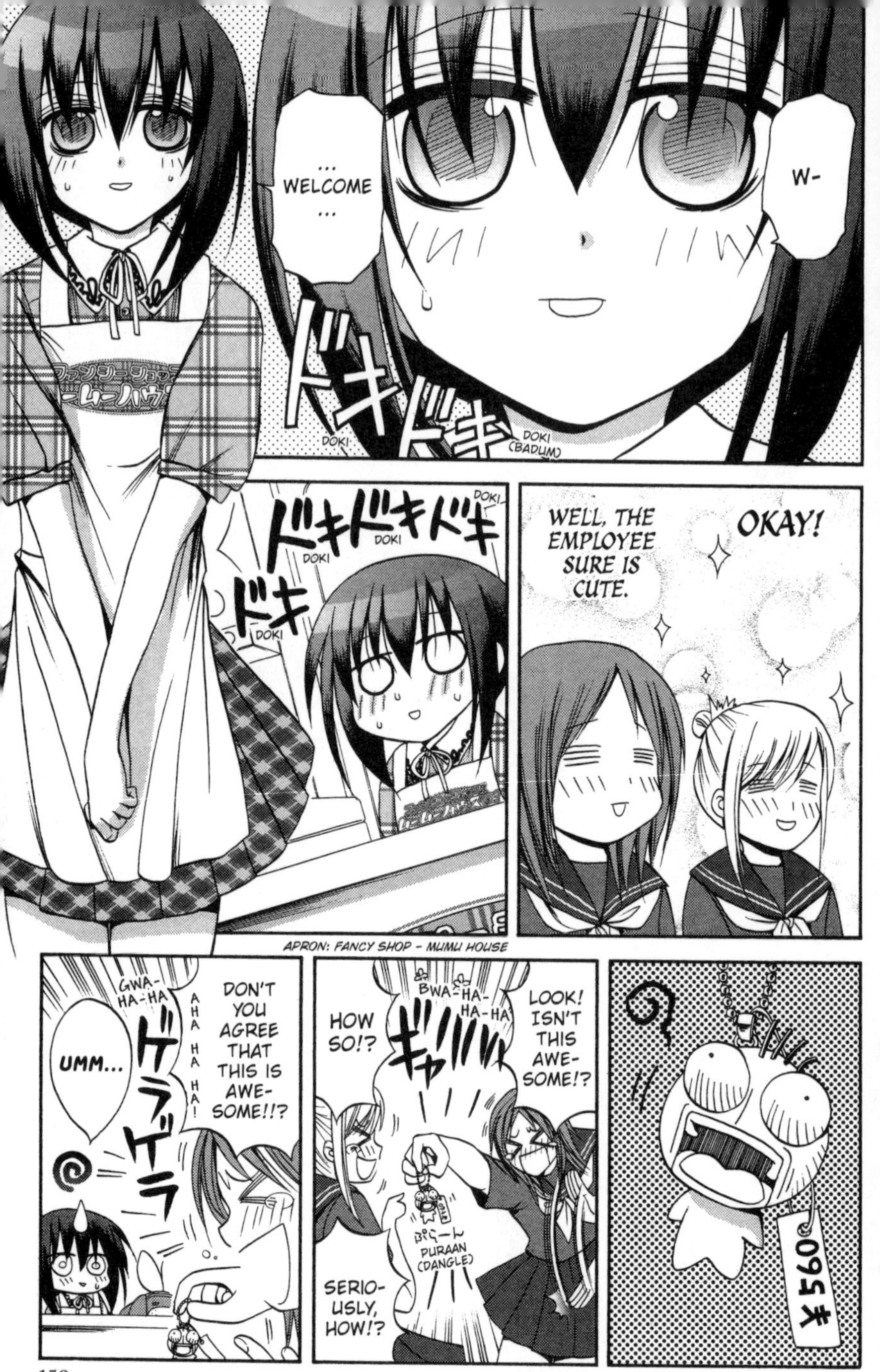
W-
... WELCOME ...
ドキドキ
DOKI
DOKI (BADUM)
OKAY!
WELL, THE EMPLOYEE SURE IS CUTE.
ドキドキドキ
DOKI
DOKI
DOKI
ドキ
DOKI
APRON: FANCY SHOP - MUMU HOUSE
LOOK! ISN'T THIS AWE-SOME!?
BWA-HA-HA-HA
HOW SO!?
ぷら〜ん
PURAAN (DANGLE)
SERIO-USLY, HOW!?
DON'T YOU AGREE THAT THIS IS AWE-SOME!!?
AHA HA HA!
GWA-HA-HA
ゲラゲラ
UMM...

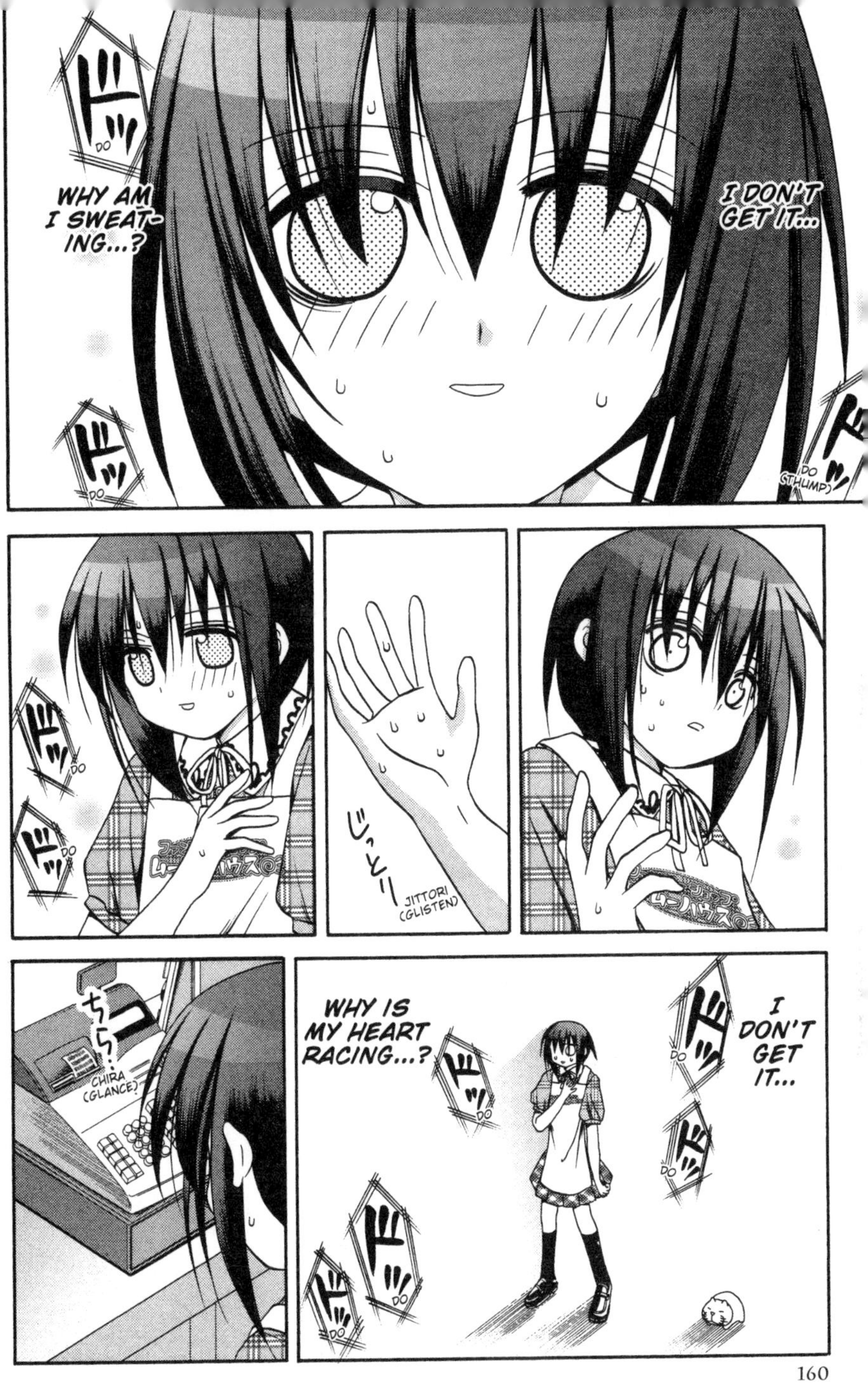
I DON'T GET IT...
ドッ
DO (THUMP)
ドッ
DO
WHY AM I SWEAT-ING...?
ドッ
DO
じっとり
JITTORI (GLISTEN)
ドッ
DO
ドッ
DO
ド
DO
I DON'T GET IT...
ド
DO
WHY IS MY HEART RACING...?
ドッ
DO
ドッ
DO
ドッ
DO
ちら…
CHIRA (GLANCE)

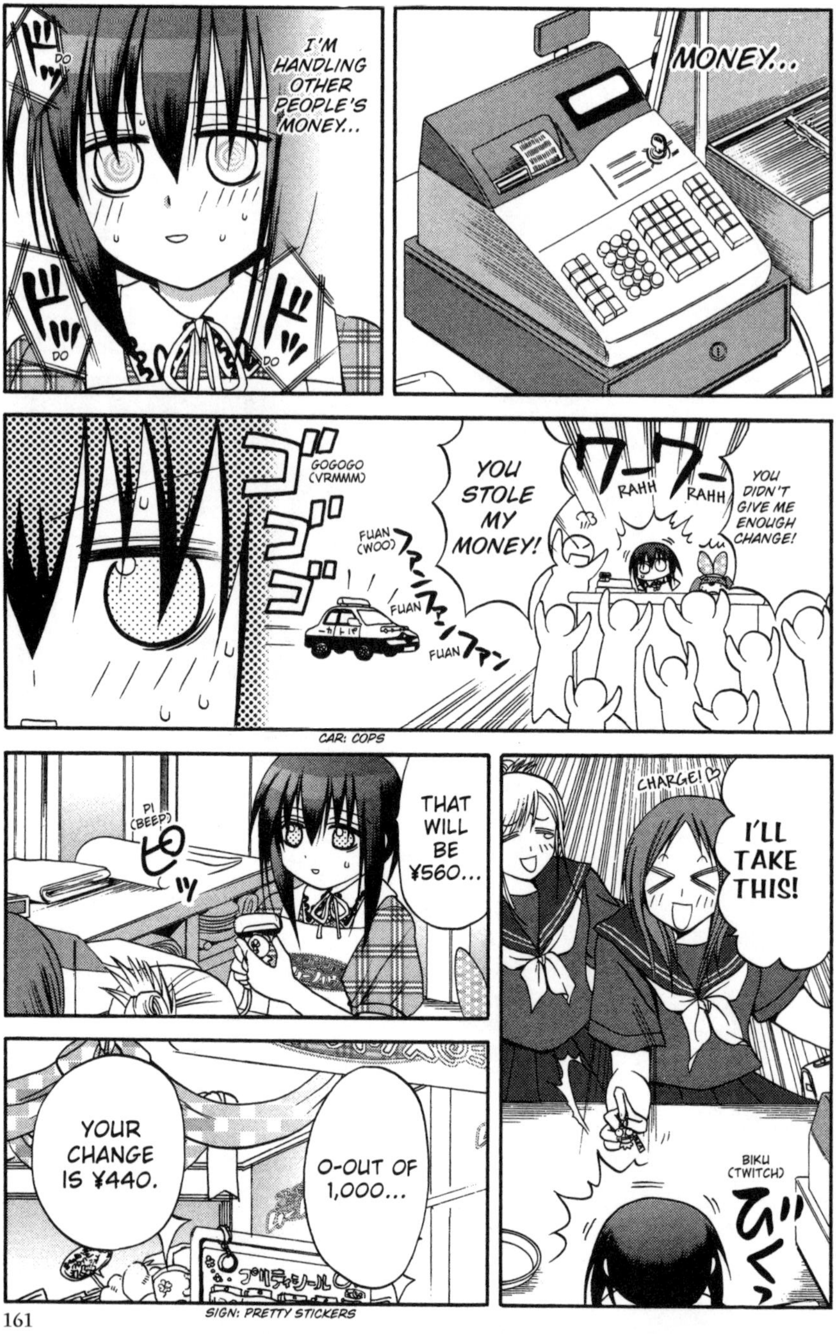
MONEY...
DO
I'M HANDLING OTHER PEOPLE'S MONEY...
DO
DO
YOU DIDN'T GIVE ME ENOUGH CHANGE!
RAHH
RAHH
YOU STOLE MY MONEY!
FUAN (WOO)
FUAN
FUAN
GOGOGO (VRMMM)
CAR: COPS
CHARGE!♡
I'LL TAKE THIS!
BIKU (TWITCH)
THAT WILL BE ¥560...
PI (BEEP)
O-OUT OF 1,000...
YOUR CHANGE IS ¥440.
SIGN: PRETTY STICKERS

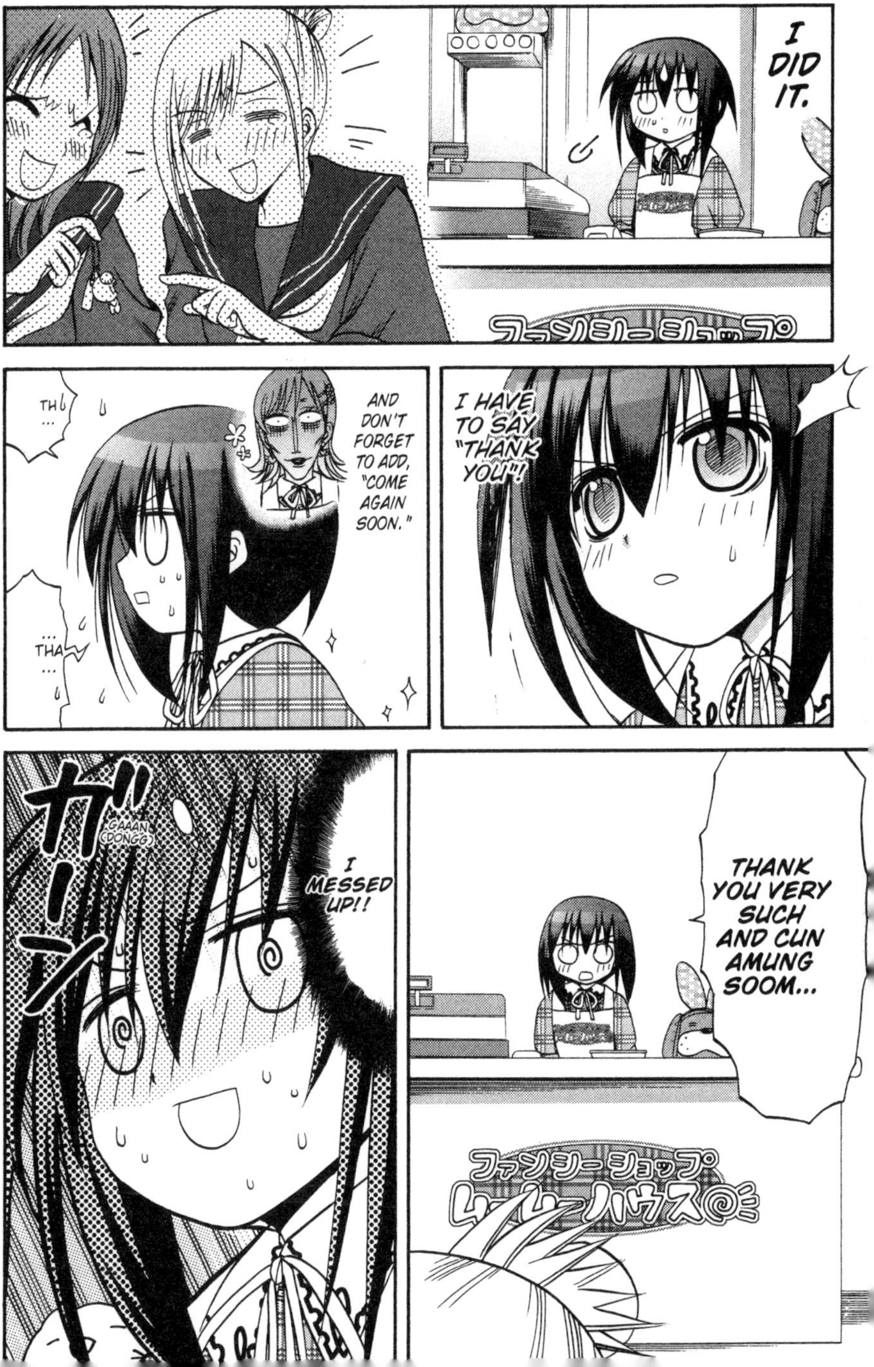
I DID IT.
I HAVE TO SAY "THANK YOU"!
AND DON'T FORGET TO ADD, "COME AGAIN SOON."
TH ...
... THA ...
THANK YOU VERY SUCH AND CUN AMUNG SOOM...
ファンシーショップ
ムームーハウス
I MESSED UP!!
ガーン
GAAAN (DONGG)

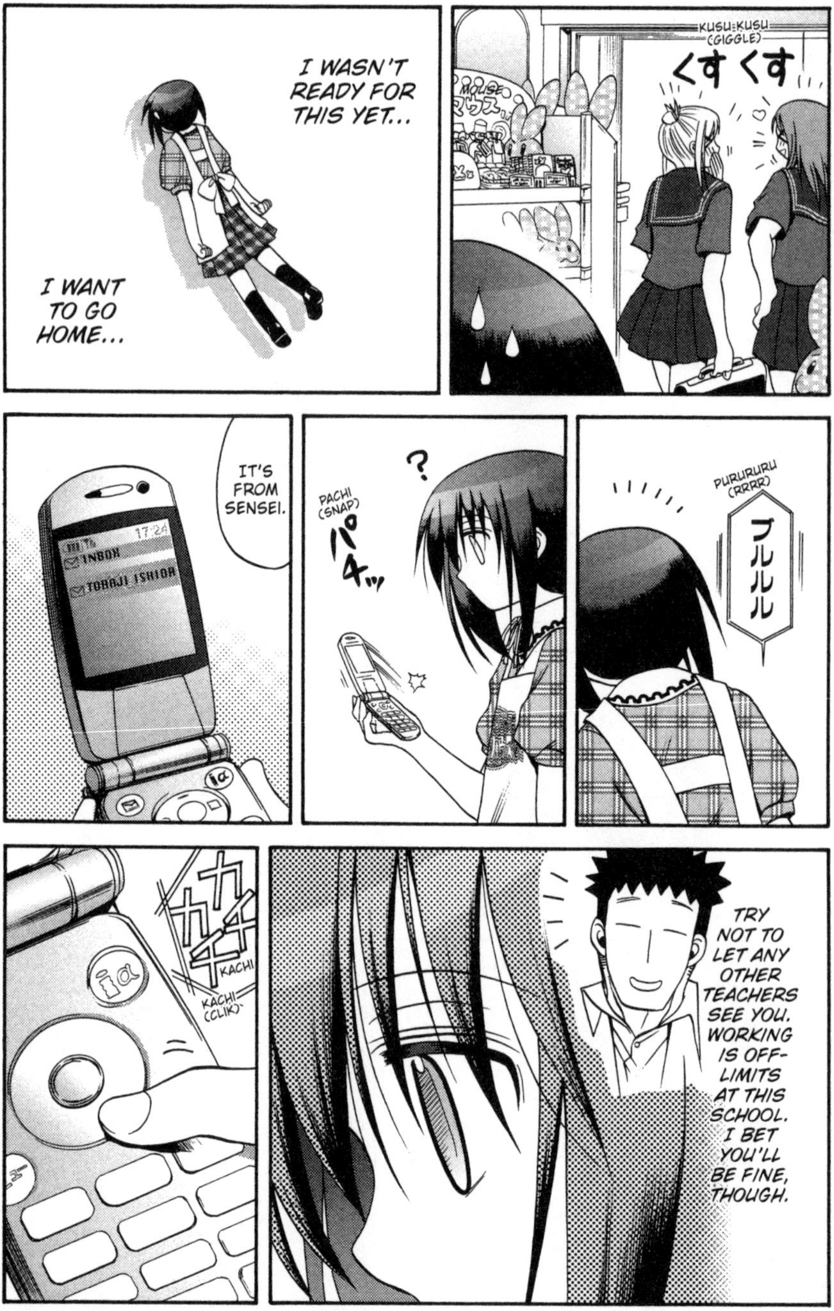
KUSU KUSU (GIGGLE)
くすくす
MOUSE
マウス
I WASN'T READY FOR THIS YET...
I WANT TO GO HOME...
PURURURU (RRRR)
ブルルル
?
PACHI (SNAP)
パチッ
IT'S FROM SENSEI.
17:24
INBOX
TRY NOT TO LET ANY OTHER TEACHERS SEE YOU. WORKING IS OFF-LIMITS AT THIS SCHOOL. I BET YOU'LL BE FINE, THOUGH.
カチカチ
KACHI KACHI (CLIK)

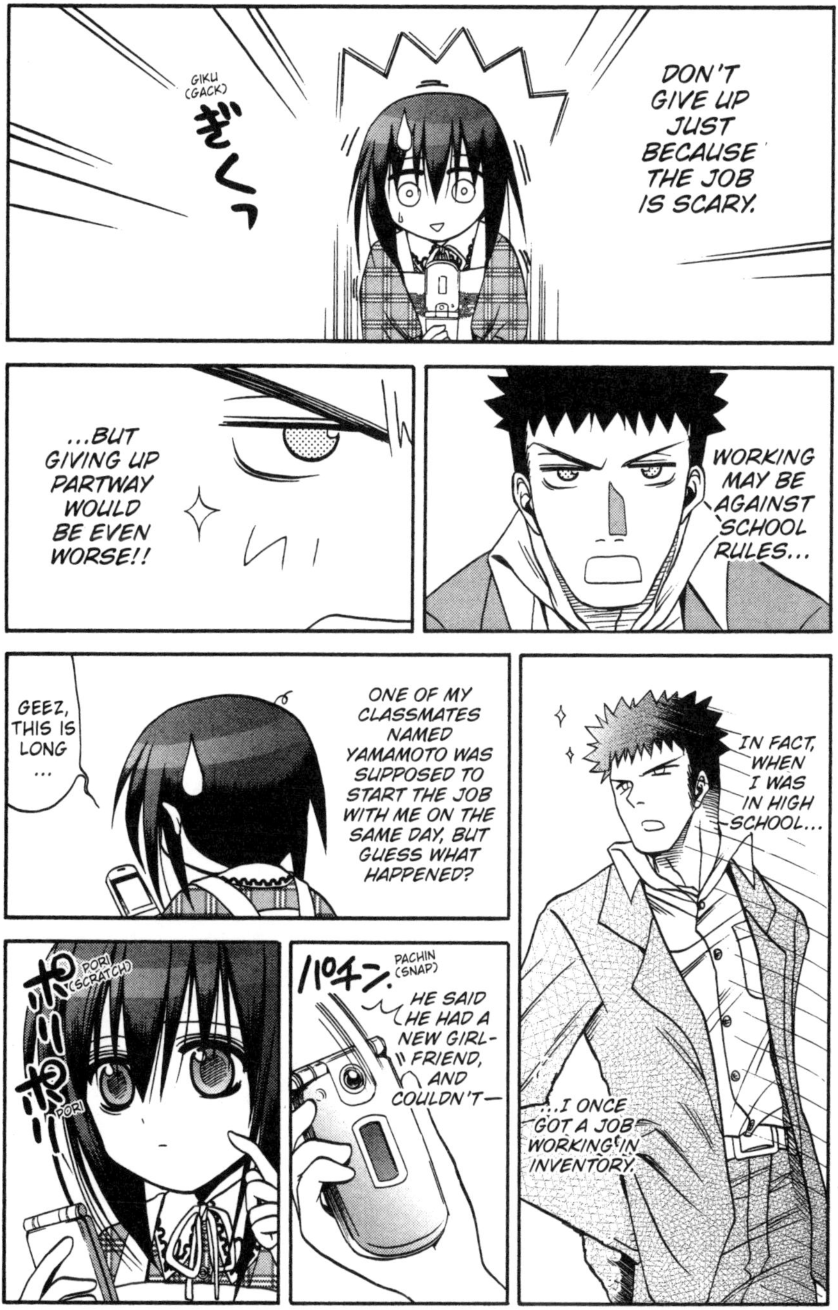
DON'T GIVE UP JUST BECAUSE THE JOB IS SCARY.
GIKU (GACK)
ぎくっ
WORKING MAY BE AGAINST SCHOOL RULES...
...BUT GIVING UP PARTWAY WOULD BE EVEN WORSE!!
IN FACT, WHEN I WAS IN HIGH SCHOOL...
...I ONCE GOT A JOB WORKING IN INVENTORY.
ONE OF MY CLASSMATES NAMED YAMAMOTO WAS SUPPOSED TO START THE JOB WITH ME ON THE SAME DAY, BUT GUESS WHAT HAPPENED?
GEEZ, THIS IS LONG ...
PACHIN (SNAP)
パチン
HE SAID HE HAD A NEW GIRL-FRIEND, AND COULDN'T—
PORI (SCRATCH)
PORI
ポリポリ

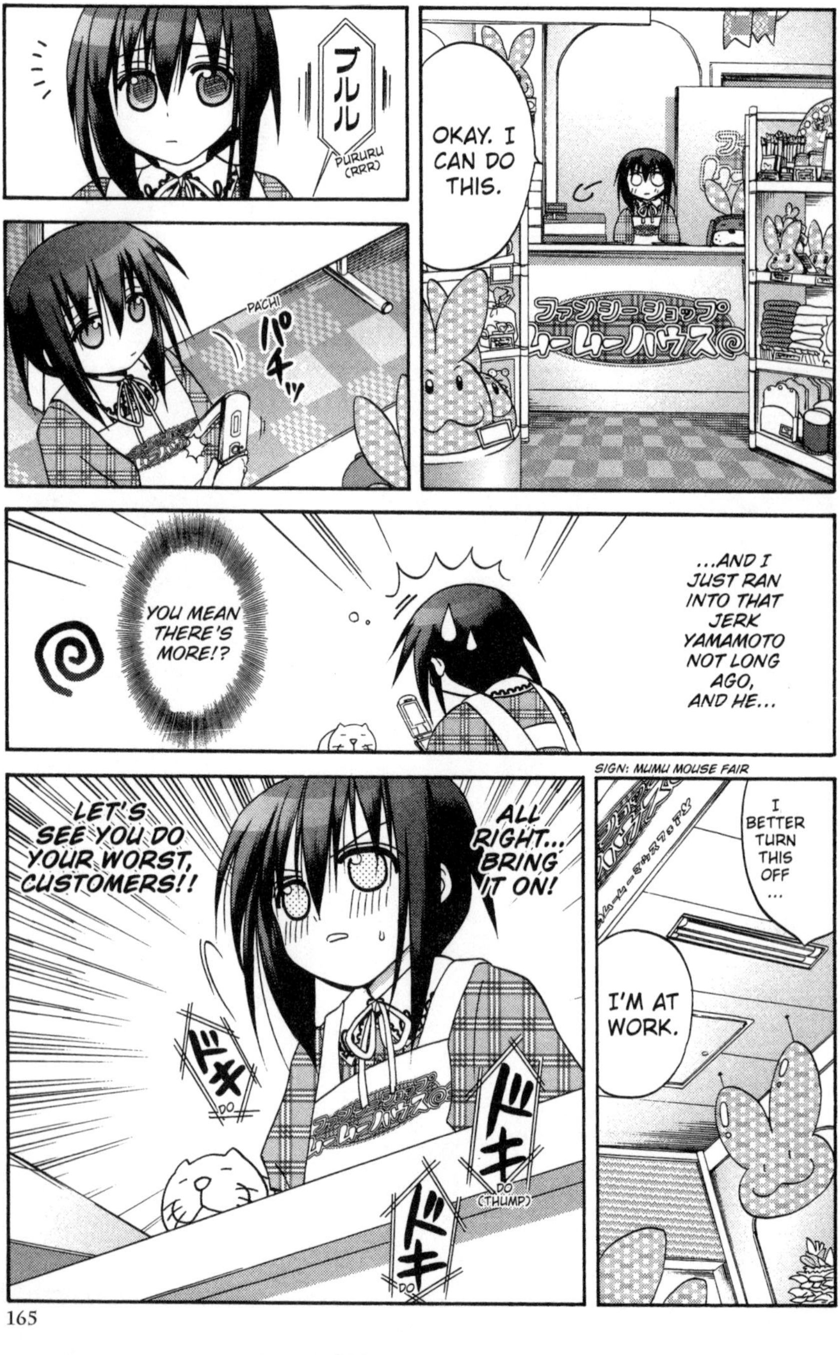
OKAY. I CAN DO THIS.
ファンシーショップ ムームーハウス
ブルル
PURURU (RRR)
パチッ
PACHI
...AND I JUST RAN INTO THAT JERK YAMAMOTO NOT LONG AGO, AND HE...
YOU MEAN THERE'S MORE!?
SIGN: MUMU MOUSE FAIR
I BETTER TURN THIS OFF...
I'M AT WORK.
ALL RIGHT... BRING IT ON!
LET'S SEE YOU DO YOUR WORST, CUSTOMERS!!
ドキ
DO (THUMP)
ドキ
DO
ドキ
DO

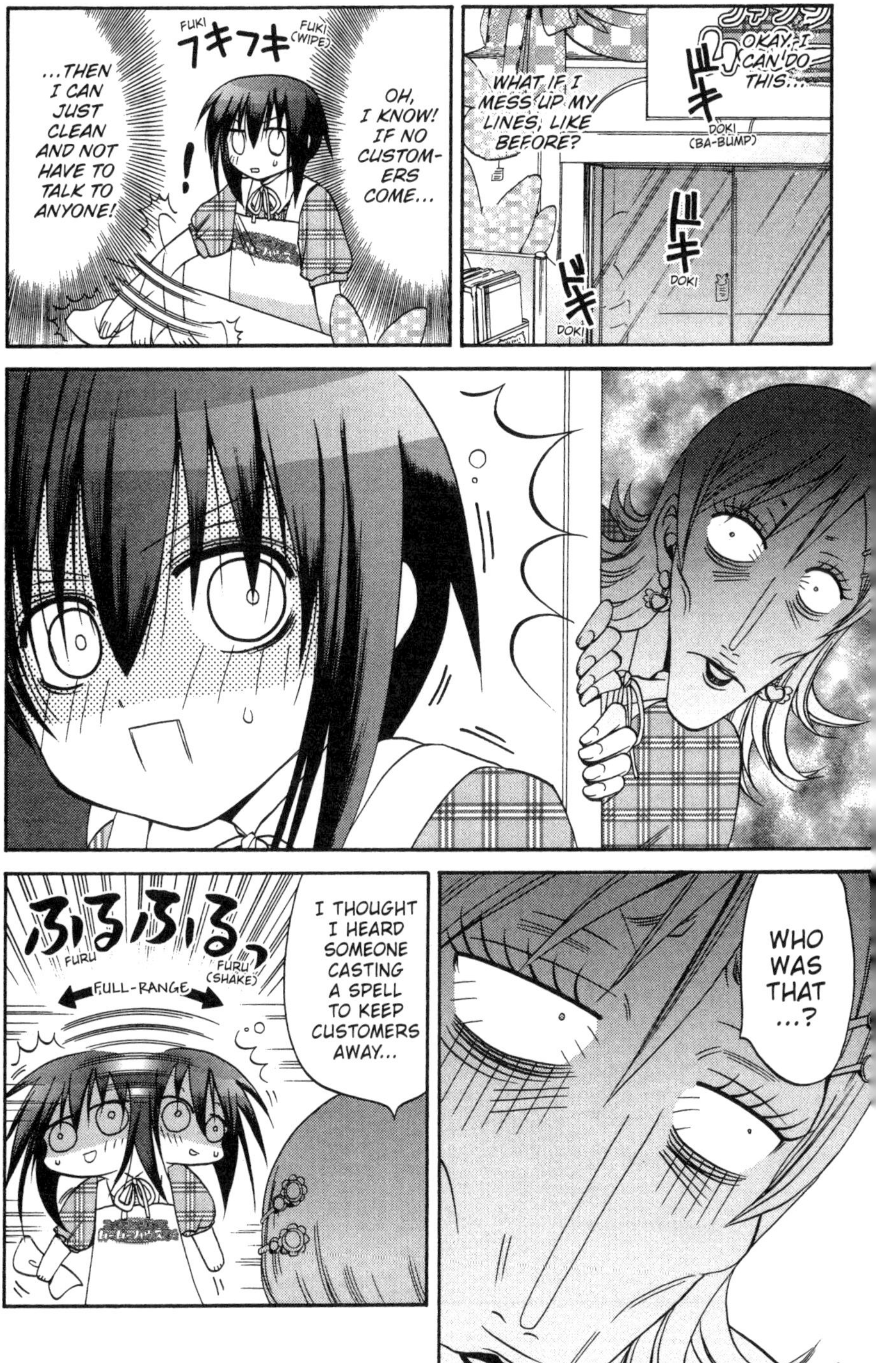
OKAY, I CAN DO THIS...
WHAT IF I MESS UP MY LINES, LIKE BEFORE?
ドキ
DOKI (BA-BUMP)
ドキ
DOKI
ドキ
DOKI
OH, I KNOW! IF NO CUSTOMERS COME...
...THEN I CAN JUST CLEAN AND NOT HAVE TO TALK TO ANYONE!
フキフキ
FUKI FUKI (WIPE)
!
WHO WAS THAT ...?
I THOUGHT I HEARD SOMEONE CASTING A SPELL TO KEEP CUSTOMERS AWAY...
ふるふるっ
FURU FURU (SHAKE)
FULL-RANGE

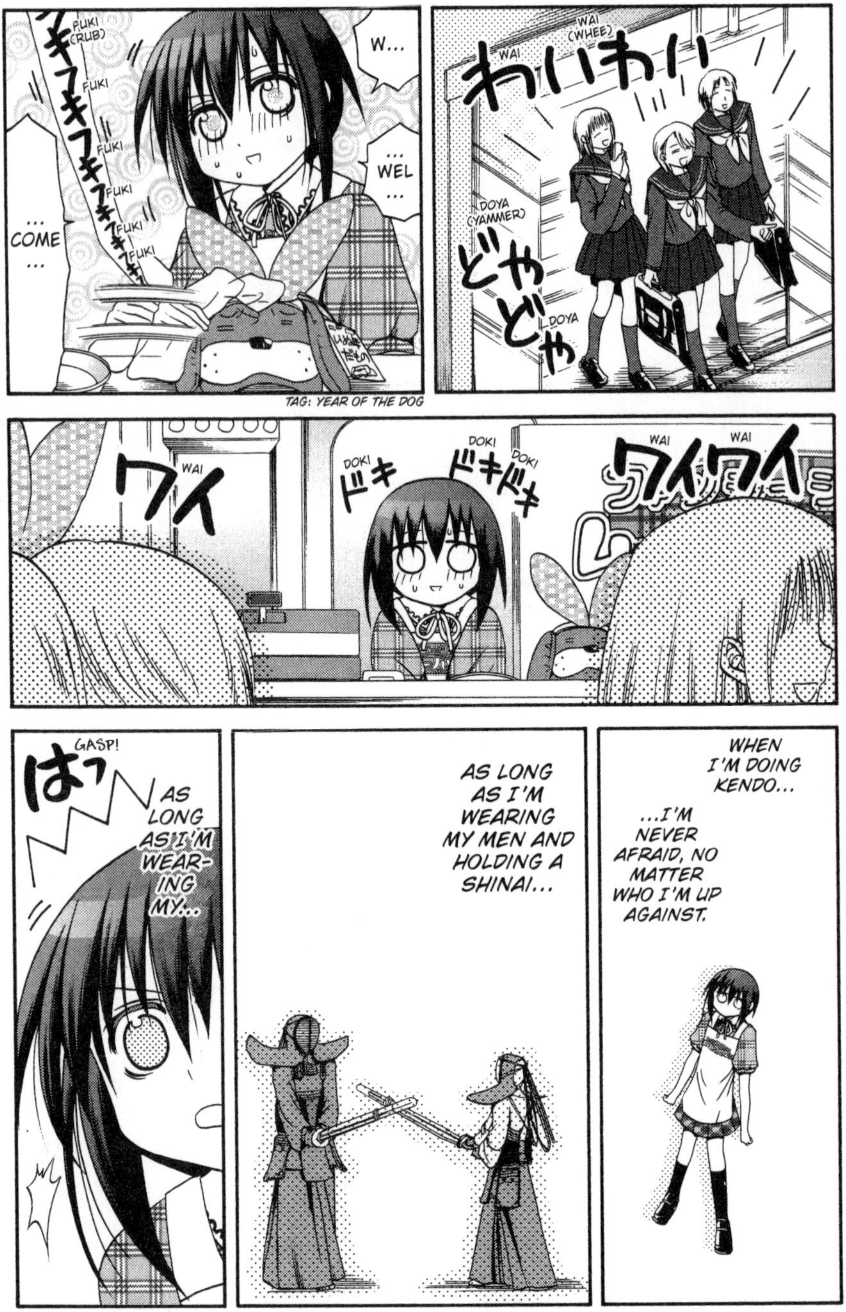
わいわい
WAI
WAI (WHEE)
どやどや
DOYA (YAMMER)
DOYA
W...
...WEL...
...COME...
FUKI (RUB)
FUKI
FUKI
FUKI
FUKI
FUKI
TAG: YEAR OF THE DOG
ワイワイ
WAI
WAI
ドキドキ
DOKI
DOKI
ドキ
DOKI
ワイ
WAI
WHEN I'M DOING KENDO...
...I'M NEVER AFRAID, NO MATTER WHO I'M UP AGAINST.
AS LONG AS I'M WEARING MY MEN AND HOLDING A SHINAI...
はっ
GASP!
AS LONG AS I'M WEAR-ING MY...

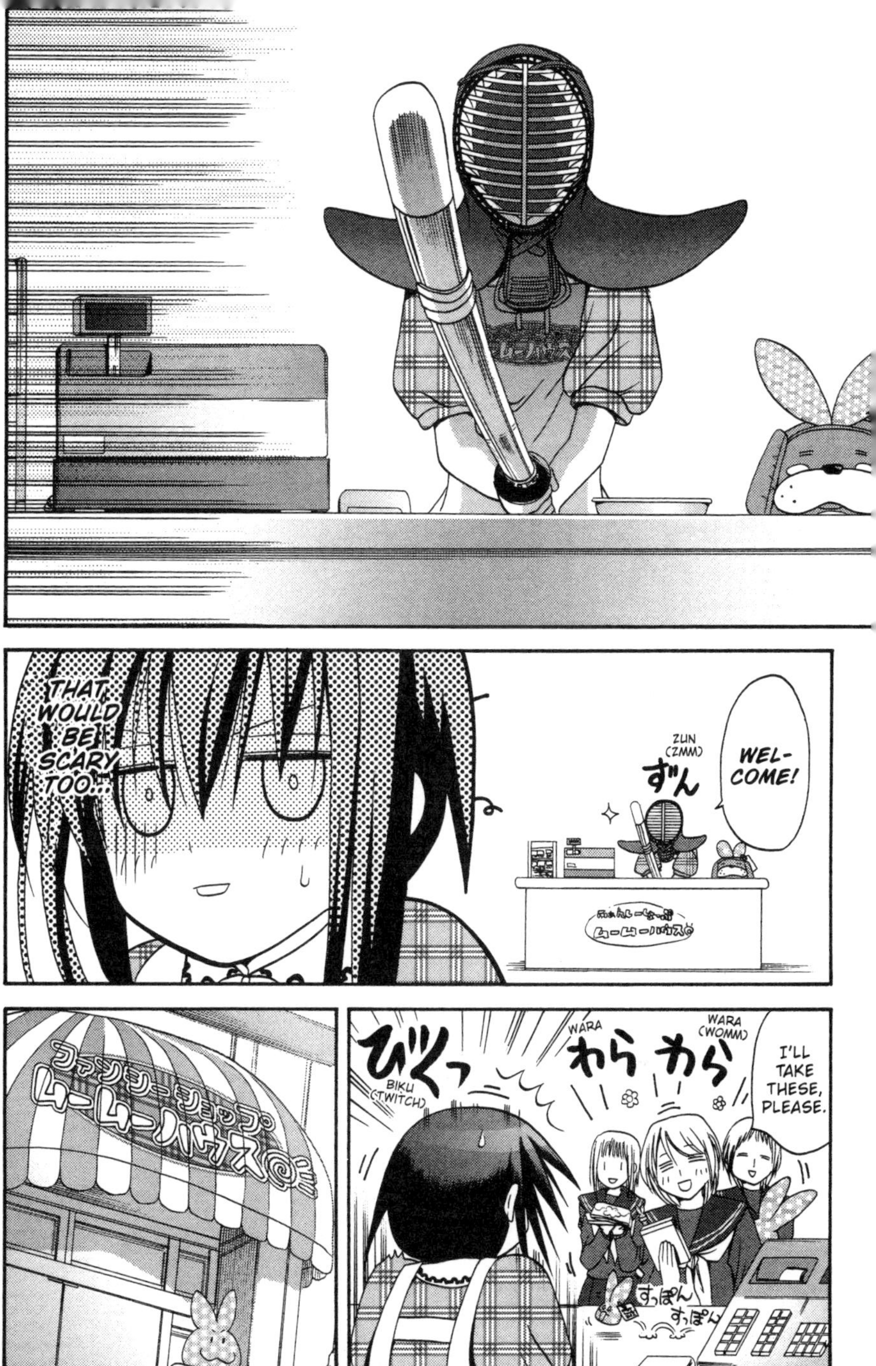
WEL-COME!
ZUN (ZMMM)
ずん
THAT WOULD BE SCARY TOO...
I'LL TAKE THESE, PLEASE.
WARA (WOMM)
わら
WARA
わら
びくっ
BIKU (TWITCH)
すっぽん
すっぽん
ファンシーショップ
ムームーハウス

SFX: SUPPON (PLOP) SUPPON

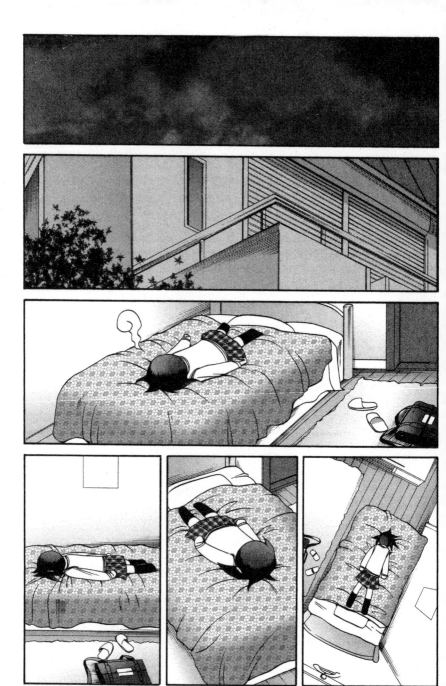

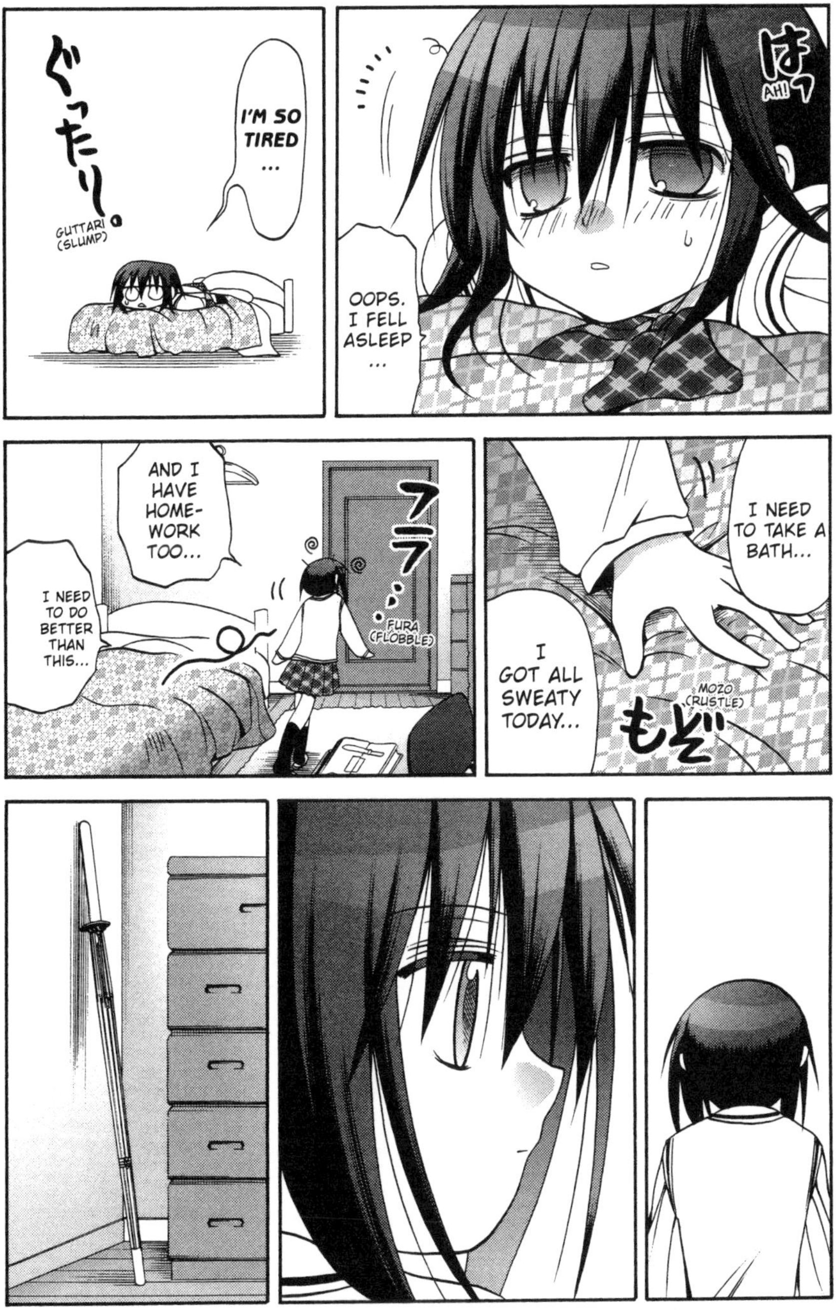
はっ
AH!
OOPS. I FELL ASLEEP ...
I'M SO TIRED ...
ぐったり。
GUTTARI (SLUMP)
I NEED TO TAKE A BATH...
I GOT ALL SWEATY TODAY...
もぞ
MOZO (RUSTLE)
AND I HAVE HOME-WORK TOO...
I NEED TO DO BETTER THAN THIS...
フラ
FURA (FLOBBLE)

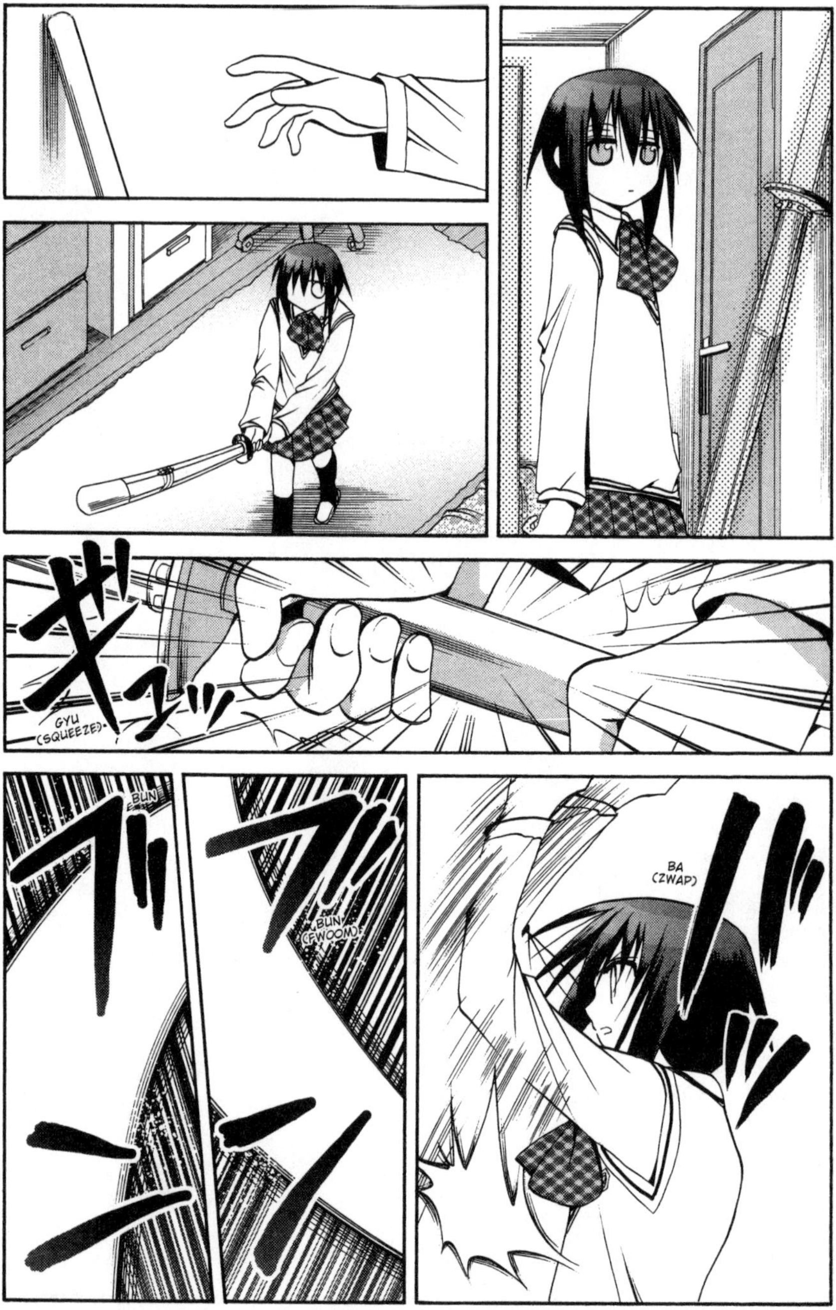
GYU (SQUEEZE)
BA (ZWAP)
BUN (FWOOM)
BUN

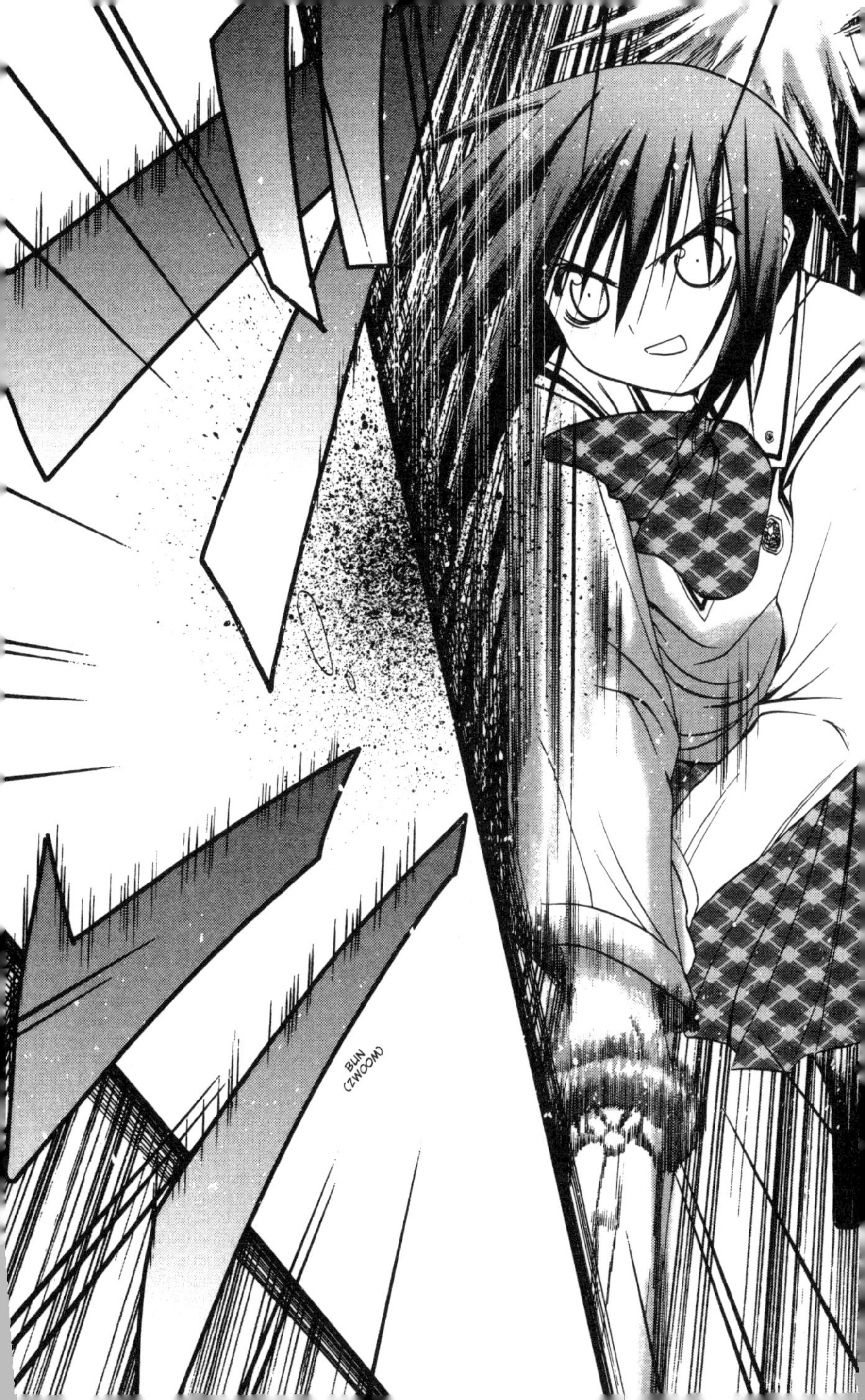
BUN
(ZWOOM)

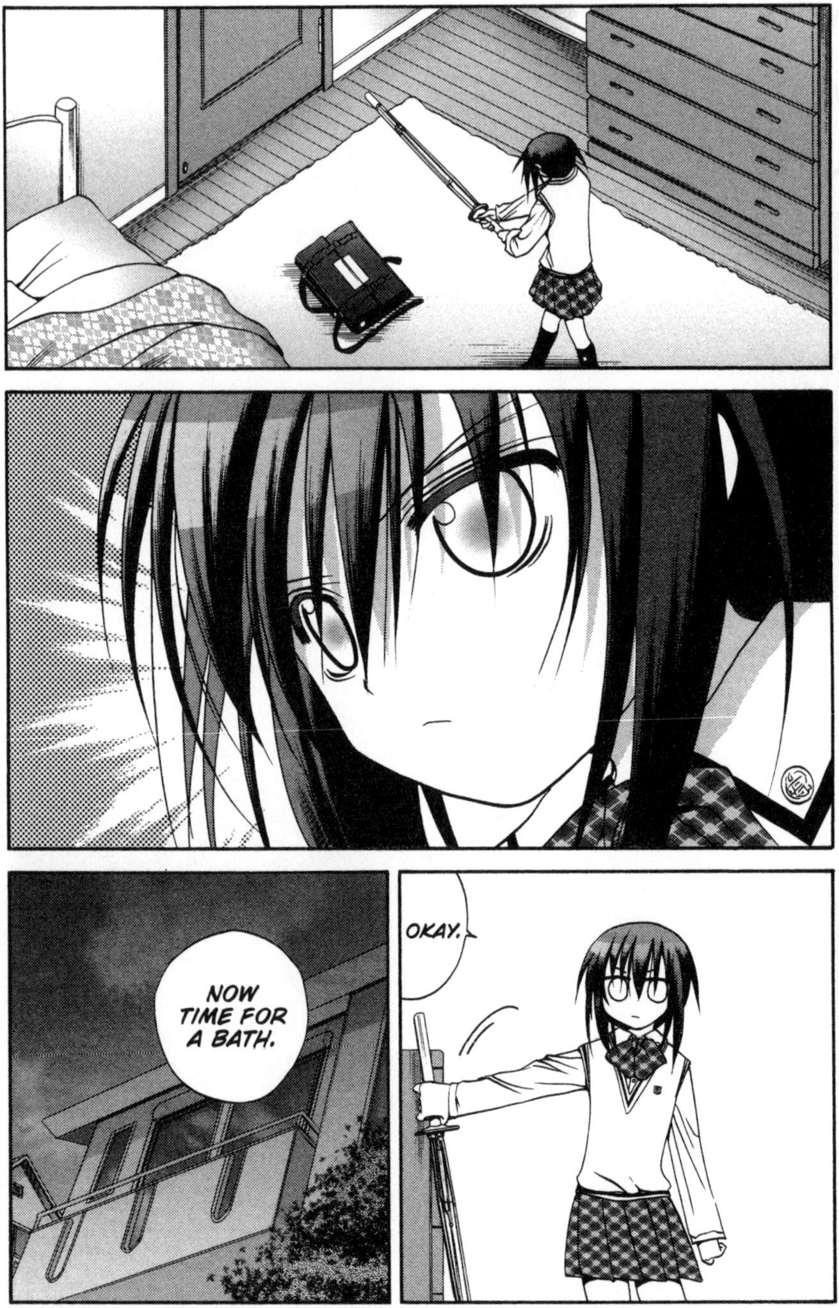
OKAY.
NOW TIME FOR A BATH.

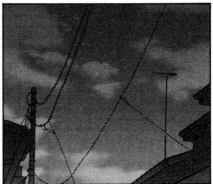

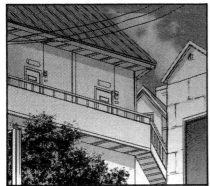

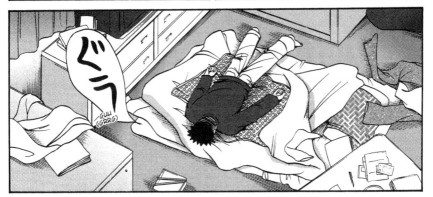

GULU
(GRRG)

OH
...

CRAP,
I FELL
ASLEEP.

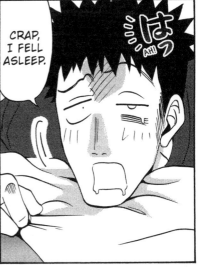

(AH)

I LEFT
THE HOT
WATER IN
MY INSTANT
NOODLES...

DAMN
...

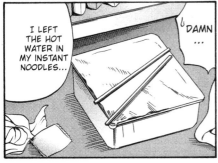

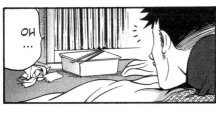

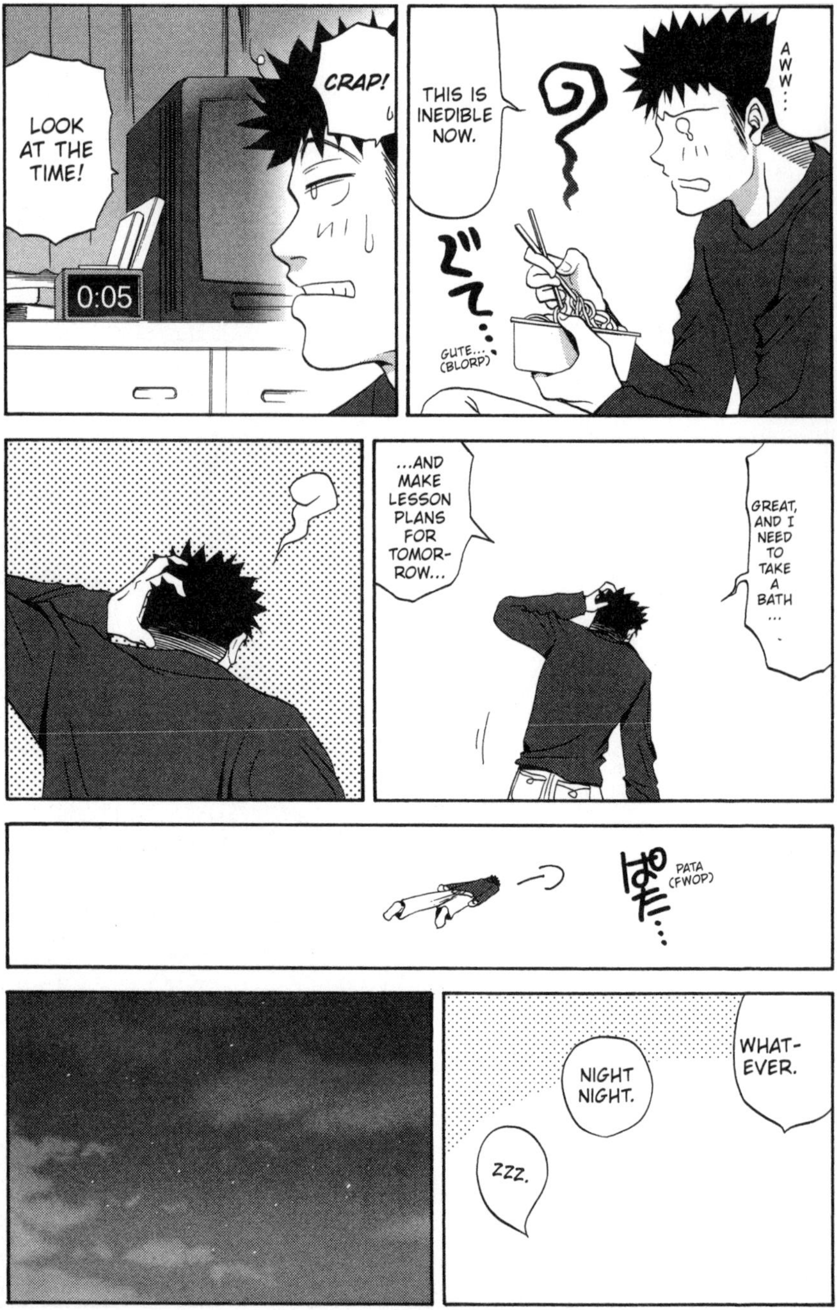
AWW...
THIS IS INEDIBLE NOW.
GUTE... (BLORP)
CRAP!
LOOK AT THE TIME!
0:05
GREAT, AND I NEED TO TAKE A BATH...
...AND MAKE LESSON PLANS FOR TOMORROW...
PATA (FWOP)
WHAT-EVER.
NIGHT NIGHT.
ZZZ.

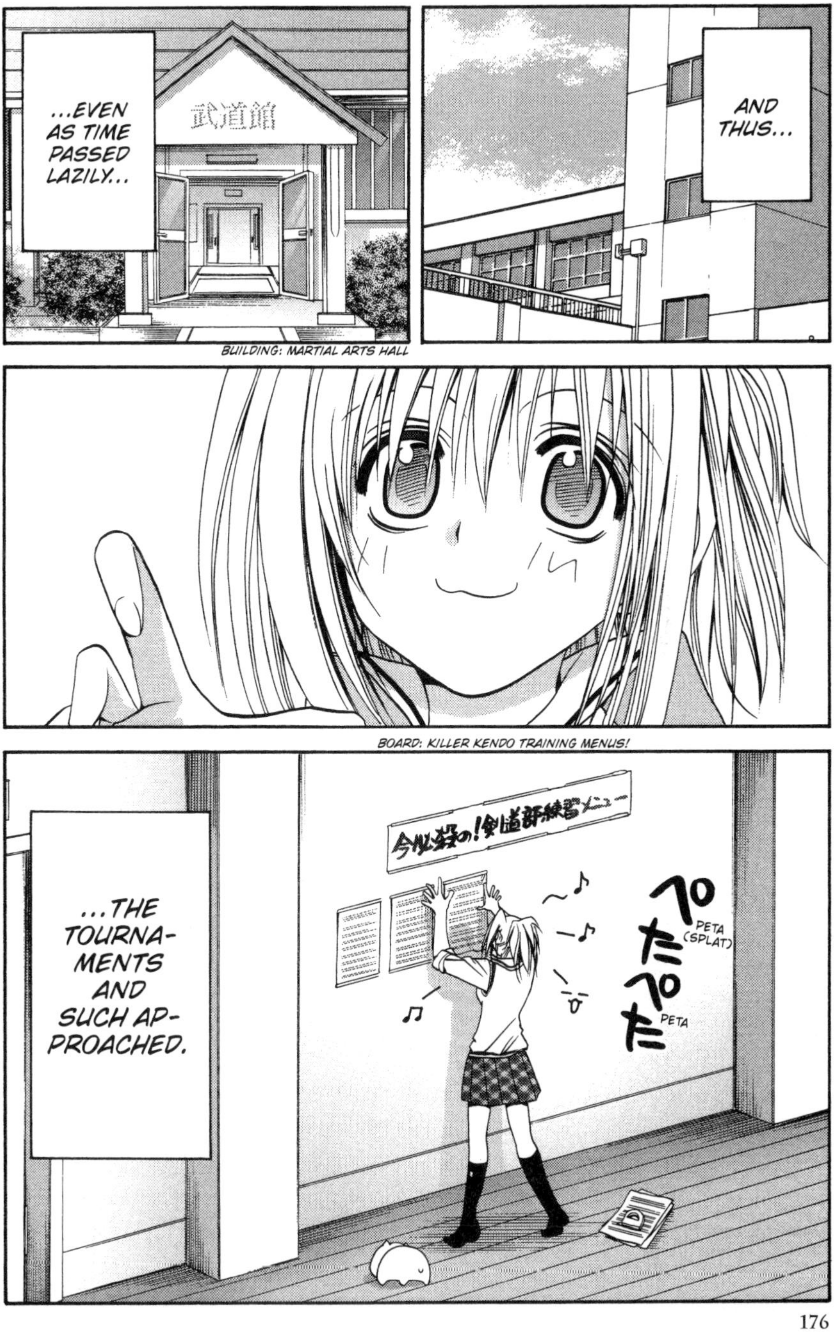
AND THUS...
...EVEN AS TIME PASSED LAZILY...
武道館
BUILDING: MARTIAL ARTS HALL
BOARD: KILLER KENDO TRAINING MENUS!
...THE TOURNA-MENTS AND SUCH AP-PROACHED.
ペタペタ
PETA (SPLAT)
PETA

BAMBOO BLADE

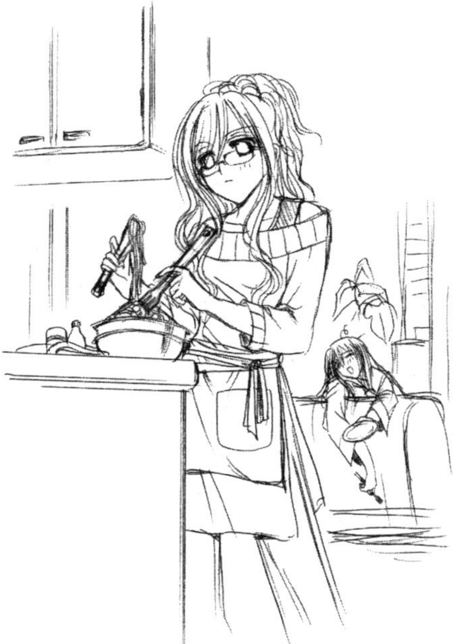

BAMBOO BLADE
バンブーブレード

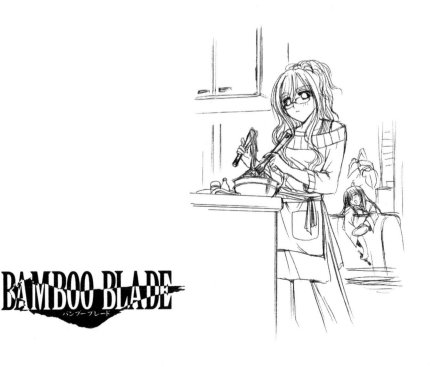

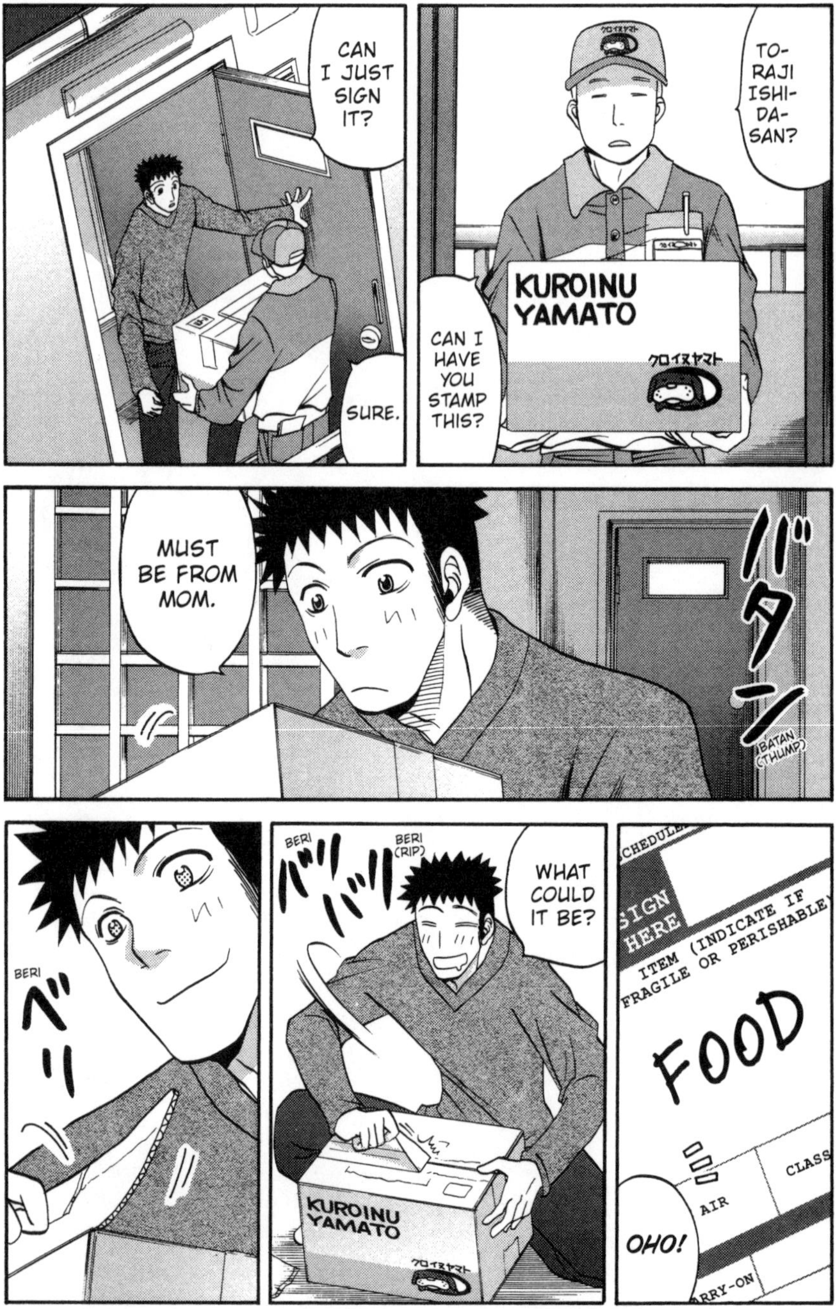
TO-RAJI ISHI-DA-SAN?
KUROINU YAMATO
クロイヌヤマト
CAN I HAVE YOU STAMP THIS?
CAN I JUST SIGN IT?
SURE.
バタン
BATAN (THUMP)
MUST BE FROM MOM.
SCHEDULE
SIGN HERE
ITEM (INDICATE IF FRAGILE OR PERISHABLE)
FOOD
CLASS
AIR
ARRY-ON
OHO!
WHAT COULD IT BE?
バリバリ
BERI BERI (RIP)
KUROINU YAMATO
クロイヌヤマト
ベリ
BERI

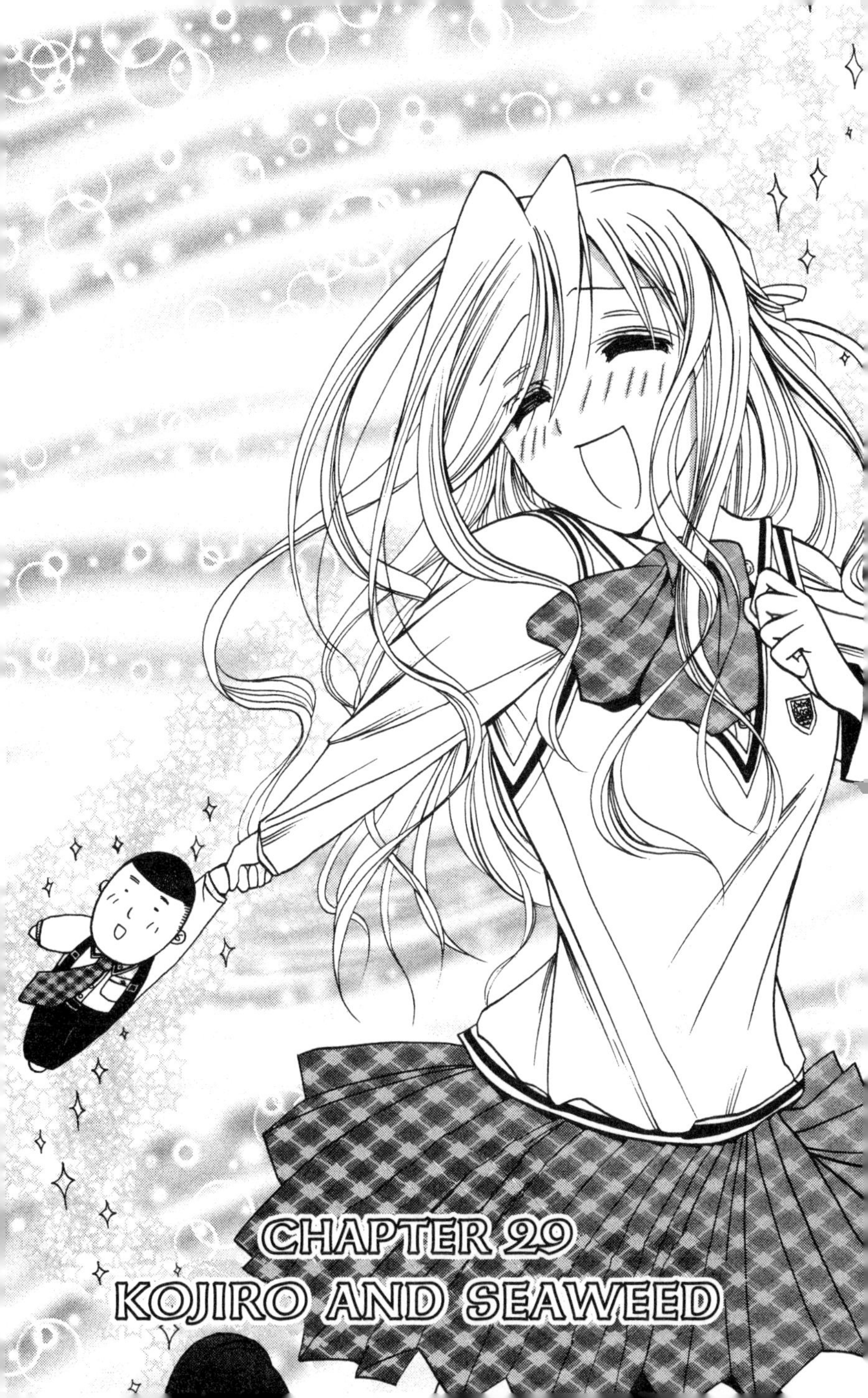
CHAPTER 29
KOJIRO AND SEAWEED

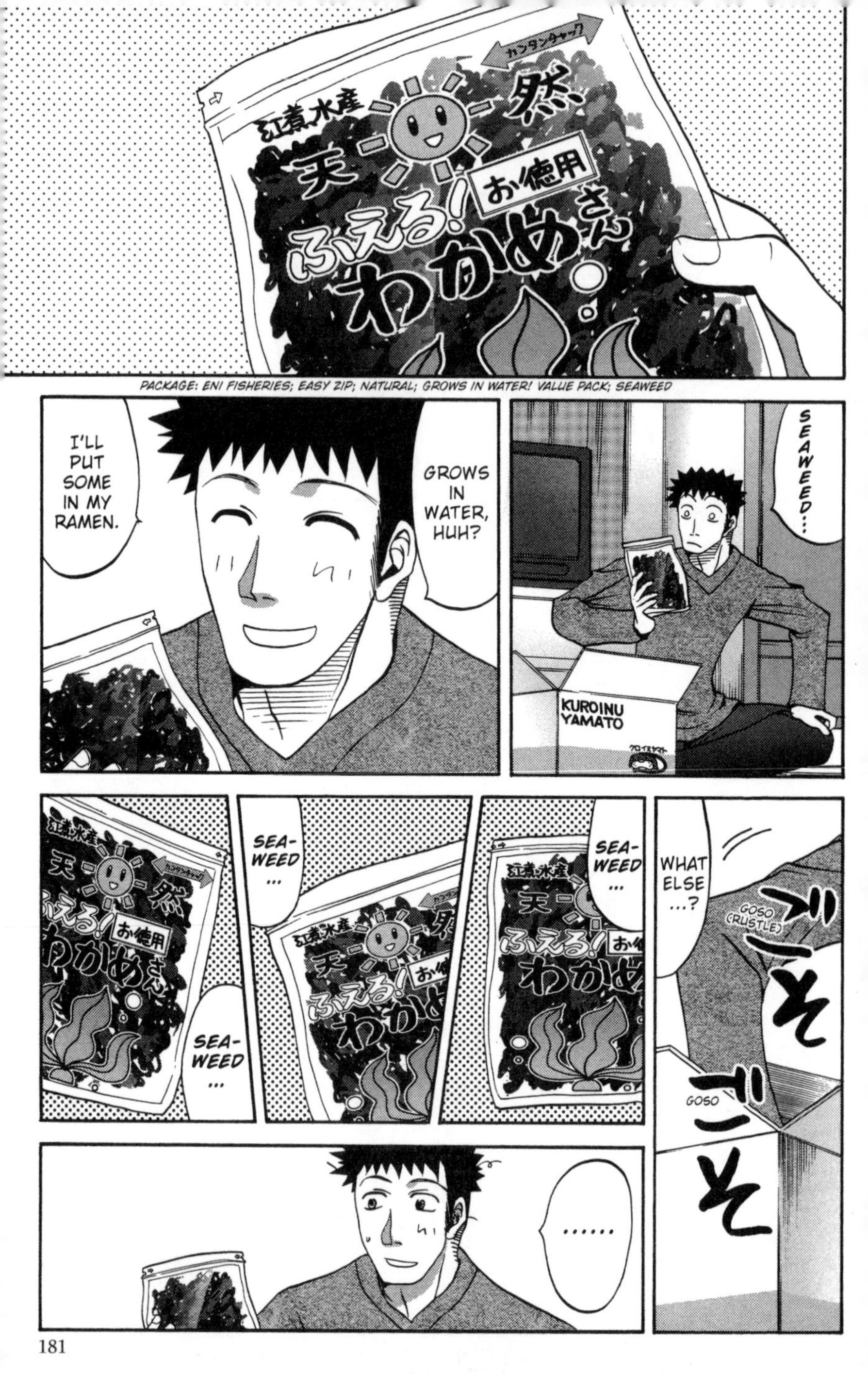
PACKAGE: ENI FISHERIES; EASY ZIP; NATURAL; GROWS IN WATER! VALUE PACK; SEAWEED
SEAWEED...
GROWS IN WATER, HUH?
I'LL PUT SOME IN MY RAMEN.
KUROINU YAMATO
WHAT ELSE ...?
ごそ
GOSO (RUSTLE)
ごそ
GOSO
SEA-WEED ...
SEA-WEED ...
SEA-WEED ...
......

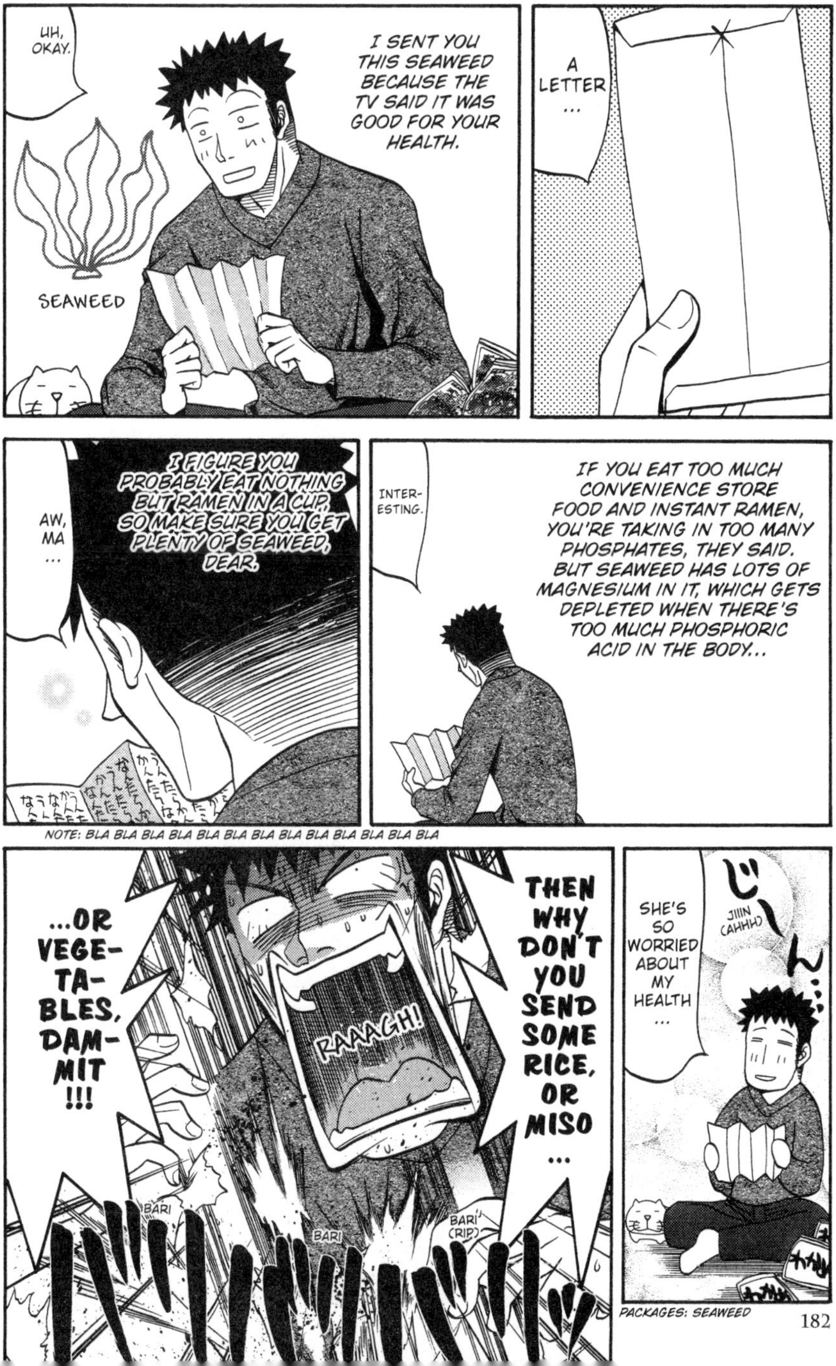
A LETTER...
I SENT YOU THIS SEAWEED BECAUSE THE TV SAID IT WAS GOOD FOR YOUR HEALTH.
UH, OKAY.
SEAWEED
IF YOU EAT TOO MUCH CONVENIENCE STORE FOOD AND INSTANT RAMEN, YOU'RE TAKING IN TOO MANY PHOSPHATES, THEY SAID. BUT SEAWEED HAS LOTS OF MAGNESIUM IN IT, WHICH GETS DEPLETED WHEN THERE'S TOO MUCH PHOSPHORIC ACID IN THE BODY...
INTER-ESTING.
I FIGURE YOU PROBABLY EAT NOTHING BUT RAMEN IN A CUP, SO MAKE SURE YOU GET PLENTY OF SEAWEED, DEAR.
AW, MA...
NOTE: BLA BLA BLA BLA BLA BLA BLA BLA BLA BLA BLA BLA BLA
SHE'S SO WORRIED ABOUT MY HEALTH...
じ～ん…
JIIN (AHHH)
THEN WHY DON'T YOU SEND SOME RICE, OR MISO...
...OR VEGE-TA-BLES, DAM-MIT!!!
RAAAGH!
BARI
BARI
BARI (RIP)
PACKAGES: SEAWEED

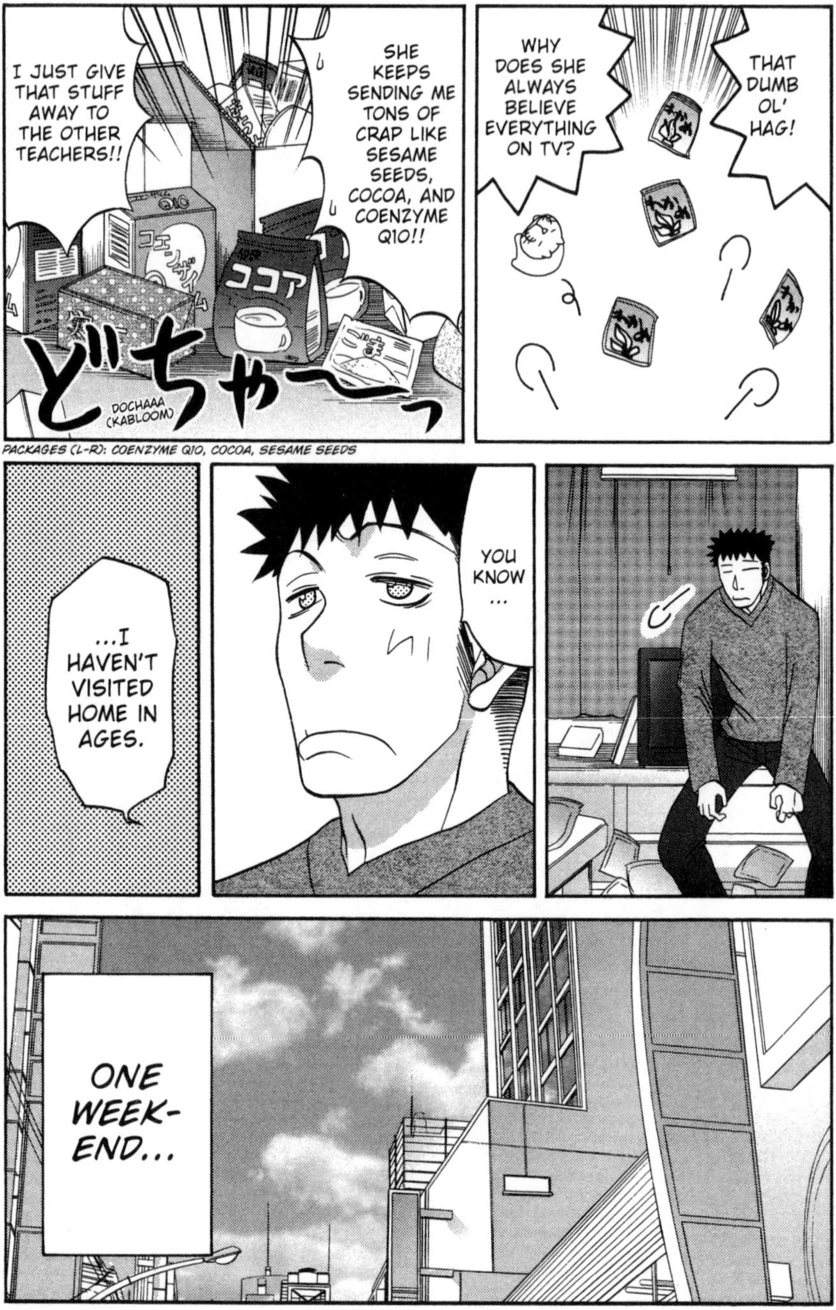
THAT DUMB OL' HAG!
WHY DOES SHE ALWAYS BELIEVE EVERYTHING ON TV?
SHE KEEPS SENDING ME TONS OF CRAP LIKE SESAME SEEDS, COCOA, AND COENZYME Q10!!
I JUST GIVE THAT STUFF AWAY TO THE OTHER TEACHERS!!
どちゃ〜っ
DOCHAAA (KABLOOM)
YOU KNOW ...
...I HAVEN'T VISITED HOME IN AGES.
ONE WEEK-END...
PACKAGES (L-R): COENZYME Q10, COCOA, SESAME SEEDS

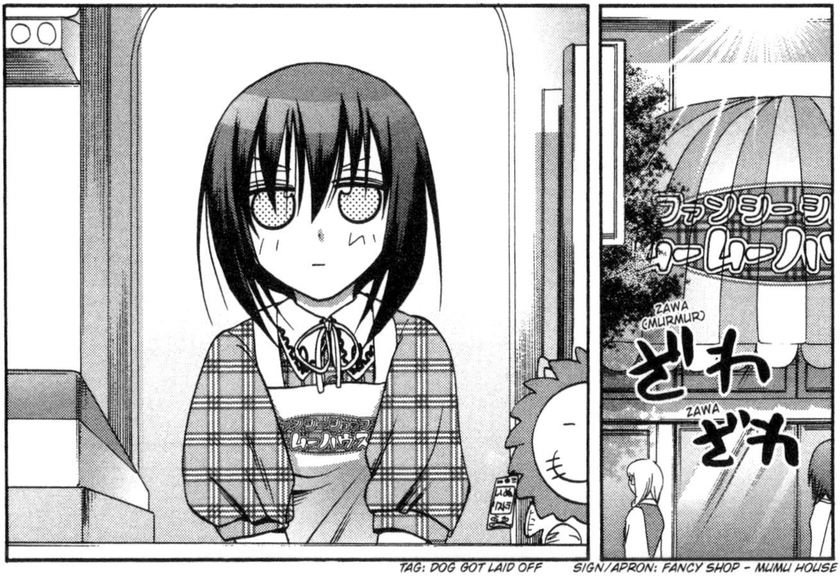
ZAWA (MURMUR)
ざわ
ZAWA
ざわ

TAG: DOG GOT LAID OFF SIGN/APRON: FANCY SHOP - MUMU HOUSE

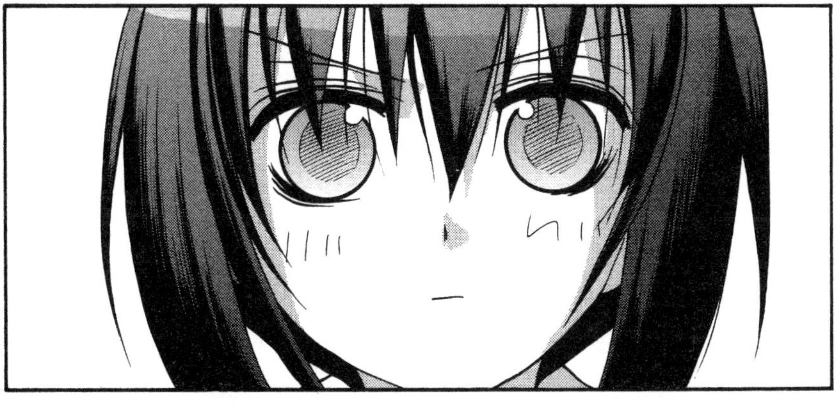

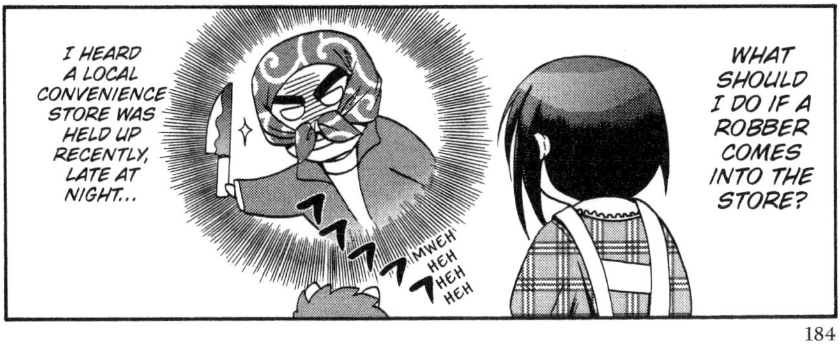
WHAT SHOULD I DO IF A ROBBER COMES INTO THE STORE?
I HEARD A LOCAL CONVENIENCE STORE WAS HELD UP RECENTLY, LATE AT NIGHT...
MWEH HEH HEH HEH

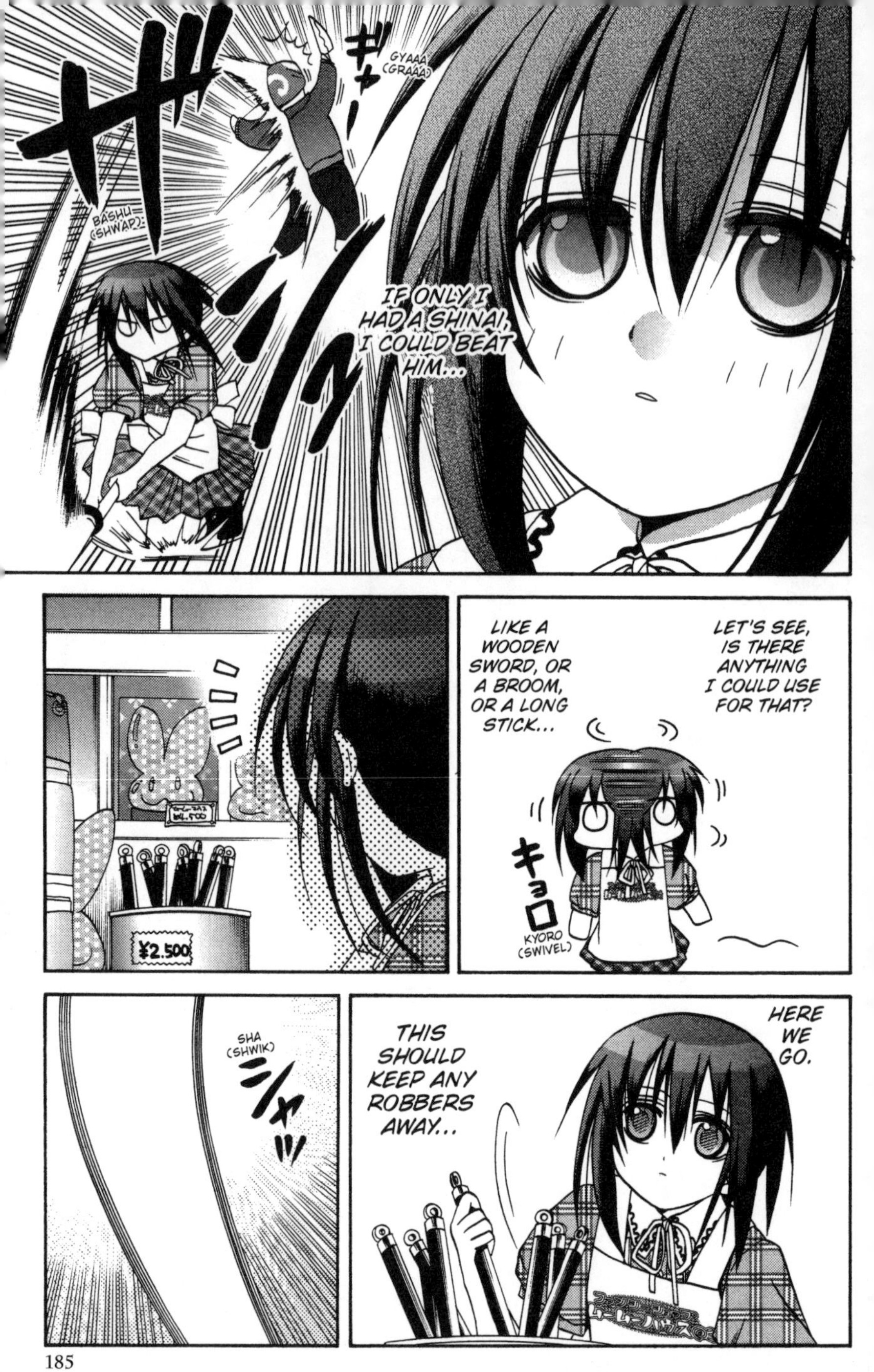
ギャー
GYAAA (GRAAA)
IF ONLY I HAD A SHINAI, I COULD BEAT HIM...
BASHU (SHWAP)
LET'S SEE, IS THERE ANYTHING I COULD USE FOR THAT?
LIKE A WOODEN SWORD, OR A BROOM, OR A LONG STICK...
キョロ
KYORO (SWIVEL)
¥4.500
¥2.500
HERE WE GO.
THIS SHOULD KEEP ANY ROBBERS AWAY...
SHA (SHWIK)
シャッ

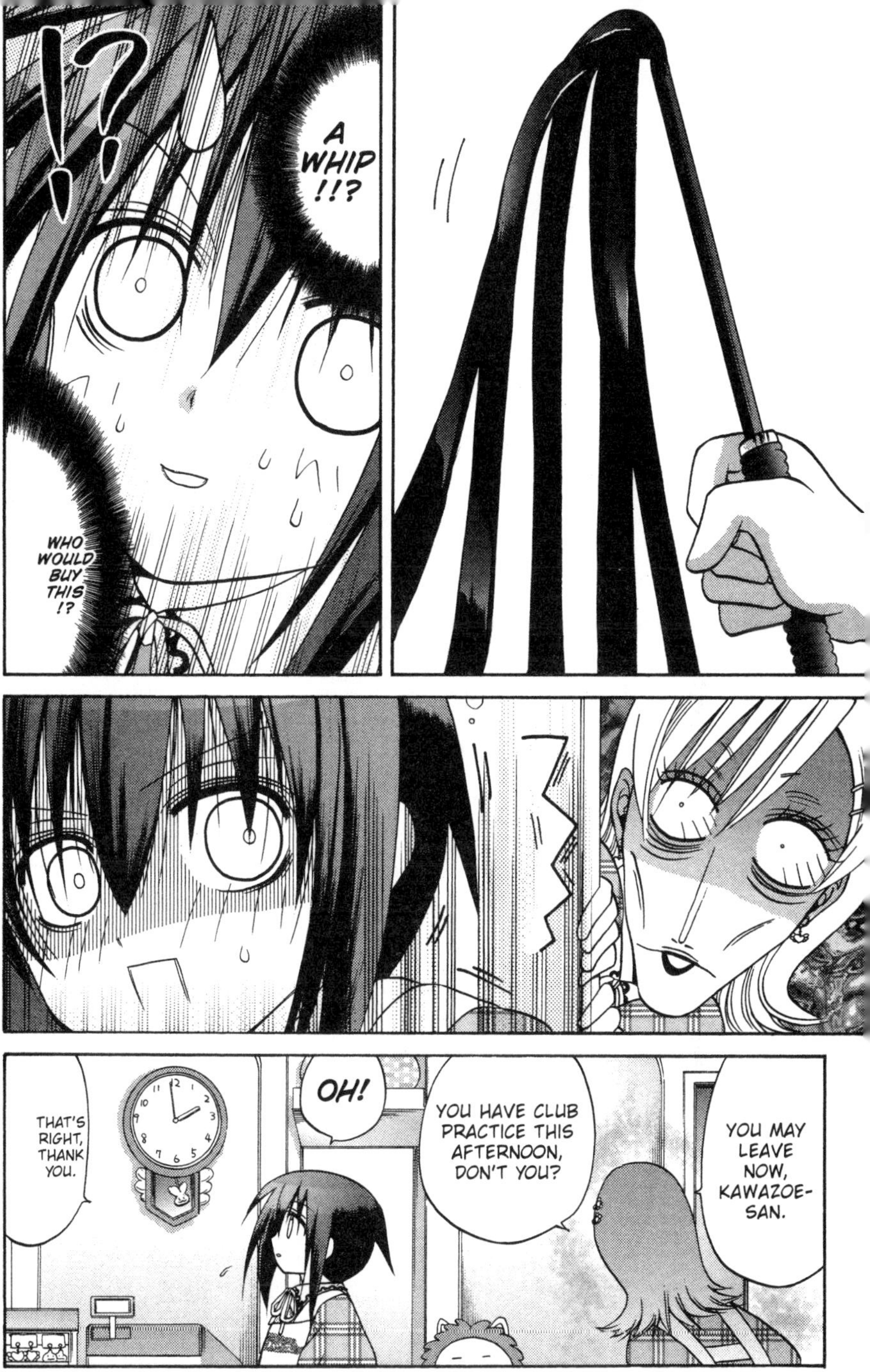
!?
A WHIP!!?
WHO WOULD BUY THIS!?
YOU MAY LEAVE NOW, KAWAZOE-SAN.
YOU HAVE CLUB PRACTICE THIS AFTERNOON, DON'T YOU?
OH!
THAT'S RIGHT, THANK YOU.

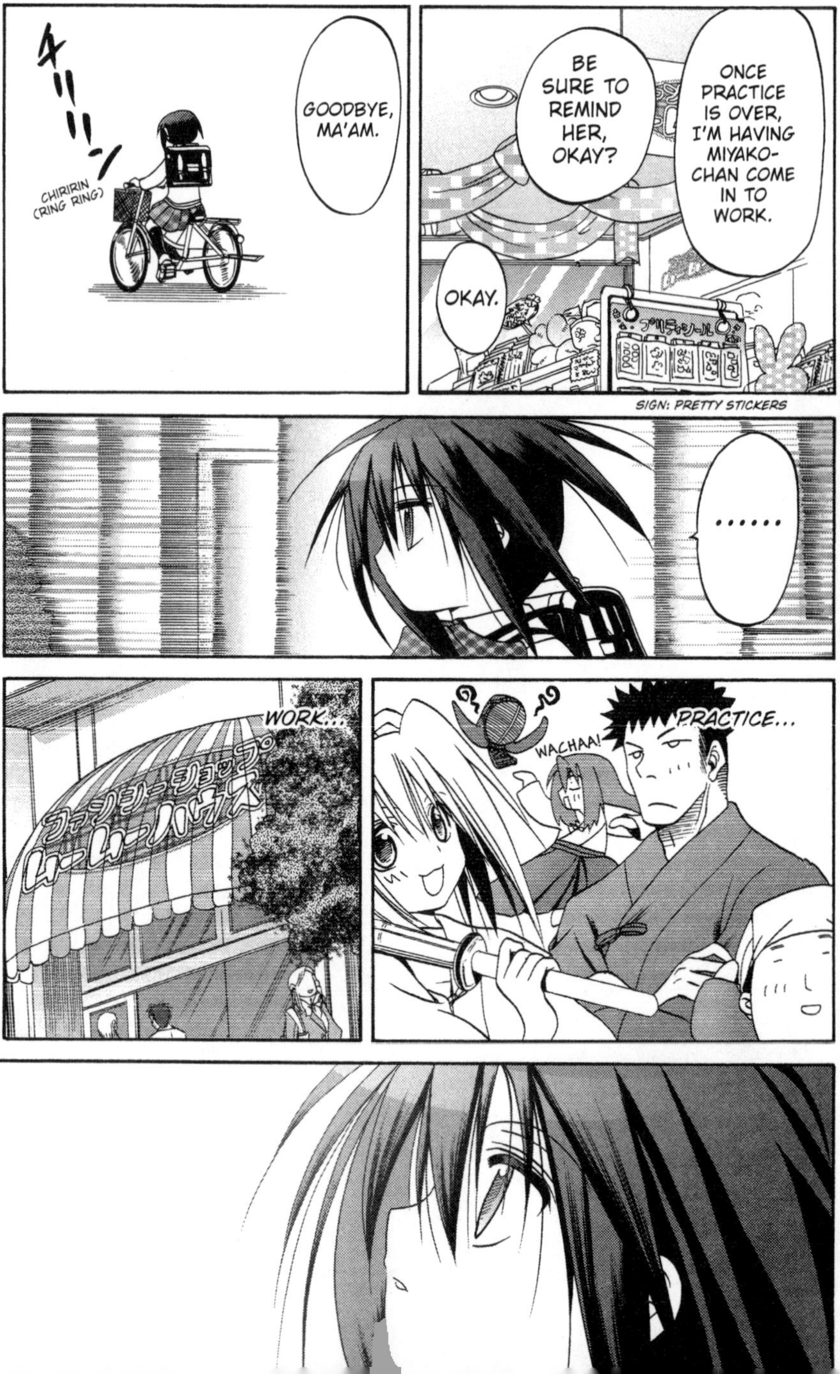
ONCE PRACTICE IS OVER, I'M HAVING MIYAKO-CHAN COME IN TO WORK.
BE SURE TO REMIND HER, OKAY?
OKAY.
SIGN: PRETTY STICKERS
GOODBYE, MA'AM.
CHIRIRIN (RING RING)
......
PRACTICE...
WACHAA!
WORK...

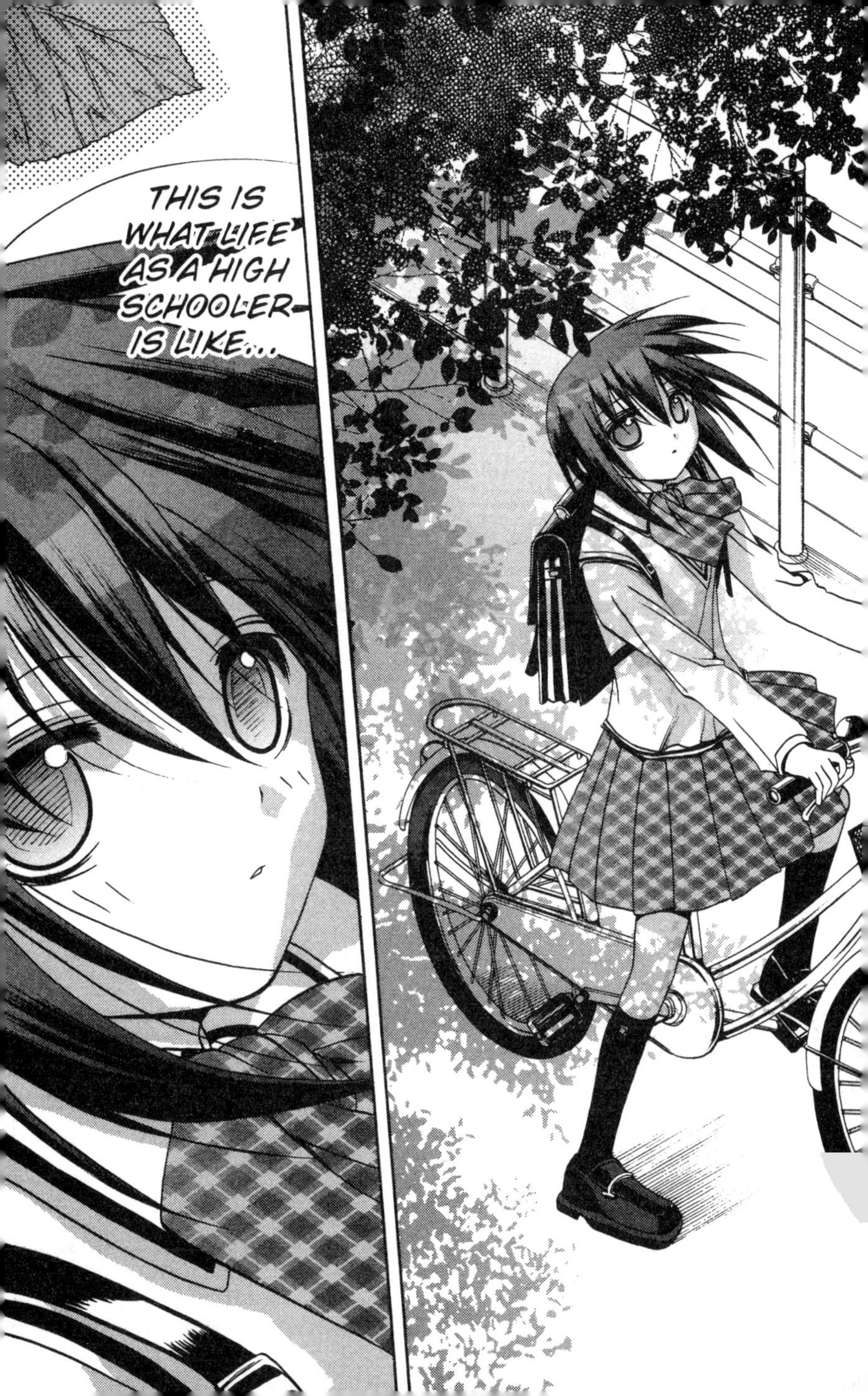
THIS IS WHAT LIFE AS A HIGH SCHOOLER IS LIKE...

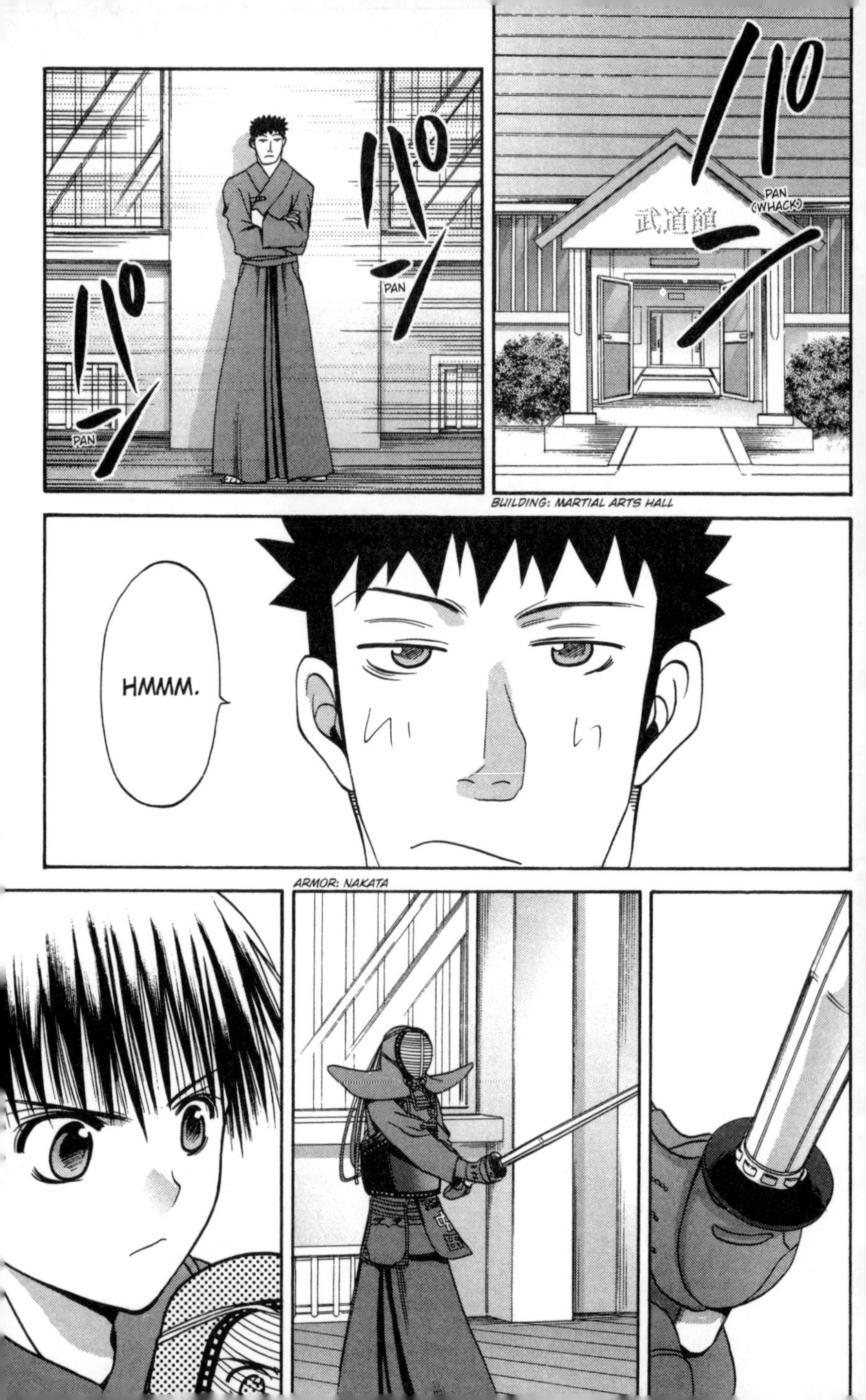
パーン
PAN (WHACK)
武道館
BUILDING: MARTIAL ARTS HALL
パーン
PAN
パーン
PAN
HMMM.
ARMOR: NAKATA

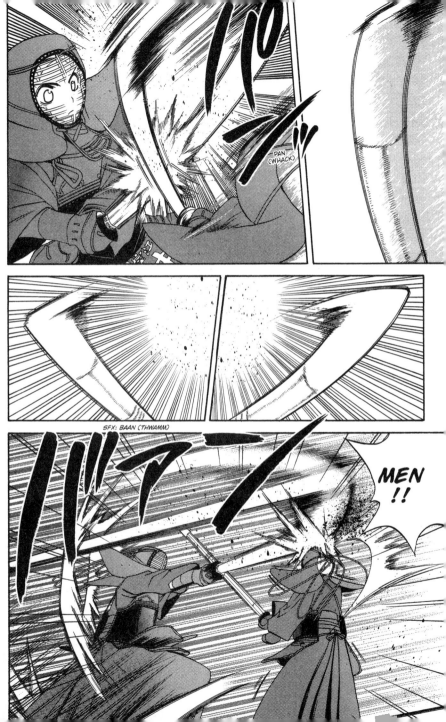

—PAN
(WHACK)

SFX: BAAN (THWAMM)

MEN
!!

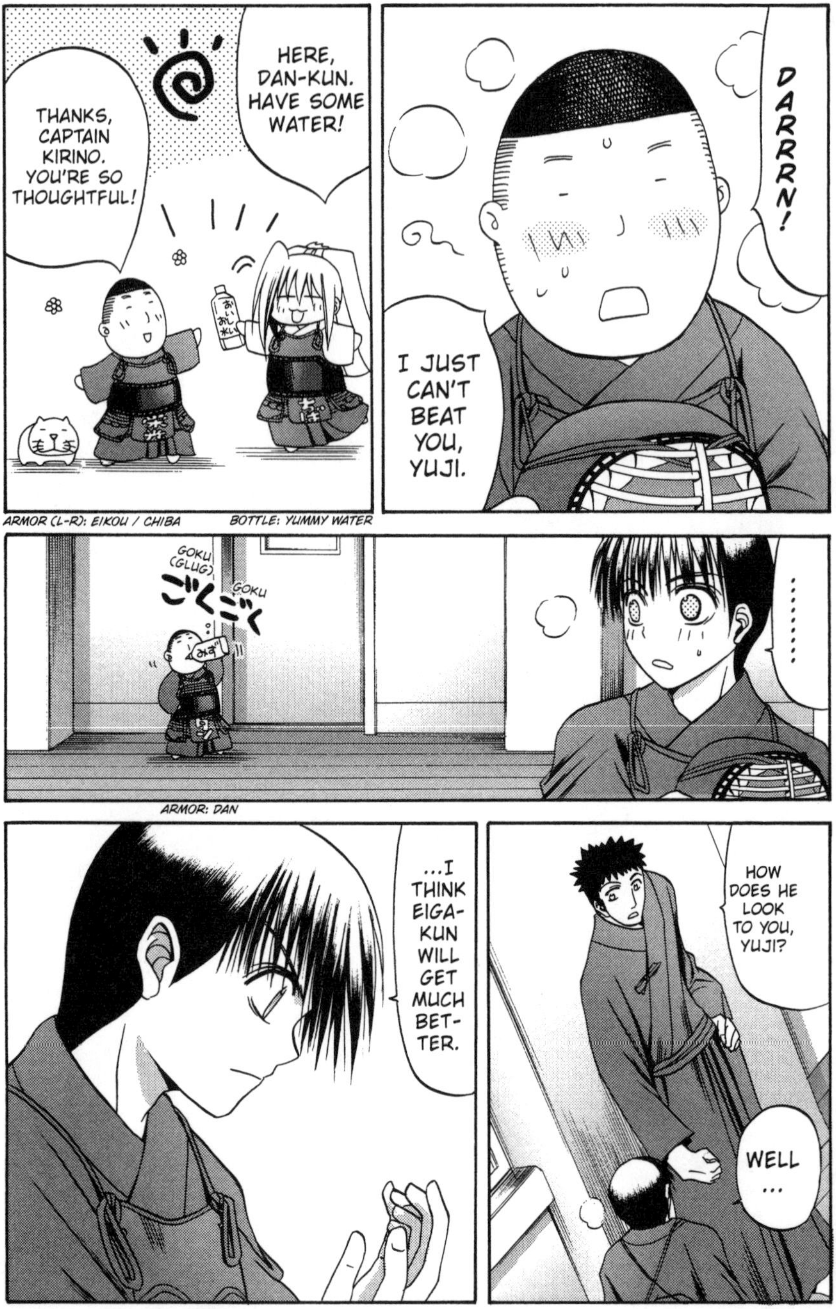
DARRRN!
I JUST CAN'T BEAT YOU, YUJI.
HERE, DAN-KUN. HAVE SOME WATER!
THANKS, CAPTAIN KIRINO. YOU'RE SO THOUGHTFUL!
ARMOR (L-R): EIKOU / CHIBA
BOTTLE: YUMMY WATER
......
ごくごく
GOKU (GLUG) GOKU
ARMOR: DAN
HOW DOES HE LOOK TO YOU, YUJI?
WELL ...
...I THINK EIGA-KUN WILL GET MUCH BET-TER.

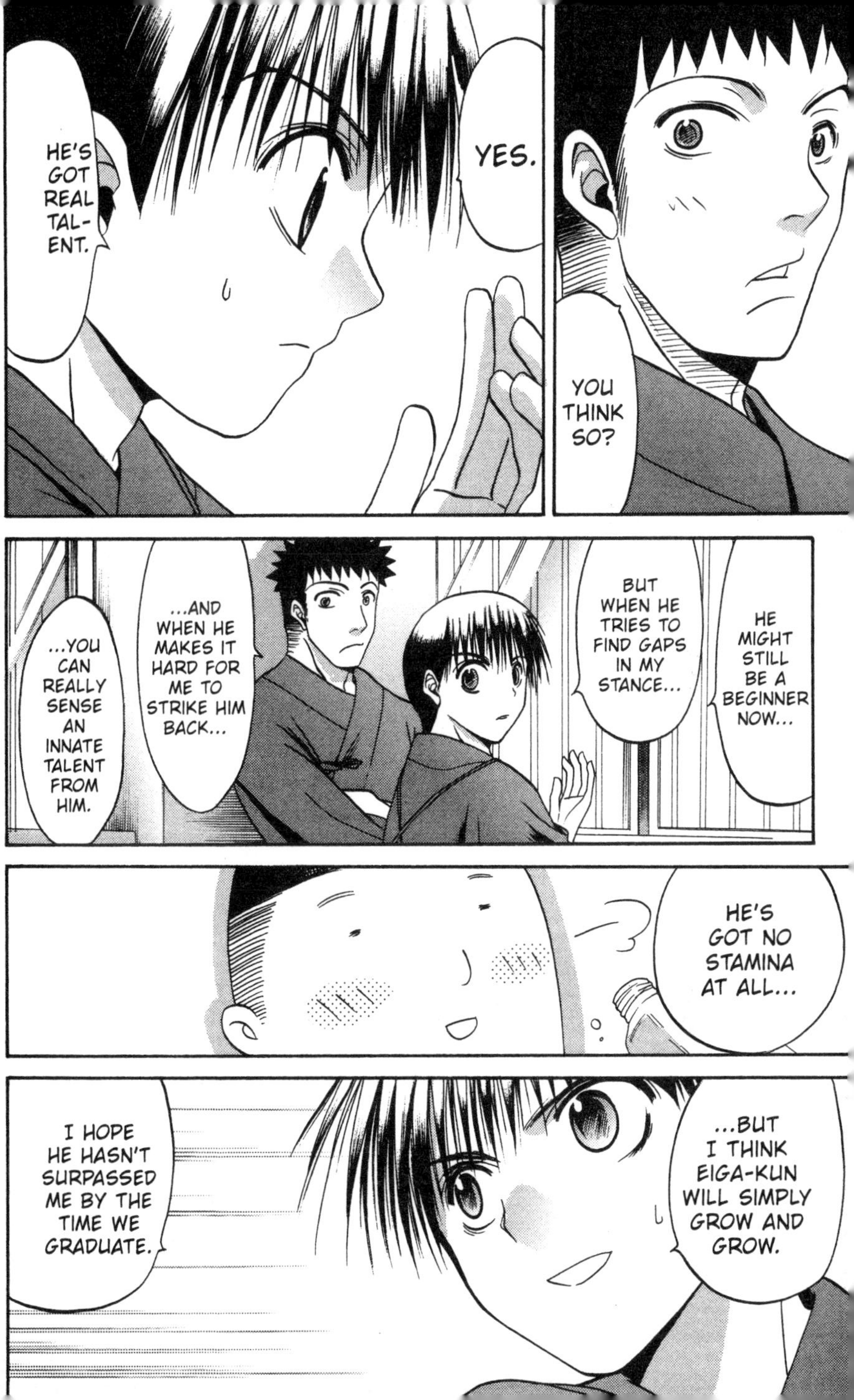
YOU THINK SO?
YES.
HE'S GOT REAL TAL-ENT.
HE MIGHT STILL BE A BEGINNER NOW...
BUT WHEN HE TRIES TO FIND GAPS IN MY STANCE...
...AND WHEN HE MAKES IT HARD FOR ME TO STRIKE HIM BACK...
...YOU CAN REALLY SENSE AN INNATE TALENT FROM HIM.
HE'S GOT NO STAMINA AT ALL...
...BUT I THINK EIGA-KUN WILL SIMPLY GROW AND GROW.
I HOPE HE HASN'T SURPASSED ME BY THE TIME WE GRADUATE.

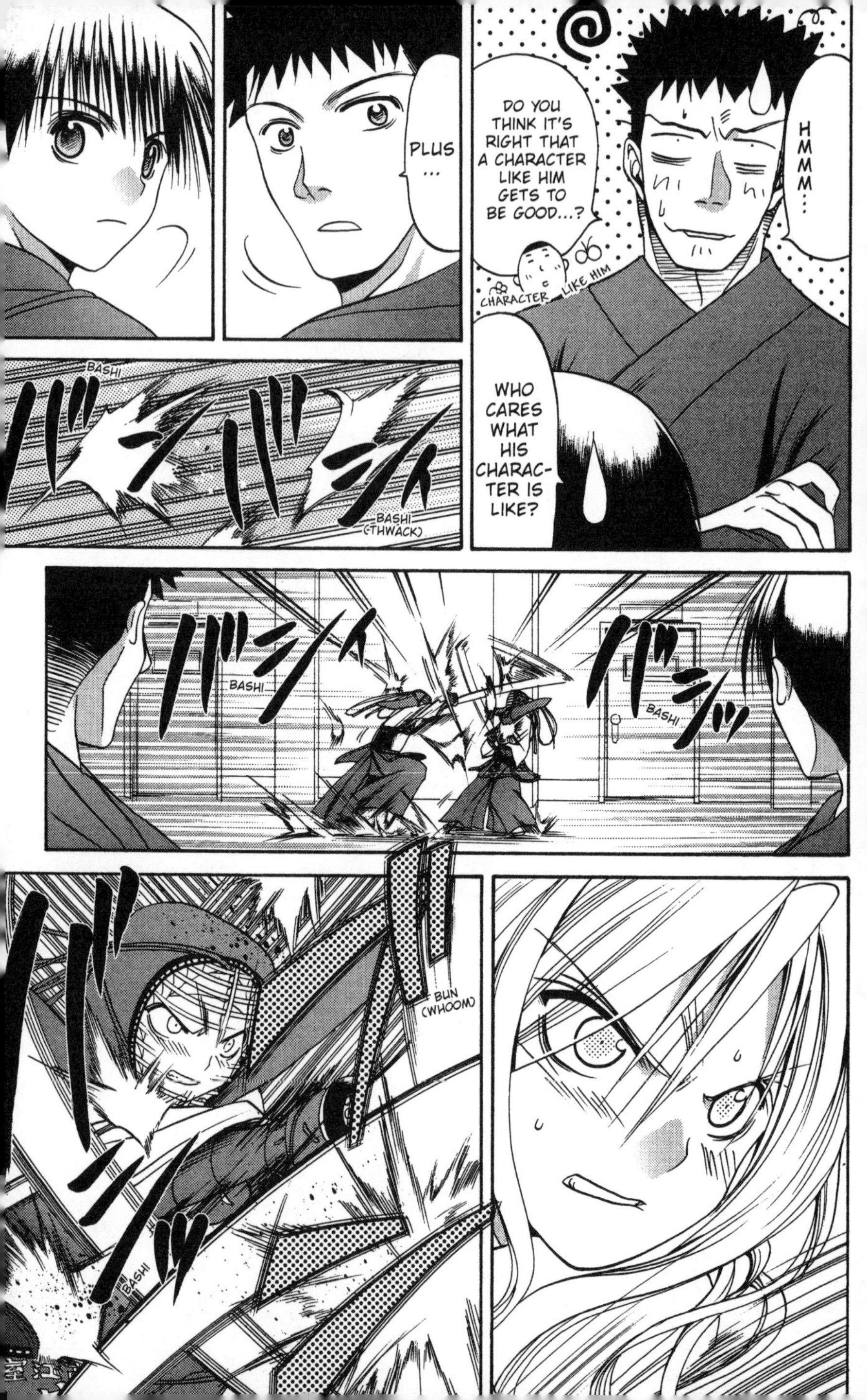
HMMM...
DO YOU THINK IT'S RIGHT THAT A CHARACTER LIKE HIM GETS TO BE GOOD...?
CHARACTER
LIKE HIM
WHO CARES WHAT HIS CHARACTER IS LIKE?
PLUS...
BASHI
BASHI (THWACK)
BASHI
BASHI
BUN (WHOOM)
BASHI

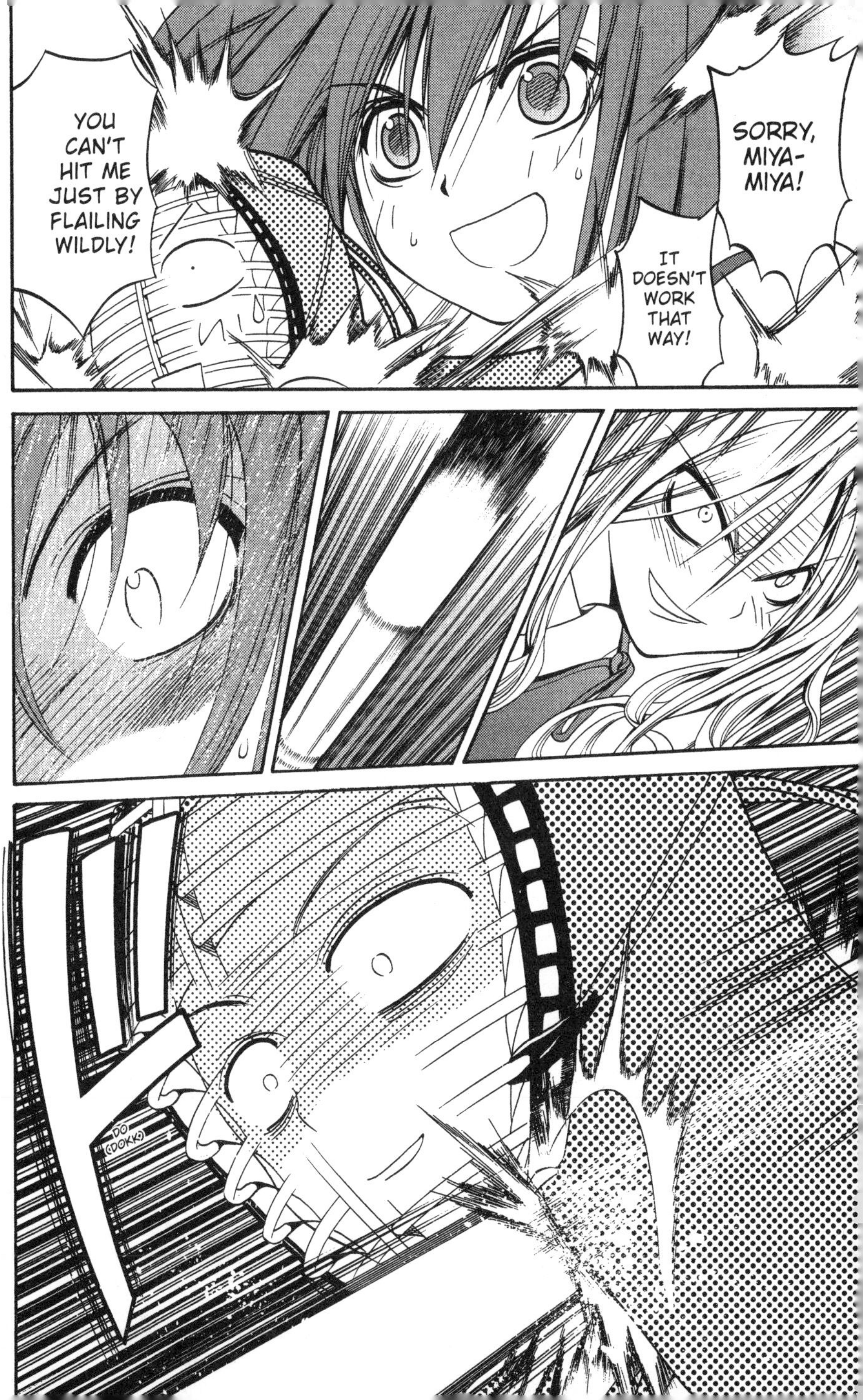
SORRY, MIYA-MIYA!
IT DOESN'T WORK THAT WAY!
YOU CAN'T HIT ME JUST BY FLAILING WILDLY!
DO (DOKK)

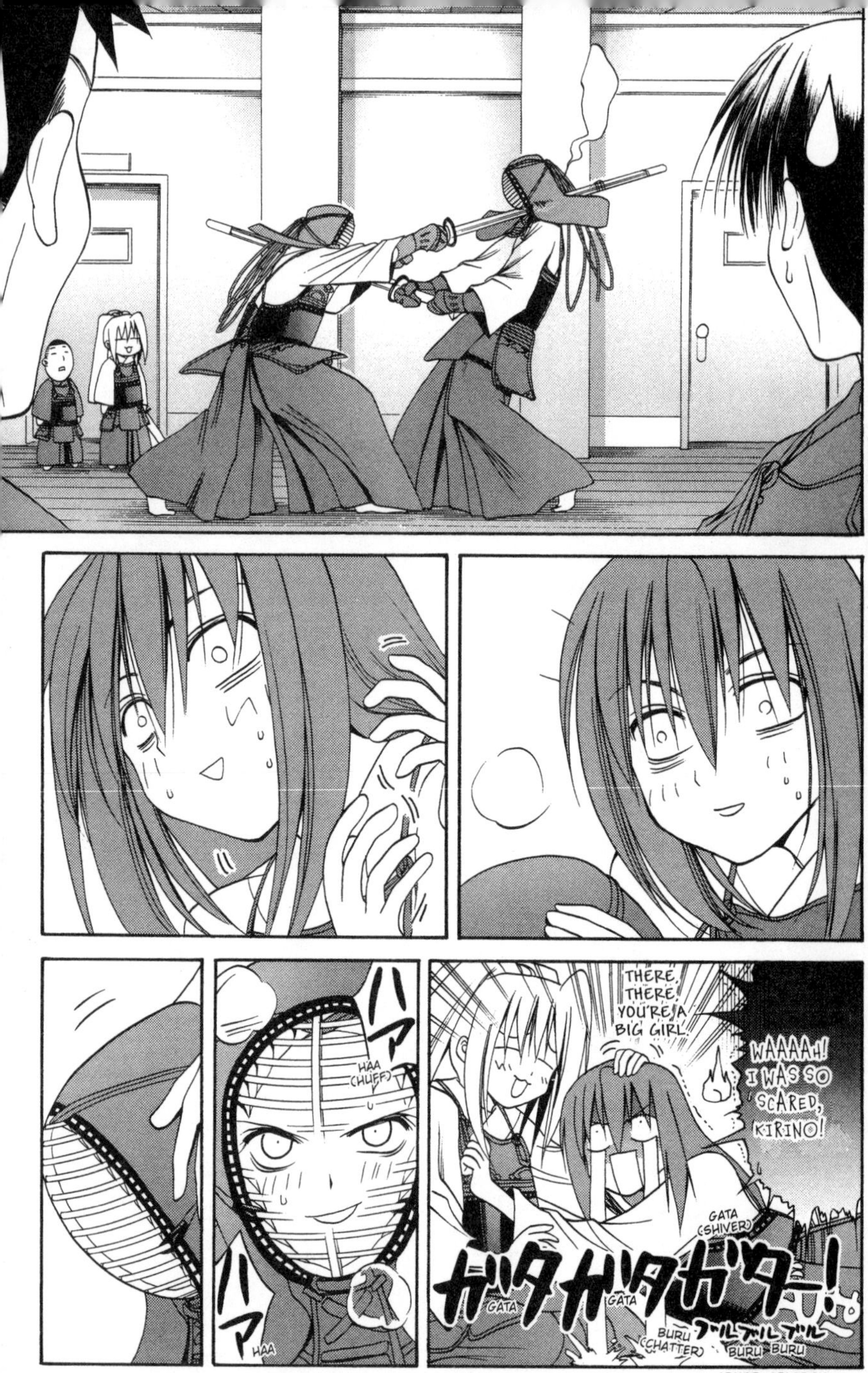
WAAAAH! I WAS SO SCARED, KIRINO!
THERE, THERE. YOU'RE A BIG GIRL.
GATA (SHIVER)
GATA
GATA
BURU (CHATTER)
BURU BURU
HAA (HUFF)
HAA

ARMOR: SPLOOSH

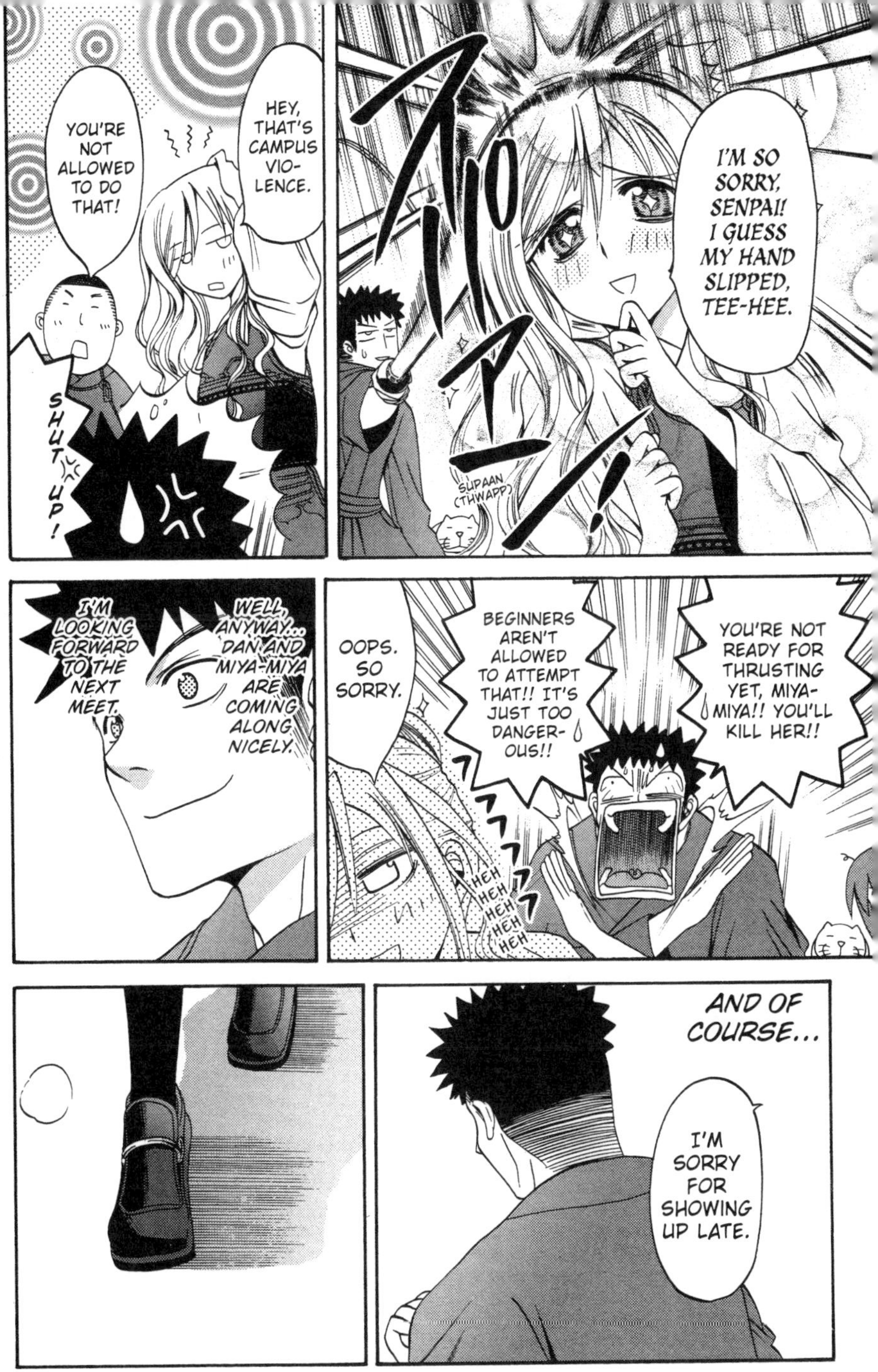
I'M SO SORRY, SENPAI! I GUESS MY HAND SLIPPED, TEE-HEE.
SUPAAN (THWAPP)
HEY, THAT'S CAMPUS VIO-LENCE.
YOU'RE NOT ALLOWED TO DO THAT!
SHUT UP!
YOU'RE NOT READY FOR THRUSTING YET, MIYA-MIYA!! YOU'LL KILL HER!!
BEGINNERS AREN'T ALLOWED TO ATTEMPT THAT!! IT'S JUST TOO DANGER-OUS!!
OOPS. SO SORRY.
HEH HEH HEH HEH HEH
WELL, ANYWAY... DAN AND MIYA-MIYA ARE COMING ALONG NICELY.
I'M LOOKING FORWARD TO THE NEXT MEET.
AND OF COURSE...
I'M SORRY FOR SHOWING UP LATE.

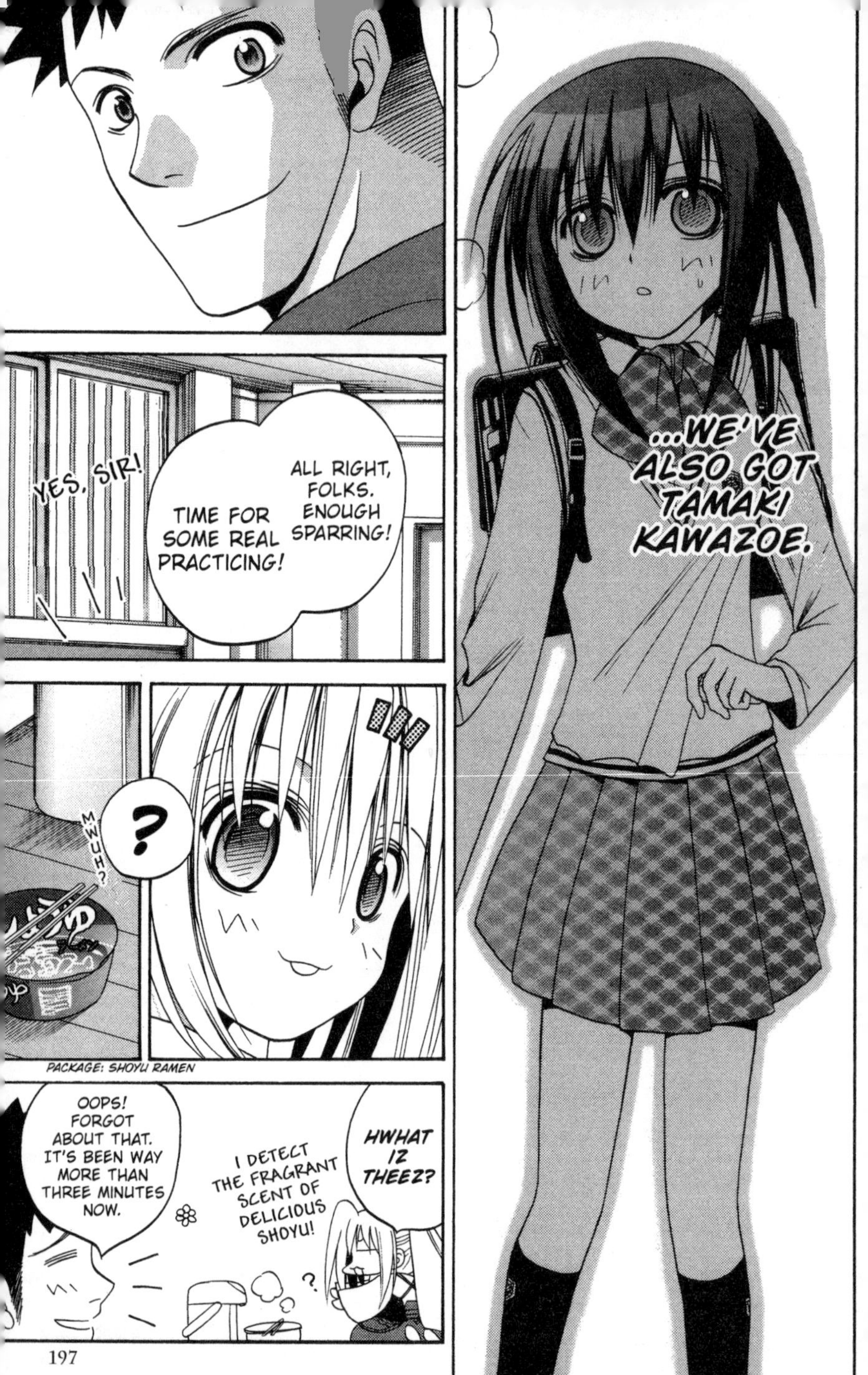
...WE'VE ALSO GOT TAMAKI KAWAZOE.
ALL RIGHT, FOLKS. ENOUGH SPARRING! TIME FOR SOME REAL PRACTICING!
YES, SIR!
?
MWUH?
PACKAGE: SHOYU RAMEN
HWHAT IZ THEEZ?
I DETECT THE FRAGRANT SCENT OF DELICIOUS SHOYU!
OOPS! FORGOT ABOUT THAT. IT'S BEEN WAY MORE THAN THREE MINUTES NOW.

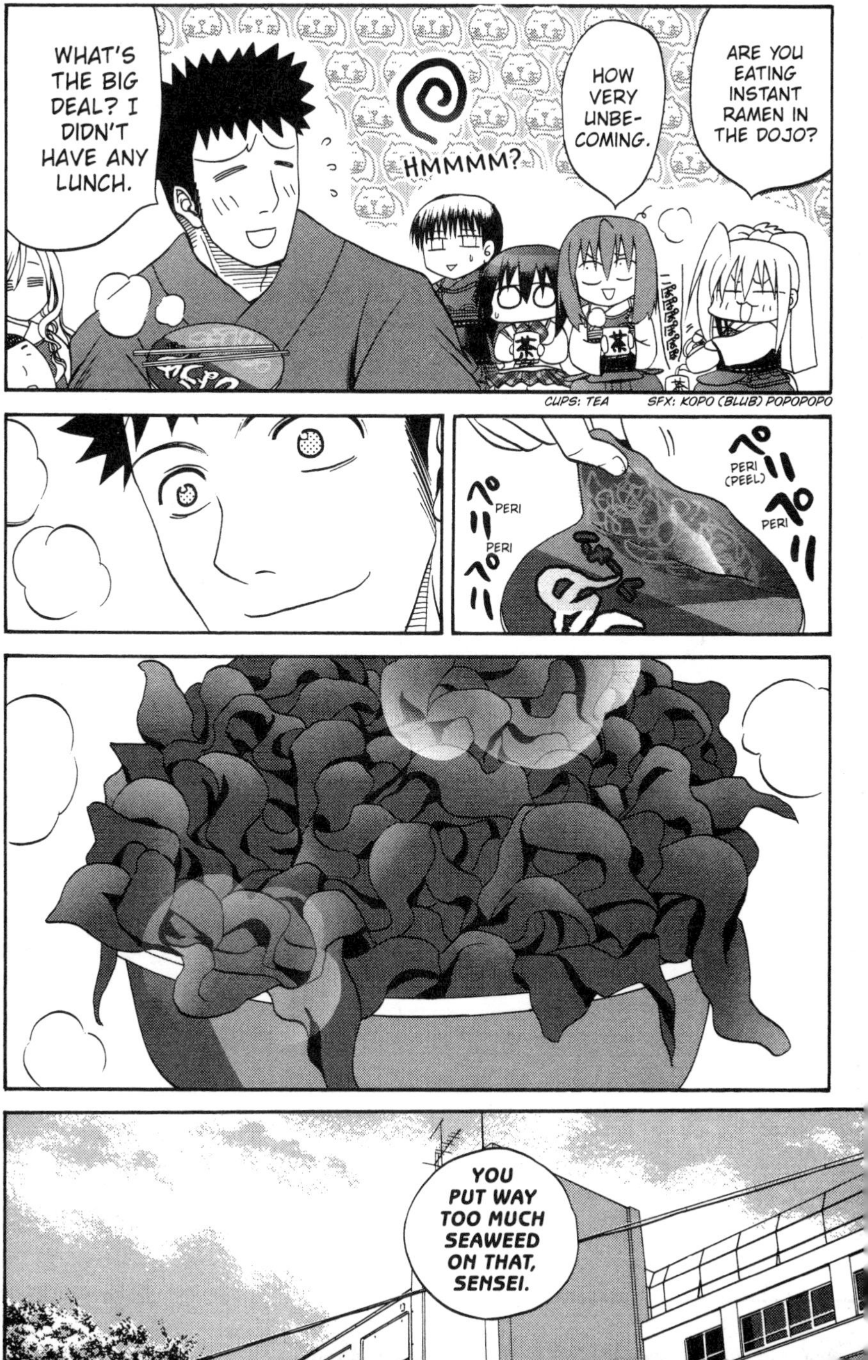
ARE YOU EATING INSTANT RAMEN IN THE DOJO?
HOW VERY UNBE-COMING.
HMMMM?
WHAT'S THE BIG DEAL? I DIDN'T HAVE ANY LUNCH.
茶
CUPS: TEA
SFX: KOPO (BLUB) POPOPOPO
ペリペリ
PERI (PEEL)
PERI
ペリペリ
PERI
PERI
YOU PUT WAY TOO MUCH SEAWEED ON THAT, SENSEI.

BAMBOO BLADE

BAMBOO BLADE
バンブーブレード

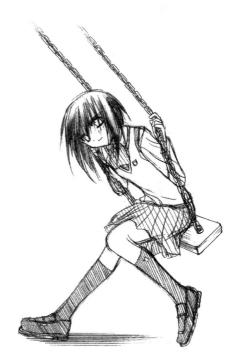

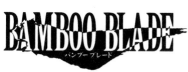

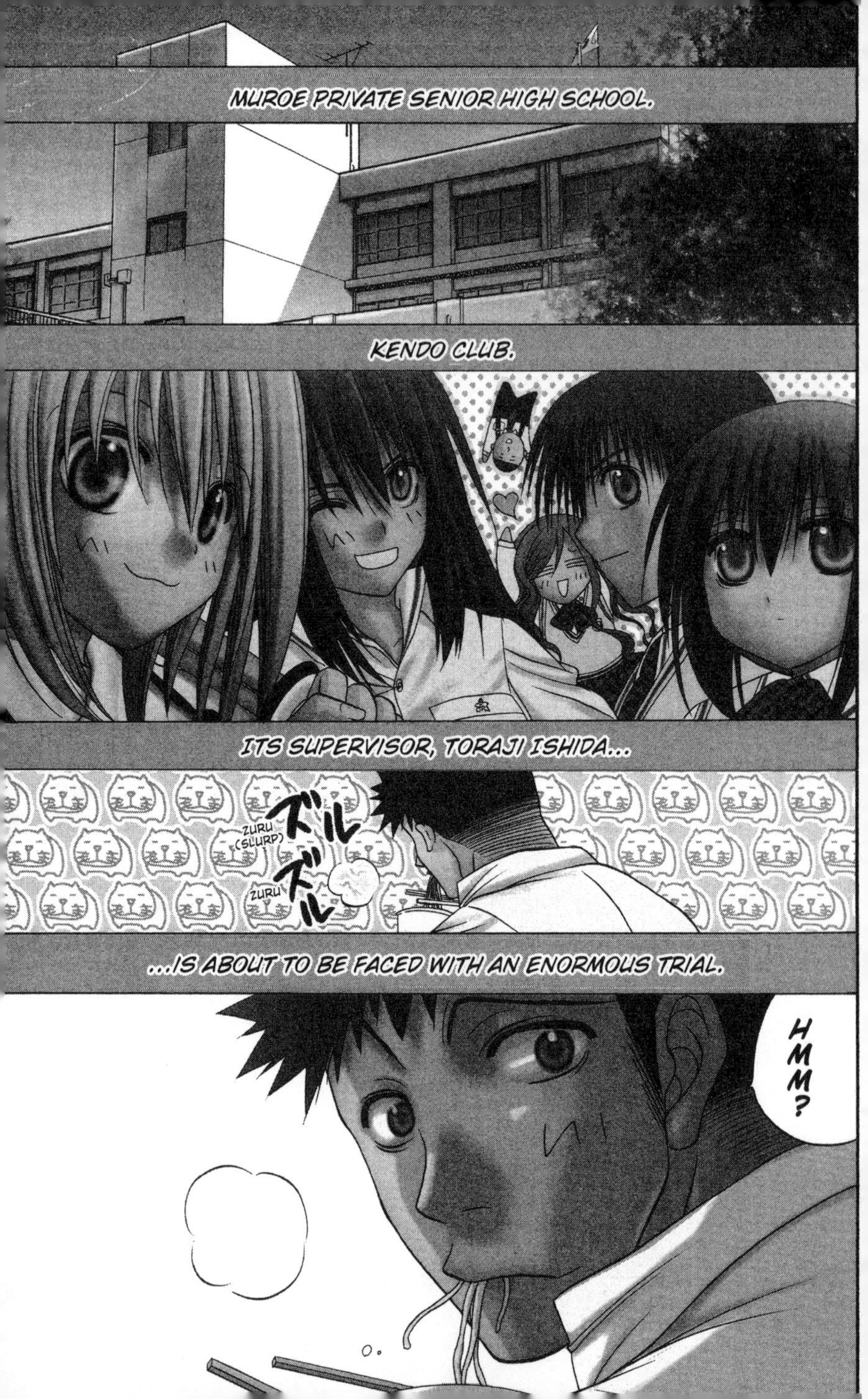
MUROE PRIVATE SENIOR HIGH SCHOOL.
KENDO CLUB.
ITS SUPERVISOR, TORAJI ISHIDA...
ズル
ZURU (SLURP)
ズル
ZURU
...IS ABOUT TO BE FACED WITH AN ENORMOUS TRIAL.
HMM?

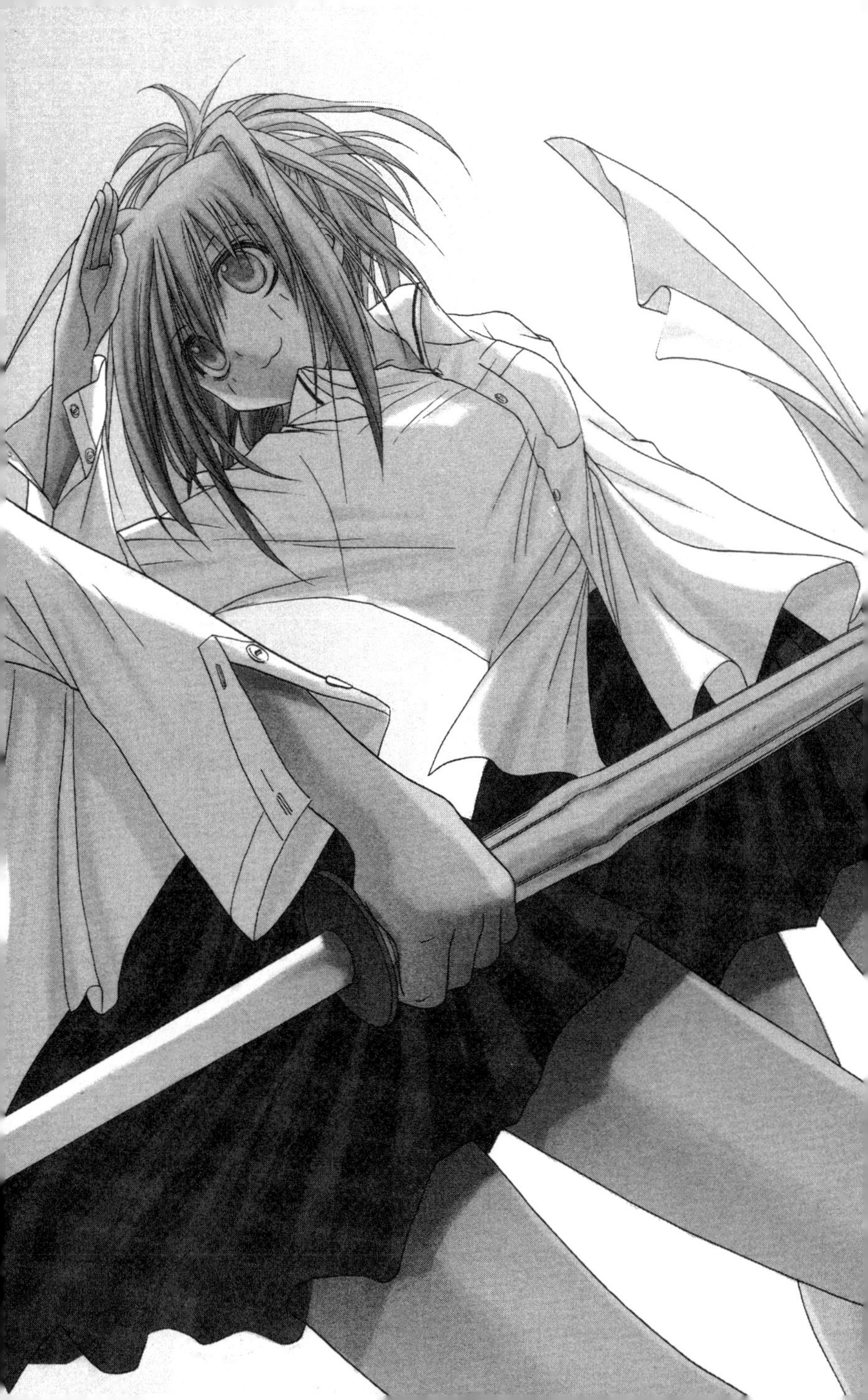

CHAPTER 30
KOJIRO AND THE BRANCHING POINT OF DESTINY

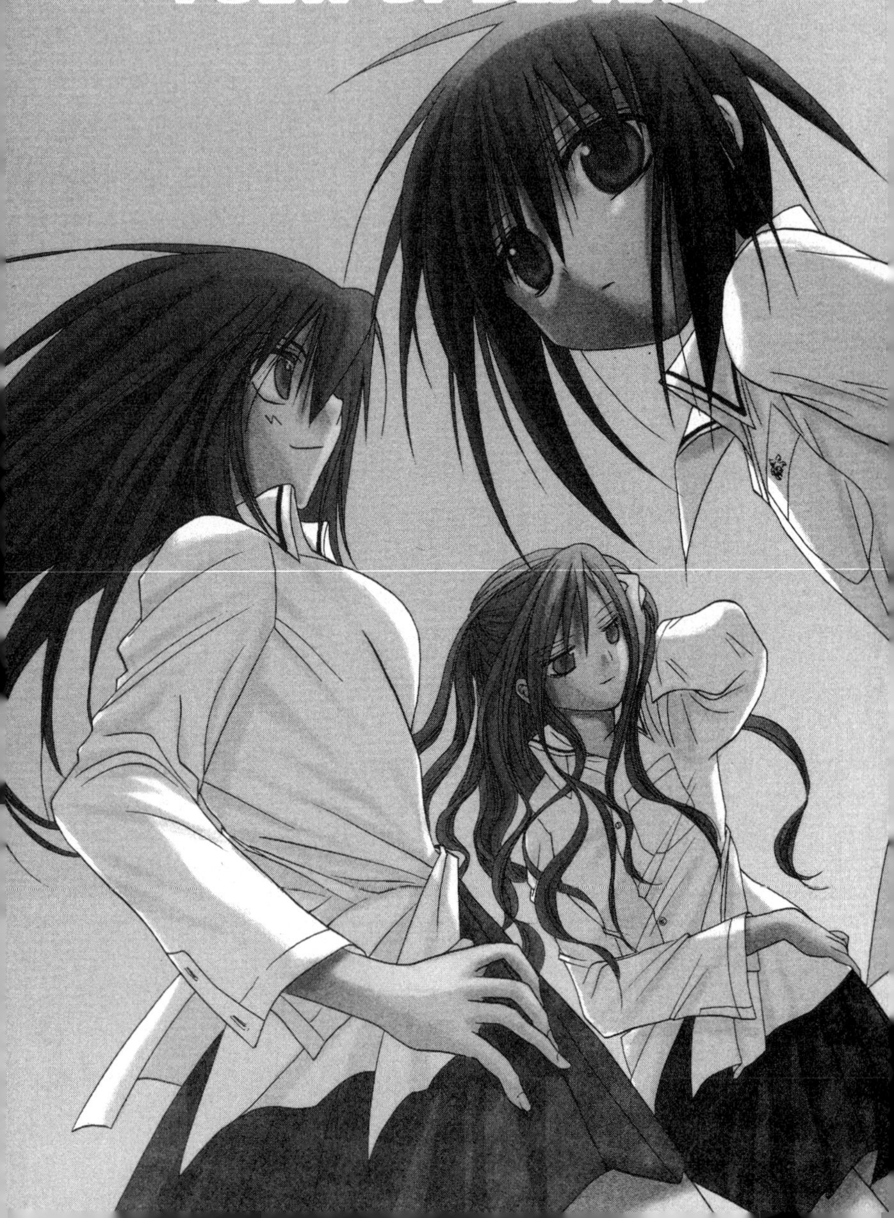

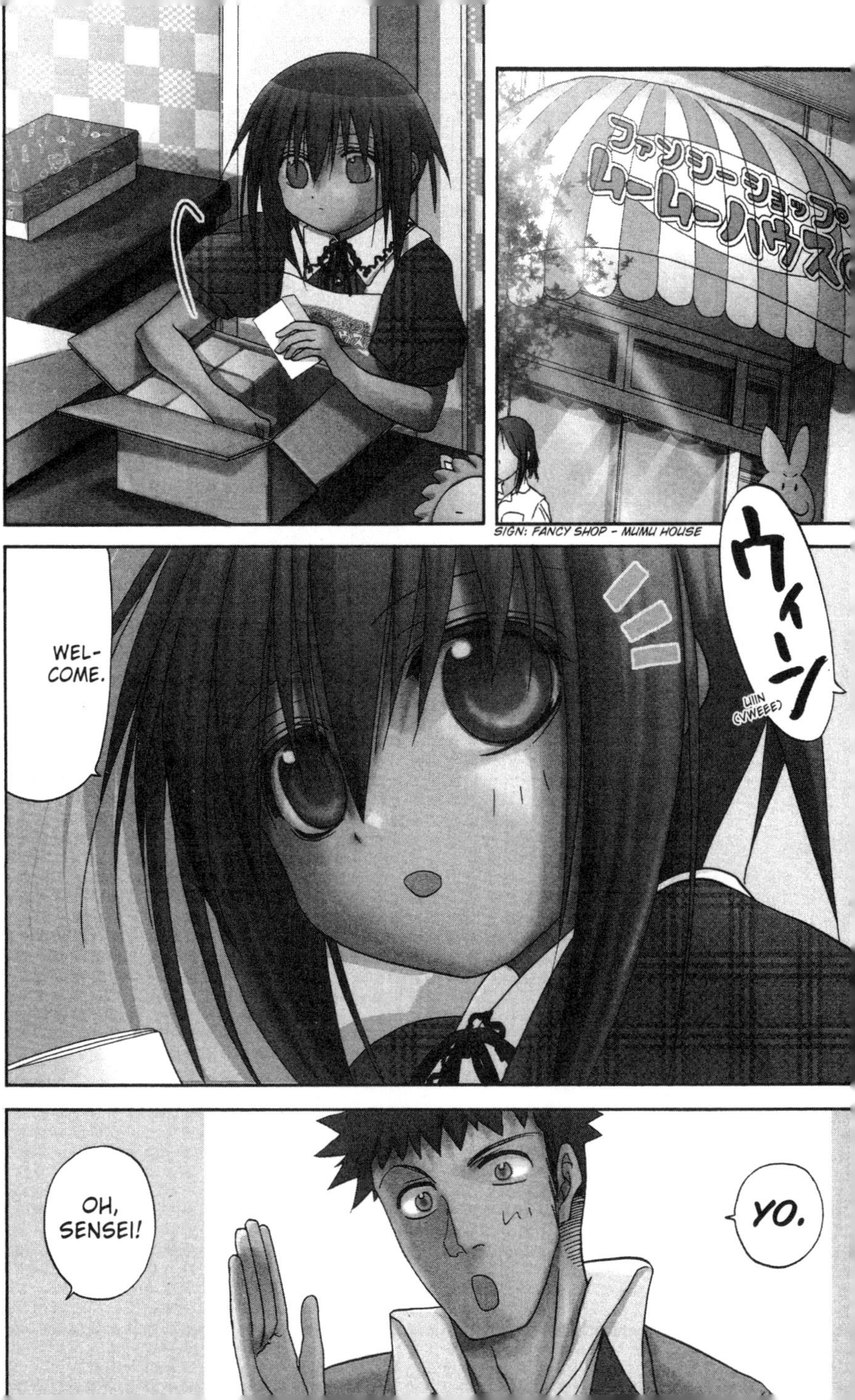
ファンシーショップ
ムームーハウス
SIGN: FANCY SHOP - MUMU HOUSE
ウィーン
UIIN (VWEEE)
WEL-COME.
YO.
OH, SENSEI!

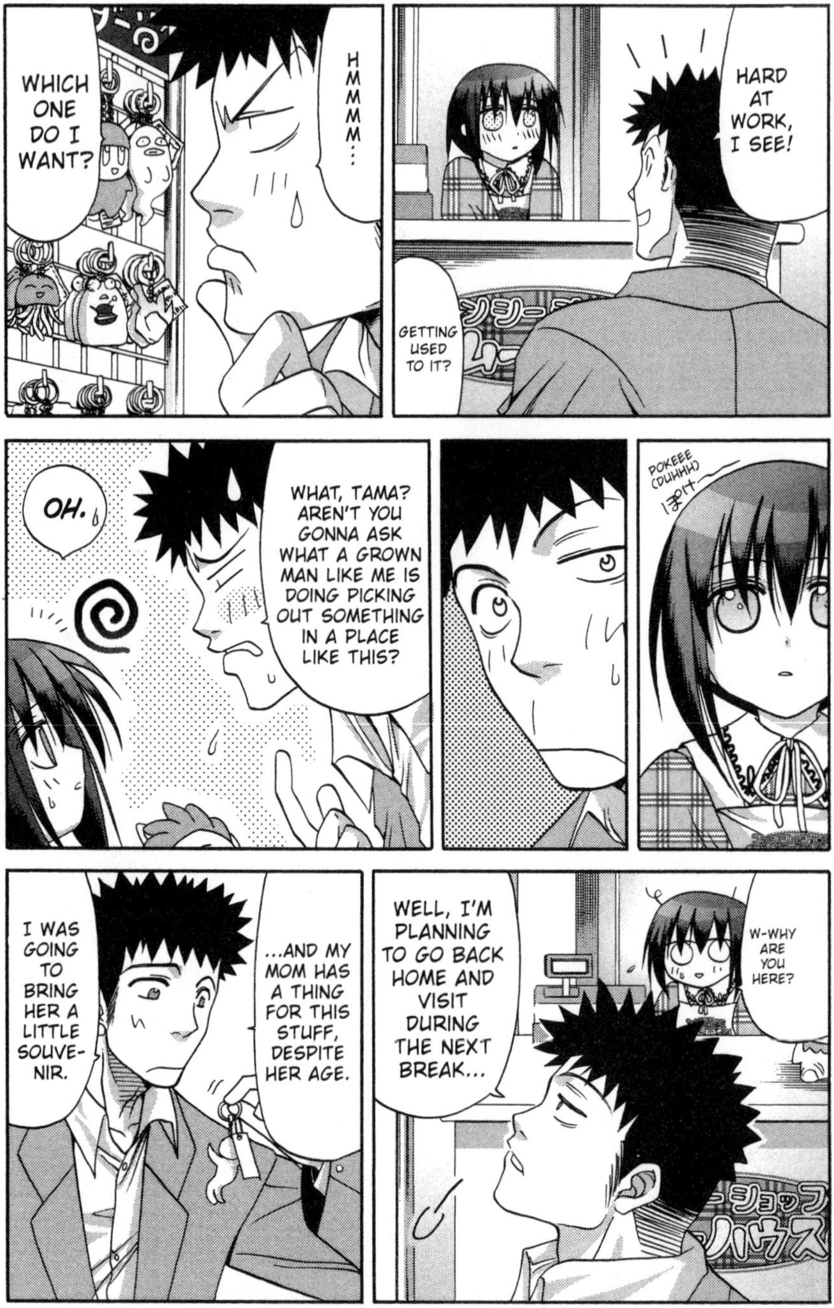
HARD AT WORK, I SEE!
GETTING USED TO IT?
HMMMM...
WHICH ONE DO I WANT?
POKEEE (DUHHH)
ぽけ
WHAT, TAMA? AREN'T YOU GONNA ASK WHAT A GROWN MAN LIKE ME IS DOING PICKING OUT SOMETHING IN A PLACE LIKE THIS?
OH.
W-WHY ARE YOU HERE?
WELL, I'M PLANNING TO GO BACK HOME AND VISIT DURING THE NEXT BREAK...
...AND MY MOM HAS A THING FOR THIS STUFF, DESPITE HER AGE.
I WAS GOING TO BRING HER A LITTLE SOUVENIR.

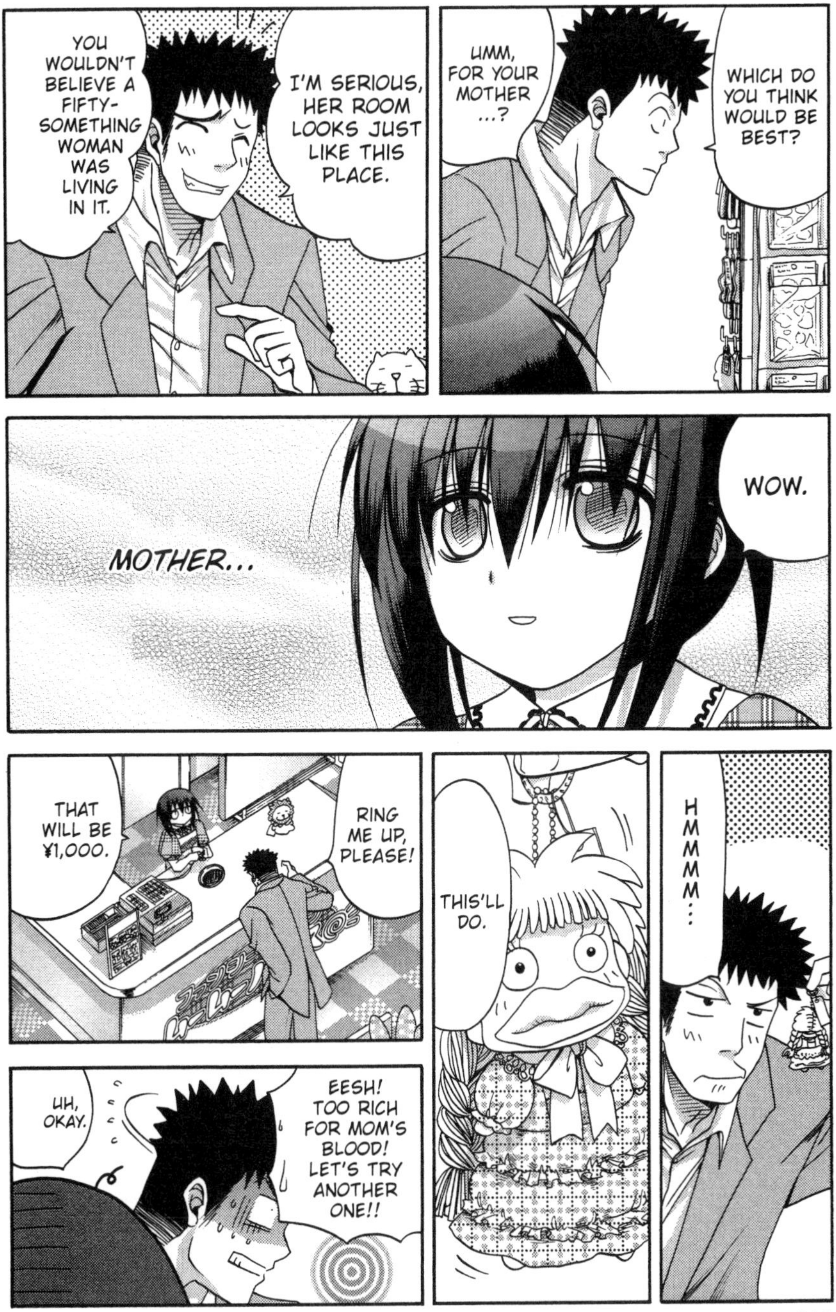
WHICH DO YOU THINK WOULD BE BEST?
UMM, FOR YOUR MOTHER ...?
I'M SERIOUS, HER ROOM LOOKS JUST LIKE THIS PLACE.
YOU WOULDN'T BELIEVE A FIFTY-SOMETHING WOMAN WAS LIVING IN IT.
WOW.
MOTHER...
HMMMM...
THIS'LL DO.
RING ME UP, PLEASE!
THAT WILL BE ¥1,000.
EESH! TOO RICH FOR MOM'S BLOOD! LET'S TRY ANOTHER ONE!!
UH, OKAY.

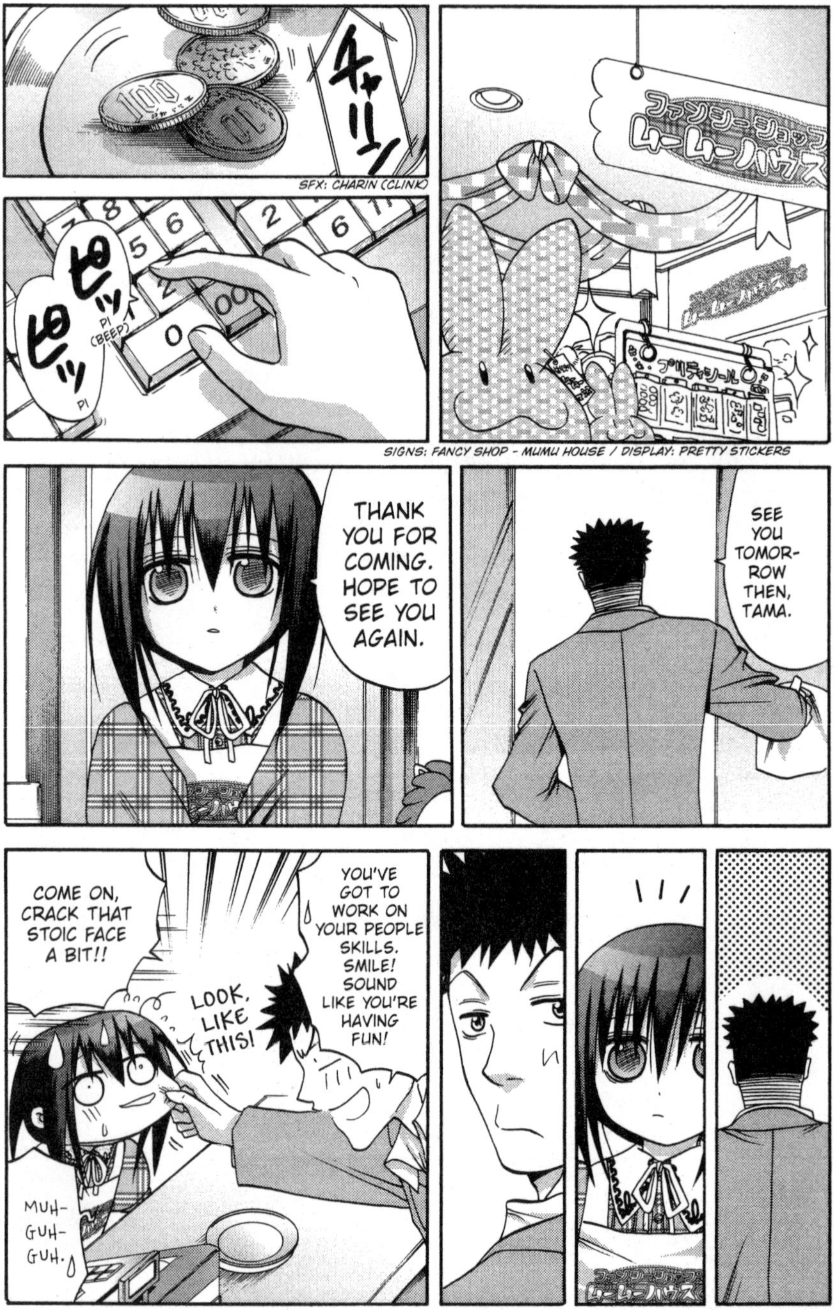
ファンシーショップ
ムームーハウス
プリティシール
SIGNS: FANCY SHOP - MUMU HOUSE / DISPLAY: PRETTY STICKERS
チャリン
SFX: CHARIN (CLINK)
ピッ
PI (BEEP)
ピッ
PI
SEE YOU TOMORROW THEN, TAMA.
THANK YOU FOR COMING. HOPE TO SEE YOU AGAIN.
YOU'VE GOT TO WORK ON YOUR PEOPLE SKILLS. SMILE! SOUND LIKE YOU'RE HAVING FUN!
COME ON, CRACK THAT STOIC FACE A BIT!!
LOOK, LIKE THIS!
MUH-GUH-GUH.

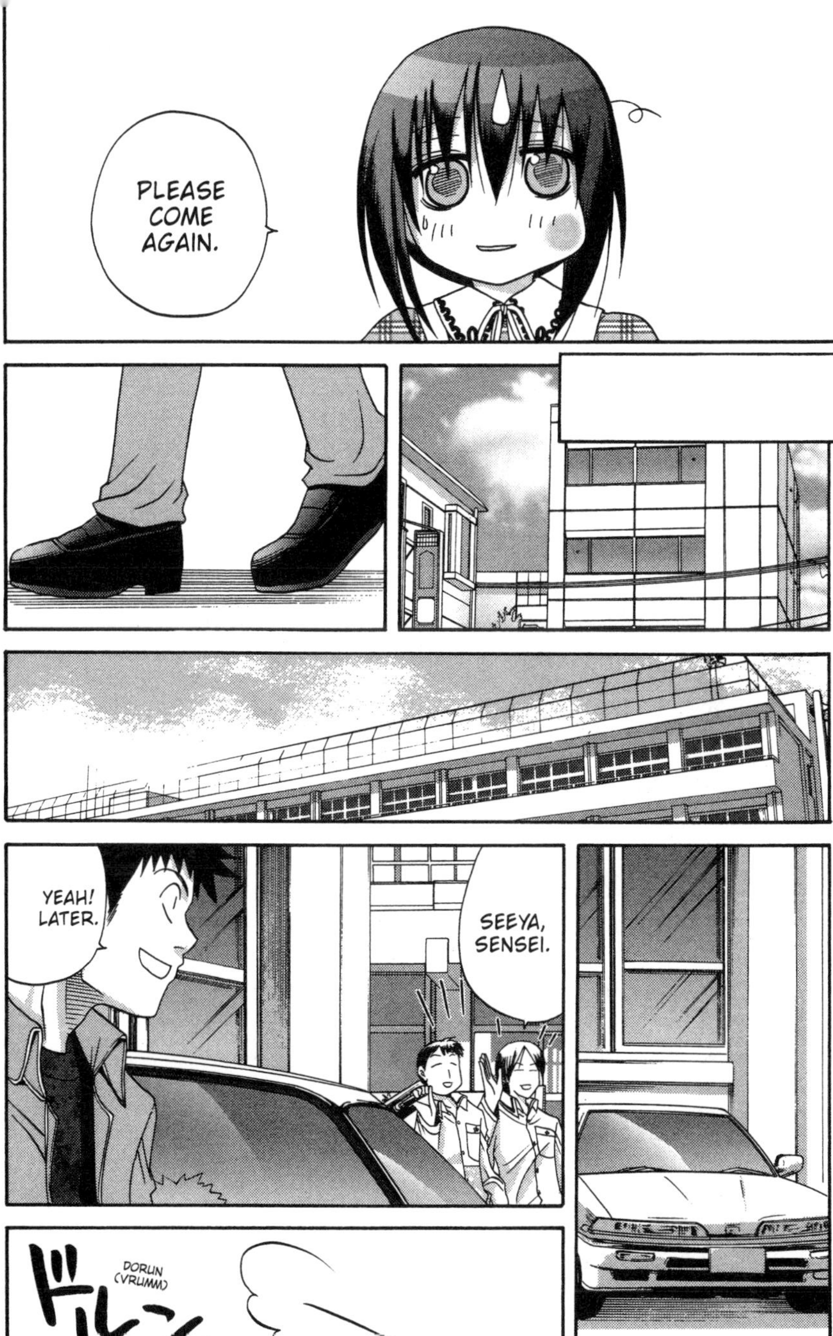
PLEASE COME AGAIN.
SEEYA, SENSEI.
YEAH! LATER.
ドルン.
DORUN (VRUMM)

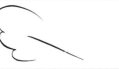

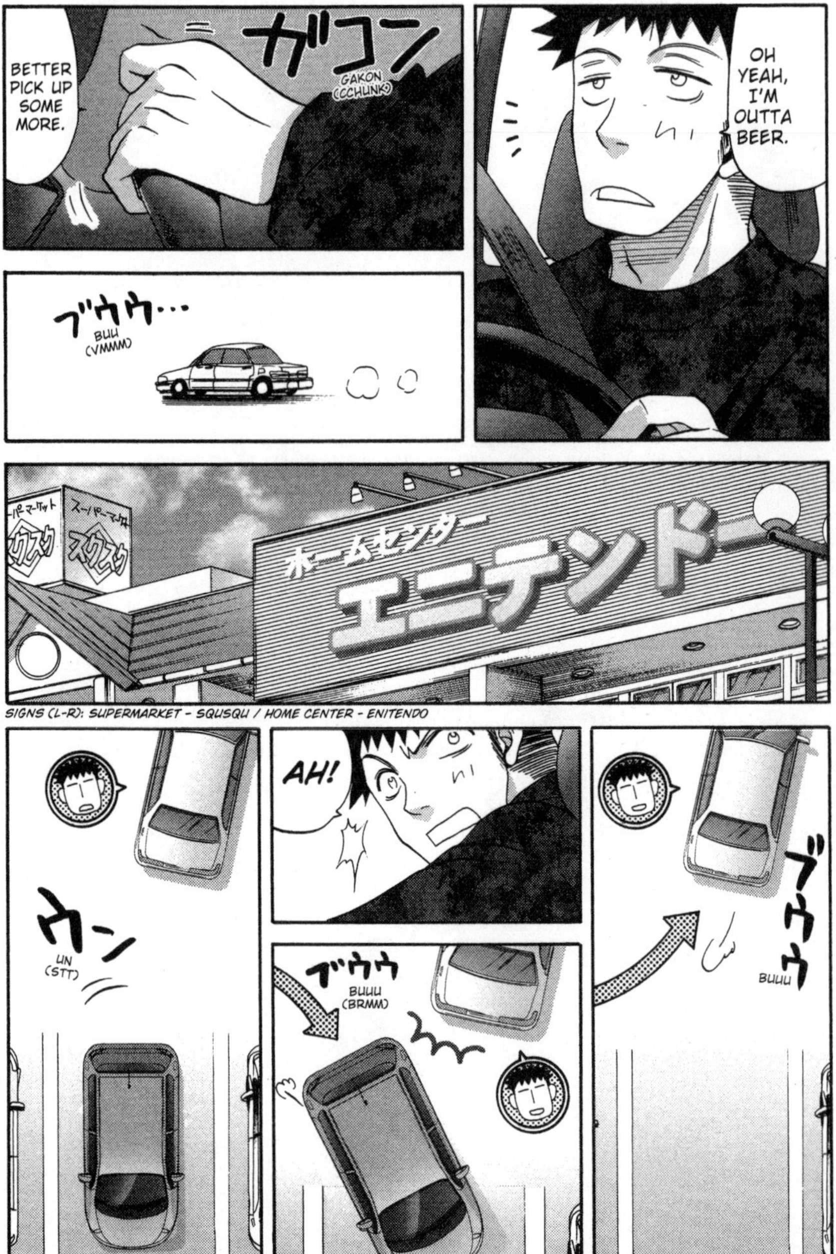
OH YEAH, I'M OUTTA BEER.
BETTER PICK UP SOME MORE.
GAKON (CCHUNK)
BUU (VMMM)
SIGNS (L-R): SUPERMARKET - SQUSQU / HOME CENTER - ENITENDO
BUUU
AH!
BUUU (BRMM)
UN (STT)

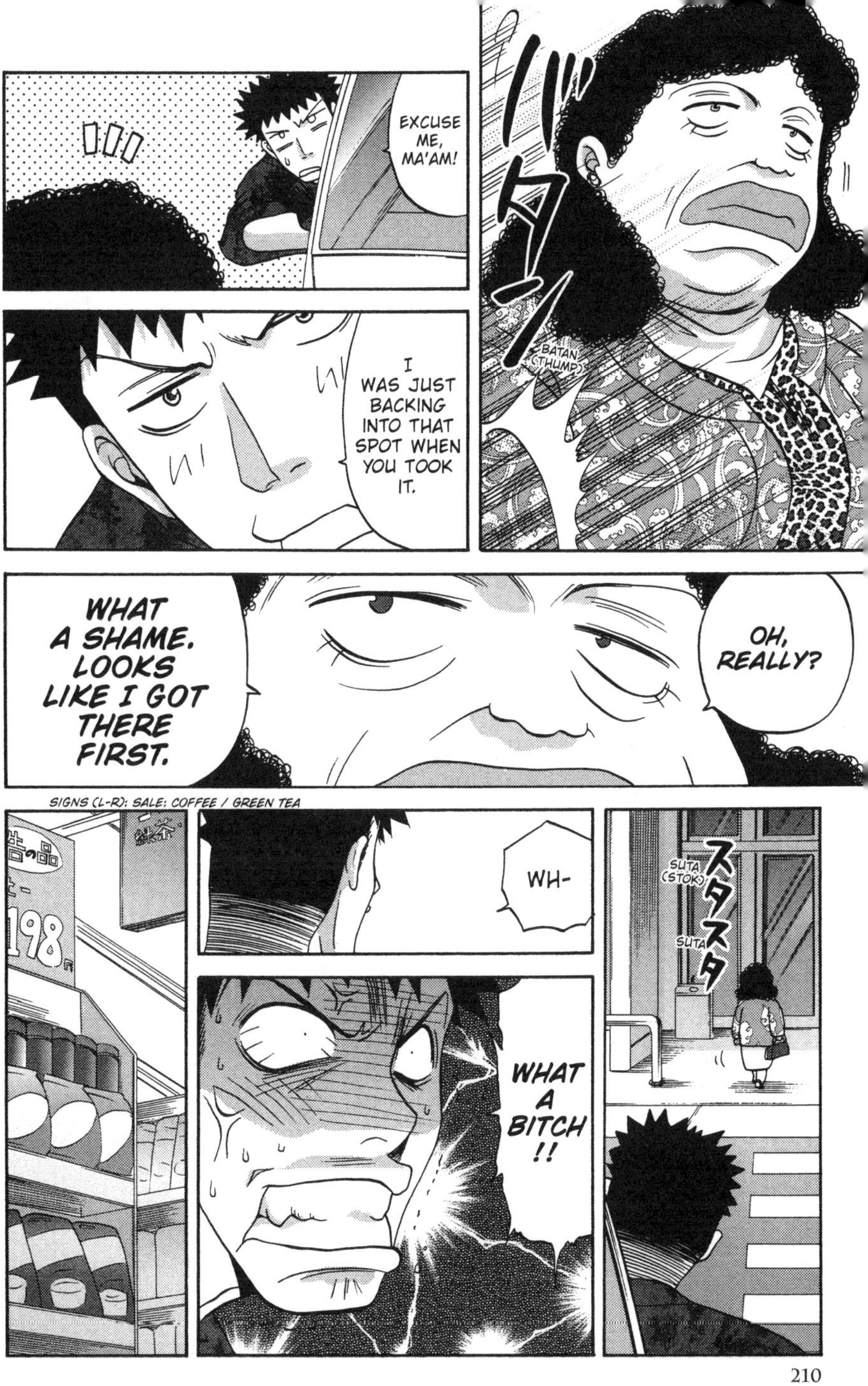
BATAN (THUMP)
EXCUSE ME, MA'AM!
I WAS JUST BACKING INTO THAT SPOT WHEN YOU TOOK IT.
OH, REALLY?
WHAT A SHAME. LOOKS LIKE I GOT THERE FIRST.
SIGNS (L-R): SALE: COFFEE / GREEN TEA
スタスタ
SUTA (STOK)
SUTA
WH-
WHAT A BITCH!!
198

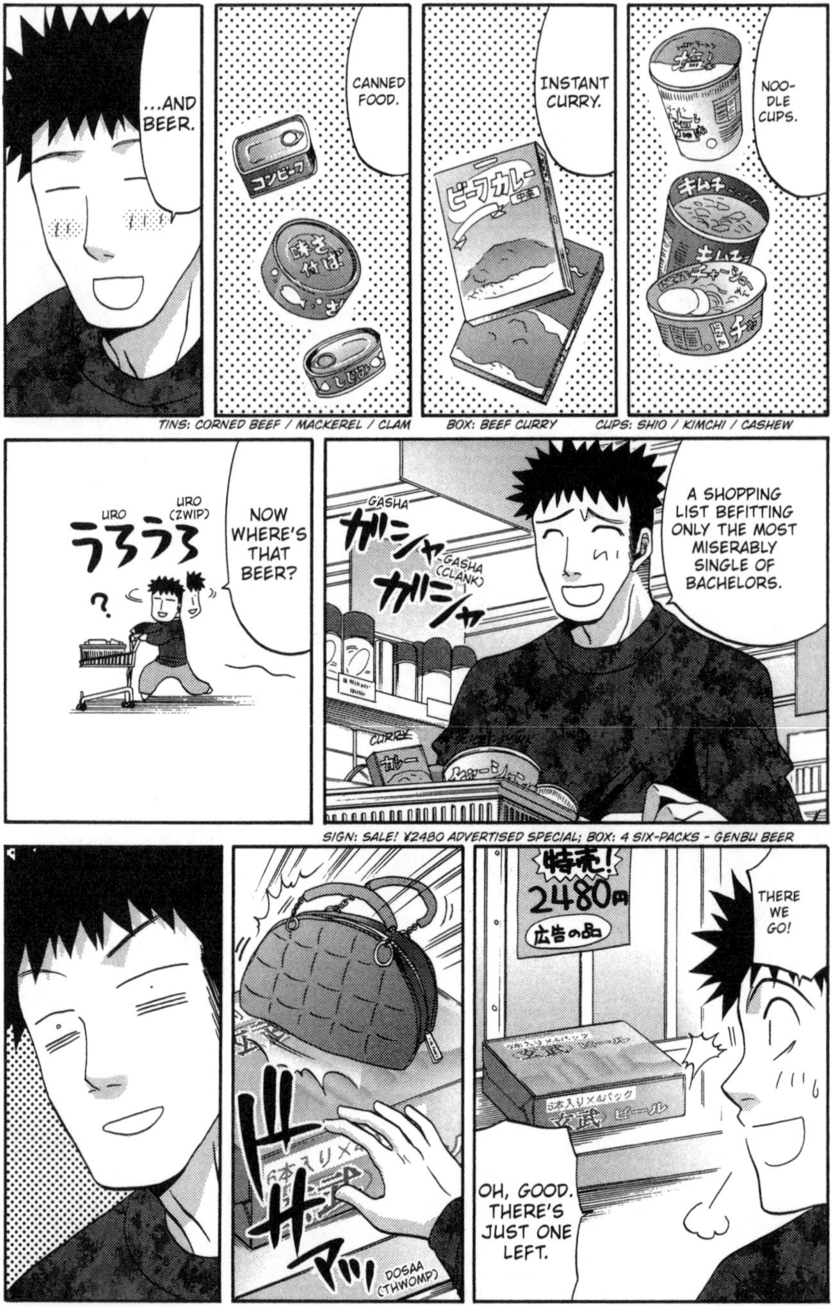
NOO-DLE CUPS.
INSTANT CURRY.
CANNED FOOD.
...AND BEER.
TINS: CORNED BEEF / MACKEREL / CLAM
BOX: BEEF CURRY
CUPS: SHIO / KIMCHI / CASHEW
A SHOPPING LIST BEFITTING ONLY THE MOST MISERABLY SINGLE OF BACHELORS.
GASHA GASHA (CLANK)
CURRY
NOW WHERE'S THAT BEER?
URO URO (ZWIP)
SIGN: SALE! ¥2480 ADVERTISED SPECIAL; BOX: 4 SIX-PACKS - GENBU BEER
特売! 2480円
広告の品
THERE WE GO!
OH, GOOD. THERE'S JUST ONE LEFT.
DOSAA (THWOMP)

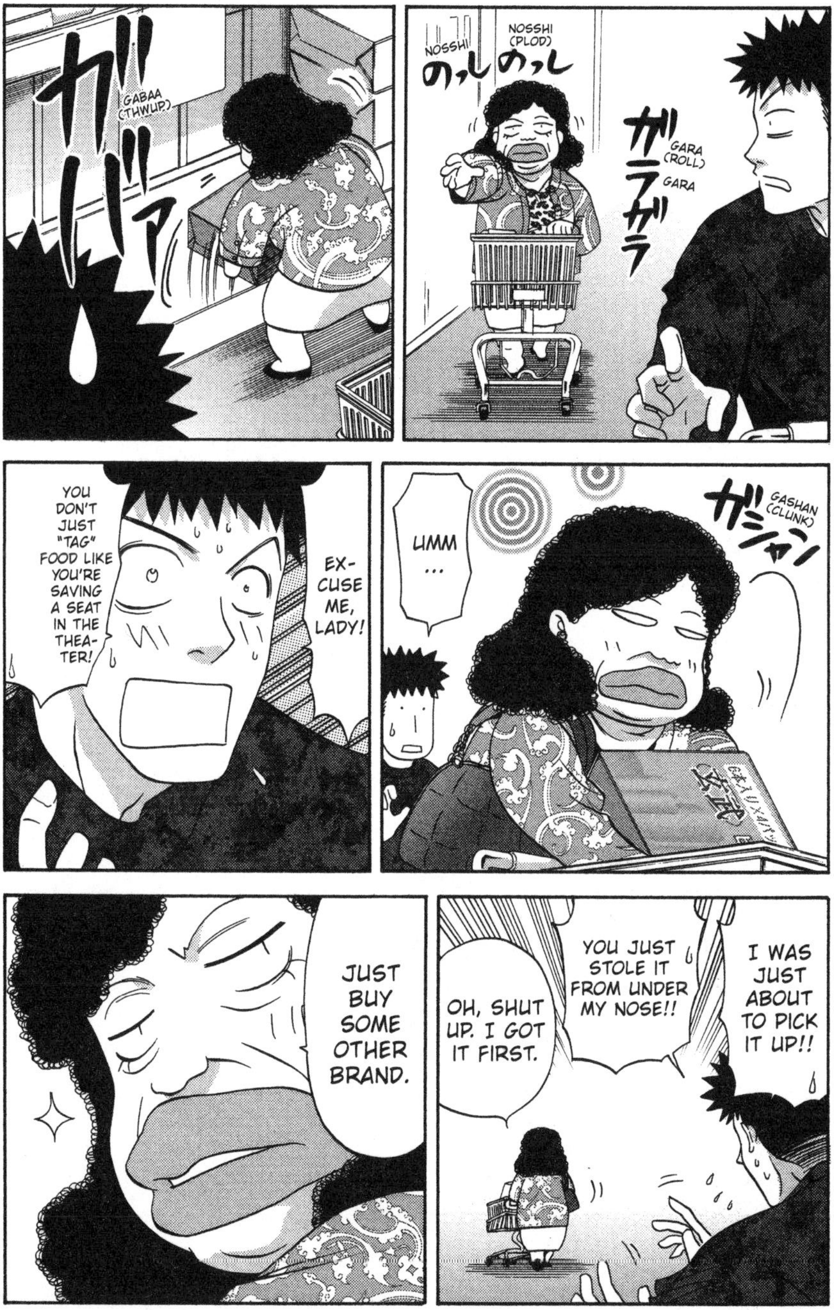
NOSSHI
NOSSHI (PLOD)
のっしのっし
GARA (ROLL)
GARA
ガラガラ
GABAA (THWUP)
ガバァ
GASHAN (CLUNK)
ガシャン
UMM ...
EX-CUSE ME, LADY!
YOU DON'T JUST "TAG" FOOD LIKE YOU'RE SAVING A SEAT IN THE THEA-TER!
I WAS JUST ABOUT TO PICK IT UP!!
YOU JUST STOLE IT FROM UNDER MY NOSE!!
OH, SHUT UP. I GOT IT FIRST.
JUST BUY SOME OTHER BRAND.

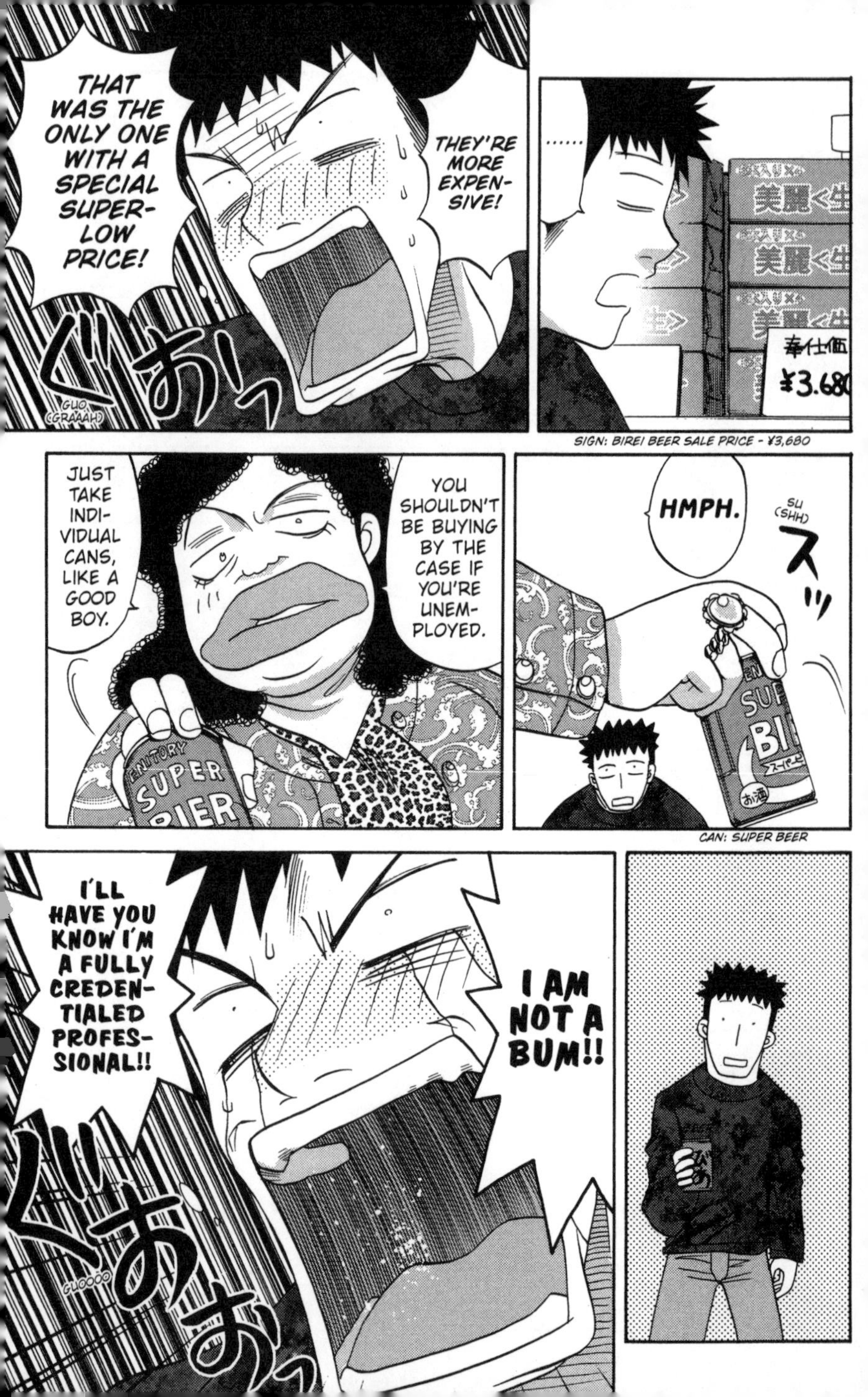
......
奉仕価
¥3.680
SIGN: BIREI BEER SALE PRICE - ¥3,680
THEY'RE MORE EXPENSIVE!
THAT WAS THE ONLY ONE WITH A SPECIAL SUPER-LOW PRICE!
ぐおっ
GUO (GRAAAH)
HMPH.
SU (SHH)
スッ
CAN: SUPER BEER
YOU SHOULDN'T BE BUYING BY THE CASE IF YOU'RE UNEMPLOYED.
JUST TAKE INDIVIDUAL CANS, LIKE A GOOD BOY.
I AM NOT A BUM!!
I'LL HAVE YOU KNOW I'M A FULLY CREDENTIALED PROFESSIONAL!!
ぐあおっ
GUOOOO

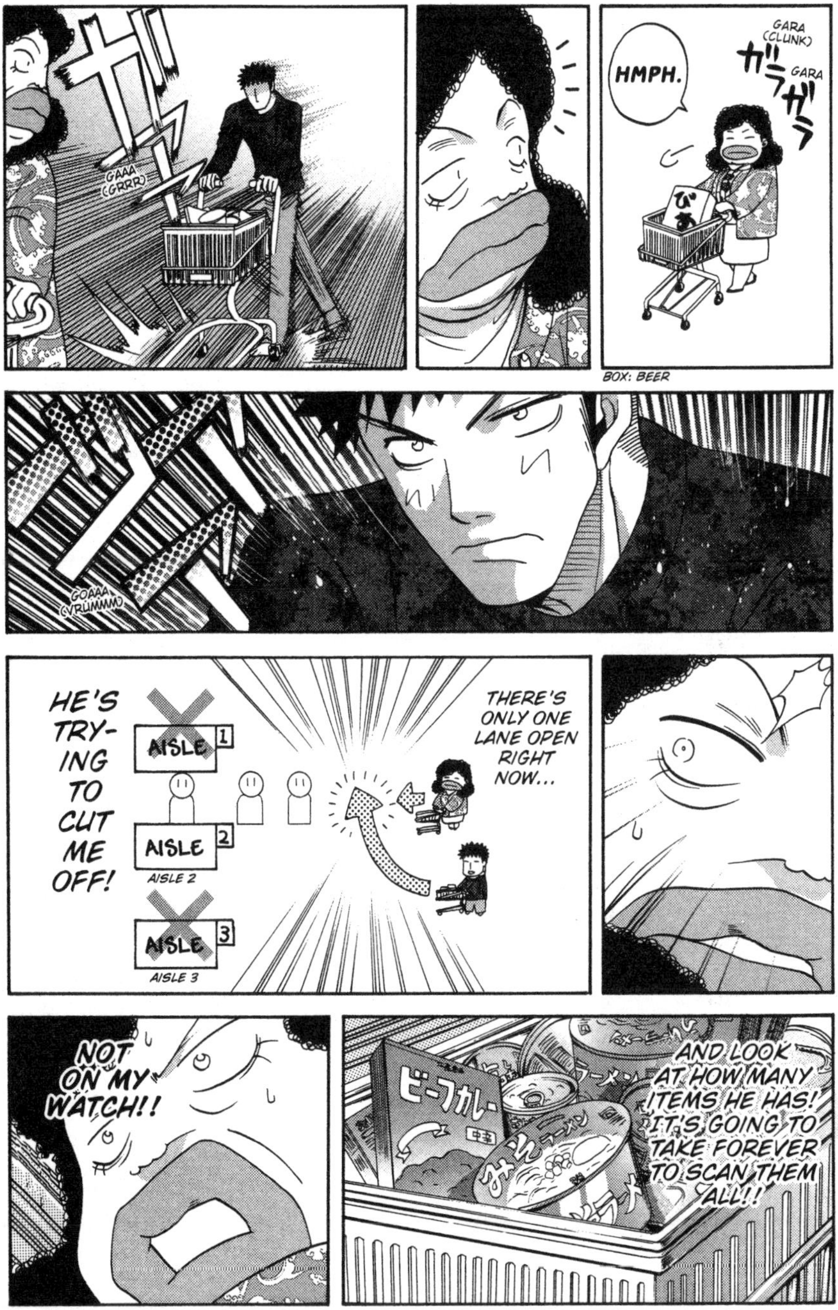
GARA (CLUNK)
GARA
HMPH.
BOX: BEER
GAAA (GRRR)
GOAAA (VRUMMM)
THERE'S ONLY ONE LANE OPEN RIGHT NOW...
HE'S TRYING TO CUT ME OFF!
AISLE 1
AISLE 2
AISLE 2
AISLE 3
AISLE 3
AND LOOK AT HOW MANY ITEMS HE HAS! IT'S GOING TO TAKE FOREVER TO SCAN THEM ALL!!
ビーフカレー
NOT ON MY WATCH!!

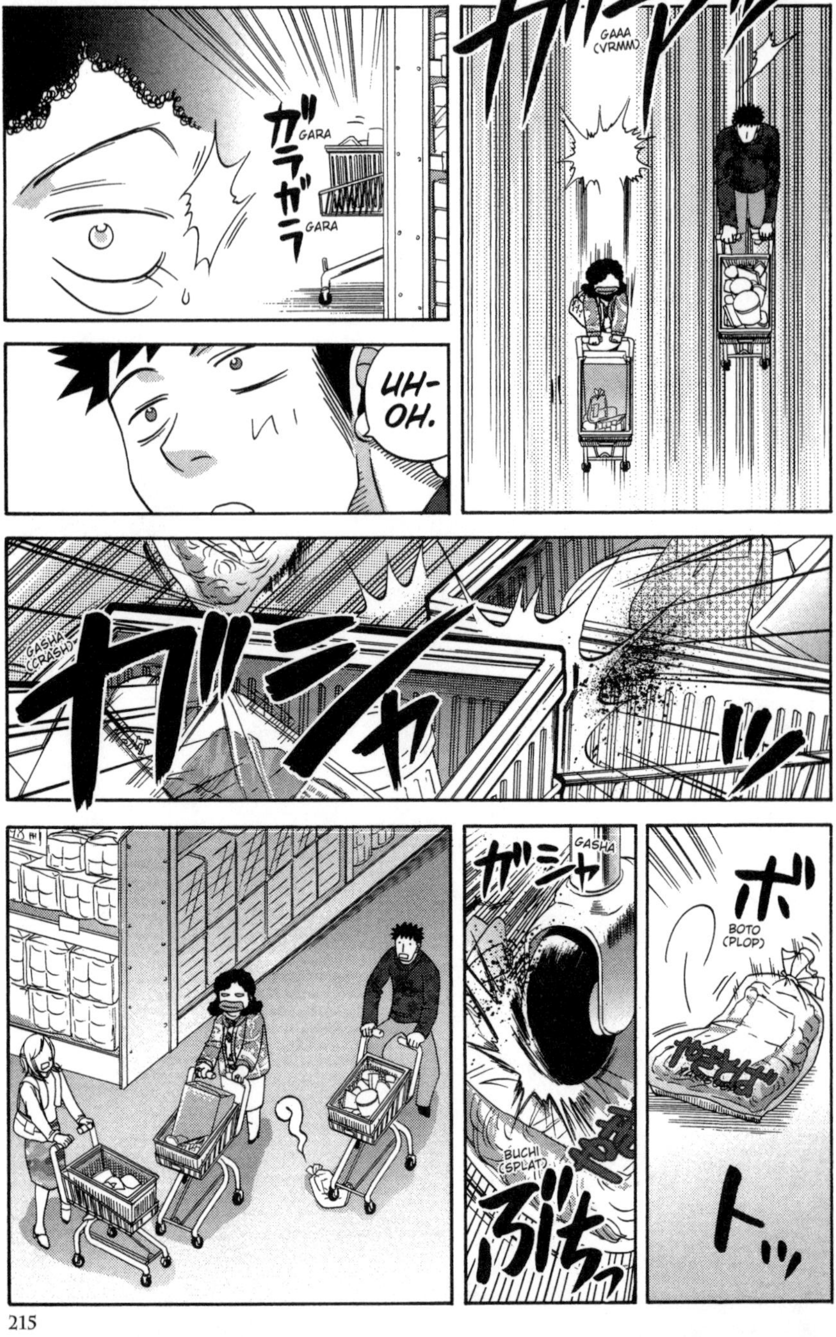
GAAA (VRMM)
ガラガラ
GARA
GARA
UH-OH.
ガシャッ
GASHA (CRASH)
ボトッ
BOTO (PLOP)
ガシャ
GASHA
ぶちっ
BUCHI (SPLAT)

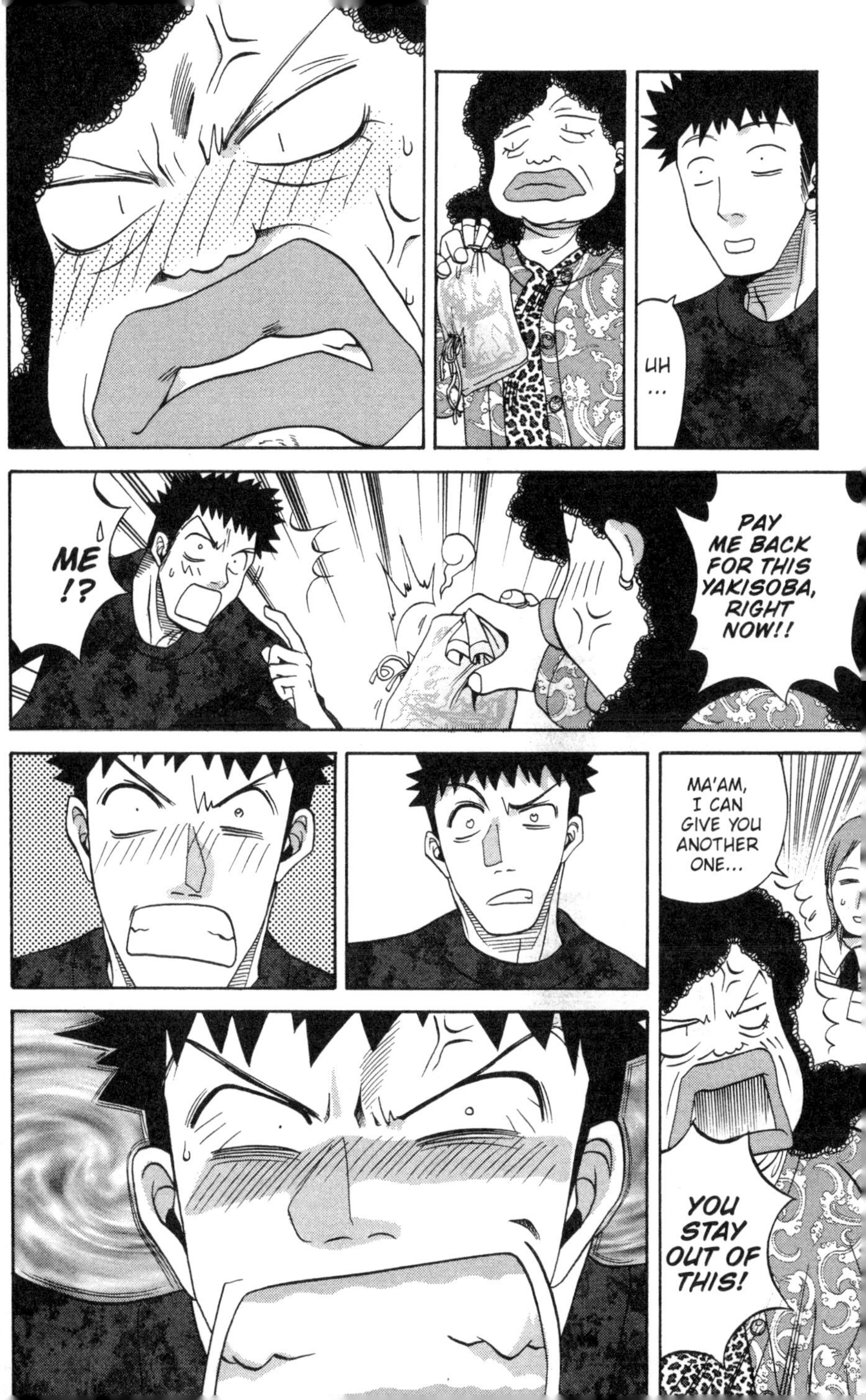
UH ...
PAY ME BACK FOR THIS YAKISOBA, RIGHT NOW!!
ME !?
MA'AM, I CAN GIVE YOU ANOTHER ONE...
YOU STAY OUT OF THIS!

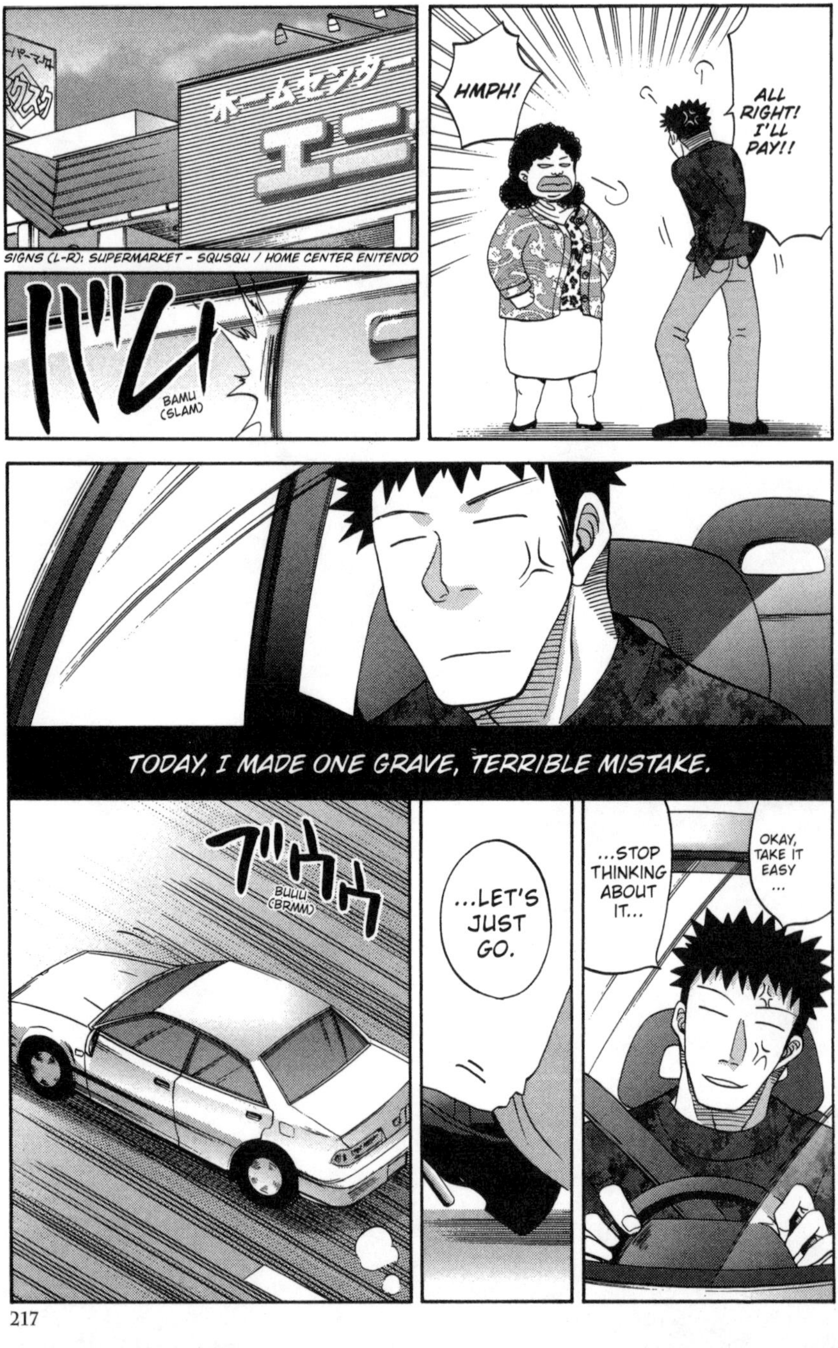
ALL RIGHT! I'LL PAY!!
HMPH!
SIGNS (L-R): SUPERMARKET - SQUSQU / HOME CENTER ENITENDO
BAMU (SLAM)
TODAY, I MADE ONE GRAVE, TERRIBLE MISTAKE.
OKAY, TAKE IT EASY ...
...STOP THINKING ABOUT IT...
...LET'S JUST GO.
BUUU (BRMM)

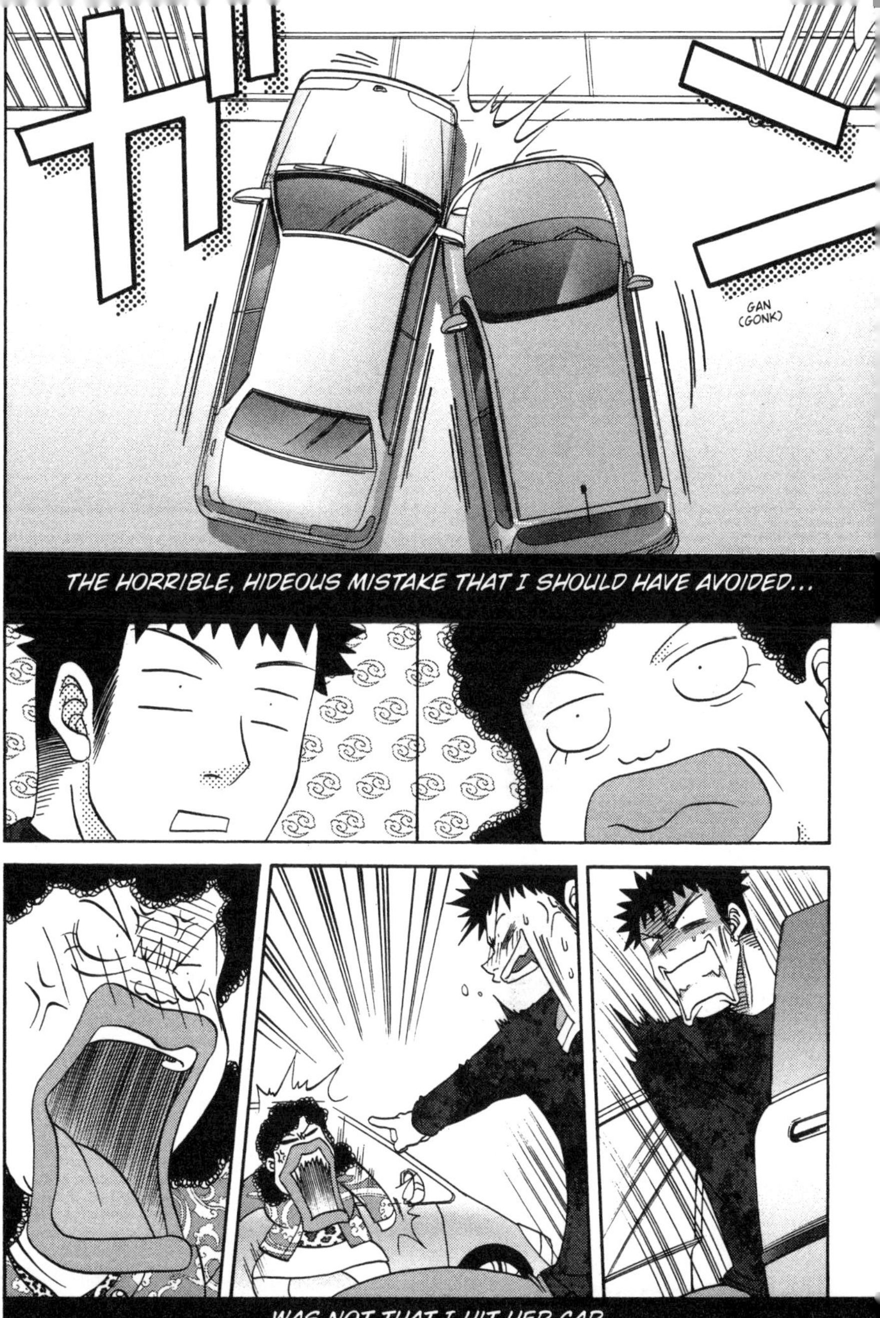
GAN
(GONK)
THE HORRIBLE, HIDEOUS MISTAKE THAT I SHOULD HAVE AVOIDED...
...WAS NOT THAT I HIT HER CAR...

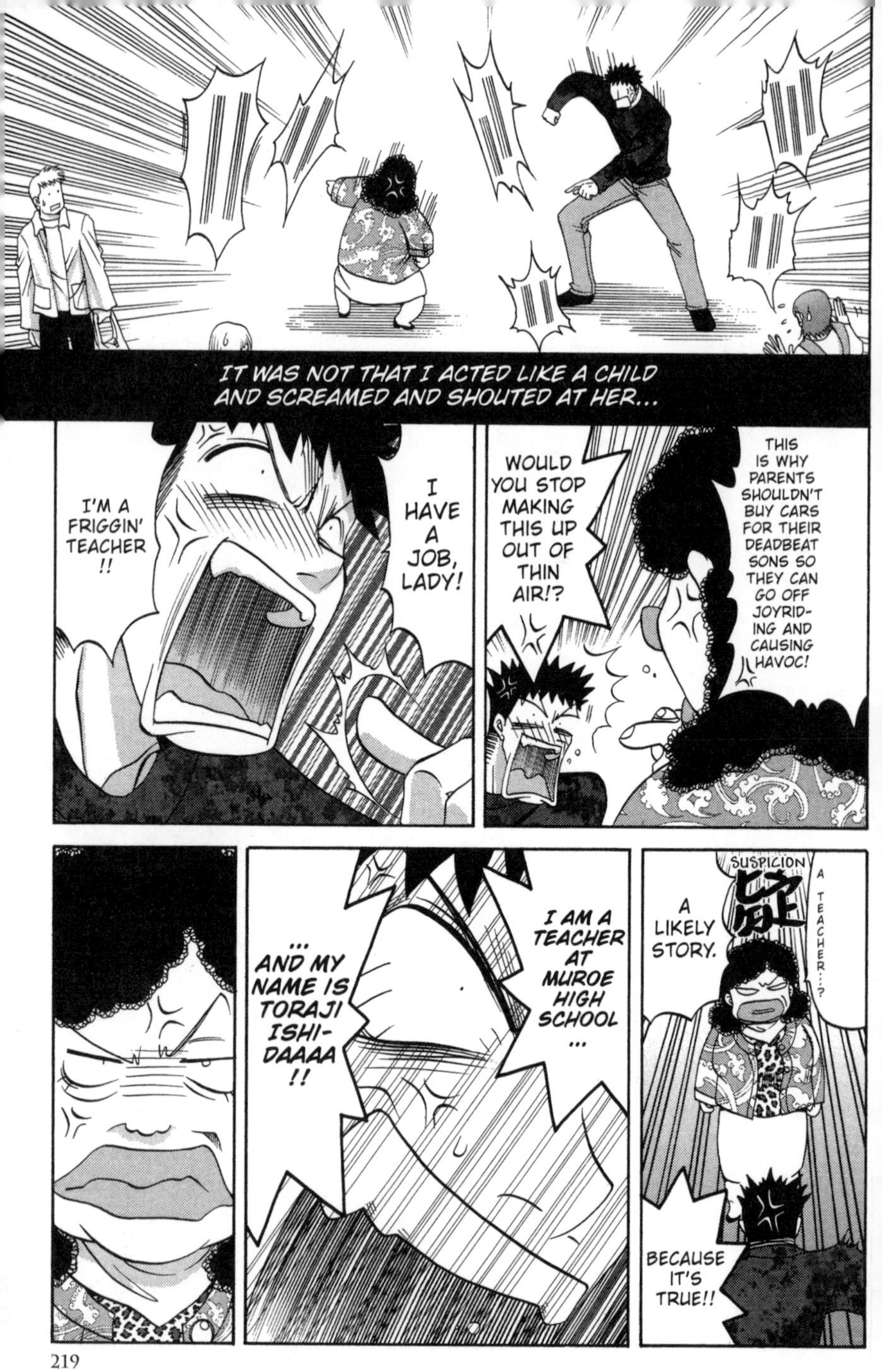
IT WAS NOT THAT I ACTED LIKE A CHILD AND SCREAMED AND SHOUTED AT HER...
THIS IS WHY PARENTS SHOULDN'T BUY CARS FOR THEIR DEADBEAT SONS SO THEY CAN GO OFF JOYRIDING AND CAUSING HAVOC!
WOULD YOU STOP MAKING THIS UP OUT OF THIN AIR!?
I HAVE A JOB, LADY!
I'M A FRIGGIN' TEACHER!!
A TEACHER...?
SUSPICION
A LIKELY STORY.
BECAUSE IT'S TRUE!!
I AM A TEACHER AT MUROE HIGH SCHOOL...
...AND MY NAME IS TORAJI ISHI-DAAAA!!

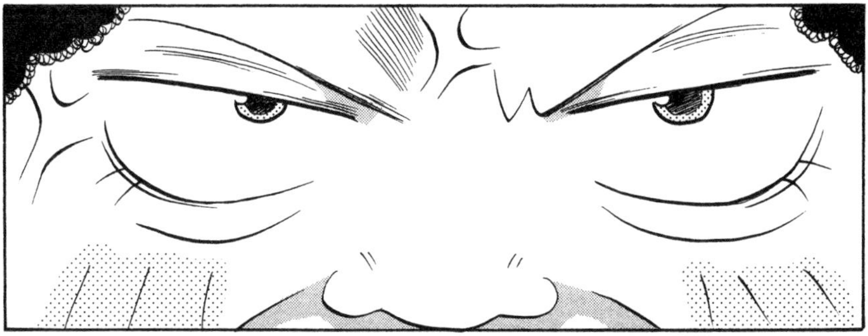

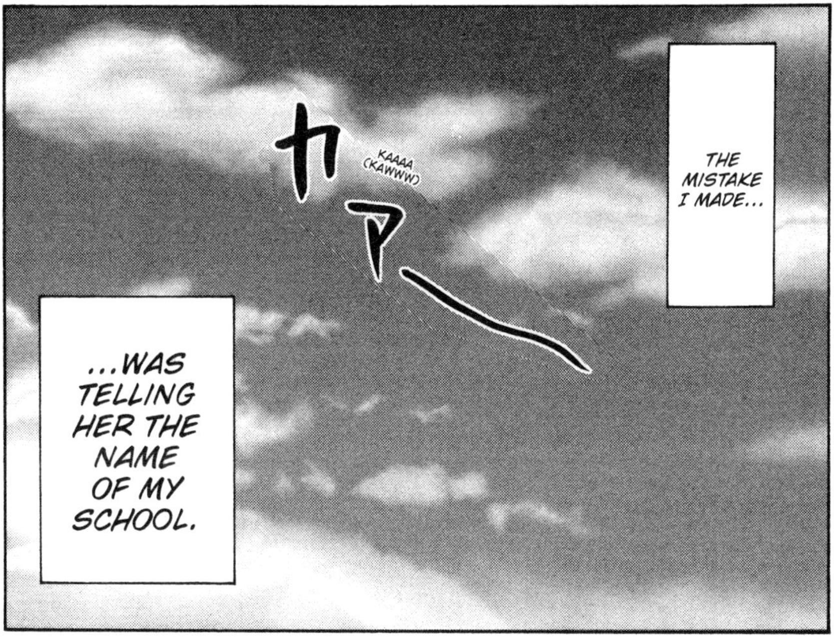
THE MISTAKE I MADE...
カァー
KAAAA (KAWWW)
...WAS TELLING HER THE NAME OF MY SCHOOL.

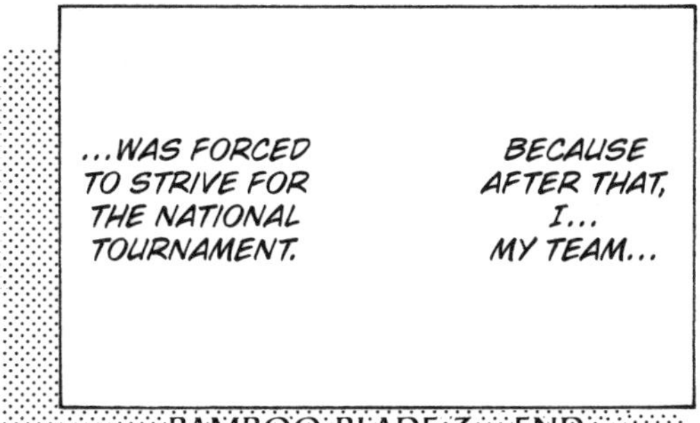
BECAUSE AFTER THAT, I... MY TEAM...
...WAS FORCED TO STRIVE FOR THE NATIONAL TOURNAMENT.

BAMBOO BLADE 3 – END

TRANSLATION NOTES

Page 8
Bureiba: This name, made up on the spot by Kojiro, is a rough approximation of the word "Braver," from Tamaki's favorite TV show, *Blade Braver*. In Japanese they are pronounced the same way — Kojiro just makes up some kanji so it looks like an official name. Of course, "Bureiba" is a totally unnatural and unlikely name for a Japanese person to have.

Page 9
&: The ampersand (&) on Andou's nameplate in the bottom left panel is playing off the fact that the Japanese pronunciation of the English word "and" is "ando."

Page 17
Natto: A traditional Japanese food of fermented soybeans in a very sticky paste. This cloying stickiness is used as a visual metaphor here to represent the exasperating inability to keep Andou away — it's like she's actually "stuck" to Kirino.

Page 48
Shobu ari: Similar to when the judge calls out "*ari*" after the location of a point scored (i.e. "*men ari*" to signify a point scored on the *men*), *shobu ari* signifies that the match is over and one combatant has won. *Shobu* is written with the kanji meaning "win and loss," and *ari* means "is." Essentially, by calling *shobu ari*, the judge is literally stating, "we have a winner and a loser."

Page 92
Okaka onigiri: An *onigiri* is a rice ball (in this case it's shaped more like a triangle), often with some kind of food in the middle. An *okaka onigiri* is stuffed with *katsuobushi*, dried tuna flakes.

Page 102
Yoko-tan: There are ways to make nicknames in Japanese that are more comprehensive than just slapping the suffix "-*chan*" on the end. One such way is the cutesy and extremely informal suffix "-*tan*." A lot of *–tan*'s usage and publicity comes from certain communities on the internet, but it is also used in real life.

Page 113
Revolving sushi: A type of sushi restaurant in which sushi is put on a conveyor belt that winds around the bar, rather than having the customers order directly from the cook on the other side.

Page 114
Ikura: Salmon roe (eggs) that are commonly served as a type of sushi.

Page 119
Engawa, mushi-ebi, iwashi: Halibut tail, steamed prawn, and sardine, respectively.

Page 122
Aburi toro, binchou maguro, botan ebi: Seared tuna, white tuna, and sweet prawn, respectively.

Page 179
Kuroinu Yamato, stamp: A parody of the well-known Japanese shipping company Yamato, which is commonly called *Kuroneko Yamato* (Black Cat Yamato) because of its logo featuring a black cat. In this case, the black cat is replaced by a black dog (*Kuroinu*). When the delivery man mentions a "stamp," he is referring to the personalized hanko stamp that most Japanese adults possess and use as a means of legal signature (though a written signature is also acceptable, of course).

Page 197
Shoyu ramen: One of the most basic flavors of ramen, *shoyu* (soy sauce) is made with a combination of soy sauce and chicken broth.

Page 211
Shio: Literally "salt," this is another basic broth flavor of ramen. It's very light and basic and made with simple chicken stock.

Page 215
Yakisoba: A dish of noodles that is fried with a special sauce and eaten with cabbage and pork. It's rather similar to lo mein.

WRITTEN BY: MASAHIRO TOTSUKA

SO, HERE'S THE THIRD VOLUME OF *BAMBOO BLADE*. NOW THAT ALL THE PRINCIPAL CHARACTERS HAVE BEEN INTRODUCED AND THE BASE OF THE STORY ESTABLISHED, THIS IS WHERE I START TO BRING OUT THE THINGS I WANTED TO DO WITH THE MANGA. NOW THE MUROE HIGH KENDO TEAM WILL BE STRIVING FOR A LARGER GOAL... ALBEIT STILL LAZILY.

KOJIRO-SENSEI'S USELESS AND FRIVOLOUS GUIDANCE MIGHT BE A HEADACHE FOR HIS PUPILS, BUT IT ALSO GUIDES THEIR PROGRESS AND PUSHES THEM ONWARD. SOMETIMES, IT'S *BECAUSE* HE'S A FRIVOLOUS TEACHER. BECAUSE WHEN THAT HAPPENS, YOU NEED TO STAND UP AND BE SERIOUS, RATHER THAN GIVING UP AS HE DOES. LEARNING THAT SENSE OF PURPOSE IS A VALUABLE TOOL IN THE PROCESS OF BECOMING AN ADULT, IN MY OPINION.

I HOPE YOU'LL CONTINUE TO FONDLY WATCH OVER KOJIRO AND TAMAKI AND THE REST. AND I HOPE TO SEE YOU AGAIN IN VOLUME 4.

- MASAHIRO TOTSUKA

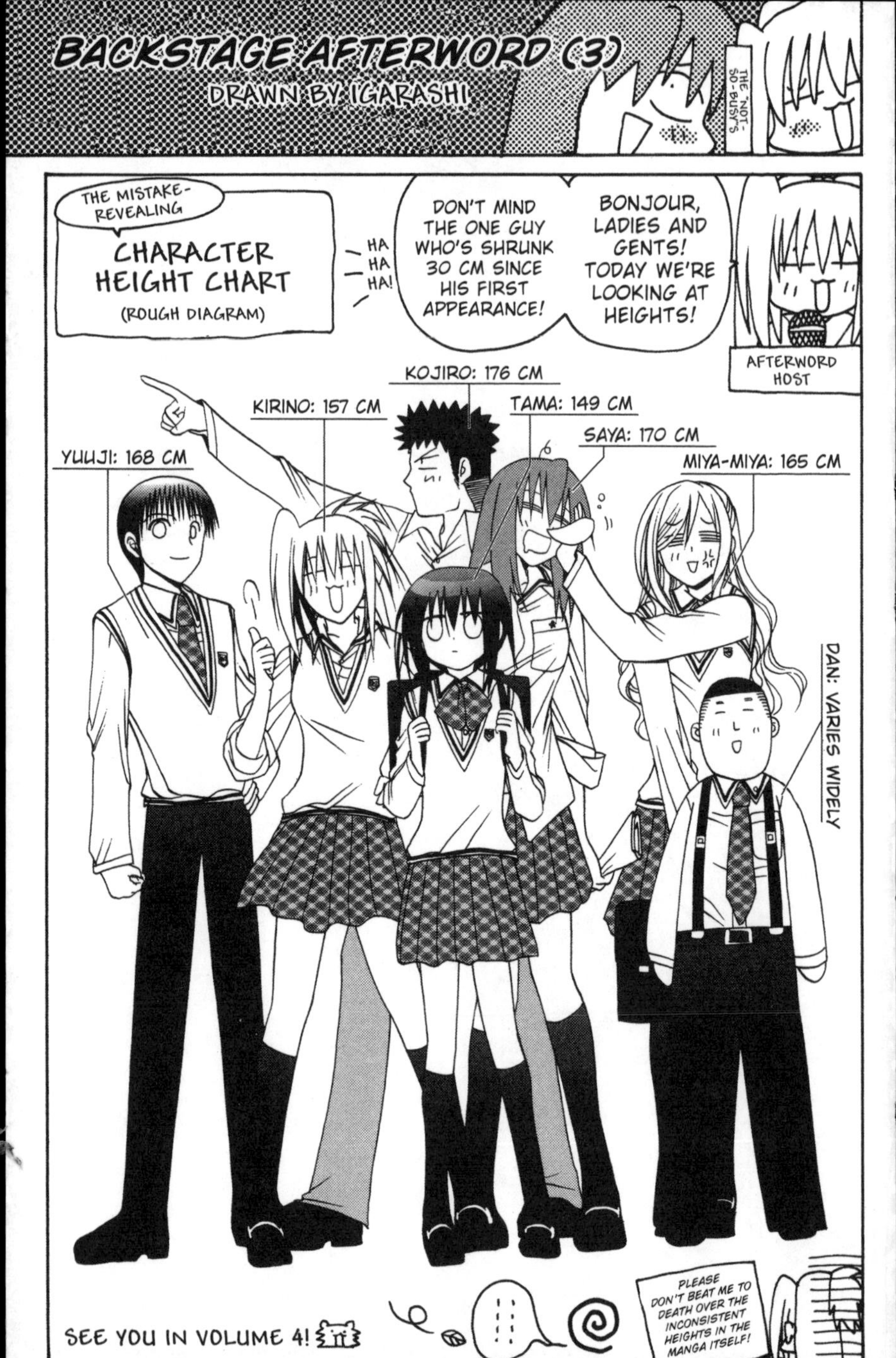
BACKSTAGE AFTERWORD (3)
DRAWN BY IGARASHI
THE "NOT-SO-BUSY'S"
AFTERWORD HOST
BONJOUR, LADIES AND GENTS! TODAY WE'RE LOOKING AT HEIGHTS!
DON'T MIND THE ONE GUY WHO'S SHRUNK 30 CM SINCE HIS FIRST APPEARANCE!
HA HA HA!
THE MISTAKE-REVEALING
CHARACTER HEIGHT CHART
(ROUGH DIAGRAM)
KOJIRO: 176 CM
KIRINO: 157 CM
TAMA: 149 CM
SAYA: 170 CM
YUUJI: 168 CM
MIYA-MIYA: 165 CM
DAN: VARIES WIDELY
PLEASE DON'T BEAT ME TO DEATH OVER THE INCONSISTENT HEIGHTS IN THE MANGA ITSELF!
SEE YOU IN VOLUME 4!

VISIT AGURI IGARASHI ON THE WEB (JAPANESE ONLY) "ANTIHEROINE NEWS" HTTP://ANTIHEROINE.COOL.NE.JP/"

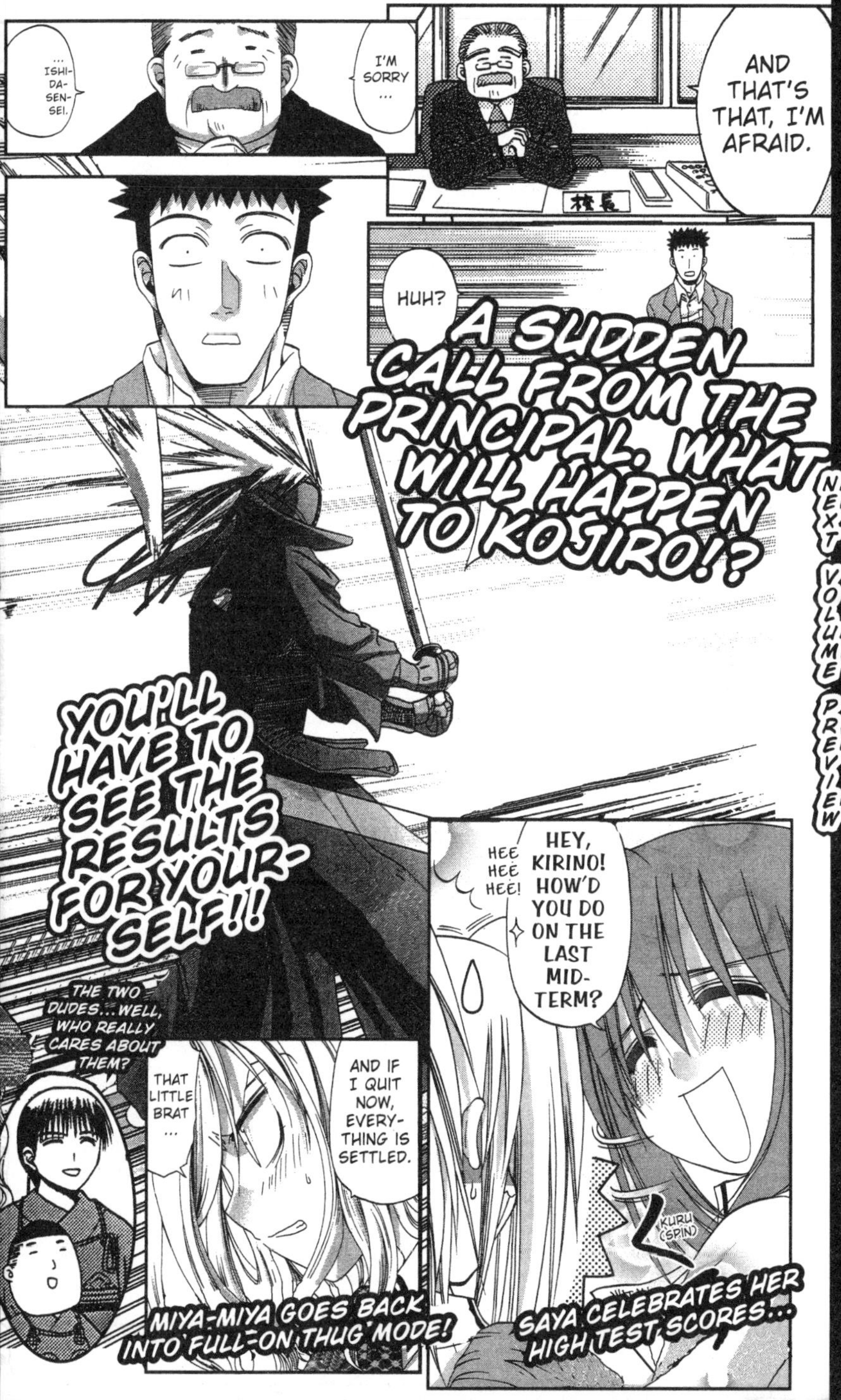
AND THAT'S THAT, I'M AFRAID.
I'M SORRY ...
... ISHI-DA-SEN-SEI.
HUH?
A SUDDEN CALL FROM THE PRINCIPAL. WHAT WILL HAPPEN TO KOJIRO!?
NEXT VOLUME PREVIEW
YOU'LL HAVE TO SEE THE RESULTS FOR YOUR-SELF!!
HEY, KIRINO! HOW'D YOU DO ON THE LAST MID-TERM?
HEE HEE HEE!
KURU (SPIN)
SAYA CELEBRATES HER HIGH TEST SCORES...
AND IF I QUIT NOW, EVERY-THING IS SETTLED.
THAT LITTLE BRAT ...
MIYA-MIYA GOES BACK INTO FULL-ON THUG MODE!
THE TWO DUDES... WELL, WHO REALLY CARES ABOUT THEM?

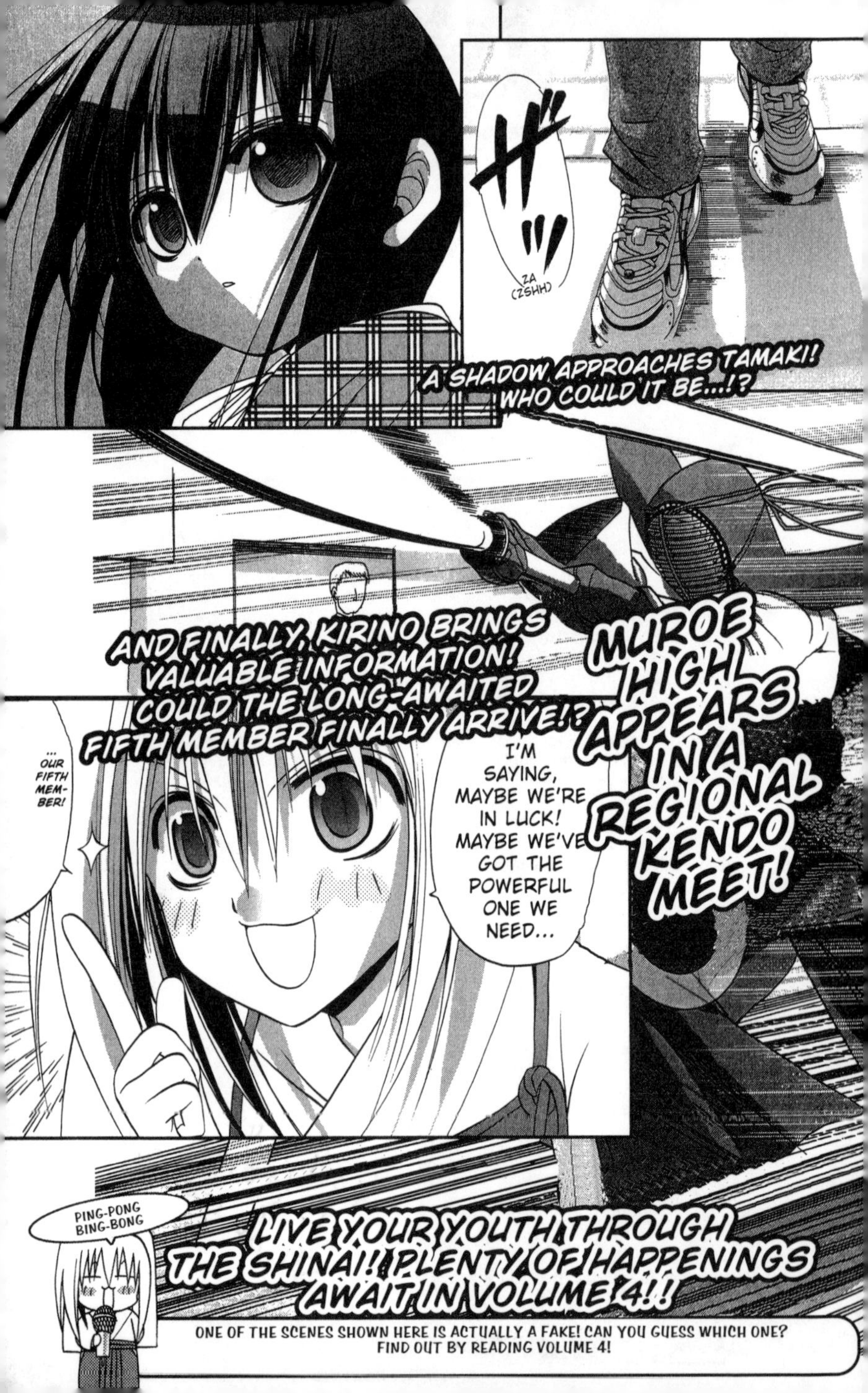
ZA (ZSHH)
A SHADOW APPROACHES TAMAKI! WHO COULD IT BE...!?
MUROE HIGH APPEARS IN A REGIONAL KENDO MEET!
AND FINALLY, KIRINO BRINGS VALUABLE INFORMATION! COULD THE LONG-AWAITED FIFTH MEMBER FINALLY ARRIVE!?
I'M SAYING, MAYBE WE'RE IN LUCK! MAYBE WE'VE GOT THE POWERFUL ONE WE NEED...
...OUR FIFTH MEMBER!
PING-PONG BING-BONG
LIVE YOUR YOUTH THROUGH THE SHINAI! PLENTY OF HAPPENINGS AWAIT IN VOLUME 4!!
ONE OF THE SCENES SHOWN HERE IS ACTUALLY A FAKE! CAN YOU GUESS WHICH ONE?
FIND OUT BY READING VOLUME 4!

BAMBOO BLADE ③

MASAHIRO TOTSUKA
AGURI IGARASHI

Translation: Stephen Paul

Lettering: Terri Delgado

BAMBOO BLADE Vol. 3 © 2006 Masahiro Totsuka, Aguri Igarashi / SQUARE ENIX CO., LTD. All rights reserved. First published in Japan in 2006 by SQUARE ENIX CO., LTD. English translation rights arranged with SQUARE ENIX CO., LTD. and Hachette Book Group through Tuttle-Mori Agency, Inc.

Translation © 2009 by SQUARE ENIX CO., LTD.

Yen Press
Hachette Book Group
237 Park Avenue, New York, NY 10017

www.HachetteBookGroup.com
www.YenPress.com

Yen Press is an imprint of Hachette Book Group, Inc. The Yen Press name and logo are trademarks of Hachette Book Group, Inc.

First Yen Press Edition: December 2009

ISBN: 978-0-7595-3047-8

10 9 8 7 6 5 4 3 2 1

BVG

Printed in the United States of America

D0182671